LITERACY RESEARCH METHODOLOGIES

Literacy Research Methodologies

Edited by

NELL K. DUKE
MARLA H. MALLETTE

THE GUILFORD PRESS
New York   London

© 2004 The Guilford Press
A Division of Guilford Publications, Inc.
72 Spring Street, New York, NY 10012
www.guilford.com

Printed in the United States of America

This book is printed on acid-free paper.

Last digit is print number: 9 8 7 6 5 4 3 2 1

Library of Congress Cataloging-in-Publication Data

Literacy research methodologies / edited by Nell K. Duke,
    Marla H. Mallette.
        p.   cm.
    Includes bibliographical references and index.
    ISBN 1-59385-060-3 — ISBN 1-59385-059-X (pbk.)
    1. Reading—Research—Methodology.   I. Mallette,
Marla H.   II. Duke, Nell K.
    LB1050.6.L58 2004
    428.4′07′2—dc22

                                                    2004009664

We dedicate this book in memory of Dr. Rebecca Barr.
As a scholar, Dr. Barr maintained the highest standards
for research. Among her many honors was receipt of
the Oscar Causey Award, the most prestigious research
award in the field of literacy. Dr. Barr was a member
of the editorial team for all three volumes of the
Handbook of Reading Research *and consistently*
valued the contributions of a range of research
methodologies to our understanding of literacy learning
and instruction.

In addition to her numerous accomplishments,
Becky Barr was an extraordinary person. Her gentle and
nurturing ways were unmistakable. She is a model as
a literacy researcher, woman, and mother. Her legacy
will always be an inspiration to us, as we hope it will
be to all.

About the Editors

Nell K. Duke, EdD, is Associate Professor of Teacher Education and Learning, Technology, and Culture at Michigan State University, East Lansing. Her research focuses on early literacy development, particularly among children living in urban poverty. Her specific areas of expertise include the development of informational literacies in young children, comprehension teaching and learning in early schooling, approaches to addressing the needs of struggling reader–writers, and issues of equity in literacy education. She has used a variety of research methodologies in her own work and teaches courses on research design. Dr. Duke has a strong interest in the preparation of educational researchers and has published and presented on this topic.

Marla H. Mallette, PhD, is Assistant Professor of Literacy Education at Southern Illinois University, Carbondale. Her research interests include literacy teacher education, literacy instruction and learning with students of culturally and linguistically diverse backgrounds, and the convergence of early literacy and technology. She is very interested in research methodologies and has used various methodologies in her own work. Dr. Mallette has also published and presented on literacy research methodologies and the preparation of literacy researchers.

Contributors

Diane M. Barone, EdD, is Professor of Educational Specialties at the University of Nevada, Reno. Her research has centered around longitudinal case studies of young children's literacy development. The first one of these studies investigated the literacy development of children prenatally exposed to crack cocaine. The second longitudinal study is nearing completion, as the students she selected to follow in kindergarten are now completing their elementary school experience as sixth graders. This work has centered on the children's literacy development as well as the instruction provided to them in their school.

James J. Bason, PhD, is an Associate Research Scientist at the University of Georgia, Athens, and Director of the Survey Research Center at the University of Georgia. He is also a Fellow at the Institute for Behavioral Research there. Dr. Bason is the author of several publications based on data collected by the Center in recent years, and is an active member of the American Association for Public Opinion Research, a past president of the Southern Association for Public Opinion Research, and a current executive committee member of the National Network of State Polls. His research interests include survey methodology, elections, and electoral behavior.

James F. Baumann, PhD, is Professor of Reading Education at the University of Georgia, Athens. His research has addressed classroom reading instruction. Dr. Baumann and his colleagues have conducted mail-survey research exploring teachers' and administrators' perspectives and practices related to elementary reading instruction.

Barbara A. Bradley, PhD, is Assistant Professor in the Department of Teaching and Leadership at the University of Kansas, Lawrence.

Her research interests include emergent literacy, language development, and teacher–child verbal interactions. Dr. Bradley has used a formative experiment approach in her research.

Adriana G. Bus, PhD, is Professor of Early Literacy at the Graduate School of Education, Leiden University, The Netherlands. Her research has focused on early reading and writing development. With Marinus van IJzendoorn, she has conducted meta-analyses on book reading, phonemic awareness, and the nonword reading deficit.

Anne E. Cunningham, PhD, is Associate Professor of Cognition and Development at the Graduate School of Education, University of California, Berkeley. Known for her research in literacy, she studies the interplay of context and instruction in reading acquisition and development across the lifespan. Her research has focused on the cognitive prerequisites for learning to read, such as phonological awareness and orthographic knowledge, as well as the cognitive consequences of reading experience. Dr. Cunningham is an elected board member of the Society for the Scientific Study of Reading and the American Educational Research Association, Division C: Learning and Instruction.

Carolyn Denton, PhD, is Assistant Professor in the Department of Special Education at the University of Texas at Austin. She is a co-principal investigator for a large-scale study of reading intervention funded by the Institute of Education Sciences of the U.S. Department of Education under the Interagency Educational Research Initiative. Dr. Denton is focused on practical school-based research and in translating research into practice for preservice and inservice teachers.

Mark Dressman, PhD, is Associate Professor in the Department of Curriculum and Instruction at the University of Illinois at Urbana–Champaign. His recent research focuses on the functions of social theory in literacy research, in particular on an analysis of the multiple theoretical frames currently used to account for the struggles of some adolescent readers.

Nell K. Duke, EdD (see "About the Editors")

Jack M. Fletcher, PhD, is Professor in the Department of Pediatrics at the University of Texas, Houston Heath Science Center, and Associate Director of the Center for Academic and Reading Skills. For the past 25 years, Dr. Fletcher, a child neuropsychologist, has completed research on many aspects of the development of reading, language,

and other cognitive skills in children, with particular attention to issues involving definition and classification, neurobiological correlates, and, most recently, intervention. He is part of a group actively
studying the correlates of reading and math development, including
intervention, with functional neuroimaging methodologies, especially
magnetic source imaging.

Susan Florio-Ruane, EdD, is Professor of Teacher Education at
Michigan State University, East Lansing. Her research includes studies of schooling and the acquisition of written literacy, reading culture in autobiography, and re-engaging low-achieving readers by
innovative professional development. Her paper "The Social Organization of Classes and Schools" won the Division K Research in
Teacher Education Award of the American Educational Research
Association. Her book, *Teacher Education and the Cultural Imagination*,
won the National Reading Conference's Fry Outstanding Book
Award. In 2003, she received the Michigan State University Distinguished Faculty Award.

Susan R. Goldman, PhD, is Distinguished Professor of Psychology
and Education at the University of Illinois at Chicago and codirector
of the Center for the Study of Learning, Instruction, and Teacher Development. Her research interests are on learning and assessment and
the analysis of written and oral discourse as a method for investigating them. Dr. Goldman is widely published in discourse, psychology,
and education journals and presently heads the Society for Text and
Discourse. She has developed and researched several technology-
based environments for learning and assessment.

Douglas K. Hartman, PhD, is Associate Professor of Curriculum
and Instruction at the University of Connecticut, Storrs. His research focuses on literacy learning from historical, sociocultural, cognitive, and technological perspectives. Dr. Hartman is currently writing a history of the International Reading Association, teaching a
doctoral seminar on the history of literacy research, and serving as
president of IRA's History of Reading Special Interest Group.

William A. Henk, EdD, is Professor of Education and Dean of the
School of Education at Marquette University, Milwaukee. In the past
decade, his scholarly work has focused on measuring affective aspects
of literacy, and this line of research led to the coauthoring of the
Reader Self-Perception Scale and the Writer Self-Perception Scale,
two public-domain instruments. More recently, Dr. Henk played a
key role in the creation of observation frameworks that assist princi-

pals and literacy supervisors in the evaluation and enhancement of reading and writing instruction in classrooms.

Katherine Hilden, BA, is a doctoral student in Learning, Technology, and Culture at Michigan State University, East Lansing. Her research interests focus on reading comprehension in the elementary grades. She is currently exploring whether verbal protocols can be successfully used to measure early elementary students' reading comprehension and, if so, what they tell us about students' comprehension processes.

Marla H. Mallette, PhD (see "About the Editors")

Sarah J. McCarthey, PhD, is Associate Professor of Language and Literacy at the University of Illinois at Urbana–Champaign. Her research focuses on the social and cultural contexts of students' literacy learning, in particular on students' identities as writers. Dr. McCarthey has conducted several studies using case study methodology and is interested in the epistemological and theoretical underpinnings of a range of research methodologies.

Michael C. McKenna, PhD, is Professor in the Department of Curriculum, Foundations, and Reading at Georgia Southern University, Statesboro. His research interests include beginning reading, content area applications, literacy and technology, and children's attitudes toward reading and writing. His research into attitudes led him to coauthor two public-domain instruments featuring the Garfield cartoon character: the Elementary Reading Attitude Survey and the Writing Attitude Survey, both published in *The Reading Teacher*.

Ernest Morrell, PhD, is Assistant Professor of Teacher Education at Michigan State University, East Lansing. His research focuses on critical pedagogy, adolescent literacy instruction, and urban education. Dr. Morrell has used critical discourse analysis to make sense of the relationship between urban youth, popular culture, and literacy development.

Andrew C. Papanicolaou, PhD, is Professor and Director of the Division of Clinical Neurosciences, Department of Neurosurgery, University of Texas, Houston Health Science Center. Dr. Papanicolaou's academic interests center on the development of noninvasive functional brain imaging procedures for mapping the brain mechanisms mediating sensory, motor, and higher psychological functions, including oral and written language comprehension.

Michael Pressley, PhD, is Professor and Director of the Doctoral Program in Teacher Education at Michigan State University, East Lansing. His career has intermingled research on basic academic cognition as well as teaching and learning in schools. Dr. Pressley has received career research awards from the National Reading Conference and the Division of Educational Psychology of the American Psychological Association as well as a number of other awards. He is now emeritus editor of the *Journal of Educational Psychology*.

Victoria Purcell-Gates, PhD, is Canada Research Chair in Early Childhood Literacy at the University of British Columbia, Vancouver. Her research has focused on early literacy development, particularly as it interacts with community and home literacy practices. Dr. Purcell-Gates has conducted several ethnographies, one of which— *Other People's Words*—was awarded the 1996 Grawemeyer Award in Education, an international award given in four categories: education, political science, music, and religion.

David Reinking, PhD, is the Eugene T. Moore Professor of Teacher Education at Clemson University, Clemson, South Carolina. He is coeditor of *Reading Research Quarterly*, one of the most highly regarded and widely circulated research journals in education. His scholarly interests focus on the relation between technology and literacy. Dr. Reinking has several publications about formative or design experiments, and he employs this methodology in his research.

Christopher Schatschneider, PhD, is Associate Professor of Psychology at Florida State University, Tallahassee, and is a faculty associate at the Florida Center for Reading Research. His research focuses on the application of appropriate research designs and statistical models to the study of individual differences in early literacy development. Dr. Schatschneider has assisted in the design of numerous quasi-experimental studies of teacher and student factors that influence growth in early literacy skills.

Panagiotis G. Simos, PhD, is Associate Professor of Developmental Neuropsychology in the Department of Psychology, University of Crete, Greece. He has developed and validated special applications of magnetoencephalography for functional brain mapping. Dr. Simos has conducted several studies investigating the brain mechanisms that support language, reading, and memory functions in normally developing children and adults and in special populations such as patients with neurological disorders and learning disabilities.

Norman A. Stahl, PhD, is Professor and Chair of the Department of Literacy Education at Northern Illinois University, DeKalb. Over the years his research has focused on postsecondary reading instruction with particular interest in the field's history. Dr. Stahl has received honors from the National Association for Developmental Education, the College Reading and Learning Association, and the College Literacy and Learning Special Interest Group of the International Reading Association for his writings pertaining to college reading and learning. He has served as president of the History of Reading Special Interest Group of the International Reading Association and recently completed his term as historian for the National Reading Conference.

Keith E. Stanovich, PhD, holds the Canada Research Chair in Applied Cognitive Science at the Ontario Institute for Studies in Education of the University of Toronto. For his work on the cognitive effects of reading experience, phonological processing, and models of reading and reading disability, Dr. Stanovich has received the Oscar Causey Award from the National Reading Conference, the Sylvia Scribner Award from the American Educational Research Association, and the Distinguished Scientific Contribution Award from the Society for the Scientific Study of Reading.

Marinus H. van IJzendoorn, PhD, is Professor of Child and Family Studies at the Graduate School of Education, Leiden University, The Netherlands. His research focuses on attachment across the lifespan. With Adriana G. Bus, he has been involved in several meta-analyses on topics in emergent literacy.

Frank R. Vellutino, PhD, is Professor of Psychology at The University at Albany, the State University of New York. He is also director of the University's Child Research and Study Center, a research and student training center. Most of his research has been concerned with reading development, the cognitive underpinnings of reading, and the relationship between reading difficulties, various aspects of language, and other cognitive functions.

Jennifer Wiley, PhD, is Assistant Professor at the University of Illinois at Chicago. Her research on text processing has focused on understanding how background variables such as prior knowledge affect learning and problem solving. Many of her studies use eye tracking and discourse analysis to gather online data about the cognitive processes that support the best learning outcomes.

Preface

This book began with our first conversation, when we, Nell and Marla, were introduced to each other at the National Reading Conference in 1999: We were having dinner with mutual friends when, as aspiring new researchers, we each began to talk about our dissertation research. We found that we shared an interest in the literacy experiences and instruction provided to poor and minority children. However, our research was conducted from very different methodological and epistemological perspectives. Rather than dismissing each other's work on the grounds of lack of commensurability, we listened to one another. We realized that we could gain a deeper understanding of the issues that perplexed us by considering the value of each other's work. We haven't lost sight of the lesson we learned that night, and we hope that the chapters in this volume, taken together, highlight that lesson—many different kinds of literacy research, conducted rigorously, have value; together they yield greater insights than any one type alone.

Several months later Nell was at a proposal review session with David Reinking. Due to a conflict of interest, she and David were excused from the review of one of the proposals. As they talked in the hallway Nell complained to David about what she viewed as the often poor preparation of graduate students to be both producers and consumers of a variety of different kinds of research. Her concerns were based, among other things, on the limited number of hours devoted to research methodologies in doctoral studies contrasted with the plethora of research methodologies being used. David suggested that issue would fit nicely into the "Critical Issues" section of the *Journal of Literacy Research* (*JLR*), of which he was coeditor at the time.

The result was a commentary, "Preparation for New Literacy Researchers in Multi-Epistemological, Multi-Methodological Times" (Duke & Mallette, 2001), that detailed our thinking about this issue.

We suggested that, as in many areas of educational research, in recent decades the field of literacy has experienced a diversification of research methodologies (Dunston, Headley, Schenk, Ridgeway, & Gambrell, 1998; Guzzetti, Anders, & Neuman, 1999). Unfortunately, this seems to be resulting in a trend toward fragmentation, a splintering off into subfields. Increasingly, particular literacy conferences are aligned with some methodologies and not others; particular literacy journals publish some methodologies with regularity but not others; those using methodologies quite different from one another seem less and less likely to be talking with one another. We argued that literacy researchers need to work actively to reverse this trend, and this work starts with the preparation of new literacy researchers.

There also appeared to us at the time to be a trend away from discussions of methodology in literacy research (our sense now is that this trend may be reversing). There seemed to be a great amount of writing and a large number of presentations focused on research methodologies during the period of "qualitative versus quantitative" debates—but since that time they have dwindled. In literacy, the one book specifically designed to provide a comprehensive account of research methodologies (Kamil, Langer, & Shanahan, 1985) is now nearly 20 years old. Yet new methodologies, and new developments in older methodologies, are being developed all the time (e.g., Putney, Green, Dixon, & Kelly, 1999). Without dedicating time and resources to understanding methodologies, including new and developing methodologies, there is the danger of misunderstanding and even being ignorant of some forms of research and their potential contributions, which in turn can lead to missed opportunities. It can position literacy researchers to focus more on explaining and defending their methodologies than on discussing the findings they yield.

Some forces are narrowing what even "counts" as "scientific" educational research at precisely the time that the pressure on educational research to yield useful insights and understandings has never been greater (Pressley, Duke, & Boling, 2004). In essence, in some forums we are being asked to do more with less, with respect to the repertoire of accepted or favored research methodologies. Of course, many educational researchers have spoken against this situation and for the value of many forms of research (Shavelson & Towne, 2002). Clearly it is essential that educational researchers understand the unique contributions as well as limitations of particular forms of research and, as important, ways in which different forms of research can work together toward useful insights and understandings. For all these reasons we believed that it was important to bring together a group of scholars well respected for their use of particular research methodologies to create this volume.

We see this volume as a way of beginning where our *JLR* commentary ended. The following concluded that piece:

> Our contention is that the field of literacy needs to emphasize or reemphasize breadth of education, particularly in the area of research method and epistemology. However, this education should reflect the changing times of literacy research. It requires deepening our understanding and appreciation of the diversification of research epistemology and method, as well as providing an historical grounding in how they came to be. (Duke & Mallette, 2001, pp. 357–358)

We hope that this volume will go some way toward building or reinforcing understanding and appreciation of many research methodologies and the contributions they make singly, and together, to knowledge in our field.

REFERENCES

Duke, N. K., & Mallette, M. H. (2001). Critical Issues: Preparation for new literacy researchers in multi-epistemological, multi-methodological times. *Journal of Literacy Research, 33,* 345–360.

Dunston, P. J., Headley, K. N., Schenk, R. L., Ridgeway, V. G., & Gambrell, B. (1998). National Reading Conference research reflections: An analysis of 20 years of research. In T. Shanahan & F. V. Rodriguez-Brown (Eds.), *47th yearbook of the National Reading Conference* (pp. 441–450). Chicago: National Reading Conference.

Guzzetti, B., Anders, P. L., & Neuman, S. (1999). Thirty years of *JRB/JLR*: A retrospective of reading/literacy research. *Journal of Literacy Research, 31,* 67–92.

Kamil, M. L., Langer, J. A., & Shanahan, T. (1985). *Understanding research in reading and writing.* Boston: Allyn & Bacon.

Pressley, M., Duke, N. K., & Boling, E. C. (2004). The educational science and scientifically-based instruction we need: Lessons from reading research and policymaking. *Harvard Educational Review, 74,* 30–61.

Putney, L. G., Green, J. L., Dixon, C. N., & Kelly, G. J. (1999). Evolution of qualitative research methodology: Looking beyond defense to possibilities. *Reading Research Quarterly, 34,* 368–377.

Shavelson, R. J., & Towne, L. (2002). *Scientific research in education.* Washington, DC: National Research Council.

Acknowledgments

We have many people to thank for this book. Most important, we thank the contributors to the book, who have helped make our vision a reality. Their willingness to focus on the core content we requested for chapters, their responsiveness to requests for revision, and the seriousness with which they took this task are all deeply appreciated. Still more appreciated are the high standards these scholars have set and met for methodology in their own research. They are truly great assets to our field.

We also thank the larger literacy research community, in particular those who go out of their way to acknowledge the contributions of a range of methodologies to literacy research. Our doctoral students deserve our thanks as well both for reinforcing our belief in the need for this book and for illustrating for us the great promise of the next generation of literacy researchers.

Chris Jennison of The Guilford Press was supportive of this book from the minute we approached him, and we are most grateful for his role in the project. It was, we think, something of a risk to commission a volume, especially a volume of this kind, with such a green editorial pair as we are. We appreciate his willingness to take that risk. Diane Barone, Bill Henk, Don Leu, Ernest Morrell, and Vicki Purcell-Gates also deserve thanks for advice regarding the book's table of contents and/or other issues that arose in putting the volume together.

Finally, we must thank those who have helped us develop as scholars and as people: our mentors and our families. If you're proud of the book, please know that you deserve credit. Where it fails, know that we will keep working to live up to the ideals you set.

Contents

CHAPTER 1.   Introduction   1
             Marla H. Mallette and Nell K. Duke

CHAPTER 2.   **Case-Study** Research   7
             Diane M. Barone

CHAPTER 3.   Inferences from **Correlational** Data: 28
             Exploring Associations with Reading Experience
             Keith E. Stanovich and Anne E. Cunningham

CHAPTER 4.   **Discourse Analysis: Conversation**   46
             Susan Florio-Ruane and Ernest Morrell

CHAPTER 5.   **Discourse Analysis: Written Text**   62
             Susan R. Goldman and Jennifer Wiley

CHAPTER 6.   **Ethnographic** Research   92
             Victoria Purcell-Gates

CHAPTER 7.   **Experimental and Quasi-Experimental** Design   114
             in Literacy Research
             Frank R. Vellutino and Christopher Schatschneider

CHAPTER 8.   Connecting Research and Practice Using   149
             Formative and Design Experiments
             David Reinking and Barbara A. Bradley

The chapters in this volume are arranged in alphabetical order by the name of the methodology, which also appears in **boldface**.

CHAPTER 9. Doing **Historical** Research on Literacy 170
Norman A. Stahl and Douglas K. Hartman

CHAPTER 10. Developing Affective **Instrumentation** 197
for Use in Literacy Research
William A. Henk and Michael C. McKenna

CHAPTER 11. **Meta-Analysis** in Reading Research 227
Adriana G. Bus and Marinus H. van IJzendoorn

CHAPTER 12. **Neuroimaging** in Reading Research 252
Jack M. Fletcher, Panagiotis G. Simos,
Andrew C. Papanicolaou, and Carolyn Denton

CHAPTER 13. **Survey** Research 287
James F. Baumann and James J. Bason

CHAPTER 14. **Verbal Protocols** of Reading 308
Michael Pressley and Katherine Hilden

CHAPTER 15. Toward a Pragmatics of Epistemology, 322
Methodology, and Other People's Theories
in Literacy Research
Mark Dressman and Sarah J. McCarthey

CHAPTER 16. Conclusion 345
Nell K. Duke and Marla H. Mallette

APPENDIX. Alphabetical Listing of the Exemplars 355

INDEX 357

CHAPTER 1

Introduction

Marla H. Mallette
Nell K. Duke

Methodology, as defined in *Webster's* dictionary, is "the science of method, or orderly arrangement; specifically, the branch of logic concerned with the application of the principles of reasoning to scientific and philosophical inquiry" (Anges, 1999, p. 906). Method, within that, is defined simply as "a way of doing anything" (Anges, 1999, p. 906). In the context of this volume, method is a way of doing literacy research. And our emphasis in this volume is on the plural, methods or methodologies. That is, there are many ways of doing literacy research.

We initially conceptualized this volume as including an exhaustive account of literacy research methodologies, but realized that it would be impossible to include every methodology and/or variation of methodology used. Thus, we include here only a partial set of literacy research methodologies currently being used in the field. The process of determining which methodologies to include began by brainstorming a list. The list was then reviewed by several colleagues who were asked to add methodologies that were noticeably missing and to reduce redundancy in methodologies already included.

Of course, methodologies do not always fall into mutually exclusive categories. Some research can be considered more than one type of research or may combine methodologies in various ways. For example, *Ways with Words* (Heath, 1983) can be considered both an ethnography and a case study and in this book is discussed in both chapters. Thus while we have attempted to minimize redundancy in constructing the table of contents and in the editorial process, we have done so with the knowledge that there has been and will continue to be both overlap among and combinations of methodologies used in literacy research.

The chapter authors in this volume have stellar reputations for use of the methodology they write about, with numerous publications of rigorous research using that methodology. Thus they are well accomplished as literacy researchers rather than solely as methodologists. This results in a volume markedly different from a general methods text. However, the authors often refer the reader to these types of texts. We hope readers will take these references seriously. By no means is the information in these chapters adequate to teach one "how to" conduct particular types of research. However, we believe the discussions within do provide meaningful information and perspective on each methodology addressed.

The chapters in this book strike a balance between maintaining each author's individual writing style and voice and achieving consistency across them. To achieve this consistency in core content, we asked authors to address the following questions[1]:

1. What is this methodology (including a definition and description of the methodology and if possible some key history of the methodology in literacy)?
2. What kinds of questions and claims is this methodology appropriate for?
3. What are standards for quality in this methodology?
4. What is one or more exemplar of this methodology (in literacy) and what makes it so good?

We suggest readers approach each chapter with these four key questions in mind. We also strongly encourage readers to gather and read the exemplar or exemplars presented for each chapter. A listing of featured exemplars appears in two places: (1) at the end of this chapter, arranged by methodology, and (2) in the Appendix, arranged in alphabetical order.

In addition to the methodology chapters, the volume includes a chapter on the role of theory and epistemology in methodology (Dressman & McCarthey, Chapter 15). We view this as an important

---

[1]The original questions posed to the authors used the word *method* as opposed to *methodology*. However, in conceptualizing the volume and considering the depth and breadth of their discussions, we recognized that *methodology* clearly was the more appropriate term.

part of understanding literacy research. All research, whether explicitly stated or not, is grounded in epistemology, or one's view of what can and cannot be known and how. To understand a research methodology, we must situate the methodology in the epistemological tenets that ground it. The chapter authors also emphasize the need to recognize epistemological strengths and weaknesses of different methodologies. They remind us that just as all methodologies have something to contribute, they also have important limitations.

The final chapter in this volume looks across methodologies. Building on the foundation provided throughout the volume, we identify five core messages about methodology in literacy research:

- Message 1: Many different research methodologies, in fact each research methodology discussed in this book and others, have valuable contributions to make to the study of literacy.
- Message 2: Different types of research are for different types of questions and claims. The match of research methodology to research questions and resulting claims is essential.
- Message 3: There are standards of quality for every type of research. There is better- and poorer-quality research of every methodology.
- Message 4: Synergy across research methodologies is possible, powerful, and advisable.
- Message 5: We must urgently and actively pursue synergy across research methodologies.

Our discussion of these messages is intended to underscore again the need for all of us to be knowledgeable about and informed by research of a broad range of research methodologies. This book, we hope, provides one tool for doing that.

REFERENCES

Anges, M. (Ed.). (1999). *Webster's new world college dictionary* (4th ed.). New York: Macmillan.

Heath, S. B. (1983). *Ways with words: Language, life, and work in communities and classrooms*. Cambridge, UK: Cambridge University Press.

APPENDIX: LISTING OF FEATURED EXEMPLARS, ARRANGED BY METHODOLOGY

Case Study

Compton-Lilly, C. (2002). *Reading families: The literate lives of urban children.* New York: Teachers College Press.

Correlational

A program of research including, among others:

Cunningham, A. E., & Stanovich, K. E. (1997). Early reading acquisition and its relation to reading experience and ability ten years later. *Developmental Psychology, 33,* 934–945.

Discourse Analysis: Conversation

Michaels, S. (1981). "Sharing time": Children's narrative styles and differential access to literacy. *Language in Society, 10,* 423–443.

Morrell, E. (2002). Toward a critical pedagogy of popular culture: Literacy development among urban youth. *Journal of Adolescent and Adult Literacy, 46*(1), 72–77.

Discourse Analysis: Written Text

Coté, N., & Goldman, S. R. (1999). Building representations of informational text: Evidence from children's think-aloud protocols. In H. Van Oostendorp & S. R. Goldman (Eds.), *The construction of mental representations during reading* (pp. 169–193). Mahwah, NJ: Erlbaum

Coté, N., Goldman, S. R., & Saul, E. U. (1998). Students making sense of informational text: Relations between processing and representation. *Discourse Processes, 25,* 1–53.

Ethnography

Dyson, A. H. (2003). *The brothers and sisters learn to write: Popular literacies in childhood and school cultures.* New York: Teachers College Press.

Lewis, C. (2001). *Literacy practices as social acts: Power, status, and cultural norms in the classroom.* Mahwah, NJ: Erlbaum.

Purcell-Gates, V. (1995). *Other people's words: The cycle of low literacy.* Cambridge, MA: Harvard University Press.

Experimental and Quasi-Experimental

Foorman, B. R., Francis, D. J., Fletcher, J. M., Schatschneider, C., & Mehta, P. (1998). The role of instruction in learning to read: Preventing reading failure in at-risk children. *Journal of Educational Psychology, 90,* 37–55.

Vellutino, F. R., & Scanlon, D. M. (1987). Phonological coding, phonological awareness, and reading ability: Evidence from a longitudinal and experimental study. *Merrill–Palmer Quarterly, 33,* 321–363

Formative and Design Experiments

Reinking, D., & Watkins, J. (2000). A formative experiment investigating the use of multimedia book reviews to increase elementary students' independent reading. *Reading Research Quarterly, 35,* 384–419.

Historical

The NRC Oral History Project (forthcoming).

Instrumentation (Affective)

Henk, W. A., & Melnick, S. A. (1995). The Reader Self-Perception Scale (RSPS): A new tool for measuring how children feel about themselves as readers. *The Reading Teacher, 48,* 470–482.

Meta-Analysis

Bus, A. G., & van IJzendoorn, M. H. (1999). Phonological awareness and early reading: A meta-analysis of experimental training studies. *Journal of Educational Psychology, 91,* 403–414.

Neuroimaging

Simos, P. G., Fletcher, J. M., Sarkari, S., Billingsley, R. L., Francis, D. J., Castillo, E. M., Denton, C., & Papanicolaou, A. C. (2004). *Early development of neuropsychological processes involved in normal reading and reading disability.* Manuscript under review.

Survey

Baumann, J. F., Hoffman, J. V., Duffy-Hester, A. M., & Ro, J. M. (2000). *The First R* yesterday and today: U.S. elementary reading instruction practices reported by teachers and administrators. *Reading Research Quarterly, 35,* 338–377.

McKenna, M. C., Kear, D. J., & Ellsworth, R. A. (1995). Children's attitudes toward reading: A national survey. *Reading Research Quarterly, 30,* 934–956.

Verbal Protocols

Brown, R., Pressley, M., Van Meter, P., & Schuder, T. (1996). A quasi-experimental validation of transactional strategies instruction with low-achieving second grade readers. *Journal of Educational Psychology, 88*, 18–37.

Wyatt, D., Pressley, M., El-Dinary, P. B., Stein, S., Evans, P., & Brown, R. (1993). Comprehension strategies, worth and credibility monitoring, and evaluations: Cold and hot cognition when experts read professional articles that are important to them. *Learning and Individual Differences, 5*, 49–72.

CHAPTER 2

Case-Study Research

Diane M. Barone

What *can* be done with thousands of children but count them? In mass, children—and the challenges they present—are faceless, nameless, and overwhelming. But these massive numbers of children are not isolated individuals; they're social participants included, or so we hope, in particular classrooms and schools, in particular institutions and communities.

—DYSON (1995, p. 51)

Dyson (1995) stated the foregoing in her response to the importance of case-study research. She continued her conversation by saying that case studies do not offer information about causality regarding teaching practices and learning, for example, but they do provide information on the "dimensions and dynamics of classroom living and learning" (p. 51). While Dyson is certainly in support of the value of case-study research, Yin (1994) noted that social scientists have stereotyped case study as "a weak sibling among social science methods" (p. xiii). Although he began his preface with this statement, his book presented an extended argument as to why this belief was wrong. The lack of status for case-study research was particularly evident after World War II when behaviorist psychology and large experimental studies were seen as the most rigorous form of research (Birnbaum, Emig, & Fisher, 2003). However, this lack of status is no longer documented and many researchers are using this design because they are dissatisfied with the limited answers they receive by studying percentages or stanines, particularly during the last 30 years (Birnbaum et al., 2003).

Clearly, case-study research is supported, maligned, and misunderstood (Merriam, 1988). While I have touched on its support and criticism, I now consider the misunderstandings attached to it. One misunderstanding centers on seeing case-study research as synonymous with single-subject design (Neuman & McCormick, 2000). Although these two are often confused, single-subject design is experimental and considers the relationship between an independent and dependent variable—it is just focused on one individual at a time—and this is where the confusion is centered. A second misunderstanding is that case-study research is the same as the cases that are used to help students and teachers understand practice. For example, Shulman, Whittaker, and Lew (2002) presented problem-centered cases on assessment for educators to consider. These cases, while illustrative of dilemmas in practice, are narratives used to explore and reflect on practice, not research studies or reports. Their goal is to allow novices to critically analyze the dimensions built into a case that demonstrate the complexity of teaching, outside the classroom situation.

So what exactly is case-study research? Stake (2000) and Merriam (1988) indicate that this question is not easy to answer. They report that all social scientists and practitioners are engaged in case exploration, sometimes known as casework or case history, in that they observe as a doctor does a patient or a reporter an event. However, case study, as described by Merriam (1988), is a research design that is descriptive and nonexperimental. A critical characteristic of case-study research is that it is a study of a bounded system that could be a child, a teacher, or a classroom, for example (Stake, 2000). Boundedness is important for it defines what is excluded or included in a study. For example, one first-grade classroom may be the focus of study and, therefore, the teacher and students in the neighboring first-grade classroom would not be considered participants.

Merriam (1988) further defines four additional characteristics, beyond the issue of boundedness, that are essential when defining this research design: (1) *particularistic* in that the study is centered on a particular situation, program, event, phenomenon, or person; (2) *descriptive* in that the researcher gathers rich description of the object of study; (3) *heuristic* as the study enriches a reader's understanding; and (4) *inductive* as the data drive the understandings that emerge from the study. In summary, case study is defined as "an intensive, holistic description and analysis of a single entity, phenomenon, or social unit" (Merriam, 1988, p. 16).

Beyond the definition of a case study, Stake (2000) describes three types of case-study research. While the focus of study is not changed based on type, the purpose of the case varies within each one. In his first type, *intrinsic*, the researcher is seeking a better understanding of a case—that is, he or she is exploring the case because it is interesting, not because it might contribute to theory building. An exemplar of this type of case study within literacy research is demonstrated in the work of Sarroub (2002). In this study, she explored the multiple uses of religious and secular text in the school, home, and community of Yemeni high school girls. Her goal was to describe their uses of literacy in multiple settings, not to build a theory around them.

Stake's second type of case study is called *instrumental*. Here the researcher is looking for insight into an issue. Stake says that in this type, the case moves to the background of interest, for it is being used to understand something else. An exemplar of this type is seen in the work of Rogers (2002). Her focus of study was an African American mother and daughter who lived in poverty and were able to successfully negotiate the literacy expectations in their home and community, although not in school. She used her study of these two individuals to explain why children from nonmainstream homes may fail to thrive in school.

The last type of case-study research is *collective case study*, or multiple case studies, where a researcher investigates numerous cases to study a phenomenon, group, condition, or event. Stake emphasizes that this type is a refinement of instrumental case study; the only difference is that the researcher is studying multiple cases. The redundancy of cases is purposeful as the researcher is building a stronger understanding and a more compelling argument for the significance of the work through the use of multiple cases. Exemplars of this type of research are seen in the work of Ladson-Billings (1994), where she studied multiple teachers and the way they supported the learning of African American students, and in Barone's research (1999) where she explored the literacy development of children who were prenatally exposed to crack cocaine. In both studies, the patterns that were observed were seen across multiple cases and in multiple settings, thus establishing additional credibility for the results.

Wolcott (1994) has criticized the third type of case study, collective case study. He compared multiple case studies with an attempt to replicate quantitative, comparative measures, and he felt that much is lost in the rich detail of the study because it is focused on comparison rather than meticulous description. Miles and Huberman (1994), on the other hand, argue that the results of multiple case studies are more compelling than single cases and contribute to literal replication (i.e., prediction of similar results). So clearly, with the multiple-case-study design, there are trade-offs that need to be considered. Certainly, as Wolcott warned, there is a loss of detail for each case, but as Miles and Huberman noted, multiple cases are often viewed as more compelling than single-case studies.

THE HISTORY OF CASE-STUDY RESEARCH IN LITERACY

Case study has a rich history in literacy research. As a way of narrowing this review I selected case studies that are book length rather than include the numerous case studies published in journals. Lea McGee and I explored book-length cases for a presentation at the National Reading Conference in 2000 and I drew from this exploration for this overview of case-study research in literacy. The majority of the studies selected focus on early literacy learning and instruction. This does not suggest that there are not other worthy case studies representing other populations; the narrow selection was meant as a way to bound the studies selected for this chapter.

The data collection for these studies varied from retrospective parent diaries to multiple sources such as observations, interviews, and artifacts. The participants also varied in that many were single-participant studies, often the researcher's child or grandchild, to studies of classrooms of students. In the majority of studies that are reported in this chapter, the researchers had an instrumental focus for their study. In other words, the case participants were selected to gain an understanding of a literacy practice, for example.

Earliest Case Studies

White (1956) wrote one of the first, book-length case studies that focused on literacy. She was a children's librarian in New Zealand and kept a retrospective parent diary of Carol's, her daughter's, interactions with books from when she was 2 years old until she was 5. Within this book, White established the precursors for response to literature research. She described her daughter's life-to-text and text-to-life experiences that were shared through reading. For example, Carol enjoyed books about babies when she had a baby sister. White commented about the significance of her descriptive work when she wrote:

> We see indeed, a twofold process at work: in some degree Carol's way of life determines the meaning she sees in the stories read to her; yet, on the other hand (and this is perhaps the more obvious), the meaning of things as it has been revealed to her through literature constantly influences the way she interprets the things that

happen around her. Seldom, I think, has the interaction of literature and life in these early years been so clearly portrayed. (pp. x–xi)

In 1975, Butler, in *Cushla and Her Books*, studied her granddaughter's interaction with books. Although there are clear similarities with the work of White, this study was a dissertation study under the guidance of Marie Clay and it focused on a child who was severely handicapped, not a *precocious* child as White described her daughter. What is particularly amazing about her work is that she connected her work to Vygotsky (1962) and highlighted the importance of social factors in a child's development. She wrote, "the effects of the particular environment to which the child is exposed—exercise some effect on the rate at which he will pass through all the essential stages, from birth onwards" (p. 90). Her work is certainly one of the first in literacy that recognized the importance of the social environment to a child's literacy development.

These early case studies focused on literature and its importance to young readers. Both researchers engaged in retrospective note taking following book-reading episodes. They looked closely at how a daughter and granddaughter made connections between books and personal experiences. And Butler set the groundwork for further exploration of the importance of social settings in the learning of young children.

The 1980s and Case-Study Research

From these early beginnings, case studies were established in the literacy community to study the reading to and interactions of young children to text. During the 1980s, case-study research took on new importance because of the work of Bissex (1980), Calkins (1983), Heath (1983), Cochran-Smith (1984), Baghban (1984), and Taylor and Dorsey-Gaines (1988), among others. These researchers laid the groundwork for research that continues to be explored into the 2000s.

Bissex (1980), in another dissertation study, studied the writing of her son David. Through this work, she helped literacy teachers and researchers understand how David learned to represent words and ideas in print. However, Bissex highlighted additional reasons as to why this study was important. Although her work is not often credited for an understanding of phonemic awareness, she wrote, "The superiority of first graders on segmentation tasks may result from their experience with the printed word" (p. 90). Her observation certainly connects with what is currently known about phonemic awareness (Ehri et al., 2001).

Bissex (1980) also spoke to the importance of case-study research. She wrote: "Case studies widen the parameters within which we view learning to read. They remind us that the methods and time schedules by which these skills are conventionally taught are not necessarily conditions for learning them" (p. 135).

This result, Bissex stated, could only be learned through careful, longitudinal case-study research. Moreover, her case study emphasized the dynamic nature of a child's learning about written language. She critiqued the notion of children accumulating discrete bits of information about written language and stated that children "evolve increasingly efficient—that is, comprehensive, informed, and practiced—strategies for understanding the relations between spoken and written language" (p. 194). And although not the remembered focus of her book, she continued in the tradition of White and Butler and shared the connections that David made between reading and writing.

Bissex's work led to numerous studies about invented spelling and error analysis. Most notable among this work are the studies that have been conducted by Henderson (1981) and his students, known as the Virginia studies, and Ehri (1997).

Shortly after Bissex's work, Calkins's (1983) *Lessons from a Child: On Teaching and Learning of Writing* was published. This work centered on the writing process and included consideration of topic choice, routines, revision and editing, and conferencing. Calkins used Susie, a student in a classroom where she observed, to present a vivid image of what revision could be for young students. Calkins's work departed from earlier case studies in two very important ways. While she studied one child, Susie, this was not her child or her grandchild. In addition, she studied Susie in her school setting and included the importance of her classroom teacher. While Butler talked about the importance of the social environment in the home, Calkins moved this importance to the classroom setting and detailed how one teacher supported the writing development of students, most particularly Susie, in her room.

As did Bissex, Calkins (1983) highlighted the importance of case-study research. She wrote:

> My hope is that through closely observing one child's growth in writing, we'll learn to watch for and to respect each child's growth in writing. My hope is that by understanding the pathways one child has taken in learning to write, we may be able to discern and

trust the pathways other children will take. Susie is representative
of all children in that she, too, is unique. (p. 7)

Calkins (1983) continued by saying that "all our students are case
studies" (p. 7).

Furthermore, Calkins bravely announced that this was "the first
study of its kind" (p. 5). This was so because she shared a day-to-day
view of how a child experienced writing and revision. This was unlike
previous work for she did not divide Susie's work into discrete categories or levels. Throughout her book, Calkins used the thoughts of
Vygotsky (1962) to explain her results, as did Butler much earlier.
She highlighted the idea of instruction preceding development and
the idea of the zone of proximal development to shed light on the importance of peer work and teacher conferencing with individual students.

Perhaps, one of the best-known case studies is *Ways with Words:
Language, Life, and Work in Communities and Classrooms* by Heath
(1983). This work crosses over and is also considered ethnography as
it was conducted over 10 years and looked at the home, community,
and school. While not spending a lot of time on this study in this
chapter, it is important to include it for it identified the importance
of family to literacy understandings and the importance of the kind
of talk and stories that were shared in homes and how they related to
children's success in schools.

Heath's work departed from the traditions of earlier case-study
research as she studied many children and families that were not considered middle class. She included their community, home, and
school experiences and enriched the more limited earlier studies that
only considered children in one setting (importantly, Bissex studied
her son in school and home settings). In her work, as described earlier by Wolcott (1994), the uniqueness of each study is secondary to
the comparisons that she provided that considered three communities as the focus. However, as can be seen by the importance of her
work into the 2000s, this limitation did not impact the importance
of her work to understandings of literacy as being broader than in-
class instruction.

Using a similar design focus, Cochran-Smith (1984) studied all
the middle-class children in one preschool classroom to learn about
the importance of storybook reading. Her study is considered instrumental and the students are secondary to the knowledge that she
wanted to acquire about this strategy. In her 18-month-long investigation, she discovered that there were two important rules about the

story-reading process: (1) a reader must read differentially depending on the audience, genre, purpose, and setting; and (2) "readers themselves contribute actively to the reading process by bringing their individual knowledge to bear upon texts (hence one book can have many realizations)" (p. 235). Perhaps, most surprising to me when reading her book were her descriptions of children talking about Superheroes such as Batman and Spiderman, or the popular culture. Her work predates the work of Dyson (1997) by 10 years or more, and certainly other researchers currently looking at this phenomenon (Alvermann, Huddleston, & Hagood, 2002; Xu, 2002).

Like White and Butler, Baghban (1984) returned to a view of her own daughter as she learned to read and write by keeping a diary centered on this development. Her study investigated this development from birth to 3 years of age and was a doctoral study similar to that done by Bissex. Her work, as has others, detailed the importance of social aspects in learning to read and write. Beyond this focus, she identified her daughter's connections with environmental print. She described how her daughter, Giti, pointed at the *K* in Special K cereal, and said "K-Mart." Baghban also identified drawing as the fifth language art. She compared writing and drawing by noting that both required motor control, were based on experiences, and moved from more contextualized experiences to decontextualized ones as the symbol systems became internalized.

Perhaps, most interesting in this work to the focus of this chapter is her rationale for using case study. She contends that case study is the best method to use when learning about individuals and it is particularly effective when studying complex phenomena in real-life situations. Further, to support her use of case study she noted that in the latest *Annual Summary of Investigations Relating to Reading, July 1, 1979 to June 30, 1980*, Weintraub (1981) claimed that because there have been so many investigations into single cases that this type of study was "no longer suspect or even unusual" (p. 7). She also extensively discussed the limited generalizability of case-study research, but then she presented conflicting thoughts when she said "with a sufficient number of such long-term case studies, generalizations have the opportunity to be validated" (p. 7). It appeared that she was arguing that with many case studies focused on the same topic, generalizations centered on the findings would be appropriate.

The last case-study research to be reported that was conducted in the 1980s is the work of Taylor and Dorsey-Gaines (1988). They, as had Heath, moved to studying low-income families when they selected black, urban families as the focus of their research. While Heath explored why low-income children had difficulty in school,

Taylor and Dorsey-Gaines turned this view inside out as they wanted to know why black, urban, poor children were doing well in first grade. They discovered that these children bridged their home literacy to school, their families supported literacy in home and in school, and their families wanted and supported their children in becoming "independent survivors in a sometimes hostile world" (p. 209).

Moreover, while Bissex was merely displeased with much of the schooling her son received, Taylor and Dorsey-Gaines were extremely critical of the instruction they observed. They wrote:

> Literacy cannot be quantified in numbers, nor is it directly related to the frequency of use. It cannot be taught through a decoding process, nor through a series of disconnected (if well ordered) exercises. We can pull language apart, but we cannot expect children to do the same. Children need to be able to create public and private text worlds with continual opportunities to use their expressive abilities to generate new meanings and maintain personal and shared interpretations of the social, technical, and aesthetic types and uses of literacy. It would be hard to dispute the assertion that, in most of our schools, few such opportunities currently exist. (p. 201)

Their argument continued as they noted that schools did not recognize the lives of students or their complex social and cognitive abilities. Schools preferred to assign exercises and tests that were not relevant to the lives of students and, perhaps more important, were limited to low-level skills. Similar arguments are seen in current research, particularly that of Kris Gutierrez (Gutierrez et al., 2002).

During the 1980s, case-study research became increasingly important to literacy researchers, and as Baghban wrote, they were "no longer suspect or unusual" (p. 7). These researchers explored writing, invented spelling, storybook reading, successful minority students, and the connections between home and school. They moved from considering their own children to larger groups of children who were frequently not considered mainstream. And as seen in the work of Bissex and Taylor and Dorsey-Gaines, a critical perspective on schools was evident.

Case-Study Research in the 1990s

In the 1990s, case-study research extended from its traditions as seen in the work of Schickendanz, Wolf and Heath, Rowe, Purcell-Gates, Martens, Dyson, Ballenger, and Barone. Their work was similar in some ways as several of these researchers explored the development of their own children (Schickendanz, Wolf and Heath, Martens, and Rowe); however, the research questions became more complex and children representing diverse backgrounds most often became the focus of study. These researchers studied writing, reading and response to literature, and diversity.

Schickendanz (1990) conducted a retrospective study centered on her son, Adam, where she wanted to learn how he came to understand how words are constructed. In much of her work, you can hear the voice of her son as he explained what he did on assignments and writing that she had saved. Adam's writing understandings began with connections between the physical relationship of things and their representation. Through extended exploration, Adam learned how to use letters to represent sounds in words "making more starts and stops, and then, finally set out a spurt of independent, phonemic-based writing" (p. 31). Schickendanz demonstrated how complicated the process of learning to represent words is when she stated, "I suspect that Adam—and other children—require considerable knowledge about phonemic segmentation and letter-sound correspondences before they can take off on their own and create spelling" (p. 27).

Shickendanz is a careful observer and her book is filled with fine-grained analysis of her son's writing. And though she has many insights about the development of writing for teachers and researchers, I found one finding of hers to be particularly important. She wrote, "Inventive spellers are not taking risks; they think they are spelling words right. The reluctant child knows more and digs in his heels" (p. 104). This finding explains why some children in school refuse to use their best efforts to spell a word; they know it has one single representation and they want to replicate that. They are dissatisfied when their teachers say just write it as best you can.

Continuing in the tradition of studying one's own child, Wolf and Heath (1992) detail and explain the responses to books that Wolf's two daughters produced. This work is reminiscent of the observations made by White and Butler. Within the two cases, those of Lindsey and Ashley, shared in this book, a reader learns about connections from life to literature and literature to life. For example, the girls scrub the floor as the children did in the *Little House* books or they explain that they are not the evil stepsister from Cinderella. Wolf and Heath highlight the difference between the act of reading and the experience of reading. In all the examples shared in the book, the reader understands how the girls brought the experiences that were read about in books to create meaning in their day-to-day experiences. They wrote about these important experiences: "Literacy is not acquired in a vacuum. Nor does it spring fully formed from our minds, like Athena from the head of Zeus. It is an evolutionary process changing from generation to generation and from life to life" (p. 24).

Within the rich descriptions, they note that Ashley preferred nonfiction text and that even in this rich, home literacy background, Lindsey had difficulty learning to decode text in first grade. Beyond these discoveries, they detail how the girls used the rich vocabulary from books. For example, Lindsey asked, "Is a bier like a grave?" after reading *Sleeping Beauty*. This discussion of vocabulary learned in text is similar to the current work being done by Beck (2002) where the importance of vocabulary for reading development and comprehension is addressed.

As with other cases already shared, Wolf and Heath (1992) compared the learning that the girls experienced at home and how they had to adapt this learning in school situations. They wrote:

> The comparatively stripped-down life of opportunities for extended discussion, and the emphasis on facts rather than interpretation bear little resemblance to what the girls knew to be reading-to-learn at home. To be successful in school, they would need to adapt their abilities to the tasks of schooling and limit their understandings to finding the prescribed answers to the relatively simple stories of basal readers and other textbooks in the classroom. (p. 191)

Wolf and Heath continued the criticism of schools in that they saw teachers asking low-level, constrained questions that took children away from real experiences with literature.

Moving away from home settings, Rowe (1994) explored the literacy learning of 21 students in a middle-class preschool. Her study is similar to Cochran-Smith's in that she was more interested in learning about the children's perspectives in general, rather than highlighting the children as individuals. Her work saw literacy as something that is "not mastered once and for all time" (p. 3). Rather, this process evolves as a child interprets the semiotic potential within text. Rowe contended that because children's perspectives and knowledge of the social world are different from those of adults, a researcher and teacher must come to understand the child's perspectives of literacy activities.

Her careful analysis is similar to Schickendanz's and she included discourse analysis as well. Through this analysis that occurred while children wrote, she discovered that "literacy activities became embedded in peer culture" (p. 119). Her work is very similar to the research done by Dyson (1997) in that she highlighted the importance of peers in literacy development.

In a departure from studying one's own children or children in middle-class preschools, Purcell-Gates (1995) engaged in inquiry centered on Donny and Jenny, a mother and son with Appalachian roots. Unlike the work of Taylor and Dorsey-Gaines (1988), she wanted to understand why this child struggled in school. And unlike earlier work, Purcell-Gates took on a critical stance when she tutored Donny and helped his mother negotiate school.

There were many interesting results to this study. First, she concluded that phonics instruction needs to be responsive to a child's knowledge. Further, she said that "new skills and strategies are learned mainly through the process of reading itself" (p. 79). Second, while Jenny wanted to and tried to help Donny with his homework, she was not able to do so. However, the school just saw Donny as lazy for he did not complete his homework. The onus for homework was totally placed with the parent and child. And third, the school used Donny's literacy struggles as further evidence that "Appalachian parents are irresponsible and uncaring about their children's education" (p. 161). While the deficit view is noted in other works, Purcell-Gates provided careful description in how this view develops when schools do not consider the needs and strengths of the families they serve.

In 1996, Martens engaged in a 3-year case study that centered on her adopted daughter, Sarah. She wanted to discover how a child viewed learning to read and write, a view that was used in the work of Schickendanz. Martens's book is filled with carefully described home events that contributed to Sarah's literacy understandings. Although there are numerous examples throughout, she highlights the importance of learning to write one's own name and acquiring the alphabetic principle to literacy development. Through these understandings, her daughter could now share her writing with others and they could gain the meaning conveyed in her messages. Sarah's story concludes with her kindergarten year where her teacher's view of literacy learning and instruction did not match home. Martens offers suggestions for early literacy teachers in which they are encouraged to observe children and teach based on these observations. What I found interesting in this case is that the mismatch between home and school literacy knowledge is most often noted for children who are from high-poverty backgrounds. In this book, a similar mismatch is observed for a child from a middle-class background, thus making the complexity of teaching literacy to young children even greater.

The next three cases (Dyson, Ballenger, and Barone) move away from consideration of one's own child or only one child. These studies consider high-poverty, language-rich children in the complexity of their classrooms.

Dyson (1997) studied second and third graders over 2 years as part of her research program that considers how children learn to write. In this study, she concentrated on how young children use Superhero stories "to feel powerful in a (pretend) danger-filled world" (p. 14). Her book is filled with events where children dealt with issues of power, romance, gender, and race in writing, the theatre enactments of their writing, and in their official and unofficial talk.

Dyson's work is powerful in that she argues for parents, teachers, and administrators to be sensitive to the "ideological as well as the social dimensions of literacy" (p. 184). She carefully crafts vignettes so that readers understand the importance of building on and responding to what children know and can do alone and with others. Her work highlights the importance of popular culture to children's personal and academic development.

Ballenger's work (1999) considered young, 3- and 4-year-old, Haitian children. In this study she was both teacher and researcher. She shared that when she first worked with these children she engaged in deficit thinking and considered them to be deficient. Throughout her book, she reflected on how she moved from this view to one where she considered each child's strengths. In her study, it was possible to see the tensions of a teacher as she tried to bring her students to middle-class understandings of book reading. Her study, unlike Dyson's with a focus on students, was concerned with the teacher's dilemmas in teaching to this group of students.

In much of her study, she discussed how she tried to make up for the lack of storybook reading that occurred in the home by reading numerous books to her students in the classroom. She shared her frustrations when children considered catalogues to be on an equal par with books. She concluded "providing storybook reading experience does not create a child who has a mainstream understanding of books" (p. 78). Rather, she believed, "storybook reading was not the same activity in this class as the one described in the literature" (p. 79). She contended that she had to understand her students' interpretations of book reading, which included not understanding that books represented stories and that they could talk throughout a book reading, before she could let them come to know her understandings. Her work extended the work of White, Butler, and Wolf and Heath in that she identified how off-topic comments may in fact help children make connections within text and between texts.

Finally, Barone's study (1999) explored the literacy development of 26 children prenatally exposed to crack cocaine. In her work, she described the children both at home and at school as she tried to understand how each child developed as a reader and writer. Her work demonstrated that children with this prenatal history could be successful in learning to read and write in their mainstream classrooms. Her work also highlighted the importance of the teacher in each child's success. And similar to Taylor and Dorsey-Gaines (1988), she found

> sharp contrasts between the classrooms of the children in schools for middle-class and poor children. I also discovered that children of color who attended middle-class schools could be the victims of discrimination. I found that what I thought were universally endorsed practices for children's literacy development were used infrequently in primary classrooms. I found that parents supported their child's learning but often were distanced from their child's teachers. I found that teachers were often unaware of the home circumstances of the children they taught. (p. 10)

The results of this study that was conducted in numerous schools and homes over 4 years, not just one classroom or home, are reminiscent of many of the case studies reported. Schools were found to not be particularly supportive of children, especially high-poverty children. The curriculum was often skills based and deficit oriented, rather than meaning based and difference oriented. Teachers did not understand the uniqueness of the children they taught and taught to the class, rather than individuals. Literacy developed in social contexts where children could talk to each other and the teacher, although these contexts were not always encouraged by teachers. Teachers were critical to each child's literacy learning—they were more important than the curricula they enacted.

Each of the cases shared provides a deeper understanding into how children develop into readers and writers. They enhance and provide rich descriptions into how this process happens. They also, as seen in the work of Bissex, provide roadmaps for the quantitative research that followed. By exploring case studies, a picture of children's learning is shared as well as the dilemmas of teaching culturally and language-rich children as particularly seen in the work of Ballenger.

The case studies that have been conducted in the 1990s are more complex than those done earlier. Like earlier studies, they considered writing, reading and response, and reading and writing development. However, they have moved from a consideration of one child, often a family member, to many children in school and home settings. And these children most often represent cultures and have home languages not considered mainstream. These cases have as their goal an understanding of home literacy practices and school literacy practices so that all children have the opportunity of developing into successful readers and writers.

In this section, the results of each study have been the focus, rather than the specific details of how the researchers structured their case studies. The exemplar studies were chosen because the researchers engaged in rigorous data collection and analysis that most often included multiple observations, interviews, and artifacts. Rather than repeatedly sharing these details, I chose to highlight the importance of their work to the literacy community. Through this foregrounding of results, the importance of case-study research to the knowledge base of literacy learning and instruction is clearly documented.

FOR WHAT KINDS OF QUESTIONS AND CLAIMS IS THIS METHODOLOGY APPROPRIATE?

Case-study research generally answers one or more questions that begin with *how* or *why* (Yin, 1994). Stake (1995) recommends that the researcher write out 10 to 20 prospective questions. From this initial list, the researcher narrows to two or three questions that guide the data collection and analysis.

Another strategy is to start with one broad question and as the study progresses other questions emerge which provide more focus. Barone (1999) did this in her study where she began with one broad question: How do children prenatally exposed to crack cocaine develop as readers and writers? During the second year of her study, she added a second question that included the classroom contexts that were established by teachers. She found that just looking at children was not sufficient as some teachers did not create learning environments that supported children's literacy learning. By just saying that a child did not enhance his or her understandings of literacy during a year presented a limited view, one that only considered the child.

McCarthey (1998) used yet another strategy when she started with one question and then used multiple lenses to explore it. She found that by using different lenses, different interpretations of the data were possible, each enriching the other. For example, if a child's identity was considered shy by the teacher, this interpretation of the child's identity was preferred. However, when this child was observed to be the leader in small-group interaction, this identity needed to be reconceptualized. Similarly, Hargreaves, Earl, and Schmidt (2002) studied alternative assessment reform from four perspectives that included technological, cultural, political, and postmodern. Thus, they gained a richer understanding of the phenomenon that could not be garnered from the use of one interpretation.

While finding the appropriate question for case study is important, it is also necessary to know when to use a case-study design. Yin (1994) described a common misconception regarding case study. He said that at one time case studies were only seen as appropriate for exploratory studies. However, today, case studies, he argues, can be used for description and explanation as well as exploration. Importantly, case studies are most often used when the researcher has no control over the behaviors that are being studied (e.g., in Dyson's study where she was investigating the writing behaviors of young students). It is misleading to believe, however, that case study can only be used to observe behavior. When a researcher assumes a critical stance, as seen in the work of Ballenger, he or she can use what is discovered during research study to improve the conditions for learning and therefore change the environment that is being investigated while the study is occurring.

Once the questions and purpose for the study are established, the researcher needs to select participants, or the unit or units for analysis. Patton (1990) discusses the need for purposeful sampling in case-study research. He recommends the selection of "information-rich cases" (p. 169). These are cases in which the researcher can learn a great deal and thoughtfully answer the question or questions posed. Yin (1994) describes the basic designs or reasons for case-study research. These include:

Single-case research

- To test a theory (single case can be used to determine if the propositions of the theory are correct)
- An extreme or unique case (often used in clinical psychology)
- Revelatory case (analyze a phenomenon previously unavailable to researchers)

Multiple-case research

- Used to predict similar results (literal replication)
- Used to produce contrasting results for predictable reasons (theoretical replication)

Simultaneously with the development of questions, purpose, and sampling, the researcher is expected to develop a rigorous design for the case study. This part includes data collection and analysis, as well as time in the field.

WHAT ARE STANDARDS FOR QUALITY
IN THIS METHODOLOGY?

Yin (1994) described several ways to determine the quality of case study. First is the use multiple sources of evidence. These might include multiple observations, interviews, and the collection of artifacts and documents. By using multiple data sources, the researcher can discover "a converging line of inquiry" (p. 92). As a result, the researcher has built a compelling case for his or her results and conclusions. Second, Yin argues for the creation of a chain of evidence. Here the researcher presents in his or her case the evidence in a linear fashion and how it contributed to the conclusions reached. In this way the reader can follow the path of data collection and analysis with the researcher. Third, the case study is reviewed by the key informant(s) before it appears in print. Through this process, the researcher is asking the key informant to correct any misconceptions that may have found their way into the report.

In addition to the strategies noted by Yin, credibility for a case study comes from length of time in the field (Merriam, 1988). Through extended time in the field, the researcher guarantees that what has been witnessed represents a pattern, rather than an aberration. Finally, the researcher needs to carefully consider ethical issues that include any biases that may be personally held and report these to the reader as well as the remedies the researcher took to hold bias in check through the interpretation of the data. Beyond personal bias, other ethical issues are relevant to case-study research. These include the researcher becoming involved with persons, issues, or events under study, maintaining confidentiality, ownership of the data, and problems with the inability to distinguish data from the researcher's interpretations (Merriam, 1988).

WHAT IS ONE OR MORE EXEMPLAR OF THIS METHODOLOGY
AND WHAT MAKES IT SO GOOD?

While there are many exemplars of this methodology in literacy research, I have chosen *Reading Families: The Literate Lives of Urban Children* by Catherine Compton-Lilly (2003) as a model. Her book represents her dissertation work that focused on parents and students and the importance of reading and how these families enacted reading in their homes. Her goal was to learn from her students and their families and to challenge the prevailing deficit views of urban families. Her work is similar to that of Taylor and Dorsey-Gaines (1988).

Her study design is a year-long multiple case study with an instrumental purpose in that she is using her 10 parent–child dyads,
randomly selected, to understand literacy. In her book she shares the
results of her 10 case studies and then uses one chapter to look
closely at one family, that of Mrs. Holt, so that readers understand
the way Bradford's (her son) "reading experiences are conceptualized
within discourse communities that operate in his home, at school,
and within the larger community" (p. 124).

Within her book, she uses one chapter to carefully lay out the
methodology that she used for her study. Unlike most examples, she
spends considerable time describing her analysis of the data. In this
description she explains how she used critical discourse analysis to
help her see "contradictions between various ideological positions
and power struggles that permeated the lives of teachers, students,
and parents" (p. 41). Her other chapters are organized along the central themes of her findings: the role of reading in the lives of students
and families, parents' and teachers' roles in helping children learn to
read, the role of social relationships in learning to read, construction
of urban reading identities, and contradictions and complexities.
Within the contradictions and complexities chapter, she shares the
contradictions that appeared in the discourse of her participants.
Through this chapter and others, she is careful not to present a singu-
lar conclusion but deals with the complexity of her results.

So why is this study good? First, Compton-Lilly uses multiple
sources of data (Yin, 1994). She had multiple student and parent interviews that occurred over time. She used classroom data that included class discussion audiotapes, guided reading group audiotapes,
student-written documents, student portfolios, and journals. Finally,
she kept daily field notes that most often reflected political disputes
centered on curriculum. She shared her tentative findings with parents throughout her study thereby creating a chain of evidence. By
sharing her work repeatedly with parents, she had confidence that
she was creating an accurate report.

Moreover, she worked with her parents throughout an entire
year, so she had sufficient time in the field to know that she was recording patterns of behavior rather than a one-time event. Compton-
Lilly also did not shy away from talking about her biases and how
they may have affected her results. She served as teacher of her students as she conducted research with them. She described this role as
one of an insider, but she coupled this with being an outsider when
she was in the homes of her students. She then reflected on the tensions that she felt when she developed curricula for her students as
she did not want to dismiss the voices and values of her students and

their families. Following this discussion, she alerted the reader to the fact that she is white and studying African American and Puerto Rican children and their families. In this discussion, she shared how hard it was to not blame families for the difficulties that students had in becoming literate. As she tried to withhold judgment about families, she was inundated with teachers who blamed parents. She wrote "arguments that blame parents can be very convincing and reassuring to a teacher concerned about efficacy; moreover, claims made in defense of parents are difficult to substantiate and sustain" (p. 43). In addition, Compton-Lilly did not try to simplify the complexity and contradictions she found in her research, particularly in her discourse analysis. She discovered ways to share this complexity and to make her study more compelling in the process. Clearly, Compton-Lilly met the criteria that make for a quality case study.

FINAL WORDS

As was evident in the overviews of case studies presented throughout this chapter, case-study research is important to our understandings of literacy. Case studies are complex because they are built around multiple data sources that must be analyzed into themes or patterns. This is no easy task as rigorous case study results in significant amounts of data that are often difficult to reconcile. However, for those who engage in this form of research, the rewards are many. Perhaps most important is this work is applicable to real life as it relates directly to the reader's experiences and facilitates understanding of complex situations, understandings that cannot be made explicit in most other research designs.

REFERENCES

Alvermann, D., Huddleston, A., & Hagood, M. (2002, December). *What could the WWF and a high school English curriculum possibly have in common?* Paper presented at the annual conference of the National Reading Conference, Miami, FL.

Baghban, M. (1984). *Our daughter learns to read and write: A case study from birth to three.* Newark, DE: International Reading Association.

Ballenger, C. (1999). *Teaching other people's children: Literacy and learning in a bilingual classroom.* New York: Teachers College Press.

Barone, D. (1999). *Resilient children: Stories of poverty, drug exposure, and literacy development.* Newark, DE: International Reading Association.

Beck, I. (2002, August). *Comprehension and vocabulary development in the early grades*. Paper presented at the Institute for Statewide Literacy Initiatives, Harvard Graduate School of Education

Birnbaum, J., Emig, J., & Fisher, D. (2003). Case studies: Placing literacy phenomena within their actual context. In J. Flood, D. Lapp, J. Squire, & J. Jensen (Eds.), *Handbook of research on teaching the English language arts* (2nd ed., pp. 192–200). Mahwah, NJ: Erlbaum.

Bissex, G. (1980) *Gnyx at Wrk*. Cambridge, MA: Harvard University Press.

Butler, D. (1975). *Cushla and her books*. Boston: The Horn Book.

Calkins, L. (1983). *Lessons from a child: On the teaching and learning of writing*. Exeter, NH: Heinemann.

Cochran-Smith, M. (1984). *The making of a reader*. Norwood, NJ: Ablex.

Compton-Lilly, C. (2003). *Reading families: The literate lives of urban children*. New York: Teachers College Press.

Dyson, A. (1995). Children out of bounds: The power of case studies in expanding visions of literacy development. In K. Hinchman, D. Leu, & C. Kinzer (Eds.), *Perspectives on literacy research and practice* (pp. 39–53). Chicago: National Reading Conference.

Dyson, A. (1997). *Writing superheroes: Contemporary childhood, popular culture, and classroom literacy*. New York: Teachers College Press.

Ehri, L. (1997). Interactions in the development of reading and spelling: Stages, strategies, and exchange of knowledge. In C. Perfetti, L. Rieben, & M. Fayol (Eds.), *Learning to spell: Research, theory, and practice across languages* (pp. 237–269). Mahwah, NJ: Erlbaum.

Ehri, L., Nunes, S., Willows, D., Schuster, B., Yaghoub-Zasdeh, Z., & Shanahan, T. (2001). Phonemic awareness instruction helps children learn to read: Evidence from the National Reading Panel's meta-analysis. *Reading Research Quarterly, 36*, 250–287.

Gutierrez, K., Asato, J., Pacheco, M., Moll, L., Olson, K., Horng, E., Ruiz, R., Garcia, E., & McCarty, T. (2002). Conversations: "Sounding American": The consequences of new reforms on English language learners. *Reading Research Quarterly, 37*, 328–347.

Hargreaves, A., Earl, L., & Schmidt, M. (2002). Perspectives on alternative assessment reform. *American Educational Research Journal, 39*, 69–100.

Heath, S. (1983). *Ways with words: Language, life, and work in communities and classrooms*. Cambridge, UK: Cambridge University Press.

Henderson, E. (1981). *Learning to read and spell: The child's knowledge of words*. DeKalb: Northern Illinois University Press.

Ladson-Billings, G. (1994). *The dreamkeepers: Successful teachers of African American children*. San Francisco: Jossey-Bass.

Martens, P. (1996). *I already know how to read: A child's view of literacy*. Portsmouth, NH; Heinemann.

McCarthey, S. (1998). Constructing multiple subjectivities in classroom learning contexts. *Research in the Teaching of English, 32*, 126–160.

McGee, L., & Barone, D. (2000, December). *Case studies of young children's literacy learning: Past, present, and future*. Paper presented at the annual meeting of the National Reading Conference, San Antonio, TX.

Merriam, S. (1988). *Case-study research in education: A qualitative approach*. San Francisco: Jossey-Bass.

Miles, M., & Huberman, A. (1994). *Qualitative data analysis: An expanded sourcebook* (2nd ed.). Newbury Park, CA: Sage.

Neuman, S., & McCormick, S. (2000). A case for single-subject experiments in literacy research. In M. Kamil, P. Mosenthal, P. D. Pearson, & R. Barr (Eds.), *Handbook of reading research* (Vol. 3, pp. 181–194). Mahwah, NJ: Erlbaum.

Patton, M. (1990). *Qualitative evaluation and research methods* (2nd ed.). Newbury Park, CA: Sage.

Purcell-Gates, V. (1995). *Other people's words: The cycle of low literacy*. Cambridge. MA: Harvard University Press.

Rogers, R. (2002). Between contexts: A critical discourse analysis of family literacy, discursive practices, and literate subjectivities. *Reading Research Quarterly, 37,* 248–277.

Rowe, D. (1994). *Preschoolers as authors: Literacy learning in the social world of the classroom*. Creskill, NJ: Hampton Press.

Sarroub, L. (2002). In-betweenness: Religion and conflicting visions of literacy. *Reading Research Quarterly, 37,* 130–149.

Schickendanz, J. (1990). *Adam's righting revolutions: One child's literacy development from infancy through grade one*. Portsmouth, NH: Heinemann.

Shulman,J., Whittaker, A., & Lew, M. (2002). *Using assessments to teach for understanding: A casebook for educators*. New York: Teachers College Press.

Stake, R. (1995). *The art of case-study research*. Thousand Oaks, CA: Sage.

Stake, R. (2000). Case studies. In N. Denzin & Y. Lincoln (Eds.), *Handbook of qualitative research* (2nd ed., pp. 435–454). Thousand Oaks, CA: Sage Publications.

Taylor, D., & Dorsey-Gaines, C. (1988). *Growing up literate: Learning from inner-city families*. Portsmouth, NH: Heinemann.

Vygotsky, L. (1962). *Thought and language* (E. Hanfmann & G. Vakar, Trans.) Cambridge, MA: Harvard University Press.

Weintraub, S. (1981). *Annual summary of investigations relating to reading July 1, 1979 to June 30, 1980*. Newark, DE: International Reading Association.

White, D. (1956). *Books before 5*. New York: Oxford University Press.

Wolcott, H. (1994). *Transforming qualitative data*. Thousand Oaks, CA: Sage.

Wolf, S., & Heath, S. (1992). *The braid of literature: Children's worlds of reading*. Cambridge, MA; Harvard University Press.

Xu, S. (2002, December). *Pre-service teachers learn to integrate student popular culture texts into literacy instruction*. Paper presented at the annual conference of the National Reading Conference, Miami, FL.

Yin, R. (1994). *Case-study research: Design and methods* (2nd ed.). Thousand Oaks, CA: Sage.

CHAPTER 3

Inferences from Correlational Data

Exploring Associations with Reading Experience

Keith E. Stanovich
Anne E. Cunningham

Every beginning student in the social sciences quickly learns the admonition that "correlation does not imply causation." Ironically, the next lesson almost immediately learned is that in many areas of the social sciences and education all we have is correlational data! Upon deeper investigation, however, this student should soon learn that correlational techniques do exist that are more complex than a simple zero-order correlation and that represent a middle ground between unqualified inference and simple correlation. In this chapter we illustrate this "middle ground" with a research problem that we have studied in depth implementing primarily correlational techniques—determining the cognitive consequences of reading experience.

THE DILEMMA OF CORRELATIONAL EVIDENCE

The power of a true experimental study comes from the integration of three essential elements: comparison, control, and manipulation. Comparison alone is not enough to justify a causal inference. Within an experimental study, a researcher is able to manipulate the hypothetical causal variable while holding other potential factors constant, thus systematically creating levels of variability that can then be compared. Factors not directly under the control of the experimenter can be controlled through randomization. Removing the elements of control and direct variable manipulation dramatically limits a researcher's ability to clearly examine the nature of the relationship between certain variables. Yet this is precisely the nature of correlational analyses. Correlational investigations attempt to compare the levels of one variable with those of another. In their most simplistic forms, they do so without trying to directly manipulate these variables or control for the presence of other variables.

Because of their lack of control and manipulation, correlational studies limit the conclusions a researcher can draw. While a researcher would ideally like to proclaim solid causal relationships between variables, this is difficult to do using correlational measures. Going back to our beginning social science student, we would reiterate that the mere existence of a relationship between two variables does not guarantee that changes in one are what causes changes in another. Here we might consider the well-worn example of the correlation between ice cream consumption and drowning deaths. The presence of this correlation does not justify a conclusion that eating ice cream causes a person to drown. But what, specifically, about correlational studies is so problematic?

Actually, two main potential problems exist that prevent us from drawing causal inferences from correlational evidence. The first is called the "third-variable problem." It occurs when a correlation between two variables arises because both variables are related to some third variable that to some degree affects both of the variables in question. This variable may not have been measured or even included in a researcher's overall theory. The correlation between ice cream consumption and drowning deaths is a perfect illustration of this problem. Eating ice cream does not cause one to drown, even though an increase in one can be linked to an increase in the other. Instead, both eating habits and cause of death are related to a third, confounding, variable: heat. As temperatures rise, more people eat ice cream and engage in water sports, thus increasing the incidences of drowning. The variable of heat, therefore, affects both ice cream consumption and drowning rates, which results in a spurious relationship between the latter two variables themselves.

The second problem is called the "directionality problem," or an inability to determine the direction of causality in a relationship between two variables. It creates potential interpretive difficulties because even if two variables have a direct causal relationship, the direction of that relationship is not indicated by the mere presence of the correlation. In short, a correlation between variables A and B could arise because changes in A are causing changes in B or because changes in B are causing changes in A. The mere presence of a correlation does little to help ascertain which of the two variables may be influencing the other. One example of this problem in education is the positive correlation between reading behaviors and reading ability. Does a student read more because he is a better reader, or has this student become a better reader because he has read more? It is impossible to tell without taking other factors into account.

THE NEED FOR CORRELATIONAL METHODOLOGY

Despite their limitations, however, correlational studies play an important role in the social sciences and education and are necessary for several reasons. Some variables, such as birth order, sex, and age, are inherently correlational because they cannot be manipulated within the parameters of a study; scientific knowledge concerning them must, therefore, be based on correlational evidence. Other variables, such as human malnutrition or physical disabilities, simply cannot be manipulated for ethical reasons. Finally, logistical difficulties inherent in carrying out research within classrooms can preclude the use of true experimental designs but leave correlational studies as a viable option.

As with any method, certain assumptions must be met. At the highest level, variables considered within a correlational analysis should be chosen with care. A sound theory that takes alternative explanations into account should be used to determine which variables are of immediate interest. Basically, any correlational model is only as good as the data to which it is applied. Correlation is based on the assumption that the variables in question are related linearly and do not suffer from multicollinearity (in which two or more variables are too highly correlated), and care must be taken to ensure that artificially restricted distributions, missing data, and deviant cases or outliers are addressed. An examination of residuals is an effective procedure to ensure that data do not suffer from these limitations.

Correlational studies also gain power when combined with other types of investigations to derive general conclusions. Particularly in the domains of classroom and curriculum research, the basis for scientific conclusions generally rest on the convergence of a variety of methodology, including correlational studies, nonequivalent control-group studies, time-series designs, and various other quasi-experimental designs and multivariate correlational designs. All these designs discussed in this volume have their strengths and weaknesses, but together, when the results are amalgamated, they are able to paint a more cohesive picture.

While limited in their most simple forms, correlational studies can be made more powerful by using statistical techniques that themselves allow for the partial control of third variables, when those variables can be measured. Correlational statistics such as multiple regression, path analysis, and structural equation modeling all fall into this category. These statistics, in essence, allow the correlation between two variables to be recalculated after the influence of other key variables are removed, or "factored out" or "partialed out." Thus, these types of correlational statistics and designs help to *rule out* certain causal hypotheses, even if they cannot demonstrate the true causal relation definitively. This is often extremely useful in science, whether education, psychology, or so-called hard sciences such as astronomy, because in many cases the leading alternative explanations (potential third variables) are known and can thus be accounted for. Given this background, we illustrate a very typical use of correlational design by discussing our own work on the cognitive consequences of literacy. The statistical technique employed is that of hierarchical multiple regression.

DIFFICULTIES IN INTERPRETING ASSOCIATIONS BETWEEN READING EXPERIENCE AND COGNITIVE OUTCOMES

Many studies in the literacy field have reported correlations between degrees of engagement in reading activities and various cognitive outcomes. However, such logic, if not supplemented with additional statistical controls, will yield data subject to an inordinately large number of alternative explanations. Historical and cross-cultural studies provide some context for understanding the problem.

Consider the international literacy campaigns conducted in nonindustrialized countries during the last three decades and how historians and sociologists used certain cultural correlates of literacy to justify these campaigns. There was, in earlier writings, a tendency to attribute every positive outcome that was historically correlated with the rise of literacy—economic development, for example—to the effects of literacy itself. However, it is now recognized that the potential for spurious correlation in the domain of literacy is quite high. Simply put, high levels of societal literacy are correlated with too many *other* positive outcomes. For example, the link between economic development and national levels of literacy has turned out to be much more complex than originally thought (Fuller, Edwards, & Gorman, 1987; Gee, 1988; Graff, 1986; Wagner, 1987). Literacy levels are as much a consequence of economic development as they are its cause.

The problem at the level of the individual reader is analogous to the problem of comparing the effects of different levels of literacy across different societies. Levels of print exposure are correlated with too many other good things. Avid readers tend to be different on a wide variety of cognitive skills, behavioral habits, and background variables. Attributing any particular outcome to print exposure uniquely is an extremely tenuous inference when based on only the presence of an unpartialed correlation. Early literacy theorists were guilty of possibly "overselling" literacy by attributing to it every positive effect with which it was correlated.

In fact, influential theorists have argued that correlations between literacy experience and cognitive outcomes are indeed largely spurious. One group of theorists has advanced what has been termed the *environmental opportunity hypothesis*, which can be illustrated by considering vocabulary growth as an example. There is considerable evidence indicating that children's vocabulary sizes are correlated with parental education and indicators of environmental quality (Hall, Nagy, & Linn, 1984; Hart & Risley, 1995; Mercy & Steelman, 1982; Wells, 1986). Thus, it has been argued that vocabulary differences are primarily the result of differential opportunities for word learning.

The environmental opportunity hypothesis is countered, however, by theorists who emphasize that differences in vocabulary are caused by variation in the efficiency of the cognitive mechanisms responsible for inducing meaning from context. This stance has been termed *the cognitive efficiency hypothesis* and proposes that superior processing abilities underlie both the cognitive outcomes obtained and the literacy experiences themselves, so that the linkage between the latter two is spurious. Proponents of the cognitive efficiency hypothesis argue that experiential factors are not implicated—or at least are of secondary importance—in explaining vocabulary differences. For example, Sternberg (1985) has argued that

> simply reading a lot does not guarantee a high vocabulary. What seems to be critical is not sheer amount of experience but rather what one has been able to learn from and do with that experience. According to this view, then, individual differences in knowledge acquisition have priority over individual differences in actual knowledge. (p. 307)

Jensen (1980) has stated the cognitive efficiency hypothesis in even stronger form:

Children of high intelligence acquire vocabulary at a faster rate than children of low intelligence, and as adults they have a much larger than average vocabulary, not primarily because they have spent more time in study or have been more exposed to words, but because they are capable of educing more meaning from single encounters with words. . . . The vocabulary test does not discriminate simply between those persons who have and those who have not been exposed to the words in context. . . . The crucial variable in vocabulary size is not exposure per se, but conceptual need and inference of meaning from context." (pp. 146–147)

It is important to realize that cognitive efficiency explanations of this type are generic and are not necessarily restricted to the domain of vocabulary acquisition. They could, in theory, apply to knowledge acquisition in virtually any domain. Ceci (1996) has discussed how in an attempt to undermine developmental theories that emphasize the importance of knowledge structures in determining intelligent performance, advocates of the cognitive efficiency hypothesis argue that "intelligent individuals do better on IQ tests because their superior central-processing mechanisms make it easier for them to glean important information and relationships from their environment" (p. 72). The cognitive efficiency hypothesis thus undercuts all developmental theories that emphasize the importance of knowledge structures in determining intelligent performance by potentially trivializing them. According to the cognitive efficiency view, these differences in knowledge bases may affect certain cognitive operations all right, but the knowledge differences themselves arise merely as epiphenomena of differences in the efficiency of more basic psychological processes. Knowledge differences thus become much less interesting as explanatory mechanisms of developmental differences because they are too proximal a cause.

THE ANALYTIC STRATEGY:
HIERARCHICAL MULTIPLE REGRESSION ANALYSIS

As part of a broad-based research program examining the impact of reading experience on cognitive development (e.g., Cunningham & Stanovich, 1997; Stanovich, 1993, 2000), we have put alternative hypotheses such as the cognitive efficiency hypothesis to test by using the logic of hierarchical multiple regression. The logic of hierarchical multiple regression analysis allows any control variables entered first into the regression equation to explain any variance that they can in the criterion variable. Following these control variables, the measures of reading experience are then entered. Thus, the procedure allows the investigator to assess whether reliable variance remains to be explained after the control variables are entered, and therefore whether exposure to print is associated with the criterion variance. In tests of the cognitive efficiency hypothesis, for example, we first regressed out ability measures (indirectly related to efficient cognitive processing) most likely to lead to spurious relationships before examining the linkage between print exposure and criterion variables. The logic of our analytic strategy is quite conservative because, in certain analyses to be described, we have actually partialed out variance in abilities that are likely to be developed by reading itself. However, the explanatory ambiguities surrounding a variable such as print exposure have led us to continue to structure the analyses in a "worst case" manner, as far as experience with print is concerned.

In a study of fourth-, fifth-, and sixth-grade children (Cunningham & Stanovich, 1991), we examined whether print exposure accounts for differences in vocabulary development (and other verbal skills) once controls for both general and specific (i.e., vocabulary-relevant) abilities were invoked. Variables were selected for analysis in this study based on contemporary theories of reading and vocabulary development. The analyses displayed in Table 3.1 illustrate some of the outcomes of this study. Three different vocabulary measures were employed as dependent variables: a word checklist measure of the written vocabulary modeled on the work of Anderson and Freebody (1983; see also White, Slater, & Graves, 1989), a verbal fluency measure where the children had to output as many words as they could that fit into a particular category (e.g., things that are red; see Sincoff & Sternberg, 1987), and a group-administered version of the Peabody Picture Vocabulary Test (PPVT).

Age was entered first into the regression equation, followed by scores on the Raven Progressive Matrices as a control for cognitive ability (general processing efficiency). As a second ability control more closely linked to vocabulary acquisition mechanisms, we entered phonological coding ability into the equation. A variable such as phonological coding skill might mediate a relationship between print exposure and a variable such as vocabulary size in numerous ways. High levels of decoding skill—certainly a contributor to greater print exposure—might provide relatively complete verbal contexts for the induction of word meanings during reading. Decoding skill might also indirectly reflect differences in short-term phonological storage that are related to vocabulary learning, particularly in the preschool years (Gathercole & Baddeley, 1989, 1993). Thus, print exposure and vocabulary might be spuriously linked via their connection with decoding ability: good decoders both read avidly and have the best

TABLE 3.1. Unique Print Exposure Variance after Age, Raven, and Phonological Coding Were Partialed Out

Step/variable	R	R^2	R^2 change	F to enter
	Word checklist			
1. Age	.103	.011	.011	1.41
2. Raven	.457	.209	.198	32.57**
3. Phonological coding	.610	.372	.163	33.49**
4. Print exposure	.683	.466	.094	22.52**
	Verbal fluency			
1. Age	.043	.002	.002	0.24
2. Raven	.231	.053	.051	6.89**
3. Phonological coding	.477	.228	.175	28.47**
4. Print exposure	.582	.339	.111	21.02**
	PPVT			
1. Age	.230	.053	.053	7.29**
2. Raven	.393	.154	.101	15.60**
3. Phonological coding	.403	.162	.008	1.21
4. Print exposure	.516	.266	.104	18.19**
	Spelling			
1. Age	.179	.032	.032	4.31*
2. Raven	.414	.172	.140	21.95**
3. Phonological coding	.656	.430	.258	58.51**
4. Print exposure	.713	.509	.079	20.42**
	General information			
1. Age	.224	.050	.050	6.84**
2. Raven	.362	.131	.081	12.05**
3. Phonological coding	.410	.168	.037	5.68*
4. Print exposure	.492	.242	.074	12.37**

Note. The spanner headings identify the dependent variables in the regression analyses. *$p < .05$, **$p < .01$.

context available for inferring new words. This spurious linkage is controlled by entering phonological coding into the regression equation prior to the measure of exposure to print. If print exposure were only an incidental correlate of vocabulary because of its linkage with phonological coding skill, then it would not serve as a unique predictor of vocabulary once phonological coding was partialed out.

The results of the first three analyses displayed in Table 3.1 indicate that for each of the vocabulary measures, exposure to print accounted for significant variance after the variance attributable to performance on the Raven and the phonological coding measure had been removed. The last two regressions indicate that this was also true for two additional criterion variables in the study: spelling ability and performance on the general information subtest of the Wechsler Intelligence Scale for Children.

In other studies (Stanovich & Cunningham, 1992, 1993), we have focused on whether content knowledge could be linked to print exposure after measures of general processing efficiency and exposure to other media sources had been partialed out, again testing theories that positioned these variables as key factors in the development of content knowledge. One study contained a particularly stringent test of the cognitive efficiency explanation of individual differences in knowledge acquisition. The subjects were 268 college students, and the strong test is displayed in Table 3.2. The criterion variable is a composite index of performance on five general knowledge measures. Four measures of general ability were entered into the regression equation prior to print exposure: high school grade point average, performance on the Raven matrices, performance on an SAT-type mathematics test, and the score on the Nelson–Denny Reading Comprehension Test. This set of tasks surely exhausts the variance attributable to any general ability construct, and general ability does account for a substantial proportion of variance in the general knowledge composite (multiple R of .63). When entered as the fifth step, a composite measure of exposure to television accounted for no additional variance. However, a composite index of exposure to print accounted for a substantial 37.1% of the variance when entered after the four ability measures and television exposure. The results thus in-

TABLE 3.2. Hierarchical Regression Analyses Predicting General Knowledge Composite

Step/variable	R	R^2 change	F to enter	Final beta	Final F
1. High school GPA	.372	.139	42.82**	.020	0.32
2. Raven	.447	.061	20.30**	.016	0.20
3. Mathematics test	.542	.094	35.07**	.165	18.19**
4. N-D comprehension	.630	.103	45.11**	.112	9.87**
5. Television composite	.630	.000	0.06	-.039	1.68
6. Print composite	.876	.371	417.63**	.720	417.63**

Note. N-D comprehension, Nelson–Denny Reading Comprehension Test.
*p < .05; **p < .01.

TABLE 3.3. Hierarchical Regressions Predicting Fifth-Grade Reading Ability

Step/variable	R	R^2	R^2 change	F to enter
Fifth-grade Stanford Reading Comprehension				
1. Iowa Comprehension (Third)	.645	.416	.416	54.06**
2. Print Exposure	.725	.526	.110	17.38**
Fifth-grade Iowa Reading Comprehension				
1. Iowa Comprehension (Third)	.545	.297	.297	33.78**
2. Print Exposure	.609	.371	.074	9.25**

Note. The spanner headings identify the dependent variables in the regression analyses.
**$p < .01$.

dicated that more avid readers in our study—independent of their general abilities (cognitive efficiency) and their television exposure—had more general knowledge.

That these analyses are conservative in entering reading comprehension before the print exposure measure is illustrated in a longitudinal study conducted by our research group (Cipielewski & Stanovich, 1992). It indicates that exposure to print is related to growth in reading comprehension ability. The regression analyses presented in Table 3.3 display the results of this study, in which growth in reading comprehension ability was tracked by administering the comprehension tests from the Stanford Diagnostic Reading Test and the Iowa Test of Basic Skills (ITBS) to 82 fifth graders who had been administered the comprehension subtest from the ITBS in the third grade (as 8- to 9-year-olds).

The regressions are hierarchical forced-entry analyses for prediction of fifth-grade reading comprehension ability. Third-grade reading comprehension was entered first, followed by a measure of print exposure. Thus, the analyses are essentially addressed to the question of whether exposure to print can predict individual differences in growth in reading comprehension from third grade to fifth grade. In both cases, print exposure predicted variance in fifth-grade reading comprehension ability after third-grade reading comprehension scores had been partialed out. In partialing reading comprehension ability in our studies (across the age range of elementary students through adults), we are undoubtedly removing some of the variance in the criterion variable that is rightfully attributed to print exposure.

Such a strict test of our hypothesis via this correlational technique, however, provides a more robust interpretation of the data patterns.

DEVELOPING A LIFETIME READING HABIT: REVERSING THE CRITERION AND PREDICTOR IN REGRESSION ANALYSES

Given that lifelong reading habits are such strong predictors of verbal cognitive growth, what is it that predicts these habits? That is, so far the analyses have treated exposure to print as a predictor variable of criterion abilities such as vocabulary and reading comprehension. However, it is generally agreed that comprehension ability and exposure to print are in a reciprocal relationship (Anderson, Wilson, & Fielding, 1988; Stanovich, 1986, 1993, 2000). We controlled for the fact that high comprehension ability leads to high levels of reading experience in a longitudinal study (Cunningham & Stanovich, 1997) in which we attempted to see whether a fast start in the early stages of reading acquisition predicted the tendency to read over and above the overall level of reading skill achieved.

In this study we had available extensive cognitive profiles of a group of children who had been tested as first graders in 1981 (see Stanovich, Cunningham, & Feeman, 1984). About one half of this sample were available 10 years later for testing as 11th graders. At that time, we administered a set of reading comprehension, cognitive ability, vocabulary, and general knowledge tasks, as well as several measures of exposure to print. We were thus able to examine what variables in the first grade predicted these cognitive outcomes in the eleventh grade.

Table 3.4 displays the results from an analysis in which we addressed the question of whether the speed of initial reading acquisition in the first grade could predict the tendency to engage in reading activities 10 years later, even after the current level of reading comprehension ability was taken into account. Entered first in the hierarchical regression is 11th-grade reading comprehension ability (Nelson–Denny performance) in order to remove the direct association between print exposure and contemporaneous reading ability. Listed next in the table are alternative second steps in the regression equation. All three measures of first-grade reading ability (Metropolitan Achievement Test, Gates, and Wide Range Achievement Test) predicted significant variance (slightly over 10%) in 11th-grade print exposure even after 11th-grade reading comprehension ability had been partialed out!

TABLE 3.4. Hierarchical Regression Analysis Predicting Exposure to Print in the 11th Grade

Step/variable	R	R^2 change	F to enter	Partial r
	Forced entry			
1. Grade 11 ND Comp	.604	.364	14.34**	—
2. Grade 1 Metropolitan	.696	.121	5.61*	.435
2. Grade 1 Gates	.681	.100	4.45*	.396
2. Grade 1 WRAT	.686	.106	4.78*	.408
2. Grade 1 Raven	.632	.035	1.39	.234
2. Grade 1 PPVT	.641	.047	1.89	.270
2. Grade 3 Metropolitan	.765	.221	11.09**	.588
2. Grade 5 Metropolitan	.719	.153	6.72*	.484

Note. ND Comp, Nelson–Denny Reading Comprehension Test.
*$p < .05$; **$p < .01$.

The table indicates that the two measures of cognitive ability administered in first grade (Raven and PPVT) did not account for unique variance in print exposure once 11th-grade reading comprehension ability had been partialed out. Finally, third- and fifth-grade measures of reading ability accounted for even more variance in print exposure than did the first-grade measures. These analyses demonstrate that an early start in reading is important in predicting a lifetime of literacy experience—and this is true regardless of the level of reading comprehension ability that the individual eventually attains. This is a strong finding because it indicates that, regardless of the student's level of reading comprehension in the 11th grade, if the student got off to a fast start in reading (as indicated by their first-grade reading ability scores) then they are more likely to engage in more reading activity as adults. Early success at reading acquisition is thus one of the keys that unlocks a lifetime of reading habits. The subsequent exercise of this habit serves to further develop reading comprehension ability in an interlocking positive feedback loop (Juel, 1988; Snow, Barnes, Chandler, Goodman, & Hemphill, 1991; Snow, Burns, & Griffin, 1998; Stanovich, 1986, 1993, 2000).

SUMMARY

This, then, is a selection of our work on the cognitive correlates of exposure to print. In this sampling, we have tried to illustrate how the logic of multiple regression can be used to pare down the number of alternative hypotheses available when a link is found between reading experience and a cognitive outcome variable. For example, in the studies we have reviewed we have demonstrated that a strong version of the cognitive efficiency account of knowledge acquisition and vocabulary growth is falsified. Print exposure accounted for a sizable portion of variance in measures of vocabulary and general knowledge even after variance associated with general cognitive ability was partialed out. Thus, at least in certain domains, and at least as measured here, individual differences in declarative knowledge bases—differences emphasized by many contemporary theories of developmental growth—appear to some extent to be experientially based. This does not mean that there might not be some other third variable operating that we have not measured. It does mean, however, that the third variables favored by the cognitive efficiency theorists have been eliminated. Some other theory with different unmeasured third variables will have to be posited to explain the association between print exposure and cognitive outcomes if the latter is to be deemed not causal. As the number of such alternative explanation decreases, they become, almost of necessity, less plausible. In many research areas, at some point the alternative explanations become less plausible than the assumption that the original association reflects a causal relationship. In this way, a series of studies using the logic of hierarchical regression (and associated techniques) can begin, ever so tentatively, to lead us to a provisional causal inference.

We have illustrated this progression toward a tentative causal inference in this chapter. Researchers and practitioners in the reading education community are nearly unanimous in recommending that children be encouraged to spend more time engaged in literacy activities outside school (e.g., Adams, 1990; Anderson, Hiebert, Scott, & Wilkinson, 1985; Cunningham & Stanovich, 2003; Manning & Manning, 1989; Morrow, 2003). From a cultural standpoint, this recommendation is virtually unassailable. What has been less clear, however, is the empirical status of the tacit model of skill acquisition that often underlies the recommendation to increase children's free reading. The tacit model is basically one of accelerating skill development via practice. It is thought that more exposure to print via home reading will lead to further growth in reading comprehension and related cognitive skills. As plausible as this tacit model sounds, until quite recently there was actually very little evidence to support it. Most of the available evidence consisted of simple correlations—for example, research demonstrating that avid readers tend to be good comprehenders (see Guthrie & Greaney, 1991, for a review)—and did not contain any statistical controls of possible third variables.

These simple correlations were ambiguous because they were open to the interpretation that better readers simply choose to read more—an interpretation at odds with the tacit model of skill development via practice that underlies efforts to increase children's free reading.

The pattern of regression results in our studies suggests that print exposure does appear to be both a consequence of developed reading ability and a contributor to further growth in that ability and in other verbal skills—thus, these studies bolster the emphasis on reading experience that currently prevails in the reading education community. The results also strengthen the case for advocating a more prominent role for reading activity in general theories of cognitive development (Booth & Hall, 1994; Guthrie, Schafer, & Hutchinson, 1991; Olson, 1994; Stanovich, 1986, 1993, 2000).

There are, in fact, several possible mechanisms by which print exposure could become a mechanism for the growth and preservation of crystalized knowledge. Reading is a very special type of interface with the environment, providing the organism with unique opportunities to acquire declarative knowledge. The world's storehouse of knowledge is readily available for those who read, and much of this information is not usually attained from other sources. Personal experience provides only narrow knowledge of the world and is often misleadingly unrepresentative. The most commonly used electronic sources of information (television, radio) lack depth. For example, most theorists agree that a substantial proportion of vocabulary growth during childhood and adulthood occurs indirectly through language exposure (Hart & Risley, 1995; Miller & Gildea, 1987; Nagy & Anderson, 1984; Nagy, Herman, & Anderson, 1985). Obviously, the only opportunities to acquire new words occur when an individual is exposed to a word in written or oral language that is outside the current vocabulary. Work by Hayes (1988; Hayes & Ahrens, 1988; see also Akinnaso, 1982; Biber, 1986; Chafe & Danielewicz, 1987; Corson, 1995) has indicated that moderate- to low-frequency words—precisely those words that differentiate individuals with high and low vocabulary sizes—appear much more often in common reading matter than in common speech.

These relative differences in the statistical distributions of words in print and in oral language have direct implications for vocabulary development. They represent the type of theoretical foundation that, when integrated with evidence which rules out some alternative third variables, can begin to lead a behavioral scientist in the direction of positing a causal hypothesis. Experiments have strong resolving power and regression analyses have weak resolving power when it comes to positing causal paths. But the weak resolving power of regression methods can be combined with theory in ways that (much more slowly than true experiments of course) lead us to some inferences that are at least stronger than those obtainable from the study of simple correlations. Thus, correlational designs can be viewed as more complex and rich than our beginning social scientist student initially conceived them and can provide a relatively powerful alternative for educational and psychological research.

ACKNOWLEDGMENTS

Research discussed in this chapter was supported by grants to Keith Stanovich from the Social Sciences and Humanities Research Council of Canada and the Canada Research Chairs Program and to Anne Cunningham from the University of California, Berkeley, Faculty Research Grant and the National Science Foundation.

REFERENCES

Adams, M. J. (1990). *Beginning to read: Thinking and learning about print*. Cambridge, MA: MIT Press.

Akinnaso, F. N. (1982). On the difference between spoken and written language. *Language and Speech, 25*, 97–125.

Anderson, R. C., & Freebody, P. (1983). Reading comprehension and the assessment and acquisition of word knowledge. In B. Huston (Ed.), *Advances in reading/language research* (Vol. 2, pp. 231–256). Greenwich, CT: JAI Press.

Anderson, R. C., Hiebert, E. H., Scott, J. A., & Wilkinson, I. (1985). *Becoming a nation of readers*. Washington, DC: National Institute of Education.

Anderson, R. C., Wilson, P. T., & Fielding, L. G. (1988). Growth in reading and how children spend their time outside of school. *Reading Research Quarterly, 23*, 285–303.

Biber, D. (1986). Spoken and written textual dimensions in English: Resolving the contradictory findings. *Language, 62*, 384–414.

Booth, J. R., & Hall, W. S. (1994). Role of the cognitive internal state lexicon in reading comprehension. *Journal of Educational Psychology, 86*, 413–422.

Ceci, S. J. (1996). *On intelligence: A bioecological treatise on intellectual development* (exp. ed.). Cambridge, MA: Harvard University Press.

Chafe, W., & Danielewicz, J. (1987). Properties of spoken and written language. In R. Horowitz & S. J. Samuels (Eds.), *Comprehending oral and written language* (pp. 83–113). San Diego: Academic Press.

Cipielewski, J., & Stanovich, K. E. (1992). Predicting growth in reading ability from children's exposure to print. *Journal of Experimental Child Psychology, 54,* 74–89.

Corson, D. (1995). *Using English words.* Boston: Kluwers Academic.

Cunningham, A. E., & Stanovich, K. E. (1991). Tracking the unique effects of print exposure in children: Associations with vocabulary, general knowledge, and spelling. *Journal of Educational Psychology, 83,* 264–274.

Cunningham, A. E., & Stanovich, K. E. (1997). Early reading acquisition and its relation to reading experience and ability ten years later. *Developmental Psychology, 33,* 934–945.

Cunningham, A. E., & Stanovich, K. E. (2003). Reading matters: How reading engagement influences cognition. In J. Flood, D. Lapp, J. Squire, & J. Jensen (Eds.), *Handbook of research on teaching the English language arts* (Vol. 2, pp. 857–867). Mahwah, NJ: Erlbaum.

Fuller, B., Edwards, J., & Gorman, K. (1987). Does rising literacy spark economic growth? Commercial Expansion in Mexico. In D. A. Wagner (Ed.), *The future of literacy in a changing world* (pp. 319–340). Oxford, UK: Pergamon Books.

Gathercole, S. E., & Baddeley, A. D. (1989). Evaluation of the role of phonological STM in the development of vocabulary in children: A longitudinal study, *Journal of Memory and Language, 28,* 200–213.

Gathercole, S. E., & Baddeley, A. D. (1993). *Working memory and language.* Hove, UK: Erlbaum.

Gee, J. P. (1988). The legacies of literacy: From Plato to Freire through Harvey Graff. *Harvard Educational Review, 58,* 195–212.

Graff, H. J. (1986). The legacies of literacy: Continuities and contradictions in western society and culture. In S. de Castell, A. Luke, & K. Egan (Eds.), *Literacy, society, and schooling* (pp. 61–86). Cambridge, UK: Cambridge University Press.

Guthrie, J. T., & Greaney, V. (1991). Literacy acts. In R. Barr, M. L. Kamil, P. Mosenthal, & P. D. Pearson (Eds.), *Handbook of reading research* (Vol. 2, pp. 68–96). New York: Longman.

Guthrie, J. T., Schafer, W. D., & Hutchinson, S. R. (1991). Relations of document literacy and prose literacy to occupational and societal characteristics of young black and white adults. *Reading Research Quarterly, 26,* 30–48.

Hall, W. S., Nagy, W. E., & Linn, R. (1984). *Spoken words: Effects of situation and social group on oral word usage and frequency.* Hillsdale, NJ: Erlbaum.

Hart, B., & Risley, T.R. (1995). *Meaningful differences in the everyday experiences of young American children.* Baltimore: Brookes.

Hayes, D. P. (1988). Speaking and writing: Distinct patterns of word choice. *Journal of Memory and Language, 27,* 572–585.

Hayes, D. P., & Ahrens, M. (1988). Vocabulary simplification for children: A special case of "motherese"? *Journal of Child Language, 15,* 395–410.

Jensen, A. (1980). *Bias in mental testing.* New York: Free Press.

Juel, C. (1988). Learning to read and write: A longitudinal study of 54 children from first through fourth grades. *Journal of Educational Psychology*, *80*, 437–447.

Manning, G., & Manning, M. (Eds.). (1989). *Whole language: Beliefs and practices, K–8*. Washington, DC: National Education Association.

Mercy, J., & Steelman, L. (1982). Familial influence on the intellectual attainment of children. *American Sociological Review, 47*, 532–542.

Miller, G. A., & Gildea, P. M. (1987). How children learn words. *Scientific American, 257*(3), 94–99.

Morrow, L.M. (2003). Motivating lifelong voluntary readers. In J. Flood, D. Lapp, J. Squire, & J. Jensen (Eds.), *Handbook of research on teaching the English language arts* (Vol. 2, pp. 857–867), Mahwah, NJ: Erlbaum.

Nagy, W. E., & Anderson, R. C. (1984). How many words are there in printed school English? *Reading Research Quarterly, 19*, 304–330.

Nagy, W. E., Herman, P. A., & Anderson, R. C. (1985). Learning words from context. *Reading Research Quarterly, 20*, 233–253.

Olson, D. R. (1994). *The world on paper*. Cambridge, UK: Cambridge University Press.

Sincoff, J. B., & Sternberg, R. J. (1987). Two faces of verbal ability. *Intelligence, 11*, 263–276.

Snow, C. E, Barnes, W., Chandler, J., Goodman, L., & Hemphill, L. (1991). *Unfulfilled expectations: Home and school influences on literacy*. Cambridge, MA: Harvard University Press.

Snow, C. E., Burns, M. S., & Griffin, P. (Ed.). (1998). *Preventing reading difficulties in young children*. Washington, DC: National Academy Press.

Stanovich, K. E. (1986). Matthew effects in reading: Some consequences of individual differences in the acquisition of literacy. *Reading Research Quarterly, 21*, 360–407.

Stanovich, K. E. (1993). Does reading make you smarter? Literacy and the development of verbal intelligence. In H. Reese (Ed.), *Advances in child development and behavior* (Vol. 24, pp. 133–180). San Diego: Academic Press.

Stanovich, K. E. (2000). *Progress in understanding reading: Scientific foundations and new frontiers*. New York: Guilford Press.

Stanovich, K. E., & Cunningham, A. E. (1992). Studying the consequences of literacy within a literate society: The cognitive correlates of print exposure. *Memory and Cognition, 20*, 51–68.

Stanovich, K. E., & Cunningham, A. E. (1993). Where does knowledge come from? Specific associations between print exposure and information acquisition. *Journal of Educational Psychology, 85*, 211–229.

Stanovich, K. E., Cunningham, A. E., & Feeman, D. J. (1984). Intelligence, cognitive skills, and early reading progress. *Reading Research Quarterly, 19*, 278–303.

Sternberg, R. J. (1985). *Beyond IQ: A triarchic theory of human intelligence*. Cambridge, UK: Cambridge University Press.

Wagner, D. A. (1987). Literacy futures: Five common problems from industrializing and developing countries. In D. A. Wagner (Ed.), *The fu-*

ture of literacy in a changing world (pp. 3–16). Oxford, UK: Pergamon Books.

Wells, G. (1986). *The meaning makers*. Portsmouth, NH: Heinemann.

White, T. G., Slater, W. H., & Graves, M. F. (1989). Yes/no method of vocabulary assessment: Valid for whom and useful for what? In S. McCormick & J. Zutell (Eds.), *Cognitive and social perspectives for literacy research and instruction* (38th yearbook of the National Reading Conference, pp. 391–397). Chicago, IL: National Reading Conference.

CHAPTER 4

Discourse Analysis

Conversation

Susan Florio-Ruane
Ernest Morrell

In this chapter we discuss research on oral discourse in education. This is not a "how-to" chapter. There is already a considerable body of published information on ways to record and analyze oral discourse, much of relevant to the classroom. There are also reviews of research containing exemplary studies of classroom discourse (e.g., Cazden, 1988). Yet it remains important for students of educational research in literacy to ask, "What is oral discourse, and why study it in research on literacy education?" There are numerous answers to this question, many of them emanating from practical concerns of curriculum, instruction, assessment, and classroom management. However, underlying these are fundamental questions about the role of oral discourse in the social construction of knowledge, power, and identity in classrooms, schools, and elsewhere in society. Our chapter focuses on such questions. *Discourse* is a technical term defined and used in a variety of ways in research on oral communication and literacy education. We use the term in two different, though related, ways in this chapter: as instructional conversation and as a social linguistic process of being in the world.

WHAT IS DISCOURSE?
WHAT DOES IT MEAN FOR LITERACY EDUCATION?

Classrooms are language-rich environments, and much of that language takes the form of talk about texts, knowledge, and ideas. In cross-cultural research on thinking, for example, Cole and his associates found that the chief way in which people who experienced formal schooling differ from those who do not is in fluency manipulating concepts in and through language—both written and oral. One way to study educational discourse within school settings is by analyzing the classroom's instructional conversations—their nature, content, and purposes. For literacy researchers, the study of oral discourse is further specified as analysis of talk within what Heath (1983) called "literacy events," those situations and activities in which written text and literate practices are central to classroom talk and activity.

A related way to think about discourse is as what linguist James Gee (1996) calls a social linguistic "identity kit." Viewed this way, discourse includes but is not limited to conversation. Although it includes language, discourse is social as well as linguistic. It is a way of behaving and making sense which includes language code (as well as dialect or speech style), use of written words, social norms and values, and practice within shared activity systems. Viewed this way, the classroom offers learners one of their first opportunities to learn a "secondary discourse" as they venture out from the primary discourse into which they have been socialized by the family. In school, language and literacy learning are part of a secondary discourse, a new identity as learners in a community in which text will be central and talk will serve instructional, curricular, and assessment purposes.

Together, discourse as educational talk and discourse as a social linguistic identity kit are far from neutral. Conversation is essential to learning and sustaining participation in a discourse, but that discourse is not neutral. It is a system of sociolinguistic identification partly created by teachers and students anew in their day-to-day interactions and partly constrained by social, historical, cultural, and political forces and factors. It is by a process of reflexivity, or the mutual construction of conversation and culture, that shared meaning is possible. This meaning is hard to make explicit for analysis because, as experienced teachers and students, we take the reflexive process of communication very much for granted. Yet, as an important factor in the development of identity and literacy which is both limiting and enabling of learning and learners' futures, it is important to study educational discourse closely and critically.

CONVERSATION AND CULTURE

It is difficult to write about analysis of discourse as educational talk without addressing three key features of conversation as a cultural activity: (1) it is jointly constructed by participants in connected oral text; (2) it is a medium for the negotiation of meaning by speakers within particular social contexts; and (3) it is rule governed in order to be held in common with others, but it is also a creative act, with improvisation necessary as conversation moves from turn to turn, topic to topic.

These features work in dynamic tension and make oral language a living cultural "artifact" which, in Cole's view (1996), weaves human and cultural development and depends on species-specific biological features in interaction with cultural practices, reflecting history and anticipating futures. Yet what makes conversation so powerful and complex also makes it hard to study. Many approaches to studying conversation are used in education, from coding systems developed a priori to analyze specific features of instructional talk to ethnographic studies in which researchers learn by means of participant observation, interview of informants, analysis of recorded speech, collaboration with teachers and students as "informants," and searching for the local meanings of discourse in context.

There is a growing interest in discourse analysis among educational researchers in Europe, Australia, and the United States. Interdisciplinary fields such as sociolinguistics (Hymes, 1974) emerged in the last half of the 20th century, along with technologies making it easy to record speech in real time and naturalistic settings. These were soon applied to the study of teaching and learning in a variety of culturally diverse educational contexts (e.g., Cazden, John, & Hymes, 1974; Heath, 1983).

In addition, with the development of the social and behavioral sciences in the last century, in part to serve its emergent institutions, the study of communication grew in importance. Researchers study literacy in relationship to linguistic and social differences in communication among members of diverse cultural groups. In contemporary life, conversation and literacy are not only local but also global phenomena in which people come together rapidly and across time and distance. Thus in talk, print, audiovisual media, and cybercommunication, researchers study the power of language to organize activities and practices of communities in contact as they shape social relations, and develop knowledge and identity (New London Group, 1996).

Just as 20th-century advances in video- and audiorecording technology made capturing sequences of oral discourse in naturalistic settings feasible, it also made oral language a wider-reaching, more powerful social, educational, and political tool. In our time, digital technology makes it possible to manipulate discourse sequences so that they can be studied, in hypermedia, in a variety of revealing ways: synchronically, diachronically, comparatively, and in conjunction with other forms of textual information relevant to the talk and context under study. Thus we are able to examine oral discourse in multiple, layered situational contexts and begin to understand learning and practice within complex, indeterminate domains such as teaching (Spiro, Feltovich, Jacobson, & Coulter, 1993/1995). This move from certainty to uncertainty raises the possibility that everyday practices can be analyzed, taught, and learned critically (Britzman, 2002).

ORAL DISCOURSE AND EDUCATION

Oral language plays an important role in schooling. We explicitly use talk in our teaching when, for example, we explain a concept or assess students by listening as they answer questions about what they have learned. However, the educational importance of talk extends far beyond these uses. It also can bring diverse people together and foster the learning of others' language codes and literate practices. To master the oral and written language systems is to be able to wield the power of language as a tool for communication, self-expression, creativity, and thinking.

If talk is to be a key tool for teaching and learning of the literacy curriculum, and teachers must plan for and enact it with youngsters in thoughtful ways, then classroom talk is clearly an area deserving of considerable educational research. Yet talk is often the most taken for granted aspect of our teaching, a part of tacit, local knowledge. There are a variety of approaches to the study of ordinary language, or conversation, in educational research, and these methods are linked to researchers' theories, interests, and questions (Schiffrin, 1994). Yet while they vary these approaches are loosely associated and often referenced by the term *analysis of discourse.* Scholars use the term *discourse* when referring to both oral and written language (both are also referred to as "text") and to both the process of talk and its functions in social life (see Goldman & Wiley, Chapter 5, in this volume, for a discussion of discourse analysis of written text).

Once we move beyond the sentence, it is difficult to understand how talk works as "text." Understanding text—discourse—involves far more than vocabulary and grammar. It involves understanding culture and social life. This is as true for the young child entering her first classroom as it is for the traveler who, armed with grammatical knowledge of a language, finds himself lost in the sea of its use by native speakers. Educators and researchers of education are interested in how people acquire, learn, and practice discourse as they learn to reason, to participate in a variety of activities, and as they attain mature and metacognitive awareness of discourse strategies. Participation in discourse involves a network of knowledge including the following:

- Understanding and using a spoken language system and a repertoire of accompanying paralinguistic and nonverbal behaviors.
- Knowledge of social contexts, roles, and activities within which conversations occur.
- The capacity to produce as well as interpret appropriate conversational behaviors and manage conversation's ensemble, improvisational, and negotiated qualities.

The study of conversational discourse has roots in several fields including anthropology, linguistics, sociology, cultural studies, child development, and critical theory. Discourse has been analyzed for purposes of understanding how children learn to speak, the process of language acquisition across diverse languages and culture, the ways people "do things with words" to, with, and in response to one another. Obviously, education in general (and literacy education in particular) is an area in which oral discourse is of central importance in part because words saturate the learning environment, much learning involves learning new discourses, much learning occurs in the medium of conversation, and language is a means for creating and sustaining social systems.

Given that, in schools, social forces operate to provide or limit access to knowledge, the study of oral discourse within the conversations of the classroom is one primary way to witness those forces in participants' talk and activity. Understanding the dynamics of educational conversation opens possibilities for reform. For this reason, there are different kinds of questions that oral discourse analysis addresses. Sometimes we are trying to find out about student understanding of particular school content, sometimes we are trying to understand how students are responding to literature, sometimes we are trying to understand power relations in a classroom. In addition, there are many kinds of discourse analysis, some of which might be called critical discourse analysis, some which resemble sociolinguistic study, and many which innovate in ways drawing on theory and method drawn from ethnography and sociolinguistics yet framing design, questions, and analysis to draw implications from research for policy and practice in a systematic way. Examples of these three approaches might be critical discourse analyses such as those collected in Barton and Hamilton's book, *Local Literacies: Reading and Writing in One Community* (1998); sociolinguistic analyses such as those by Michaels (to be detailed later), and many of the studies of reading instruction among Hawaiian youngsters conducted by Kathryn Au and reviewed in detail in a review chapter by Florio-Ruane and McVee (2000) in the *Handbook of Reading Research*. Although the length and purpose of this chapter precludes detailed review of all of these, we briefly examine several exemplars of research illustrating different approaches to analysis of discourse in literacy education later in this chapter.

DOING THINGS WITH WORDS

Early studies of language in use involved anthropologists in theorizing language acquisition and use within cultures. In the mid-20th century, linguists, philosophers, anthropologists, and psychologists shared an interest in this question because to answer it would shed light on language, culture, and thought. Ordinary language philosophers in the mid-20th century were interested in referential use of talk as but one way that oral discourse functions. Linguists studying conversation found, related to this insight, that speakers often used the same form of talk to accomplish a range of different social functions (and vice versa). Thus learning to hold a conversation was about far more than taking turns or giving words to experience; it was also about shaping, reinforcing, repairing, and re-creating social life, power relations, identity, and social norms. Because, as Heath (1983) pointed out in her book on the subject, *Ways with Words*, we do so much with our talk, teachers need both knowledge of conversation's complexities and the disposition to recognize differences in discourse practices rather than to assess differences as disability or ignorance.

The analysis of oral discourse inside classrooms, families, and other social groups and settings came into its own in the United States in the mid-20th century, when both funds and public concerns converged on problems of inequality—especially unequal access to learning in school. At the same time, many disciplines were asking not only how people acquire language but how they acquire social competence—or the ability to use language to communicate. There was a burgeoning of interest in language variation of all kinds—and in the tremendous amount of experience and local knowledge encapsulated in even the simplest slice of discourse. Finally, there were learning questions of another sort—how, out of the language we exchange, are we creating, sustaining, and possibly re-creating social relationships?

Embedded in each speech act is not only referential information and culturally appropriate reading of it but a large store of situational knowledge and a local drama in which people make the sense they make out of a potentially ambiguous exchange. These are the expression of our norms, or rules for treating one another in particular ways, our values about what is important, what and who deserves our respect, our sense of etiquette, and our biases and prejudices. In the past decade, critical linguists have focused on these dimensions of conversation and their role in equity and education.

From the outset, the application of the study of discourse to teaching and learning was colored by concerns about and interest in social norms. By studying discourse we could get a window on what people believe—and how they negotiate, construct, and reconstruct their beliefs. This is at the core of examining differential treatment and access to knowledge and it is also potentially at the core of social change. One exemplar of sociolinguistic research on oral language in a literacy event in a diverse primary classroom was conducted by Sarah Michaels (1981) and illustrates this convergence.

EXEMPLAR 1: "SHARING TIME" RESEARCH BY MICHAELS

In this research, close study of the conversation of teacher and pupils in a primary classroom's "sharing time" uncovered some troubling patterns. The teacher's schema for an appropriate oral sharing was brief and topic-centered—a spoken paragraph. Some children, mainly from middle-class backgrounds and European American speech communities knew that this was the appropriate way to share in school—even without having to be told by the teacher. They were making manifest in their talk not only the information they had to share but also a great deal about their social standing.

Students who did not already know or who for other reasons did not produce the school-appropriate sharing talk tended to tell longer, more complex, and thematically linked stories. These would be appropriate in nonschool contexts and perhaps in particular speech communities. However, in this context, they were inappropriate. The teacher did not explicitly address their structure with an explanation of rules for talk, but she did offer them different kinds of responses—less topically relevant and more related to the structure of their narratives. The public, evaluative nature of this kind of classroom conversation produces not only differential access to knowledge but also different available personae to participants. The less school-appropriate narratives were offered most often by lower-income pupils of color. These narratives might well be assessed as showing lack of readiness for school literacy work, especially writing, and also as less mature participation.

Because talk is permeable and improvised and is related to the shifting landscape of identity and activity, participants have options in how they will participate—and some of these options are influenced by their participation in discourse communities, including families, ethnic communities, gendered groups, and occupations. Idealized views of conversation, particularly when applied to communication in educational activities, are limited because they imply a closed system with few options—initiation, reply, evaluation.

Cazden (1988) notes that while this system may well be the "default" mode in Euro-American education, it is not universal and, moreover, it can be altered by explicit effort. Burbules (1993) offers two ways of thinking about such alteration in democratic classrooms: (1) the idea that within even a single conversation, participants may apply diverse conversational "genres" to accomplish the work of reasoning; and (2) the idea that these genres reflect shifting perspectives on "who we are and what we are doing." In some cases, consensus is the aim; in others it is divergence of thinking.

Of research findings such as those of Michaels, Gee (1996) (who has contributed additional analyses of Michaels's data in his own writing about social linguistics) argues that the subtle yet powerful dynamics of sharing time—both as a social event and as an oral preparation for topic-centered writing—illustrates the power of our words to shape both learning and social identity. Further, he argues that these data illustrate the ways that tacitly the wider social context of teacher–student interaction in an activity as apparently simple as sharing time can make a big difference in students' public identities and opportunities to learn, as well as in the recapitulation of social inequality based on race. Vivian Paley in her book, *White Teacher* (2000), analyzed her own practice and made similar findings. Describing the problem she discovered as hers, not that of her pupils, Paley's narrative recounted her efforts to come to terms with her own biases and pay close attention to talk and learning in her classroom as a part of her responsibility as an educator.

In that vein, Gee (1996) not only urges us to analyze classroom talk to understand this problem better but also suggests that when we recognize a situation in education in our society in which some members of a community are harmed or disadvantaged by dominant discourse practices we have a moral and ethnical responsibility to engage in critical discourse analysis to identify the sources of inequality and in reform of practice to redress them.

CRITICAL DISCOURSE ANALYSIS:
AN EXAMINATION OF LANGUAGE AND POWER

Critical linguists are those linguists who wish to analyze texts and conversations for political purposes. Because they argue that language is a central vehicle in the process whereby people are constituted as individuals and as social subjects, and because language and ideology are closely imbricated, the close systematic analysis of the language of texts can expose some of the workings of texts and, by extension, the way that people are oppressed within current social structures. They are attempting to integrate poststructuralist questions of power, truth, and knowledge within their linguistic analytical methods (Mills, 1997). Their definition of discourse draws heavily on the work of French philosopher and social theorist Michel Foucault (1926–1984), although they provide a substantial modification of the term because they are concerned with a more ground-level approach to language than Foucault; they thus provide more working models and concrete examples of how texts and conversations work to create inequalities of power and are more concerned with the mechanics of discursive functioning.

Terrain of critical discourse analysts has included an interrogation of the politics of representation and exclusion in the popular media. Fairclough (1989, 1995), for example, examines the media depictions of the actions of prominent politicians such as Ronald Reagan and Margaret Thatcher. Kress (2003) discusses the relationship between the proliferation of new media literacies and the confluence of spoken language and textuality in developing a Foucaultian-inspired framework of discourse analysis that could be applied to a conversation among peers or an examination of the nightly news. According to Kress (2003), no text, whether a conversational text or new media text, escapes the shaping influence of discourse (p. 47). Douglas Kellner (1995) examines how media discourses socialize and define identities in ways that both reproduce and resist existing power relations. Kellner's work critically examines the functions and usage of spoken language in films, youth music, and television news and entertainment. His work is not only descriptive but also prescriptive in articulating a method to be used by discerning citizens to make sense of their positioning vis-à-vis dominant media discourses.

The Construction of Knowledge in Discourse

Foucault believed that one of the most productive ways of thinking about discourse is not as a group of signs or a stretch of text but as "practices that systematically form the objects of which they speak." In this sense, discourse is something which produces something else, rather than something which exists in and of itself and which can be analyzed in isolation. Foucault (1981) also believed that each society has its regime of truth, its general politics of truth: that is, the types of discourse it harbors and causes to function as true. Truth, therefore, is something societies have to work to produce rather than something that appears in a transcendental way.

Discourses do not exist in a vacuum but are in constant conflict with other discourses and other social practices which inform them over questions of truth and authority. Foucault was not interested in which discourse is a true or accurate representation of the real; rather, he was concerned with the mechanics whereby one becomes produced as the dominant discourse. Foucault argued for the imbrication of power with knowledge, so that all the knowledge that exists is the result or the effect of power struggles. Most theorists of power have seen individuals as either benefited or oppressed by existing power relations, but Foucault saw them as the effects or instances of power relations. This is why Foucault's archaeological analysis of discourse is so important; he was not interested in simply analyzing the discourses that circulate in our society but challenges us to see the arbitrariness of this range of discourses, the strangeness of those discourses, in spite of their familiarity. He also charted the development of certain discursive practices, so that we can see that, rather than being permanent, as their familiarity would suggest, discourses are constantly changing and their origins can be traced to certain key shifts in history.

Talk and Perspective

More recent work in discourse analysis and in critical linguistics has shown that utterances do not simply mean one thing and that they cannot be interpreted from the standpoint of the speaker or hearer alone. Fairclough (1995) assumes that each of the participants will view the functioning of utterances from a standpoint made up of different interests and preoccupations—the analyst has therefore to be careful not to elide his or her position of analysis with that of one of the participants. Critical linguists have therefore been concerned with inflecting Foucault's analysis of discourse with a political concern with the effects of discourse (e.g., the way that people are positioned into roles through discursive structures and the way that certain people's knowledge is disqualified or not taken seriously in contrast to authorized knowledge). It is the shift away from mere description to a more analytical and critical perspective which is a significant reinterpretation of Foucault's work through the matrix of linguistics' concern for replicable, verifiable analyses.

Fairclough believes that Foucault's work is so important to critical linguistics because of his work's emphasis on the major role of discourse in the constitution of social subjects. Fairclough argues that Foucault's work on discourse can be usefully drawn on by linguists for two main insights: (1) the constitutive nature of discourse—discourse constitutes the social, including "objects" and social subjects; and (2) the primacy of interdiscursivity and intertextuality—that discursive practice is defined by its relations with others, and draws on others in complex ways. A concern for the relation between the individual interaction and the wider discursive and social structure not only makes for a form of analysis that is complex and finely nuanced but also makes for an analysis that is self-critical in terms of its own claims to "truth," and is aware of the dangers of naively ascribing meaning to texts. It is this type of fusion of larger social questions with smaller-scale analytical questions which holds the greatest potential for future work in this field.

Michel Pecheux (1982) views a discourse as a particular area of language use identified by the institutions to which it relates and by the positions from which it comes and which it marks for the speaker. The position does not exist by itself, however. Indeed, it may be understood as a standpoint taken up by the discourse through its relation to another, ultimately an opposing, discourse. Most critical approaches consider discourses to be principally organized around practices of exclusion. Pecheux's work on discourse is important in that he tries to analyze the meanings of words and their relations to larger structures without assuming that words and sentences had a meaning in themselves. Pecheux's work is also important in that he stresses more than Foucault the conflictual nature of discourse; that is, it is always in dialogue and conflict with other positions. He stresses the fact that ideological struggle is the essence of discourse structure.

Pecheux is concerned that, for example, people who are not privileged within a class system, through lack of access to education, knowledge, and familiarity with information networks and capital, are similarly prevented from having easy access to discourses. Discourses structure both our sense of reality and our notion of our own identity. For Pecheux in particular, discourses do not exist in isolation but are the object and site of struggle. Discourses are thus not fixed but are the site of constant contestation of meaning.

Feminist and postcolonial scholars have drawn on the French discourse analysis of Foucault and Pecheux for overtly political ends. Feminists, for instance, have used discourse analysis to move away from conceptions of women as victims of male domination to examine the ways in which power manifests itself and is resisted in everyday life (Mills, 1997). Postcolonial theorists are able to use discourse analysis to map historical, cultural, and political shifts in relations between subaltern cultures and the West through examination of discursive representations (Loomba, 2001). Similar to the feminists, postcolonial theorists also resist simple characterizations between dominant and subordinate groups and have used discourse analysis not only to characterize contemporary relations but to challenge problematic and disempowering historical narratives.

EXEMPLAR 2:
CRITICAL DISCOURSE IN EDUCATION BY MORRELL

An exemplar of research on literacy education approaching discourse in terms of institutionalized power, inequality, and historical narrative is Morrell's (2002) research on the experience of urban youth learning literacy in high school. Morrell researched integration of study of the high school's literary canon with students' popular culture as a way to tap the competence, motivation, and considerable background knowledge students can bring to literature study when it is linked to salient experiences in their lives outside school.

In his critical research on discourse in literacy education at the high school level, Morrell (2002, 2004) has worked at the borders of discourse communities, tapping expertise in one discourse (that of popular culture among urban youth) not only to master canonical high school curriculum but to enter even more explicitly powerful discourse of political and social activism in one's community. Morrell finds that incorporating study of the discourses of popular culture has two important outcomes for urban students. First, he was able to demonstrate connections between the way students talk about music and film and the ways that students are required to talk about canonical texts such as poems and novels. Students had developed schemas for close textual analysis and critical conversations in one arena that could be tapped into in another arena, namely, school. The second important outcome of the research with discourses of popular culture was that students were able to apply this analytical tool to be more discerning consumers of a set of cultural practices that were simultaneously representative and co-opting (Lipsitz, 1994; Storey, 1998).

Morrell's work is echoed in the ethnographic and sociolinguistic research of Moll (2000), who prepared teachers to become ethnographers in the home communities of their pupils and learn about the "funds of knowledge" within those communities which might be brought into the classroom to embody the school curriculum in the knowledge and practice of important adults in the child's life and mother tongue. Similarly, Gutiérrez, Baquedabi-Lopez, and Tejada (1999) have identified by means of discourse analysis in bilingual classrooms those activity settings in which students are able to bridge home and school and often transcend the norms of either community to forge a powerful linguistic and educational synthesis. Gutiérrez calls these third spaces, and advances both research and recommendations for practice based on her research among youngsters for whom English is a second language.

In all three of these examples, researchers tackle not only discourse analysis in ethnographic perspective but the move toward innovation and intervention as they attempt (or encourage and study) innovative practices that seem to break the frame of our taken for granted assumptions about how language and literacy are constituted within the established institution of U.S. public schooling. Each study also exemplifies the ways that the researchers followed rigors of analysis of discourse in its social and cultural context as part of developing, implementing, and studying innovative curriculum and instruction within the institution of schooling.

To work at this level of depth and sensitivity, a researcher must take pains to collect data among speakers engaged in authentic activities (in addition to other kinds of data based on surveys or tests or analysis of artifacts). He or she must look at social, political, and historical contexts as frames for interpretation. He or she must sample extensively from the speech data available within a particular discourse community or speech event and report analyses both descriptively and analytically, giving evidentiary warrant for the interpretation/descriptions as he or she has written it, and considering both alternate readings of the same data and disconfirming examples. Florio-Ruane (1987, p. 195) summarized the following maxims as important features to include when conducting or assessing research on classroom discourse:

- Go to the people.
- Pay attention to what is said and done.

- Plan your recording carefully.
- Proceed inductively.
- Be alert to interpretation.
- Find locally meaningful units of analysis.
- Balance explanation with narration and verbatim examples.
- Look for disconfirming evidence and discrepant cases.
- Think about your informants.

We judge the adequacy of research on oral discourse by its closeness to speakers, their speech, and the cultural contexts of their social and linguistic activities. Research of this kind is concerned with identification of local meaning in speakers' terms but also with its power. Having done this, many researchers move from descriptive, analytical, and critical studies to innovations aimed at educational improvement.

TALK, POWER, AND INSTITUTIONAL CHANGE

Again, we judge analysis of discourse (both defined as extended sequences of talk and as the social process of identification by means of talk) by its closeness to speakers and speech—by its concern for identification of local meaning in speakers' terms but also by its power to see the multiple form/function relationships possible in a language system and the ways that disambiguation of those relationships depends on cultural knowledge—especially that knowledge acquired in use and by participation. Ultimately, we value a study of oral discourse in terms of its pertinence to the educational questions asked. It is especially useful in addressing the following sorts of question in education: What is happening, specifically, in the social action that takes place in this particular setting? What do these actions mean to the actors involved in them, at the moment that they are taking place? How are the happenings organized in patterns of social organization and learned cultural principles for the conduct of everyday life—how, in other words, are people in the immediate setting present to each other as environments for one another's meaningful actions? How is what is happening in this setting as a whole (i.e., the classroom) related to happenings at other system levels outside and inside the setting? How do the ways everyday life is organized in this setting compare to other ways of organizing social life in a wide range of settings and at other times? (Erickson, 1986, p. 121).

From these examples and rigors it should be evident that the study of discourse in education is not a static, decontextualized process. It is a study of people actively engaged in communicating information and also negotiating roles, statuses, and identities. This line of inquiry leads us to look at the social organization of inequality, the ways language is used to sustain particular norms, and the ways metalinguistic awareness can foster critique and reasoning about complexity. Finally, the tool is useful for studying—and designing and assessing transformative discourse situations and practices generative of new possibilities for thought, action, and identification. For these reasons, it is an important tool for research on learning and education.

REFERENCES

Barton, D., & Hamilton, H. (1998). *Local literacies: Reading and writing in one community*. New York: Routledge.

Britzman, D. (2002). *Practice makes practice* (rev. ed.). New York: Teachers College Press.

Burbules, N. C. (1993). *Dialogue in teaching: Theory and practice*. New York: Teachers College Press.

Cazden, C. B. (1988). *Classroom discourse*. Portsmouth, NH: Heinemann.

Cazden, C., John, V., & Hymes, D. (1974). Functions of language in the classroom. New York: Teachers College Press.

Cole, M. (1996). *Cultural psychology: A once and future discipline*. Cambridge, MA: Harvard University Press.

Erickson, F. (1986). Qualitative methods in research on teaching. In M. C. Wittrock (Ed.), *Handbook of research on teaching* (3rd ed., pp. 119–161). New York: Macmillan.

Fairclough, N. (1989). *Language and power*. London: Longman.

Fairclough, N. (1995). *Critical discourse analysis: The critical study of language*. London: Longman.

Florio-Ruane, S. (1987). Sociolinguistics for educational researchers. *American Educational Research Journal, 24*(2), 185–197.

Florio-Ruane, S., & McVee, M. (2000). Ethnographic approaches to literacy research. In M. L. Kamil, P. B. Mosenthal, P. B., Pearson, P. D., & & R. Barr (Eds.), *Handbook of reading research* (Vol. 3, pp. 153–162). Mahwah, NJ: Erlbaum.

Foucault, M. (1981). The order of discourse. In R. Young (Ed.), *Untying the text: A postructuralist reader*. London: RKP.

Gee, J.P. (1996). *Social linguistics and literacies: Ideology in discourses* (3rd ed.). London: Routledge.

Gutiérrez, K., Baquedano-Lopez, P., & Tejeda, C. (1999). Rethinking diversity: Hybridity and hybrid language practices in the third space. *Mind, Culture, and Activity, 6*, 286–303.

Heath, S. B. (1983). *Ways with words: Language, life, and work in communities and classrooms.* Cambridge, UK: Cambridge University Press.

Hymes, D. (1974). *Foundations in sociolinguistics: An ethnographic approach.* Philadelphia: University of Pennsylvania Press.

Kellner, D. (1995). *Media culture: Cultural studies, identity and politics, between the modern and the postmodern.* New York: Routledge.

Kress, G. (2003). *Literacy in the new media age.* London: Routledge.

Lipsitz, G. (1994). History, hip-hop, and the post-colonial politics of sound. In *Dangerous crossroads: Popular music, postmodernism, and the poetics of place* (pp. 23–48). New York: Verso.

Loomba, A. (2001). *Colonialism/postcolonialism: The new critical idiom.* London: Routledge.

Michaels, S. (1981). "Sharing time": Children's narrative styles and differential access to literacy. *Language in Society, 10,* 423–443.

Mills, S. (1997). *Discourse: The new critical idiom.* London: Routledge.

Moll, L. (2000). Inspired by Vygotsky: Ethnographic experiments in education. In C. Lee & P. Smagorinsky (Eds.), *Vygotskian perspectives on literacy research: Constructing meaning through collaborative inquiry* (pp. 256–268). Cambridge, UK: Cambridge University Press.

Morrell, E. (2002). Toward a critical pedagogy of popular culture: Literacy development among urban youth. *Journal of Adolescent and Adult Literacy, 46*(1), 72–77.

Morrell, E. (2004). *Linking literacy and popular culture: Finding connections for lifelong learning.* Norwood, MA: Christopher-Gordon.

New London Group. (1996). A pedagogy of multiliteracies: Designing social futures. *Harvard Educational Review, 66*(1), 60–92.

Paley, V. (2000). *White teacher.* Cambridge, MA: Harvard University Press.

Pecheux, M. (1982). *Language, semantics, and ideology.* MacMillan.

Schiffrin, D. (1994). *Approaches to discourse.* London: Blackwell.

Spiro, R. J., Feltovich, P. J., Jacobson, M. L., & Coulson, R. L. (1993/1995). Cognitive flexibility, constructivism, and hypertext: Theory and technology for the nonlinear and multidimensional traversal of complex subject matter. In D. Nix & R. J. Spiro (Eds.), *Cognition, education, and multimedia* (pp. 163–205). Hillsdale, NJ: Erlbaum.

Storey, J. (1998). *An introduction to cultural theory and popular culture.* Athens: University of Georgia Press.

CHAPTER 5

Discourse Analysis
Written Text

Susan R. Goldman
Jennifer Wiley

Written text can be approached from a variety of disciplinary perspectives and purposes. In the context of this volume, we approach discourse analysis of written text by asking why written texts are of concern to literacy researchers, why they need to be analyzed, and how the texts and their analyses inform theoretical and empirical research in literacy. Written texts are of concern to literacy researchers because the ability to read and understand them is definitional to literacy, at least in Western culture. But *written text* is far from monolithic. There are any number of written text genre, differentiated by their purpose or function as well as their structure or form (e.g., narrative, poetic, persuasive, and informative). And within a genre, texts vary in both their form and their content. A primary goal of the analysis of written text is to describe structure and content. It is important to do so because well-established empirical findings indicate that structure and content affect how readers read, understand, remember, and learn from written texts (Goldman, 1997; Goldman & Rakestraw, 2000; Hiebert, Englert, & Brennan, 1983; Lorch, 1989). The discourse analysis of written text provides a method for systematically describing texts that students read as well as those they write.

To get a sense of what we might want our analysis of written text to capture you should read over example texts 1 and 2. They each deal with the topic of river ecosystems and were written to introduce young adolescents (11- to 13-year-olds) to the ideas of interdependence and environmental pollution. As we read them, you should think about how you might describe their characteristics, their similarities, and their differences. (Do this now before reading on in the chapter.)

Text 1: The Tupelo River Mystery

In the spring of 1999, a new nuclear power plant in the town of Bregsville went into operation. Local citizens and environmentalists were concerned because the power plant was located along a branch of the Tupelo River. They knew that a river is a very fragile **ecosystem**. The word ecosystem connects the idea of *eco*, which means a habitat or environment, with that of *system*, which means a set of relationships. Environmentalists were worried that the nuclear power plant would upset the balance of relationships among everything in the Tupelo River ecosystem.

There are many parts of the Tupelo River's ecosystem. Some are organisms such as fish, insects, animals, and plants. They live in and around the river. River systems also contain non-living things such as water, the rocks on the bottom, and the mud on the banks of the river. The most important concept about any ecosystem, including the Tupelo River's, is that everything depends on everything else. A change in one part of the ecosystem could introduce changes in all parts of the ecosystem. There was concern that the operation of the nuclear power plant would introduce changes.

Text 2: Ecosystems

Any group of living and nonliving things interacting with each other can be considered as an ecosystem. Within each ecosystem, there are habitats that may vary in size. A habitat is the place where a population lives. A population is a group of living organisms of the same kind living in the same place at the same time. All of the populations interact and form a community. The community of living things interacts with the non-living world around it to form the ecosystem. The living members of a river's system are the plants and animals that live around and within the river—and they are all connected to each other in what is called a food web.

Anything that is added to the water of our aquatic ecosystems that is not a normal part of the systems, and that should not be there, is a type of water pollution. There are many sources of water pollution. Some types of pollution can be traced directly to a particular spot, such as a factory, or industrial plant. These sources of water pollution are easier to control, because the actual point where the pollution is being added to the water can be identified.

Here are some of the things you might have come up with to describe the characteristics and the differences.

1. Text 1 is a story about a town; text 2 is more straight "content."
2. They both define ecosystem but they do it differently.
3. They are both about the same length and have the same number of paragraphs.
4. Text 2 talks about water pollution in general; text 1 talks about the impact of the nuclear power plant but doesn't say it is a potential source of pollution.
5. Text 2 talks about the food web, but text 1 just says that things in an ecosystem depend on each other.

We suspect that as you engaged in the analysis and comparison process you were unsure of precisely how to describe what you were noticing. Discourse analysis provides a means to more systematically engage in the descriptive analysis and comparison of written texts. The particular perspective we take in this chapter assumes that discourse analysis is informed by knowledge of the content domain(s) that the text is about. In other words, the method is not "content free."

WHAT IS THE METHOD?

Discourse analysis of written text is a method for describing the ideas and the relations among the ideas that are present in a text. The method draws on work in a variety of disciplines, including rhetoric, text linguistics, and psychology. These disciplines provide ways to describe and analyze how the structure and content of the text encodes ideas and the relations among the ideas. In describing these relations it is important to initially define the genre to which the text belongs because structures differ across genre. For example, narrative stories differ from persuasive essays; news articles have a different form than editorials; and fiction texts have different structures than do nonfiction. Differences in structure imply different relations among the ideas in the texts, especially at the global level. With respect to the differences between the example texts 1 and 2, the first difference we listed reflects just such genre differences.

The global level of relations is often referred to as the rhetorical structure of the text. Different rhetorical structures are appropriate for different genres. For example, the rhetorical structure of many stories involves the occurrence of a problem that protagonist(s) attempt to resolve and, in "happy ending" stories, are successful at resolving. The story typically consists of a series of episodes that are causally related. A common form of episode relations occurs when there are a number of preconditions that must be met in order to resolve the overall problem. In other narrative rhetorical structures, the interepisode relations may be temporal, with one episode succeeding another but with goals that are not particularly related. (For further information about narrative structure, refer to Bamberg, 1997; Bloome, 2003; Mandler & Johnson, 1977; McCabe, 1997; Stein & Albro, 1997; Stein & Glenn, 1979; Trabasso & van den Broek, 1985.)

The global structure of nonfiction texts contrasts with those of fictional ones, and there is less agreement about the rhetorical structures that apply. Meyer (1985) proposed a set of five "top-level" rhetorical structures in an attempt to systematize the structure of the major genre of expository texts. These were collection or list, description, causal, comparative, and problem/solution (see also Weaver & Kintsch, 1991). These rhetorical structures may be signaled by particular words or phrases but do not have to be. Example text 2 is a description. Example text 1 is a bit more complicated, but we think it may be best described as a nonfiction narrative perhaps similar to a feature article in a news magazine or newspaper.

The analysis of written text is also concerned with understanding the local relations among the ideas conveyed in a text (i.e., relations among information in sentences occurring relatively close together in the text). It is precisely the relations among ideas that define the coherence of the text and make it more than the sum of its parts. Indeed, Sanders, Spooren, and Noordman (1992), defined coherence relations as the "aspect of meaning of two or more discourse segments that cannot be described in terms of the meaning of the segments in isolation. In other words, it is because of this coherence relation that the meaning of two discourse segments is more than the sum of its parts" (p. 2). There are a number of ways coherence relations are established. Halliday and Hasan (1976) identified four primary logical connector relations: temporal as in an ordered sequence of events (e.g., the steps in a mathematical proof), additive as in elaborations of an idea (e.g., main idea followed by details), causal as in antecedent and consequent events, and adversative, as in the juxtaposition of contradictory information.

A number of discourse markers (also called linguistic cues) are relevant to understanding local relations among ideas. A specific class of discourse markers, called connectives, express, signal, or cue the underlying conceptual coherence relations. Examples of connectives are *because, furthermore,* and *however.* Other kinds of signaling devices (Lorch, 1989) signal the relationships of sentences to paragraphs, and paragraphs to one another and to the overall theme of the text.

Lorch (1989) distinguished signaling devices from those aspects of a text that communicate the semantic content: Signals *emphasize* particular aspects of content or structure, but they do not add content (Lorch, 1989). Signaling devices help readers pick out what to selectively attend to and how to differentiate the importance of different information in the text (Goldman & Duran, 1988; Goldman & Saul, 1990; Guthrie, 1988; Lorch & Chen, 1986; Lorch & Lorch, 1996). Lorch provided a list of signaling devices used in expository prose that included titles, headings and subheadings; repetition of content to emphasize, preview, or summarize; function indicators (pointer words such as *thus,* pointer phrases such as *in summary,* pointer sentences such as *let me summarize what has been said*); relevance indicators (*let me stress that*); enumeration devices; and typographical cues (underlining, boldface, and spatial layout such as indenting, centering).

A large body of empirical research indicates that some genres and content structures are more difficult for readers to understand than others. For example, knowledge of narrative structure generally appears earlier than knowledge of expository structure (Crowhurst, 1990; Engelhard, Gordon, & Gabrielson, 1992; Grabe, 2002; Langer, 1986; Scott, & Windsor, 2000; Tolchinsky, Johansson, & Zamora, 2002). Of course, this may be a result of typical instructional practices of concentrating on narrative text in primary grades and not introducing expository forms until later (Duke, 2000; Pappas, 1993). When readers have knowledge of informational content structures and use that information to guide their processing of text, their understanding and memory are better than in the absence of such knowledge (Carrell, 1992; Englert & Hiebert, 1984; Garner et al., 1986; McGee, 1982; Meyer, Brandt, & Bluth, 1980; Taylor & Beach, 1984; Taylor & Samuels, 1983). Although literacy researchers have always been aware of genre, content, and structure differences among texts, historically there was far less recognition of the role that such differences might play in outcomes for readers and the implications for literacy education. This is no longer the case. Thus, it is critical for literacy educators to describe and understand the content and structure of written texts, the demands they place on readers, and the relationship between written texts students read and those they write.

THE ANALYSIS OF WRITTEN TEXT

The goal of analyzing written text is to arrive at systematic descriptions that provide a basis for comparing written texts with one another. But what kind of description? There are a number of issues to consider in answering this question, the most important of which is what questions the researcher wishes to address with the analysis. If, for example, interest is in how much of the text a student remembers exactly as it was presented, counting the number of words that can be reproduced in correct order and position might be all that is necessary. Of course, even word counting can become more complex (e.g., if location in the text—beginning, middle, end—was important). Indeed, early work on memory for written text used the word-counting method (Clark, 1940, cited in Carroll, 1972; Gomulicki, 1956; King, 1960, 1961, cited in Carroll, 1972). Word counting might also be useful if interest is in a simple measure of fluency of producing written text.

A fairly common reason for wanting a systematic description of written text is to determine the reading difficulty of a passage, referred to as passage *readability*. Traditional readability formulas such as the Flesch Reading Ease index make extensive use of word complexity (assessed via number of syllables), number of sentences, and number of sentences per 100 words (see Klare, 1974–1975, for review). However, readability formulas do not correspond well with how easy the text makes it to understand the concepts and ideas. One reason for this is that making explicit the local relation between ideas sometimes results in longer sentences. Consider the contrast between examples 1 and 1a:

1. Torrential rains fell on Saturday. The road collapsed.
1a. The road collapsed because of the torrential rains that fell on Saturday.

Even though 1a is a longer sentence readers find it easier to understand the causal connection than in sentence 1 (Pearson, 1974–1975).

Traditional readability formulas also fail to consider the familiarity of the concepts in the passage. More recently, the lexile has been used to assess readability (Stenner & Wright, 2002). The lexile determines readability using sentence length and word frequency. Word frequency is a rough index of concept familiarity and is being widely used. (For additional information, see *www.Lexile.com*.) In addition to underestimating the impact of readers' knowledge of the passage topic, readability formulas do not take into account the text as a whole. That is, texts have global structure that transcends the individual words and sentences. It is perfectly obvious, for example, that the meaning of a text is entirely different when we reorder the sentences.

To illustrate the limitations of text descriptions that are based only on readability formulas, we need only refer back to the example texts 1 and 2. A number of the differences we noted would have been masked if all we had done was look at word counts and readability indices. The relevant data are 190 (text 1) versus 201 (text 2) words; 12 versus 11 sentences; 15.8 versus 18.2 words per sentence; 6 versus 5.5 sentences per paragraph; 47.3 versus 58 for the Flesch Reading Ease; 10.5 versus 9.6 for the Flesch Kincaid grade level; and 970 versus 1030 for the Lexile measure. On the basis of these data the two texts are hard to distinguish. Thus, readability formulas provide only a rough descriptive and comparative index and miss many of the important characteristics of texts.

Typically, it is the ideas in text and their interrelations that are of interest to the literacy researcher. Some ideas can be conveyed in a word or two; others require several sentences and paragraphs. How then do we systematically describe the ideational content and structure of written text?

The most commonly accepted unit of analysis among literacy researchers is some form of the proposition, a construct that appeared in the work of a number of linguists, psychologists, and computer scientists during the 1970s (e.g., Anderson, 1976; Fillmore, 1968; Frederiksen, 1975; W. Kintsch, 1974; Kieras, 1981; Kintsch & van Dijk, 1978; Meyer, 1975; Schank, 1972; van Dijk, 1972). A widely used formulation, and the one we favor, is that of Kintsch and van Dijk (1978). Specifically, van Dijk and Kintsch (1983) defined the proposition as a theoretical unit that corresponds roughly to the meaning of a clause. A whole text is represented by organizing the set of propositions derived from the clauses and sentences in the text. Different forms of organizing the propositions include hierarchical lists, semantic networks, or procedural networks. The proposition itself consists of the simple concepts or *atomic propositions* and the *propositional scheme* (or complex proposition) into which the atomic propositions are arranged. The propositional scheme consists of a *predicate* and one or more *arguments*. Predicates are main verbs of clauses or connectives between clauses. Arguments have functional roles with respect to the predicate (e.g., agent, patient, and object location) or can be embedded propositional schemes. A proposition refers to a state, an event or an action. The psychological plausibility of clause-level propositional schemes has been demonstrated in a variety of research studies although we do not review them here (Anderson & Bower, 1973; Graesser, 1981; Kintsch & Keenan, 1973; Ratcliff & McKoon, 1978).

In Figure 5.1, we present a schematic of the propositional scheme for the first sentence in example text 1: *In the spring of 1999, a new nuclear power plant in the town of Bregsville went into operation.* To generate the propositional representation shown in Figure 5.1, we analyze its elements and decide whether it is an event or a state. As shown in Figure 5.1, the decision we reach is that it is an EVENT.

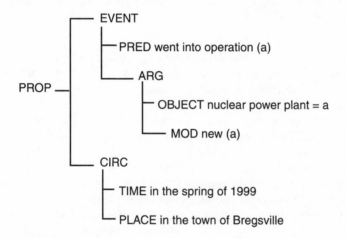

PROP = propositional scheme; PRED = predicate; ARG = argument; MOD = modification; CIRC = circumstances.

Atomic Propositions
AP1: In (x1, AP6)
AP2: spring of 1999 = x1
AP3: new (x2)
AP4: nuclear power (x2)
AP5: plant = x2
AP6: went into operation (x2)
AP7: in (x5, AP6)
AP8: town = x5
AP9: of Bregsville (x5)

FIGURE 5.1. Propositional scheme representation for the sentence *In the Spring of 1999, a new nuclear power plant in the town of Bregsville went into operation.*

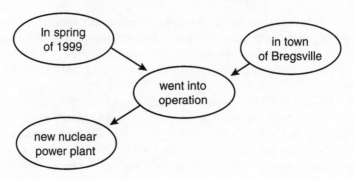

FIGURE 5.2. Semantic network representation of the propositional scheme for the sentence *In the Spring of 1999, a new nuclear power plant in the town of Bregsville went into operation.*

The decision is based on our understanding that the words *went into operation* mark a change in state of some entity, in this case *a new nuclear power plant*. Because it is an inanimate entity, we refer to the plant as an Object. We also know that events occur in time and space and indeed the first sentence provides us with this information. Time and place are indicators of the circumstances of the event. The structure of the propositional scheme conveys these relations. But the schematic in Figure 5.1 does not accurately reflect the *atomic level* of analysis. The atomic level, resulting from further analysis of the phrases in the schematic, is shown in the lower portion of Figure 5.1. The atomic level can be considered the basic, core level of meaning, and although it may be useful from linguistic or philosophical perspectives to capture this level, it is often too detailed for purposes of looking at understanding and learning. For our purposes we typically represent propositions at the more molar level shown in Figure 5.1.

Figure 5.2 shows the same sentence represented as a semantic network. We have left the links unlabeled, but they could be labeled with object, time, and location.

While it is useful for didactic purposes to work out several sentences at the level of detail shown in Figure 5.1, it is often impractical to draw such structures for every sentence in a written text. The typical way in which we create the propositions of a text is in a list format as shown here.

   i. Went into operation (OBJECT: new nuclear power plant, TIME: ii, PLACE: iii)
   ii. in the spring of 1999
   iii. in the town of Bregsville

We refer to the proposition labeled *i* as the predicate proposition; *ii* and *iii* specify the time and place of the main action. We use indentation to show that propositions *ii* and *iii* are subordinate to the predicate proposition. Depending on the discourse analyst, there might be additional propositions reflecting the adjectival modifiers of *plant*. For example, *iv.* TYPEOF plant: nuclear power; and *v.* MOD plant: new. These would also be indented to show that they are subordinate to the main action. The level of detail needed in the proposition specification depends on the questions the researcher is addressing. The next sentence in the paragraph would be similarly represented, as shown in Figure 5.3. In sentence 2 there are two clauses that are causally related, shown in the figure as a BECAUSE node (cross-hatched and rectangular). The argument *power plant* is common to sentences 1 and 2; this overlap is shown in Figure 5.3 by having the node, shaded for emphasis) linked to the predicate of each sentence. Similarly, sentence 2 and 3 share an argument (*local citizens and environmentalists*). Understanding this connection requires the resolution of the referent for the pronoun *They* in sentence 3. Note that showing node overlap in the list format can get messy, but arrows are often used to show which cross-sentence overlaps exist. Illustrations of this can be found in a number of published papers (e.g., Goldman & Varnhagen, 1986; Goldman, Varma, & Coté, 1996; Goldman, Varma, Sharp, & CTGV, 1999; Trabasso & van den Broek, 1985).

If we carried out the process demonstrated in Figures 5.2 and 5.3 for the remainder of the sentences in the paragraph and passage, the result would be an organized network or list of propositions connected on the basis of the meaning relations among the ideas. Organizing the individual clauses into a network or list depends on the semantic relationships among the ideas, often producing a hierarchically organized structure of super- and subordinated ideas. The title and first several sentences usually establish concepts that are subsequently repeated throughout the passage as more information about them is provided. Subsequent incoming information "attaches" to these concepts creating the subordinate or supporting relation, as illustrated in Figures 5.1, 5.2, and 5.3. Sentences that have many subsequent sentences connected to them take on more superordinate, thematic status in the passage (e.g., Goldman et al., 1996; Kintsch & van Dijk, 1978; Meyer, 1975).

Texts in which the individual clauses are explicitly connected have high cohesiveness (Halliday & Hasan, 1972). Example 1a, previously discussed, is a highly *cohesive* sentence. *Coherence* is reflected in the connectedness among propositions in readers' representations. In example 1, readers might infer the causal relation that is explicit in

Identification of the clauses in the first two sentences
1. In the spring of 1999, a new nuclear power plant in the town of Bregsville went into operation.
2.1 Local citizens and environmentalists were concerned
2.2 because
2.3 the power plant was located along a branch of the Tupelo River.
3.1 They knew 3.2
3.2 that a river is a very fragile ecosystem.

Shorthand of the Propositional Schemes in the first three sentences.
    1.1. went into operation (OBJECT: new nuclear power plant, TIME: 1.2, PLACE: 1.3)
         1.2. in the spring of 1999
         1.3 in the town of Bregsville
    2.1 were concerned (AGENTS: local citizens and environmentalists)
    2.2 because (2.1, 2.3)
    2.3 was located (OBJECT: power plant, LOC: 2.4)
         2.4 LOC: 2.3, along a branch of the Tupelo River
    3.1 They knew 3.1
    3.2 is (OBJECT: river, OBJECT: ecosystem)
         3.3 very fragile (ecosystem)

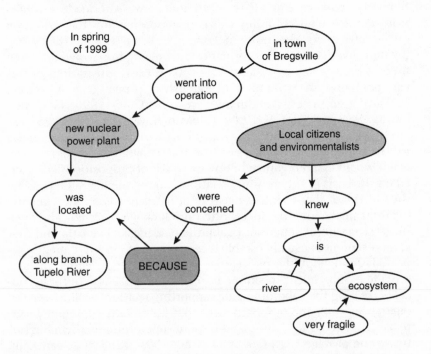

FIGURE 5.3. Construction of the representation of the initial part of text 1.

1a, in which case the representation would be similarly coherent for 1 and 1a. Similarly, in Figure 5.3, we noted that the reader needs to make an anaphoric reference to resolve the referent for *they* in sentence 3. If readers do not make that connection, they might make one between *Tupelo River* in sentence 2 and *river* in sentence 3, an inference based on the specific river being an instance or example of the general class of rivers. If readers failed to make either the anaphoric or the general-to-specific inference the two sentences would be unconnected and a gap in local coherence would exist. Lack of coherence in readers' representations of text make it difficult to understand the meaning of the text as a whole; information remains in bits and pieces, so to speak.

To foster the development of coherent representations, texts often supply cues (cohesive devices) in the text. This should make it easier to establish coherence but only for those readers who understand how to interpret the cues (Goldman & Rakestraw, 2000). Texts that have few cohesive devices require that readers work to fill in the gaps among ideas. Doing so frequently requires that readers have requisite prior knowledge of the content domain or knowledge of the genre of the text. If they do not and the text has few cohesive devices, understanding is often not very good. As might be expected, comprehension by readers who know little about the topic of a text is aided by cohesive text. However, researchers have found that readers who have high content knowledge achieve deeper understanding of a text in which the cohesion is not obvious as compared to those in which cohesion is explicit (E. Kintsch, 1990; McNamara, Kintsch, Butler-Songer, & Kintsch, 1996; Voss & Silfies, 1996). Discourse analysis permits researchers to compare texts in terms of propositional structure and the ease with which connections across propositions, hence coherence, can be achieved.

The Role of Prior Knowledge

Why should it be the case that readers with high knowledge of the topic achieve deeper understanding when they have to create coherence? Answering this question involves expanding our discussion of text representation to include an interpretive level. Researchers in the early 1980s recognized a distinction between creating a representation of the text itself and integrating the information in the text with prior knowledge, thereby constructing a representation of the situation described by the text. The representation of the text itself, labeled the *textbase*, is what we have been constructing thus far (see Figure 5.3). The representation of the situation is referred to as a *mental*

(Johnson-Laird, 1983) or *situation model* (van Dijk & Kintsch, 1983) and reflects readers' interpretations of the meaning of the text (Perfetti, 1989), constructed by integrating prior knowledge with the ideas in the textbase. Interpretations come about through elaborative, explanatory, and evaluative processes. To conclude that learning has occurred, evidence of a situation model representation is needed (Kintsch et al., 1993; McNamara et al., 1996). Assessment of learning thus involves going beyond reproductive or recognition memory; readers need to demonstrate that they have formed a coherent model of the situation described in the text. This can be demonstrated in a variety of ways such as by applying the information to a new situation, providing verbal explanations or drawings that illustrate how something works (e.g., Chi, De Leeuw, Chiu, & Lavancher, 1994), or successfully carrying out a procedure (Mills, Diehl, Birkmire, & Mou, 1995).

Discourse Analysis of Texts Produced by Readers and Learners

Written discourse is not only a medium of information presentation. It is also a window into the mental model of the learner. Frequently, readers and learners are asked to produce text, sometimes to demonstrate what they have learned from reading a particular textbook selection, passage, or set of passages. These learner-produced texts can be analyzed and compared to what learners read or were presumed to have read. Other times learners produce written discourse "spontaneously" and in the absence of some just read "stimulus" material. In these situations, the written discourse communicates writers' content knowledge, beliefs, feelings, and command of the language. In the discussion that follows, we focus on learner-produced writing in the context of presented texts and only briefly discuss spontaneous writing.

Writing in Response to Presented Text

When learners produce essay responses to open-ended questions, their writing samples can be analyzed with respect to "how close" they are to the presented text and how much they go beyond what was "in" the text through inferences and elaborations. We can look for evidence of coherence in the mental model and of appropriate integration of new and prior knowledge, both important benchmarks of understanding (Coté, Goldman, & Saul, 1998; Coté & Goldman, 1999). As such, they act as a window into the internal representations that readers have constructed. By comparing texts, learners write to those they have read it is possible to characterize comprehension and understanding. For example, we might want to know the degree to which they have accurately understood the meaning of the text or how they have interpreted the information, as reflected in elaborations and explanations. To facilitate such analyses, we want to conduct discourse analyses of the written texts produced by readers and learners and do so in a form that is compatible with the representation of the material that they read and from which they learn.

Responses to Specific Prompts and Questions

Consider the three student-produced written texts provided in Table 5.1. These are the responses of three seventh-grade students who had read *The Tupelo River* text in its entirety. They were asked to respond to the specific probe question, "Explain the idea of an ecosystem." The researchers (Oney et al., 2003; Goldman et al., 2003) used this type of probe because they were interested in what students had understood about ecosystems. They were not interested in learners' memory for the story per se, so rather than asking for recall of what they remembered from *The Tupelo River Mystery*, the researchers asked a targeted question.

To understand the students' writing samples, it is important to know the gist of *The Tupelo River Mystery* beyond the two paragraphs in the example at the beginning of the paper. (Full text is available at *http://litd.psch.uic.edu/docs/river_7th.doc*). Briefly, scientists decided to monitor the river to see if any changes in the ecosystem occurred. Over a 10-month period they found that the Mayfly population had declined by over 70% and the Rainbow Darter by 50%, but the Elodea plant had increased by 20%. This was explained in terms of a food chain in which the Mayflies were central, serving as food for the Darter and eating the Elodea. The cause of the food chain disruption was a 5-degree increase in the river temperature, resulting in less dissolved oxygen and the negative impact on the Mayfly population. The scientists traced the rise in temperature to thermal pollution from the nuclear power plant.

We noticed several things about the seventh graders' responses. (Before reading on you might want to take the researcher's role and read over the responses, thinking about similarities and differences among them and between each and the passage.) First, the responses differ in length; however, longer is not necessarily better. Student 3 has the shortest response but perhaps the best explanation of an ecosystem. Student 2 likens an ecosystem to the food chain and includes

TABLE 5.1. Three Seventh-Grade Students' Responses to the Prompt "Explain the Idea of an Ecosystem" Based on *The Tupelo River Mystery* Passage

Student 1

An ecosystem is kind of like a cycle. A cycle that depends on its self. For example the insects that live in the water play in an important in the cycle. The insects eat a certain plant which helps the water in certain ways. Also the insect is a major food source for a certain species of fish. This insect does a very important part in keeping this ecosystem [flawless?]. If you remove this insect there will eventually be no fish and a huge surplus of plants. This is what I believe an ecosystem is.

Student 2

The ecosystem is like a chain that connects different species together and the different animals depend on each other and if one species becomes endangered then that mess the whole system up and the other animals won't be able to live right. When pollution is occurred it can kill off lots of animals and destroy the whole ecosystem. An ecosystem is also similar to a food chain because if one species die or if a certain type of plant isn't growing any more then it will knock off the whole system. If an animal kills another species than that also will affect the ecosystem as well. Also if one animal dies then the other animal won't be able to eat and then the next animal will die off and then the whole system will be gone.

Student 3

An ecosystem is the relationship among the things in an environment. In an ecosystem, everything is related to one another. If one thing is removed, many other things are effected. In the story, the water temperature increased and it caused Mayflies to die. Fishes that feed on Mayflies began to die too. In contrast, the plants the Mayflies ate increased in number. That's an example of a food chain in the ecosystem.

a number of specifics about how the death of one animal or plant will affect what happens to others. Student 2 seems to have accurate details but lacks the more interpretive understanding that student 3 seems to have achieved. Finally, student 1 seems to have bits and pieces of what the text contained but they are not connected in ways that show the interrelationships. If we were to paraphrase student 1's response, it might go something like the following: "An ecosystem is a cycle in which insects are important. They eat plants and are a food source for certain fish." Thus the more general notion of an ecosystem is missing. This contrasts dramatically with student 3, who uses the specifics in the story to exemplify the general principles of an ecosystem.

If we want our analyses of these data to be capable of revealing the differences among these three kinds of responses, how are we to accomplish this? We need to specify the conceptual elements of an ecosystem as they are communicated in the text and look for correspondences in the students' responses. We start by dividing the responses into clauses, just as we did the text, and ask whether these clauses are meaning preserving of propositions from the passage. We would also look at how the relations among the concepts are expressed and whether they are organized in a way that conveys a coherent situation or mental model of an ecosystem. This is the advantage of student 3's response over that of the other two. Student 3 has inferred a set of core principles about ecosystems based on the information in the text ("An ecosystem is a relational environmental system. In an ecosystem, everything is related to one another. If one thing is removed, other things are effected.") These principles are then exemplified with the specific species and causal chain (water temperature increase → decrease in Mayfly → decrease in fish and increase in plant) that is described for the Tupelo River ecosystem. Student 3 seems to have used information from throughout the whole text in developing a mental model. In contrast, student 1 appears to be largely focused on the information contained in the two paragraphs in the text about the food chain. Like student 1, student 2 seems to draw on these paragraphs but is less tied to the specifics of insects and fish, suggesting more integration with prior knowledge of endangerment and interdependence in an ecosystem. These ideas are similar to the principles student 3 expresses, yet student 2 does not abstract them beyond specific animals. We might conclude that student 2 has a more concrete or specific situation model than student 3.

Specific prompts such as the one illustrated for *The Tupelo River Mystery* and other kinds of open-ended questions are one way to elicit information from learners and are quite similar to the kinds of questions teachers might pose to students on end-of-unit classroom tests for purposes of assessing learning. The recall task is another method that researchers commonly use to elicit text from students.

Writing in Response to Presented Text: Recall

The recall (or retell) task asks students to write down (or say) what they remember from the text they have heard or read. This task is quite commonly used with many text genres. Here we focus on recall of an informational passage on metabolism typical of those used by many researchers. In research with passages of this genre, subjects typically recall about 25% to 40% of the predicate propositions from the textbase. In crediting students with recalling propositions, researchers need to decide whether to adopt a stringent or a looser criteria. A stringent criteria means that for credit to be given the student wording must be very close to the passage wording. More commonly looser criteria are used so that credit for inclusion of a proposition is based on comparability of meaning across the passage and students' productions. Comparability of meaning is usually based on the core idea of the predicate proposition.

The *Metabolism* passage shown in Table 5.2 has been used in research with children ranging in age from 8 to 12 years (Coté et al., 1998; Coté & Goldman, 1999). The *Metabolism* passage, and several others that were used in the same experiment, was written to begin in the style of a feature article in a newsmagazine and to conform to a specific content structure (Coté et al., 1998; Coté & Goldman, 1999). For example in the *Metabolism* passage (Table 5.2), the first paragraph reported a new scientific invention, which we hoped would provide students with a reason for wanting to learn more about metabolism. From there, the passage structure is typical of the informational text genre. The second paragraph provided definitional information on metabolism; the next four paragraphs provided information on "four factors that affect metabolic rate." The final paragraph related back to the first in stating how the new invention would measure metabolism. For the most part each sentence contained one predicate proposition and in cases where there were two clauses in a sentence we focused on the predicate that introduced new information. (For example, in sentence 4, _Different people have different metabolic rates_ that indicate how easily they can produce energy, the new information and the main predicate we focused on was the underlined portion because the information in the second clause had already been given in the passage.)

Also in Table 5.2 are two examples that are representative of recall protocols obtained when students read the passage and were subsequently asked to recall "everything you remember." Several differences between the two recalls and between the recalls and the passage are evident. First, both recalls leave out much of the information in the passage. Student 1 wrote everything in a single paragraph and student 2 created a list, using up and down arrows that we assumed meant increase and decrease, respectively. What about content? Both students have changed much of the wording from the exact wording of the passage. This is fairly typical and researchers often adopt the *meaning preserving* criterion: Does the statement in the re-

TABLE 5.2. Metabolism Passage and Recalls by Undergraduates

Metabolism

Customers in many pharmacies may soon be seeing the latest in new devices for the health conscious. A sports physiologist is developing the metabometer, a device that he hopes will measure the human body's ability to produce energy efficiently.

The rate at which the body produces energy is called metabolism. Different people have different metabolic rates that indicate how easily they can produce energy. The same person may have different metabolic rates, depending on the circumstances. Different species of animals also have different metabolic rates.

There are several factors that affect metabolic rate. One factor is the type of food a person or animal eats. For example, some foods are hard to digest, such as complex carbohydrates like rice. The body has to work harder to get energy from rice. If a person ate a steady diet of rice, the result would be a higher metabolic rate.

Another factor affecting metabolism is the climate of the environment. Temperature may cause the metabolism to change. People and animals that live in cold environments need to produce more energy in order to keep warm. Most animals that live in polar regions have high metabolisms. If people move from a warm to a cold climate, /their metabolic rates will increase.

Metabolic rate also differs depending on activity level. Changing the level of activity may cause the body to change its metabolism /because different activities require different amounts of energy. For example, basketball players use more energy than golfers so their metabolic rates are generally higher.

To some degree, metabolic rate is influenced by genetic inheritance. Children of parents who have high metabolic rates tend to have high metabolic rates also. This is because the body chemistry of the children is a combination of the body chemistry of the parents.

Metabolism is regulated by hormones produced by the thyroid gland, a tiny gland located at the base of the neck. These hormones regulate the behavior of all the cells in the body so that enough energy is produced. The metabometer will work by measuring hormone levels in the blood.

Student 1

A sports physiologist is trying to measure the metabolic rate by creating the metabolar. Metabolism is affected by many things. It depends on what someone eats. Rice is hard to digest, so the metabolism would be high for someone on an all-rice diet. Climate accounts for metabolism. People in colder climates have higher metabolic rates than people in warm climates. Genetics is responsible for metabolism too. If a child's parents both have high metabolic rates, the child will have a high metabolic rate too. Activity changes the metabolism. A golfer will have a lower metabolic rate than a basketball player because Golf does not require as much energy as Basketball.

(continued)

TABLE 5.2 *(continued)*

Student 2

Metabolism: Deals w/ability of body to produce energy
Influenced by 4 things:
1. <u>Diet</u>: harder food to digest = ?? metabolism
2. <u>Climate</u>: ?? temperature = ?? metabolism
3. <u>Physical activity</u>: ? activity = ?? metabolism
4. <u>Genetic</u>: hormone released from thyroid, located at bottom of neck ?
The new "metabometer" measures the hormones being released.

---

call capture the meaning that was in the passage. If so, the student is credited with having remembered the information. By the *meaning-preserving* criterion, each student would be credited with remembering the four factors. In addition, student 1 included information from the passage to convey the impact the factor has on metabolism. In contrast, student 2 just indicated the relationship. Notice, however, that the way student 1 expressed these relationships is not identical to the propositions in the text. To take just one example, the passage stated:

> For example, <u>some foods are hard to digest</u>, such as complex carbohydrates like rice. The body has to work harder to get energy from rice. If a person ate a steady diet of rice, the result would be a higher metabolic rate.

Student 1 wrote:

> Rice is hard to digest, so the metabolism would be high for someone on an all-rice diet.

Student 1 received credit for remembering the underlined portions of the passage. Student 2 received credit for the same underlined information even though *rice* was not mentioned. Although other researchers might argue with this scoring decision, the important point is that such decisions need to be made on a principled and reliable basis. To achieve this, we have found it not only useful but necessary to keep a log of coding decisions so that inter- and intrarater reliability can be achieved.

In general, the task of deciding on *meaning preserving* is nontrivial because of the variability in how people recall information they have read, even when they are accurate. As these two student examples illustrate, people combine multiple sentences and produce summary statements; they combine ideas from parts of different sentences; they make accurate as well as inaccurate inferences; and they express what they remember in different structural forms. To the degree that learners combine information and add information that goes beyond what is present in the text, we would credit their recall as reflecting situation-model-level understanding. (For a more detailed discussion, see Coté et al., 1998; W. Kintsch, 1994, 1998; McNamara & Kintsch, 1996; van Oostendorp & Goldman, 1999; and van Dijk & Kintsch, 1983.)

In the analysis of the responses to *The Tupelo River* and *Metabolism* texts, we have attempted to model the kind of thinking that researchers need to do when they are attempting to understand what students have learned from reading a passage or set of passages on specific topics. You might have noticed that this thinking depends on understanding the conceptual domain as well as how that information is encapsulated in the specific passage. If one goal of reading informational text is to enable learners to acquire conceptual knowledge, the content and structure of that conceptual domain must be part of the discourse analysis of written text. This is as true for the analysis of passages and what they afford in the way of opportunities to learn concepts and relations in a particular domain as it is for understanding the situation models that are suggested by what learners write about these topics after reading.

Spontaneous Production of Written Discourse

The analysis of written text is often useful for assessing learners' prior knowledge, beliefs, feelings, and facility with the writing process. As indicated previously in our discussion, prior knowledge has a powerful impact on the way learners process, understand, and write about what they read. For informational text it is important to have a model of the conceptual domain in order to analyze both informational passages learners are provided with and what they learn as manifest in their written work. It is also possible to analyze essays that learners produce prior to any instruction in a topic area. These can be analyzed with respect to a conceptual model of the domain to estimate the contents and organization of learners' preinstruction grasp of the domain. This information can be used in several ways, two of which are extremely important from the standpoint of literacy and instruction: as baseline assessments of domain understanding that can be compared to understanding at a later time; to select materials that are optimally suited to learners' incoming knowledge level. (See Wolfe et al., 1998, for an alternative method for matching texts to readers.)

Written productions can also be quite informative with respect to children's cognitive and social development. Both content knowledge and knowledge of linguistic conventions, especially genre, are evident in children's writing. For example, in a study by Chapman (1994, 1995), first graders' productions during "writer's workshop" were analyzed in terms of what genres they represented. Chapman noted that over the course of the year children's writing became increasingly differentiated in terms of genre. Dyson (1997, 2003) examines the ways in which children construct their roles and relationships in text. In work with children in urban neighborhoods she documented both challenges to, and adoption of, gendered and cultural stereotypes (Dyson, 2003). From an instructional perspective, reader response logs are frequently advocated as a means by which children can develop engagement and enjoyment in text as well as comprehension and reflective processes (Barr, Blachowicz, Katz, Kaufman, & Wogman-Sadow, 2001).

Subjective but Scientifically Sound

Discourse analysis of written text is a necessarily subjective activity. Subjectivity does not, however, mean idiosyncratic or arbitrary. Scientifically sound discourse analysis follows principles and processes that ensure the rigor and reliability of the endeavor. For example, discourse analysis needs to follow the standard procedures for developing coding schemes that can be used reliably by multiple coders (e.g., Strauss, 1987; Strauss & Corbin, 1998). These processes bring a greater degree of objectivity to the analysis. As mentioned previously, logs of decisions or difficult cases can help a rater maintain consistency across samples. In addition, it is standard practice to include some measure of interrater reliability. Reliability measures may be reported as simple correlations between raters, or when there is a finite set of possible observations, and one can compute both hits and misses in the coding of observations, Cohen's Kappa may be used (Cohen, 1960). The purpose of having a second person code the data is to ensure that codes are applied in a principled manner. If two people can concur in their use of a coding scheme, it seems more likely that the coding scheme represents an objective set of criteria for differentiating among examples, and that differences in coding are meaningful and not just *arbitrary or subjective* judgments. With such evidence of reliability, discourse analysis can fulfill its promise as a tool for description and distillation of important similarities and differences in written texts.

AN EXEMPLAR OF THE ANALYSIS OF WRITTEN DISCOURSE

Goldman and colleagues (Coté & Goldman, 1999; Coté et al., 1998) conducted a series of studies on learning from informational texts that we discuss as an example of how the theoretical and methodological issues introduced in the previous sections of this chapter can be applied to yield insights into student thinking and learning. The studies were designed to reveal how fourth and sixth graders think about informational texts similar to the *Metabolism* example (see Table 5.2) and what strategies they engage in as they attempt to learn from such texts. To gather information about their thinking, the students were asked to think aloud as they read the texts (for additional discussion of think-aloud or verbal protocols, see Pressley & Hilden, Chapter 14, this volume). Specifically, they were asked to verbalize what they were thinking as they tried to understand the written passage, and what they were doing to understand the passage, what they found easy or hard and to describe any comprehension problems they had and what they were doing about them. Thus, oral discourse samples provided information about students' thinking about written discourse. Following the think-aloud, students were asked to create a report on what they had learned. They dictated the report to a researcher who typed it into a computer as the students watched. They were free to edit the text on the screen as they wished until they said they were satisfied with it.

Theoretical Framework

The approach in these studies assumes that (1) readers attempt to construct multiple levels of representation from written text, especially textbase and situation-model levels; (2) different kinds of processing support the construction of different levels of representation; (3) processing focused on the information in the written text supports textbase model construction; (4) processing focused on connecting prior knowledge with information in the written text supports situation-model construction; (5) processing that focuses on creating connections among propositions in the text and between propositions in the text and prior knowledge propositions leads to more coherent representations; and (6) more coherent representations support better performance on retention and learning tasks. The main goal of these studies was to examine these assumptions through detailed analyses of students' thinking during comprehension and the relation of that thinking to the resulting representation. We were also interested in the impact of difficulty of the written text (easier and harder within each grade) on the kinds of processing in which readers engaged. These goals informed the selection and adaptation of passages for use in the study.

Passage Content and Structure

We chose topics and content that we thought would be unfamiliar to students and used a three-pronged validation process (readability, curriculum experts' ratings, and ease of comprehension ratings collected from other fourth- and sixth-grade students) to establish that the passages met our familiarity and difficulty level requirements (for details see Coté et al., 1998). Passages conformed to a content structure like that of the *Metabolism* passage. We included explicit signals in the text to help readers understand the relations among the ideas. Those used in the *Metabolism* text are underlined in Table 5.2.

Analytic Process

A coding system was developed to describe the types of processing that students engaged in as they constructed a representation of the text. Think-aloud statements were assigned to one of five categories: self-explanations, comprehension monitoring for problems, predictions, paraphrases, and irrelevant associations. In a second analysis, the degree to which children made connections among the elements in the text or among text and statements in the think-alouds was examined. Such connections reflect reinstatements and rereadings of previously processed information.

We looked at the prevalence of each category as well as profiles of readers based on the combination of categories in their think-alouds. The reports that students generated were used as indicators of their representations. These were coded with respect to the inclusion of information from the presented passages as well as the coherence of the reports as texts themselves. Coté et al. (1998) provide information on the reliability process we used in each of these analyses.

Findings

Goldman and colleagues were able to show through parametric and nonparametric statistical tests in conjunction with case profiles of individual students that there were predictable relationships between the kinds of thinking students did during processing and the representations that resulted as reflected in the contents and coherence of their reports. We mention several noteworthy findings here. First, there was evidence that the majority of students on both easier and harder texts were integrating prior knowledge with the information in the text. However, these were local integrations in that they tended to focus on a single sentence and did not serve to connect across other parts of the text. Second, students used a range of strategies (e.g., use prior knowledge, ignore, reread, read ahead, and reread prior sentence) in efforts to resolve comprehension problems and tended to be more successful at doing so on the easier passages. Third, when students read passages silently with no think-aloud (Experiment 2, Coté et al., 1998), better recall performance was predicted by the number of times a sentence was accessed and by longer processing times. Coté et al. (1998) interpreted these measures obtained during silent reading as consistent with more elaborative processing and cross-sentence connections. Fourth, Coté and Goldman (1999) found that number of reinstatements and number of self-explanations were positively correlated. This pattern tended to be associated with more coherent reports of the information. Finally, the case analyses provided concrete manifestations of processing patterns associated with good and poor textbase construction and different levels of prior knowledge integration. Thus, the analyses of students' discourse as they processed written discourse yielded both quantitative and qualitative data that resulted in the identification of several patterns of processing and coherence in what was learned.

This line of research illustrates the rich information that can be gleaned by analyses of written text—in this case the texts children read as well as the texts they produced themselves following the reading. It also meets standards of quality associated with discourse analysis of written text in three ways. First, the theory underlying the analyses has been carefully articulated and grounded in relevant models of text comprehension. Second, multiple methods and coding schemes were developed to characterize the texts that were read and to capture the phenomena that were observed. Third, the coding schemes were used systematically and resulted in high levels of interrater reliablity (between .80 and .92) on various measures. As a result, this research serves as an excellent example of scientifically sound discourse analysis and its utility for understanding text processing, learning, and their relationships.

CONCLUDING COMMENTS

The approach to analysis that we have illustrated here provides a more complex picture of written discourse and students' understanding of it than is provided by a typical "right answer" approach to scoring students' responses. Although more complex, the approach conveys information about specific concepts and ideas that students understand and how deeply they understand them. It also conveys information about how students' thinking differs from the information conveyed in the text, their misconceptions, and gaps in their understanding. As such, discourse-analytic approaches provide information that could guide instructional decision making in the classroom in ways that points on a multiple-choice or short-answer test cannot. In the future, we hope that the discourse-analytic approach will be more tractable for teachers to use in classroom instruction and assessment. There are some research efforts under way that are attempting to address this challenge through the use of various computational technologies (e.g., Foltz, Lahm, & Landauer, 1999; Golden et al., 2003; Goldman et al., 2003; Kintsch, Steinhart, Stahl, & LSA Research Group, 2000; Wolfe et al., 1998).

In closing, we wish to stress that researchers undertaking discourse analysis of written texts need to understand that it is an iterative process. It is driven by both theoretical and conceptual orientations and by the contents of the written discourse. In other words, even when researchers collect data with a priori ideas about the features or relationships that might be important, these ideas change as researchers engage in careful, scientific analysis of the written text that people produce. Discourse analysis is a process that successively approximates ways to adequately capture systematicity and variance across written texts and draw inferences about knowledge and learning.

ACKNOWLEDGMENTS

The development and research on the ecosystem materials was supported by a grant from the National Science Foundation (#RECOI13669) to the first author, although no official endorsement by NSF should be inferred.

REFERENCES

Anderson, J. R. (1976). *Language, memory, and thought.* Hillsdale, NJ: Erlbaum.

Anderson, J., & Bower, G. (1973). *Human associative memory.* Washington, DC: Winston.

Bamberg, M. A. (1997). A constructivist approach to narrative development. In M. Bamberg (Ed.), *Narrative development: Six approaches* (pp. 89–132). Mahwah, NJ: Erlbaum.

Barr, R., Blachowicz, C. L. Z., Katz, C., Kaufman, B., & Wogman-Sadow, M. (2001). *Reading diagnosis for teachers: An instructional approach* (4th ed.). New York: Pearson Allyn & Bacon.

Bloome, D. M. (2003). Narrative discourse. In A. C. Graesser, M. A. Gernsbacher, & S. R. Goldman (Eds.), *Handbook of discourse processes* (pp. 287–320). Mahwah, NJ: Erlbaum.

Carrell, P. L. (1992). Awareness of text structure: Effects on recall. *Language Learning, 42,* 1–20.

Carroll, J. B. (1972). Defining language comprehension: Some speculations. In J. B. Carroll & R. O. Freedle (Eds.), *Language comprehension and the acquisition of knowledge* (pp. 1–30). Washington, DC: Winston.

Chapman, M. L. (1994). The emergence of genres: Some findings from an examination of first-grade writing. *Written Communication, 11*(3), 348–380.

Chapman, M. L. (1995). The sociocognitive construction of written genres in first grade. *Research in the Teaching of English, 29*(2), 164–192.

Chi, M. T. H., De Leeuw, N., Chiu, M., & Lavancher, C. (1994). Eliciting self-explanations improves understanding. *Cognitive Science, 18,* 439–477.

Cohen, J. A, (1960). A coefficient of agreement for nominal scales. *Educational Psychology Measurement, 20,* 37–46.

Coté, N., & Goldman, S. R. (1999). Building representations of informational text: Evidence from children's think-aloud protocols. In H. Van Oostendorp & S. R. Goldman (Eds.), *The construction of mental representations during reading* (pp. 169–193). Mahwah, NJ: Erlbaum.

Coté, N., Goldman, S. R., & Saul, E. U. (1998). Students making sense of informational text: Relations between processing and representation. *Discourse Processes, 25,* 1–53.

Crowhurst, M. (1990). The development of persuasive/argumentative writing. In R. Beauch & S. Hynds (Eds.), *Developing discourse practices in adolescence and adulthood* (pp. 200–223). Norwood, NJ: Ablex.

Duke, N. (2000). 3.6 minutes per day: The scarcity of informational texts in first grade. *Reading Research Quarterly, 35,* 202–224.

Dyson, A, H. (1997). *Writing superheroes.* New York: Teachers College Press.

Dyson, A, H. (2003). *The brothers and sisters learn to write: Popular literacies in childhood and school cultures.* New York: Teachers College Press.

Englehard, G., Gordon, B., & Gabrielson, S. (1992). The influence of mode of discourse, experiential demand, and gender on the quality of student writing. *Research in the Teaching of English, 26,* 315–336.

Englert, C. S., & Hiebert, E. H. (1984). Children's developing awareness of text structure in expository materials. *Journal of Educational Psychology, 76,* 65–74.

Fillmore, C. J. (1968). The case for case. In E. Bach & R. T. Harms (Ed.), *Universals of linguistic theory.* New York: Holt, Rinehart & Winston.

Foltz, P. W., Laham, D., & Landauer, T. K. (1999). The intelligent essay assessor: Applications to educational technology. *Interactive Multimedia Electronic Journal of Computer-Enhanced Learning, 1*(2). Retrieved January 10, 2003, from http://imej.wfu.edu/articles/1999/2/04/index.asp

Frederiksen, C. H. (1975). Representing logical and semantic structure of knowledge acquired from discourse. *Cognitive Psychology, 7,* 371–458.

Garner, R., Alexander, P., Slater, W., Hare, V. C., Smith, T., & Reis, R. (1986). Children's knowledge of structural properties of expository text. *Journal of Educational Psychology, 78,* 411–416.

Golden, R. M., Goldman, S. R., Thomas, C., Oney, B., Macleod, S., & Lauterbach, M. (2003, June). *Modeling text understanding: Applications for diagnostic assessment of reading.* Invited talk, International Conference on Higher Level Language Processes in the Brain: Inference and Comprehension Processes, Hanse Institute for Advanced Study, Delmenhorst, Germany.

Goldman, S. R. (1997). Learning from text: Reflections on the past and suggestions for the future. *Discourse Processes, 23,* 357–398.

Goldman, S. R., & Durán, R. P. (1988). Answering questions from oceanography texts: Learner, task and text characteristics. *Discourse Processes, 11,* 373–412.

Goldman, S. R., Golden, R. M., Thomas, C., Oney, B., Macleod, S., & Lauterbach, M. (2003, June 26–28). *Applications of text processing models to diagnostic assessment of reading.* Paper presented at the 13th annual meeting of the Society for Text and Discourse, Madrid, Spain.

Goldman, S. R., & Rakestraw, J. (2000). Structural aspects of constructing meaning from text. In M. L. Kamil, P. B. Mosenthal, P. D. Pearson, & R Barr (Eds.), *Handbook of reading research* (Vol. III, pp. 311–335). Mahwah, NJ: Erlbaum.

Goldman, S. R., & Saul, E. U. (1990). Flexibility in text processing: A strategy competition model. *Learning and Individual Differences, 2,* 181–219.

Goldman, S. R., Varma, K. O., Sharp, D., & Cognition and Technology Group at Vanderbilt. (1999). Children's understanding of complex stories: Issues of representation and assessment. In S. R. Goldman, A. C. Graesser, & P. van den Broek (Eds.), *Narrative comprehension, causality, and coherence: Essays in honor of Tom Trabasso* (pp. 135–160). Mahwah, NJ: Erlbaum.

Goldman, S. R., Varma, S., & Cote, N. (1996). Extending capacity-constrained construction integration: Toward "smarter" and flexible models of text comprehension. In B. K. Britton, & A. C. Graesser (Eds.), *Models of understanding text* (pp. 73–114). Mahwah, NJ: Erlbaum.

Goldman, S. R., & Varnhagen, C. K. (1986). Memory for embedded and sequential story structures. *Journal of Memory and Language, 25,* 401–418.

Gomulicki, B. R. (1956). Recall as an abstractive process. *Acta Psychologica, 12,* 77–94.

Grabe, W. (2002). Narratives and expository macro-genres. In A. M. Johns (Ed.), *Genre in the classroom: Multiple perspectives* (pp. 249–267). Mahwah, NJ: Erlbaum.

Graesser, A. C. (1981). *Prose comprehension beyond the word.* New York: Springer Verlag.

Guthrie, J. T. (1988). Locating information in documents: Examination of a cognitive model. *Reading Research Quarterly, 23,* 178–199.

Halliday, M. A. K., & Hasan, R. (1976). *Cohesion in English*. London: Longman.

Hiebert, E. H., Englert, C. S., & Brennan, S. (1983). Awareness of text structure in recognition and production of expository discourse. *Journal of Reading Behavior, 15,* 63–79.

Johnson-Laird, P. N. (1983). *Mental models*. Cambridge, MA: Harvard University Press.

Kieras, D. E. (1981). Component processes in the comprehension of simple prose. *Journal of Verbal Learning and Verbal Behavior, 20,* 1–20.

Kintsch, E. (1990). Macroprocesses and microprocesses in the development of summarization skill. *Cognition and Instruction, 7,* 161–195.

Kintsch, E., Steinhart, D., Stahl, G., & LSA Research Group. (2000). Developing summarization skills through the use of LSA-based feedback. *Interactive Learning Environments, 8,* 87–109.

Kintsch, W. (1974). *The representation of meaning in memory*. Hillsdale, NJ: Erlbaum.

Kintsch, W. (1994). Text comprehension, memory, and learning. *American Psychologist*, pp. 294–303.

Kintsch, W. (1998). *Comprehension: A paradigm for cognition*. New York: Cambridge University Press.

Kintsch, W., Britton, B. K., Fletcher, C. R., Kintsch, E., Mannes, S. M., & Nathan, M. J. (1993). A comprehension-based approach to learning and understanding. In D. L. Medin (Ed.), *The psychology of learning and motivation: Advances in research and theory* (Vol. 30, pp. 165–214). New York: Academic Press.

Kintsch, W., & Keenan, J. (1973). Reading rate and retention as a function of the number of propositions in the base structure of sentences. *Cognitive Psychology, 5,* 257–274.

Kintsch, W., & van Dijk, T. A. (1978). Towards a model of text comprehension and production. *Psychological Review, 85,* 363–394.

Klare, G. R. (1974–1975). Assessing readability. *Reading Research Quarterly, 1,* 63–102.

Langer, J. A. (1986). *Children reading and writing: Structures and strategies*. Norwood, NJ: Ablex.

Lorch, R. F., Jr. (1989). Text signaling devices and their effects on reading and memory processes. *Educational Psychology Review, 1,* 209–234.

Lorch, R. F., Jr., & Chen, A. H. (1986). Effects of number signals on reading and recall. *Journal of Educational Psychology, 78,* 263–270.

Lorch, R. F., Jr., & Lorch, E. P. (1996). Effects of organizational signals on free recall of expository texts. *Journal of Educational Psychology, 88,* 38–48.

Mandler, J. M., & Johnson, N. S. (1977). Remembrance of things parsed: Story structure and recall. *Cognitive Psychology, 9,* 111–151.

McCabe, A. (1997). Developmental and cross-cultural aspects of children's narration. In M. Bamberg (Ed.), *Narrative development: Six approaches* (pp. 137–174). Mahwah, NJ: Erlbaum.

McGee, L. M. (1982). Awareness of text structure: effects on recall of expository text. *Reading Research Quarterly 17,* 581–590.

McNamara, D. S., Kintsch, E., Butler-Songer, N., & Kintsch, W. (1996). Are good texts always better? Interactions of text coherence, background knowledge, and levels of understanding in learning from text. *Cognition and Instruction, 14,* 1–43.

McNamara, D. S., & Kintsch, W. (1996). Learning from texts: Effects of prior knowledge and text coherence. *Discourse Processes, 22,* 247–288.

Meyer, B. (1975). *The organization of prose and its effects on memory.* Amsterdam: North-Holland.

Meyer, B. (1985). Prose analysis: Purposes, procedures, and problems. In B. K. Britton & J. Black (Eds.), *Analyzing and understanding expository text,* (pp. 11–64, 269–304). Hillsdale, NJ: Erlbaum.

Meyer, B. J. F., Brandt, D. M., & Bluth, G. J. (1980). Use of top level structure in text: Key for reading comprehension of ninth grade students. *Reading Research Quarterly 16,* 72–103

Mills, C. B., Diehl, V. A., Birkmire, D. P., & Mou, L. (1995). Reading procedural texts: Effects of purpose for reading and predictions of reading comprehension models. *Discourse Processes, 20,* 79–107.

Oney, B., Goldman, S. R., Lauterbach, M., Braasch, J., Kusumgar, R., Brodowinska, K., & Golden, R. (2003, April). *Assessing complex comprehension through computer based and paper and pencil testing.* Paper presented at the annual meeting of the American Educational Research Association, Chicago.

Pappas, C. C. (1993). Is narrative primary? Some insights from kindergarteners' pretend readings of stories and information books. *Journal of Reading Behavior, 25,* 97–129.

Pearson, P. D. (1974–1975). The effects of grammatical complexity on children's comprehension, recall and conception of semantic relations. *Reading Research Quarterly, 10,* 155–192.

Perfetti, C. A. (1989). There are generalized abilities and one of them is reading. In L. B. Resnick (Ed.), *Knowing, learning, and instruction: Essays in honor of Robert Glaser* (pp. 307–333). Hillsdale, NJ: Erlbaum.

Ratcliff, R., & McKoon, G. (1978). Priming in item recognition: Evidence for the propositional structure of sentences. *Journal of Verbal Learning and Verbal Behavior, 17,* 403–417.

Sanders, T. J., Spooren, W. P. M., & Noordman, L. G. M. (1992). Toward a taxonomy of coherence relations. *Discourse Processes, 15,* 1–35.

Schank, R., & Abelson, R. (1977). *Scripts, plans, goals and understanding.* Hillsdale, NJ: Erlbaum.

Schank, R. C. (1972). Conceptual dependency: A theory of natural language understanding. *Cognitive Psychology, 3*(4), 552–631.

Scott, C., & Windsor, J. (2000). General language performance measures in spoken and written narrative and expository discourse of school-age children with language learning disabilities. *Journal of Speech, Language, and Hearing Research, 43,* 324–339.

Stein, N. L., & Albro, E. R. (1997). Building complexity and coherence: Children's use of goal-structured knowledge in telling stories. In M.

Bamberg (Ed.), *Narrative development: Six approaches* (pp. 5–44). Mahway, NJ: Erlbaum.

Stein, N., & Glenn, C. (1979). An analysis of story comprehension in elementary school children. In R. Freedle (Ed.), *New directions in discourse processing* (Vol. 2, pp. 53–120). Norwood, NJ: Ablex.

Stenner, A. J., & Wright, B. D. (2002). *Readability, reading ability, and comprehension.* Retrieved July, 24, 2003, from http://www.lexile.com/about_lex/tech-papers/documents/ReadabilityPaper.pdf

Strauss, A. (1987). *Qualitative analysis for social scientists.* Cambridge, UK: Cambridge University Press.

Strauss, A., & Corbin, J. (1998). *Basics of qualitative research techniques and procedures for developing grounded theory* (2nd ed.). London: Sage.

Taylor, B. M., & Beach, R. W. (1984). The effects of text structure instruction on middle grade student comprehension and production of expository text. *Reading Research Quarterly, 19,* 134–146.

Taylor, B. M., & Samuels, S. J. (1983). Children's use of text structure in the recall of expository material. *American Educational Research Journal, 40,* 517–528.

Tolchinsky, L., Johansson, V., & Zamora, A. (2002). Text openings and closings: Textual autonomy and differentiation. *Written Language and Literacy, 5,* 219–254.

Trabasso, T., & van den Broek, P. (1985). Causal thinking and the representation of narrative events. *Journal of Memory and Language, 24,* 612–630.

van Dijk, T. A. (1972). *Some aspects of text grammars.* The Hague, Netherlands: Mouton.

van Dijk, T. A., & Kintsch, W. (1983). *Strategies of discourse comprehension.* New York: Academic Press.

van Oostendorp, H., & Goldman, S. R. (Eds.). (1999). *The construction of mental representations during reading.* Mahwah, NJ: Erlbaum.

Voss, J. F., & Silfies, L. N. (1996). Learning from history text: The interaction of knowledge and comprehension skill with text structure. *Cognition and Instruction, 14,* 45–68.

Weaver, C. A., III, & Kintsch, W. (1991). Expository text. In R. Barr, M. L. Kamil, P. Mosenthal, & P. D. Pearson (Eds.), *Handbook of reading research* (Vol. 2, pp. 230–243). New York: Longman.

Wolfe, M. B., Schreiner, M. E., Rehder, B., Laham, D., Foltz, P. W., Kintsch, W., & Landauer, T. K. (1998). Learning from text: Matching readers and texts by Latent Semantic Analysis. *Discourse Processes, 25,* 309–336.

CHAPTER 6

Ethnographic Research

Victoria Purcell-Gates

Literacy researchers who operate out of a theoretical frame that views literacy as cultural practice are particularly drawn to *ethnography* as a methodological tool. This is because ethnography is grounded in theories of culture and allows researchers to view literacy development, instruction, learning, and practice as it occurs naturally in sociocultural contexts.

Ethnography contributes to the quilt of research methodologies in that it allows literacy researchers to explore and come to understand phenomena about which little is known. As such, it provides those researchers who are so inclined a method for exploration and making sense of their data that is scientific and trustworthy. If done appropriately, the results, or outcomes, of ethnographies provide critical understandings of language and literacy *in situ*. They offer hitherto unknown maps and perspectives on literacy learning and development, without which teachers and researchers would be operating more or less blindly, in the dark, as they plan for and implement instructional strategies that "should" work according to other research paradigms.

Ethnographies provide the landscapes and the details of worlds. They aim to discover, understand, and describe human behavior holistically, as it occurs naturally within social and cultural contexts. In so doing, ethnographers can look for patterns and themes that ethnographic consumers can take away and use to enhance their own understandings of similar actors and contexts.

While much of the data collected by ethnographers, though not all, is *qualitative*, ethnography is distinguishable within the category of qualitative research in that ethnography is rooted in the concept of culture. This is not true of all qualitative research. As LeCompte and Schensul (1999a) emphasize, "Ethnography generates or builds theories of cultures—or explanations of how people think, believe, and behave—that are situated in local time and space" (p. 8).

LeCompte and Schensul (1999a, p. 9) list seven characteristics of ethnography that are useful when conceptualizing this methodology and differentiating it from others:

- It is carried out in a natural setting, not in a laboratory.
- It involves intimate, face-to-face interaction with participants.
- It presents an accurate reflection of participants' perspectives and behaviors.
- It uses inductive, interactive, and recursive data collection and analytic strategies to build local cultural theories.
- It uses multiple data sources, including both quantitative and qualitative data.
- It frames all human behavior and belief within a sociopolitical and historical context.
- It uses the concept of culture as a lens through which to interpret results.

Our understandings of literacy and literacy learning have been enhanced and advanced by an array of ethnographies over the years. In the following sections I draw on several of these to illustrate methodological points. I used several criteria for the ethnographies I have chosen for illustrative purposes: (1) the study has won awards; (2) the author is particularly well-known for methodological rigor; (3) the ethnographic findings are recognized as of high significance to the field of literacy; or (4) I am particularly familiar with the work because it is my own and I can "think aloud" about research decision making in ways I could not do with the work of others [rueful smile].

QUESTIONS PARTICULARLY SUITED TO ETHNOGRAPHIC INQUIRY

As is true for other research methodologies, ethnography follows from particular types of research questions or, more appropriately for ethnography, research foci. Because ethnography seeks to *explain, describe*, and *provide insight* into human behavior in context, it is appropriate for questions that ask *why, how, what is happening,* and *what does it look like?* It is *not* appropriate for inquiries that seek to isolate factors for causal implication (experimental/quasi-experimental). Nor is it appropriate for studies that seek to describe, count, or index items, groups, or events that are identified as of interest prior to the research (descriptive), although descriptive data may be incorporated within an ethnography.

Ethnography is not for researchers who already know what they are seeking or for those who have strong hypotheses to test. Rather, it is for those researchers who are truly wondering, seeking, curious about some aspect of literacy as it occurs naturally in sociocultural contexts. These contexts can be schools, classrooms, homes, communities, workplaces—any naturally occurring context for literacy use. Theoretically, even the context of a scientific laboratory is considered a sociocultural context and ethnographic inquiry would be appropriate given the research focus of coming to understand and describe literacy use as it occurs and is practiced within the culture of a scientific lab.

In her award-winning ethnography (The Ed Fry Award, presented at the 2002 annual meeting of the National Reading Conference in Miami, Florida), *Literacy Practices as Social Acts: Power, Status, and Cultural Norms in the Classroom* (2001), Cynthia Lewis, states as her research focus or goal: "*To understand* (emphasis mine) the ways that the literacy culture of a classroom is created within the interwoven social contexts of classroom and community" (p. xi). She elaborates by describing her focus on response to literature as it occurs in peer groups and by including issues of power and status in her lens.

Anne Haas Dyson, in her latest book, *The Brothers and Sisters Learn to Write: Popular Literacies in Childhood and School Cultures* (2003), proposes similar research actions in her description of her "broad research aims . . . *to document* the cultural landscape . . . *to analyze how* . . . ; *to trace changes* (all emphases mine) in how . . . ; to examine the consequences of . . ." (p. 25).

Shirley Brice Heath in her landmark ethnography that has been so influential in the literacy field, *Ways With Words: Language, Life, and Work in Communities and Classrooms* (1983), describes her research focus as follows: to explore answers to the questions, "*why* students and teachers often could not understand each other, *why* questions were sometimes not answered, and *why* habitual ways of talking and listening did not always seem to work" (p. 2) in communication attempts among three different cultural groups in the Piedmont region of the Carolinas. Related to these goals was the research focus on the need to fully *describe*:

the primary face-to-face interactions of children from community cultures other than (the) mainstream one. The ways of living, eating, sleeping, worshiping, using space, and filling time which surrounded these language learners would have to be accounted for as part of the milieu in which the processes of language learning took place. (p. 3)

In summary, ethnographic design calls for research questions, or research foci, that seek to situate the researcher into a cultural landscape for the purpose of exploration and discovery of answers to questions like *why, what is happening, what does it look like, how does it work,* and so on.

It is important to note that ethnographic questions do not emerge spontaneously or serendipitously. Rather, as for other types of research, they need to surface within a theoretical framework and to relate to issues recognized by others as significant and interesting. Schensul, Schensul, and LeCompte (1999) also stress that it is important to build the research focus and theoretical models in conjunction with the local population with which the research is going to be conducted. This involves learning as much as possible about this population at this early stage through study and interactions with members of the group.

Due to space constraints, it is impossible to represent the broad range of different types of ethnography that are available to literacy researchers in this chapter. The reader is strongly encouraged to consult other sources which address this research methodology more fully and with more detail. Sources that have been especially helpful for me include (1) Schensul and LeCompte (1999), (2) Goetz and LeCompte (1984), and (3) Miles and Huberman (1994).

ETHNOGRAPHIC LENSES REPRESENTED IN LITERACY RESEARCH

Not all literacy ethnographies result from research conducted within the same epistemological paradigm. Many of them incorporate a phenomenological or interpretive stance. Others, though, represent more of an ecological perspective. Two relatively new paradigms, but growing ones, in the literacy field are those of (1) critical research and (2) network research. Although each of these approaches exists more or less independently of the others, readers may encounter literacy ethnographies that include a synthesis of two or more. This is a reflection of the important-to-understand fact that ethnography, as a method, can be approached and conducted in many different ways, making it difficult to describe technically. Following, I provide brief descriptions of each of the approaches. I am indebted to LeCompte and Schensul (1999a) for these categorical distinctions.

Phenomenological Approach

The researcher taking primarily an interpretive or phenomenological approach is concerned with coming to understand the world from the participants' perspectives. This lens assumes that knowledge, beliefs, and values are socially constructed through social interaction and thus are constantly changing and evolving. To understand participants' perspectives, the researcher must live in the world of the participants as a participant, interacting with group members, observing, and interviewing. My study of the urban Appalachian family (awarded the Grawemeyer Award in Education, 1996) in which no one read or wrote (Purcell-Gates, 1995) reflects this perspective. My goal was to understand how a young child from this family takes and does not take from traditional literacy instruction in school and how this helps to explain his successes and his struggles in learning to read and write. In the process of this study, I worked as his tutor, as well as an occasional tutor for his mother. This was my way of entering and participating in the family and ultimately the community as I complemented the tutoring with participation in daily routines, meals, and informal conversational interviews.

Ecological Approach

The researcher from the ecological perspective studies the ways that individuals and groups are defined by social structures at different levels of influence (LeCompte & Schensul, 1999a). These are structures such as family, peers, school, work, community, and society. While the interpretive researcher strives to participate in the community of interest, the ecologically framed researcher remains more detached and objective. His or her goal is to observe behavior and elicit participant perspectives so that the analysis of systemic structures and meanings can proceed. Barton and Hamilton's (1998) ethnography of reading and writing in a neighborhood of Lancaster, England, reflects an ecological frame in that it documents the many different ways that people in that community use literacy and how those literacy practices are shaped and interact with such social factors as role, domain, institutions, power relationships, and historical contexts.

Critical Approach

Researchers who take a critical stance view the world through a lens that forefronts inequality, oppression, and marginalization that result from unequal power relationships. This research is focused on uncovering and describing these inequalities and oppressive sociopolitical structures with the goal of bringing about change. Within this, researcher and researched inform each other and work together for empowerment and ultimate resolution of the unequal power relationships. The researcher is very much involved in the lives of the participants and works with them to understand power and oppression. As such, this research approach can be described as activist as well as educative. Ellen Cushman's (1998) ethnography of the ways in which inner-city women used literate strategies to empower themselves within oppressive systems is an example of this type of research.

Network Approach

Literacy can also be studied as it is influenced and occurs within social networks within specific cultural domains. This is a relatively new research approach to literacy researchers. Sociologists, however, have employed this lens for a number of years and analytic frames for social network data have been developed and employed for a wide variety of research questions. Wasserman and Faust, authors of *Social Network Analysis: Methods and Applications* (1994), state that "the network perspective allows new leverage for answering standard social and behavioral science research questions by giving precise formal definition to aspects of the political, economic, or social structural environment" (p. 3). Deborah Brandt's *Literacy in American Lives* (2001) probably comes closest to a social network approach in the existing corpus of ethnographies of literacy. This historical study documents how families pass on literacy to their children within times of social and technological change as well as the social impact on literacy skills of adults.

ESSENTIAL ELEMENTS OF ETHNOGRAPHIES

Clearly, there are many different lens researchers can use to approach ethnographic research. Also, there is no one way to conduct an ethnography within any one of these lens. However, there are generally agreed-upon elements to ethnographic research that researchers must consider to ensure rigor, validity, and reliability for their data, data analysis, and final conclusions and interpretations. I list these later. First, however, I provide a brief discussion of the constructs of validity and reliability as they apply to ethnographic research because they do not hold the same meanings, nor are they arrived at in the same ways, as for experimental research.

Validity

Validity in ethnographic research refers to the degree to which one's data and interpretation correspond to the "way it is" within the phenomenon being investigated. Granted this is a very fuzzy concept, but ethnographers have procedures for approaching it to guarantee rigor. One procedure that is absolutely required to ensure validity is that of *triangulation*. Triangulation is the gathering of data from different sources to confirm the validity of data. For example, if one is documenting through observation that a participant in a book-club discussion group feels disempowered by the group, one would want to cross-check that with, perhaps, interviews with the participant, and examples of her journal writing that would relate to this observation. In my book *Other People's Words* (Purcell-Gates, 1995), I concluded that Jenny, the nonliterate urban Appalachian mother whose son I was tutoring, could not penetrate the world of print partly because the structure and vocabulary of written language was so unfamiliar, and thus nonfunctional, for her. This conclusion was based on several sources of data: (1) my documentation that, while she was young, no one in her family read or wrote in ways that were visible to her; (2) many statements from her to the effect that the way she talked was not the way the books "talked"; and (3) discourse analysis of a taped session with her in which I helped her to read and answer a printed parent survey from the school; and (4) her report of difficulty with vocabulary in church material and my own observations as she tried to read this and other texts.

Reliability

The construct of reliability in ethnographic research is closely related to that of validity. If instruments are being used in the study, they, of course, should have demonstrated reliability, both internal and test–retest. However, observational data also need to be considered reliable. One of the more trusted ways to achieve this reliability is to build in the factor of time when designing a study. To ensure that behaviors coalesce to constitute patterns, the research needs to continue over a long enough period. This allows one to watch for recurrence, to observe similar behaviors in different contexts, and to enable the revelation of behaviors, thoughts, and feelings that may have been repressed due to the presence of the researcher. One of the things to guard against is the phenomenon of seeing only what the researcher expects to see and, perhaps, wants to see. Building in enough time in the cultural context of interest will allow the researcher to stop seeing the world through his or her eyes and begin to see it also through those of the participants.

Procedures for ensuring validity and reliability are built into all aspects of the ethnographic research process as becomes clear as I discuss field entry, data collection, data analysis, and informant checks below.

Field Entry

Entering the field involves the researcher forming the types of relationships that allow for the learning that needs to take place during the course of the study. It involves learning the language, the social customs, and the patterns of behavior that exist in a setting that is new in many respects to the researcher. Field entry depends on building rapport with the participants and this is dependent on trust and reciprocity. Most ethnographers find some way to "give back" to the communities they study. This may be in the form of contributing expertise to community problems, materials for community use, or simply time to help out with chores or errands, as needed. These types of activity also contribute to the process of becoming a participant in the community of study as well as to help develop reciprocity. Occasionally some ethnographers may pay informants for their time.

Field entry always involves some type of initial approach, or cover story. For the researcher, this is often an uncomfortable aspect of the ethnographic research process. Schensul et al. (1999) make the point, however, that few people in the research setting pay attention to the initial explanation of the project or study. Rather, "Rapport ultimately rests on the connections through which ethnographers have been introduced to the community setting, how comfortable researchers are with the people in the field, how well they maintain confidentiality, and how fast they learn local customs and norms" (p. 75).

While much literacy ethnography takes place in classrooms, it is important for researchers to realize that although they may have been students and teachers themselves, it does not obviate the need to view each new classroom as a new and unfamiliar community.

Care must be taken to develop trusting relationships and rapport with classroom members. Time must be devoted to coming to see the world of the classroom through *these* participants' eyes, guarding against assuming realities that come from the researcher's past experiences. Anne Haas Dyson, who has conducted many in-depth ethnographies of children learning in classrooms (1989, 1993, 1997, 2003), reports that she always devotes many days and weeks to just sitting in a new classroom and observing before she knows what she is seeing well enough to begin to call them data.

SAMPLING

There are as many different ways to approach selecting who to research as there are types of ethnographies. Schensul et al. (1999) list and describe up to 14 different approaches to sampling for ethnographic research, ranging from extreme case selection to random selection. (Note that the topic of ethnographic research is much broader and inclusive than I am able to attend to in this chapter. Many good sources are available for the student of ethnography, and those who wish to explore the topic beyond this introductory treatment of ethnographic literacy research are urged to consult them.)

The type of study and the goals of the study determine the selection procedure. The type of sample, further, determines the degree to which the findings can be generalized.

Ethnographies of literacy have for the most part involved sampling that could be described as "convenience samples that fit the research focus or question." For example, the classroom in which Lewis conducted her study of the social dynamics of peer response was selected because (1) the teacher was known for valuing and teaching for peer response to literature; and (2) the teacher and the school was available to Lewis both in proximity and willingness to participate in research. However, within the classroom, Lewis reports that she chose five focal children who were representative of the population of the classroom and who would provide contrasting characteristics. Thus, Lewis was attending to *representation* to expand the generalizability of her findings and to *contrast* to achieve the variation needed for increased validity. This could be labeled both *representative sampling* and *contrastive sampling*.

Dyson, on the other hand, samples primarily to find instances in which she can examine her construct of interest: how young children construct their understandings of symbolic communication, including learning to write. She therefore purposively seeks teachers whose instruction is "open" enough to allow children's own constructions of their understandings to surface in an accepting environment. Within such classrooms, she seeks child informants who not only take advantage of such an instructional context by visibly producing their evolving constructions of writing but also who are open and relaxed enough with her to talk about their work and to answer her questions about what they are doing. This type of sampling is sometimes referred to as *purposive sampling*.

I selected Donny and his mother Jenny to study (Purcell-Gates, 1995) because I was interested in how the literacy that young children learn in their homes before school help them learn to read and write in school. Jenny conveniently presented herself to me as a nonreader and wanted her son, Donny, to be tutored in the Literacy Center I directed. Perhaps this is an instance of what can be termed *providential sampling*!

Other literacy researchers select whole communities as their sample, depending on their research focus. David Barton and Mary Hamilton (1998), for example, selected the Lancaster, England, community to study "local literacies" because it was representative of working class communities and because it was close by the university where they both worked.

Generalizing from Ethnographic Research

Ethnographic research is not designed or intended to provide statistical generalizability of results. However, the degree to which readers of such research can generalize the findings depends on the type of sampling (e.g., representative sampling affords a different level of generalizability than does convenience/purposive), context, and characteristics of the participants. Readers are usually advised to consider the degree to which these factors are similar to or different from their own situations when considering issues of generalizability. Always, however, the ethnographic researcher provides insights into issues of concern that others can take away and ponder, applying them as seems appropriate to their own situations.

ETHNOGRAPHIC DATA COLLECTION

Participant Observation

Traditionally the ethnographic researcher collects data as a participant observer in the community of study. The relationship between *participant* and *observer* is often described as a continuum, with the researcher, depending on the design of the study and on the community being studied, locating herself at varying points along this continuum. For studies that call for, and communities that allow, full participation, the researcher finds ways to immerse him- or herself in the community. Again, the researcher must take care to learn the language, language patterns, social customs and behaviors quickly in order to become as unobtrusive a presence as possible. At the same time, the researcher needs to ensure that he or she has a regular time to withdraw from participation in order to write up notes on what he or she has been observing.

For researchers studying in settings that are very different from their own, participation to the fullest extent possible is often the best way to begin to see and understand a different cultural context. My co-researcher and coauthor of the book *Now We Read, We See, We Speak* (2000), Robin Waterman, followed this immersion approach to our study of literacy development in a women's literacy class in rural El Salvador. Our purpose with the study was to explore how learners developed their reading and writing abilities within a class framed by the pedagogy of Paolo Freire (1993). Robin lived in the community (she spoke fluent Spanish) in a mud-walled hut like the other community members. She shared in community events, attending religious services and *asambleas*; she bathed and washed her clothes in the river with the other women; she took her water from the same pipe; and she carried food and other necessities on foot from the bus stop on the paved highway, 1-hour walking away from the community. Her role in the rural district was to train adult literacy teachers, and within the village, she taught the class herself while apprenticing a local teacher. Almost every afternoon or evening, she would write up her notes for the research study, sending them to me by courier about every 2 weeks.

Classroom ethnography, on the other hand, often positions the researcher closer to the observer end of the continuum. The ethnographer in classrooms is often interested in such things as teacher–student transactions, learner beliefs and interpretations, peer-group response, the ways that teachers use texts with different students, and so on. While acknowledging their own influence on these different aspects of classroom life, classroom ethnographers strive to understand phenomena as they happen naturally. This compels many of them to adopt more of an observer position and work to make themselves as unobtrusive as they can to the ordinary life of the classroom. Several common techniques are employed to achieve this goal: Being present over long periods so that participants begin to ignore them, and adopting a nonparticipatory stance in the life of the class. Let's look at the Lewis and Dyson studies as examples.

Cynthia Lewis (2001), in her study of peer-group response to lit-erature in a middle school classroom, wished to avoid influencing the instruction by assuming any authoritative role as a teacher. She was also worried that assuming a "teacher" status would make the stu-dents more guarded in sharing their beliefs with her. On the other hand, she did not want to influence the nature of the student re-sponse by participating as a member of the response groups. She did not want them to exclude her either. Thus, she chose to take a friendly observer stance, describing this by quoting Bogdan and Biklen (1992): "given the challenge of researching children, the best option may be to establish oneself, not as an authority figure, and not as a peer, but as a "quasi-friend" or "tolerated insider in chil-dren's society" (p. 88).

Anne Haas Dyson takes a similar stance with very young chil-dren. In *The Brothers and Sisters Learn to Write* (2003), Dyson de-scribes how she positioned herself in the classroom so as to be unob-trusive and yet interested in what the children were doing and in what they could tell her about themselves:

> . . . I made no effort to become one of the gang. I was "busy" with writing in my notebook, I was "interested" in "children," and I wouldn't "tell on them." So, as Rita taught a lesson, circulated among the children, or modeled working on her product, I sat, pen in hand, legal pad on lap, watching and writing without looking at the pad (a feat that never fails to impress first graders). (p. 21)

Lewis conducted her research over the course of a full school year, as did Dyson. Lewis began the year with full-day, everyday ob-servations, cutting back to three times a week for the rest of the year during the literature class. Dyson observed the children 4–6 hours a week for the year during their language arts period. She also followed them out to the playground during recess and occasionally stayed all day.

Beginning Observation

As stated, ethnographic observation needs a length of time before re-searchers can be reasonably sure that what they are observing is "nat-ural" and before they can begin to ascribe meaning to it from the par-ticipants' perspectives. This means that there is always a period at the start of observation that must be devoted to orienting. Detailed, descriptive notes can be taken at this time to document what the re-searcher is seeing during these early days. This activity is often re-ferred to as documenting: "Census, Map, and Calendar." This refers to the fact that the researcher will be noting who the participants are/ who is "there," details of the setting—such as for classrooms, the arrangement of desks, blackboards, bookshelves, and so on—and the events and event sequences. Diagrams can be drawn; the day's and class activities can be noted; the names and descriptions of students, teachers, aides, and so on can be noted.

The Census, Map, and Calendar procedures will ground the observations to follow and make it easier to take field notes by providing the researcher with a shorthand way of documenting the context for the observations. For example, once the routine of "Daily Morning Message" is established through observation, the researcher need not document the routine and players each time something is observed during this activity. He or she can simply note for context something like DMM. Of course, any alteration in the routine would need to be documented and noted.

Field Notes

The writing of field notes is the backbone of ethnographic data collection. In the field notes, researchers note what they are observing. There are many different forms for recording field notes, and most of them have some way of recording on each page: (1) Date; (2) Time; (3) Setting; (4) Observer; (5) What was observed; and (6) Researcher's comments.

Good field note procedure requires that behaviors should be noted as they happen and are observed, without the researcher's interpretation of them. For example, if the researcher is noting that William is sitting at his desk, squirming, yawning, and glancing around the room, these behaviors should be noted as such. It is inappropriate, and a threat to the validity of the data, to record these behaviors as "William is restless and bored and not paying attention." The researcher's interpretation of the behaviors should be recorded, if needed, in the section of the field note form set aside for such comments.

Many literacy researchers supplement field notes with audiotaping activity. Audiotapes provide back up for researchers who may not be able to capture in field notes complex, fast-moving events such as classroom teaching, peer-group work, or play. They are also a source of language and exact quotes to be used in the final written report of the study. Some literacy ethnographers also incorporate videotaping into their data collection procedures. Videotapes serve many of the same purposes for the ethnographer as do audiotapes. They provided the additional benefit of capturing interaction visually complete with body language and paralinguistic behaviors.

Interviews

Interviews are almost always a part of ethnographic data collection. They allow the researcher to elicit insider information from informants and to explore topics in greater detail. Interviews can be informal, off-the-cuff question–answer events or more structured and carefully planned.

Many questions for informal interviews occur to the researcher during early stages of data analysis as the researcher is reading over field notes and looking for patterns and demonstrations of local meaning. When the next available opportunity comes up for asking a participant about the meanings of a term or about the history of an event, the researcher is prepared.

More formal, semistructured interviews are often used later in the data analysis to further clarify and/or triangulate interpretations. The content of the preformulated questions can come from both the goals and focus of the study and the conclusions or interpretations of the researcher. Some general considerations to keep in mind when constructing semistructured interview protocols include the following:

- Avoid asking questions that elicit a "yes" or "no" answer. Instead, begin questions with phrases such as "Tell me about . . . ," "If I asked you what X means, what would you say?", or "Why do you think . . . ?"
- Be sure to use language that is familiar and comfortable to your informant.
- Include possible probes with questions to allow you to follow up on answers to achieve more information. Sample probes would be "Tell me more . . ." or "That's fascinating! What about. . . ."
- Ask less sensitive or threatening questions early in the interview and save the more threatening ones for the end. Remember the cultural context of your community when deciding the subjects that are more or less threatening.
- During any interviewing process, strive to maintain the rapport and reciprocity you have developed with your informants and within the community. This may mean volunteering and sharing information about yourself as your informant answers your questions. It also often happens, if the atmosphere is relaxed enough, that the informant will ask her own questions of you in turn as the interview proceeds.

Readers are referred to the following for more detail regarding ethnographic interviewing: Babbie (1995), Fink (1995), Levy and Holland (1998), Schensul et al. (1999), Sudman and Bradburn (1982).

Artifact and Archival Data

The final type of data I describe, and the type that is used often by ethnographic researchers of literacy, is artifacts and archival data. *Artifacts* for literacy researchers usually mean physical evidence of literacy instruction, learning, or practice. Examples include copies of worksheets, writing samples, book reports, test results, drawings, and so on. Artifacts are sought by literacy ethnographers to triangulate observation data and to document literacy learning much as a portfolio would.

Archival data are defined by Schensul et al. (1999) as "materials originally collected for bureaucratic or administrative purposes that are transformed into data for research purposes" (p. 202). Examples of these would include census data, demographic data, surveys, records of governmental expenditures, and so on. These data are used by ethnographers to build context for their studies as well as to contribute valuable information to the researcher to be used in the analysis of the observational and interview data. For *Now We Read, We See, We Speak* (2000), Waterman and I used archival data to construct the historical context of the civil war in El Salvador, the literacy rates as they evolved over time, and the current context of the Peace Accords and their impact on the lives of the participants.

DATA ANALYSIS

Analysis of ethnographic data begins in the field and continues past the time the researcher has left it. LeCompte and Schensul (1999b, p. 3) quote Patton (1987) on the results of analysis:

- It brings order to the piles of data the ethnographer has accumulated.
- It turns the big piles of raw data into smaller piles of crunched or summarized data.
- It permits the ethnographer to discover patterns and themes in the data and to link them with other patterns and themes.

Intersubjectivity

An important distinction needs to be drawn about a fundamental difference between analysis of ethnographic data and that of causal, correlational, and descriptive data. This lies in the epistemological lens used by ethnographers. Ethnographers admit to, and use, the fact that research data and analysis is always affected by the researcher. Regarding study design and data collection, Dobbert (1982) explains it this way:

> All scientific information is filtered; first, through the scientist's cognitive model; second, by any collecting instruments; and third, through the sense modalities of the recording scientist. The presence of this filtering process is not a weakness in scientific procedure. If human beings did not design research and filter data through their natural modes of perception, the results would be both useless and meaningless. (p. 6)

Data analysis in ethnography is also considered interpretive, filtered through the researcher's culturally learned frames for interpretation (Erickson, 1986). Several procedures are used to ensure that inappropriate conclusions are not drawn from this perspective. The first is the search for disconfirming evidence. This procedure is intended to prevent the researcher from accepting early, or sometimes favorite, interpretations that arise from the data analysis without double-checking that evidence may exist to disconfirm these perhaps biased findings. The search for negative evidence also allows the researcher to discover nuances and variation in the data that may lead to the discovery of new patterns and categories of interest.

Another procedure that ensures greater validity of the data analysis and interpretation is that of informant checking. For this procedure the researcher shares their evolving interpretations of the data with participants in the study to gain the informants' perspective. Through this process, the researcher can often gain new insights into local meanings from the participants and community members. These may deepen the final analysis as well as guard against overenthusiasm about the researcher's favorite interpretations.

Finally, to ensure that readers of ethnographies do not inappropriately interpret the researcher's interpretation, the authors of these studies need to engage in what has been termed *location*. This means that the author includes in the write-up a section in which she shares "the basis of one's subjectivity in approaching (her) research problem; i.e. making clear one's theoretical, methodological, and personal preferences and biases to the extent that they may affect research processes and outcomes" (Dobbert, 1982, p. 6). These authors also often illuminate these preferences and biases with short histories of their lives as they relate to the research and research focus. Following are a few statements of location from different ethnographies:

> I am a middle-aged White woman and I study in local schools, in which the social category of race, and its links to socioeconomic class, is consistently enacted. (Dyson, 2003, p. 20)

> My own assumptions as a researcher include a belief that context is dynamic, shifting, and manifold. Although the site for this study lacked diversity as it is often defined (i.e., ethnic or racial diversity), my goal has been to examine this context in ways that reveal its complexity and reconsider the meaning of diversity. (Lewis, 2001, p. 183)

> One of my first decisions was, for ethical reasons, to place my role of teacher above that of researcher. . . . This sometimes meant that I did not gather information that would inform the research at all or at the appropriate time if I felt that the act of obtaining the data would hinder Jenny's or Donny's progress. (Purcell-Gates, 1995, p. 203)

In the Field

Analysis of the data begins in the field as the researcher *cooks his or her field notes* (i.e., the process of going through the handwritten notes from the field, cleaning them up, clarifying, perhaps synthesizing audiotaped data, and entering them into a data base, perhaps, or rendering them in a typed or word-processed form), organizes the artifacts, transcribes audiotapes and/or videotapes, and organizes artifacts. It is imperative that the researcher begin this type of work early and stay on top of it to avoid drowning in a sea of data. I learned early in my career to organize and type my field notes for the day before I allowed myself to go to sleep. The few times this discipline wavered, I regretted it for months as I sought to catch up. In addition to avoiding feeling overwhelmed, cooking notes and organizing data on a continuous basis allow the researcher to identify emerging patterns and areas of interest in a timely fashion. This enables the creation of new data-collection procedures to investigate these insights. This is the recursive nature of ethnographic data collection and analysis.

Coding

Coding, or categorizing, the data to reduce them to manageable form follows the initial cleaning up. Early coding begins while the researcher is in the field but not until after the research has reached the point where patterns are beginning to emerge and researcher enculturation is well on its way.

Coding is done both inductively and deductively as the researcher, focusing on the research area of interest, categorizes events, behaviors, indications of beliefs, and so on. Inductive coding, or bottom-up, involves some form of organizing events, players, settings, and so on that are present in the data. Deductive codes for the data for *Other People's Words* (Purcell-Gates, 1995) marked categories such as "writing attempts," "reading attempts," "reading refusals," "notes from teacher," and "using signs to navigate space." As analysis proceeded, these deductive codes became more differentiated but still marked categories of interest to the research focus that existed in the data.

Deductive coding categorizes and patterns events, actions, beliefs, and so on from domains of interest or theories held by the researcher. Often these are built in to the research questions or focus. For example, inductive codes for *Other People's Words* included "experience with print in names," "evidence of lack of knowledge of semiotic role of print," and "attribution of failure to spoken dialect."

As coding proceeds, both top-down and bottom-up, the researcher recursively checks and rechecks all of his or her data, moving toward more refined and nuanced insights regarding the research focus and toward grounded theory which is based on specific observations which provide the basis for generalization. The researcher is well-served to keep notebooks for (1) codes and their meanings; (2) coding decisions, including the date each was made and the data one was analyzing when the decision was made; and (3) evolving hypothesis or thoughts about the progress of the analysis.

Interpretation

While even the coding process is inevitably interpretive, most ethnographers identify the separate analytic phase of interpretation. This is the final phase where the researcher arrives at, and presents in written form, the meaning of the results of the analysis. The interpretation goes beyond description of a phenomenon. It imposes meaning to categories and patterns of behaviors, values, and beliefs. It puts the pieces of the puzzle together to create a whole. It answers the questions: What's going on here? Why does what happens here happen here? What are insights we can take away from this?

Interpretation of ethnographic results requires going beyond the data in a principled way in order to ascribe meaning to them. It involves speculating and drawing implications. It is helpful, always, to return to the original, or evolved, research questions to focus the interpretation. Reviewing the theoretical and research literature around the issue at hand helps to place the results and the interpretation in the scientific field and clarify them for the reader. One way to think about interpretation of ethnographic results is "this is what we can learn from this study and I can support this with concrete, specific examples."

WRITING UP ETHNOGRAPHIC RESULTS

Ethnographies, at least in the field of literacy, often are written in book form rather than articles, although the latter certainly do appear. Authors may choose to present their studies in books because the complexity of results that result from ethnographic research is difficult to compress into research article form.

The final presentation of the results of an ethnography are often referred to a the "telling of a story." This refers to the responsibility of the researcher to pull together the pieces of the study and results into a meaningful whole—the interpretation. Thus, key elements of the final report are usually organized around the elements of the interpretation. This differs somewhat from other empirical research write-ups for which the data collection, analysis, results, and discussion are presented separately and in assumed temporal order. The ethnographic write-up, on the other hand, uses the interpretation as the organizing frame.

Another distinguishing aspect of the final presentation of ethnography is the amount of space given to descriptions of context. This, of course, reflects the underlying epistemology of ethnography that behaviors, values, and beliefs can never be viewed or analyzed outside sociocultural contexts. Usually, several chapters of book-length ethnographies are devoted to establishing the historical, geographical, and social contexts of the communities of interest.

Finally, readers of ethnographies should be able to find chapters related to the issue under consideration with the appropriate relevant literature cited and discussed. They should also find chapters or sections (often appendices) devoted to a description of the methodology and the location of the author(s).

STANDARDS FOR QUALITY

I am asked by the editors of this volume to provide a summary of the standards for quality in ethnographic research which have been presented throughout this chapter. This is undoubtedly worthwhile, perhaps, because this particular research methodology is sometimes considered to be an easy way out by researchers who do not like the quantitative requirements of other types of research or by consumers of research who tend to disregard anything that does not include numbers. Good ethnography, though, is arguably one of the most labor-intensive and cognitively challenging types of research to carry out.

High-quality ethnography demands the following:

- A deep understanding of, and the ability to shape, theory.
- Sharp and insightful observational skills.
- The ability to decenter to the degree needed to identify and come to understand the perspectives of others.
- Strict adherence to rules for valid and rigorous data collection, data management, and data analysis.
- The ability to think generatively as well as analytically.
- The ability to write engagingly and vividly so that readers can see and grasp the meanings that the ethnography has discovered, or interpreted.

The "story" that emerges at the end of the research process is not only a story, to be read and enjoyed and then discarded. Rather, it is a bringing together again into a whole that which the researcher has taken apart, struggled over in the search for meaning, double- and triple-checked for bias, and worked to discover the threads of meaning that can be pulled together to inform theory and future research.

Each of the exemplars used in this chapter to illustrate and illuminate methods that help to guarantee high-quality ethnography meets these demands. They have either won national or international awards as exemplars of research, or they were written by authors who have won such awards in the past. Readers are referred to these texts, and particularly to their methodology sections, for examples of ethnographic methodology that is publicly held up as exemplary.

REFERENCES

Babbie, E. (1995). *The practice of survey research* (7th ed.). Belmont, CA: Wadsworth.

Barton, D., & Hamilton, M. (1998). *Local literacies: Reading and writing in one community.* New York: Routledge.

Bogdan, R. C., & Biklen, S. K. (1992). *Qualitative research for education: An introduction to theory and methods* (2nd ed.). Boston: Allyn & Bacon.

Brandt, D. (2001). *Literacy in American lives.* Cambridge, UK: Cambridge University Press.

Cushman, E. (1998). *The struggle and the tools: Oral and literate strategies in an inner city community.* New York: State University of New York Press.

Dobbert, M. L. (1982). *Ethnographic research.* New York: Praeger.

Dyson, A. H. (1989). *Multiple worlds of child writers: Friends learning to write.* New York: Teachers College Press.

Dyson, A. H. (1993). *Social words of children learning to write in an urban primary school.* New York: Teachers College Press.

Dyson, A. H. (1997). *Writing superheroes: Contemporary childhood, popular culture, and classroom literacy.* New York: Teachers College Press.

Dyson, A. H. (2003). *The brothers and sisters learn to write: Popular literacies in childhood and school cultures.* New York: Teachers College Press.

Fink, A. (1995). *How to ask survey questions.* Thousand Oaks, CA: Sage.

Freire, P. (1993). *Pedagogy of the oppressed* (new rev. 20th anniversary ed.). New York: Continuum.

Goetz, J. P., & LeCompte, M. D. (1984). *Ethnography and qualitative design in educational research.* Orlando, FL: Academic Press.

Heath, S. B. (1983). *Ways with words: Language, life, and work in communities and classrooms.* Cambridge, UK: Cambridge University Press.

LeCompte, M. D., & Schensul, J. J. (1999a). *Designing & conducting ethnographic research.* Walnut Creek, CA: AltaMira Press.

LeCompte, M. D., & Schensul, J. J. (1999b). *Analyzing & interpreting ethnographic data.* Walnut Creek, CA: AltaMira Press.

Levy, R. I., & Holland, D. W. (1998). Person-centered interviews. In H. R. Bernard (Ed.), *Handbook of methods in cultural anthropology* (pp. 333-364). Walnut Creek, CA: AltaMira.

Lewis, C. (2001). *Literacy practices as social acts: Power, status, and cultural norms in the classroom.* Mahwah, NJ: Erlbaum.

Miles, M. B., & Huberman, M. (1994). *Qualitative data analysis: An expanded sourcebook* (2nd ed). London: Sage.

Patton, M. Q. (1987). *Qualitative evaluation methods.* Newbury Park, CA: Sage.

Purcell-Gates, V. (1995). *Other people's words: The cycle of low literacy.* Cambridge, MA: Harvard University Press.

Purcell-Gates, V., & Waterman, R. (2000). *Now we read, we see, we speak: Portrait of literacy development in an adult Freirean-based class.* Mahwah, NJ: Erlbaum.

Schensul, J. J., & LeCompte, M. D. (1999). *Ethnographic toolkit*. Walnut Creek, CA: AltaMira Press.

Schensul, S. L., Schensul, J. J., & LeCompte, M. D. (1999). *Essential ethnographic methods*. Walnut Creek, CA: AltaMira Press.

Sudman, S., & Bradburn, N. M. (1982). *Asking questions*. San Francisco: Jossey-Bass.

Wasserman, S., & Faust, K. (1994). *Social network analysis: Methods and applications*. Cambridge, UK: Cambridge University Press.

CHAPTER 7

Experimental and Quasi-Experimental Design in Literacy Research

Frank R. Vellutino
Christopher Schatschneider

$\mathbf{A}$ccording to many historians and philosophers, the experimental approach to scientific inquiry dates back to at least the 16th and 17th centuries and was ushered in with the seminal experiments of such notable students of nature as Galileo, da Vinci, Gilbert, and Copernicus (Drake, 1981). The work done by these and other experimenters in the natural sciences during this period represented a distinct departure from the approach used by philosophers in the Aristotelian tradition, whose writings and teachings about natural phenomena were based largely on inductive reasoning and intuition rather than systematic observation and empirical evidence. This work broke with tradition in three ways. First, scientific inquiry during the 16th and 17th centuries increasingly questioned rather than supported explanations of natural phenomena based on dogma. Second, passive observations of nature were increasingly accompanied by deliberate attempts to manipulate entities and elements in the physical world so as to produce changes that might provide useful information about cause–effect relationships. Third, experimenters during this period became increasingly appreciative of the need to take into account and possibly control extraneous influences that might compromise the investigator's objectivity, or constrain, in unintended ways, observations and interpretations of causal relationships. As a consequence, relevant procedures to accomplish these objectives were developed and implemented with positive effects in given areas of inquiry and controlled experimentation became firmly entrenched in disciplines that adopted the experimental method, especially in natural sciences such as astronomy, chemistry, and physics.

However, it soon became evident that controlled experimentation was more easily accomplished in laboratory sciences such as physics and chemistry than in field-based sciences such as public health, sociology, economics, psychology, and education. As researchers in these fields began employing the experimental method to study causal relationships, they increasingly discovered sources of bias that called for different methods of controlling extraneous influences that might compromise the integrity of their experiments. As a result, new methods of controlling extraneous influences were developed, such as random assignment to treatments (Fisher, 1925, 1935), the use of control groups, pre- and postexperimental assessment, and/or statistical control. In the related disciplines of psychology and education, much has been learned about research methodology in terms of the constraints imposed on the investigator by the research questions typically addressed in these fields, relative to the populations, experimental designs, technologies, and resources available to address those questions practically and meaningfully. Much of this work has been done by pioneers such as Lee Cronbach, Donald Campbell, Julian Stanley, and Thomas Cook, whose influential ideas have been summarized and significantly expanded in an excellent text concerned with generalized causal inference (Shadish, Cook, & Campbell, 2002). We have drawn generously from this text in preparing this chapter and acknowledge its influence on our thinking (see also Campbell & Stanley, 1963).

In the sections that ensue, we discuss methodologies for establishing causal relationships, focusing on two experimental approaches that have been used for this purpose: experimental and quasi-experimental research designs. We first discuss the experimental method in general terms, in the interest of providing some basic understanding of key concepts that define this approach to scientific inquiry. We then discuss the concept of validity in experimentation and describe different types of validity that must be considered in establishing and generalizing causal relationships. We then discuss experimental and quasi-experimental designs and provide examples of these designs that have been used in literacy research. We should point out, however, that because of space constraints, our treatment of these topics must necessarily be limited, both in scope and depth.

However, it is hoped that we provide the reader with enough incentive to explore these and related topics more comprehensively.

THE EXPERIMENTAL METHOD: SOME BASIC CONCEPTS AND DISTINCTIONS

Counterfactual Inference

For the purposes of this chapter, an experiment can be defined as a deliberate attempt to administer a treatment in order to observe the effects of that treatment. To be able to infer if an experimental treatment has any effect(s), it is crucial that we have some knowledge of what would have happened if the treatment had not been administered. Inferring treatment effects by comparing them to what would have happened if the treatment had not been administered is called *counterfactual inferencing* (Shadish et al., 2002). The idea of counterfactual inferencing was first explicitly stated by Hume (1748/1999) and expounded upon by Mill (1843) and, more recently, by Lewis (1973). The main idea of counterfactual inferencing is that we can only know if event C caused event E if it were the case that if C had not occurred, E would not have occurred.

Obtaining appropriate counterfactual information is difficult. In practice, once a treatment is delivered, it cannot be undelivered. In most (if not all) cases, it is impossible to know exactly what would have occurred had the treatment not been delivered. The main goal of experimental and quasi-experimental design is to create hypothetical counterfactuals (Dawes, 1994) that approximate, as closely as possible, what would have happened if the treatment had not been administered. How this approximation is obtained is the main distinction between experimental and quasi-experimental designs. Experimental designs employ random assignment of units to conditions as the methodology for generating hypothetical counterfactuals. That is, some units (e.g., children or classes) are assigned at random (using tables of random numbers, found in most statistics texts or software) to receive the treatment and some are not. We then infer that what happened to a unit that did not receive the treatment—the control group—reflects what would have happened to the other group of units had they not received the treatment. Quasi-experimental designs do not randomly assign units to conditions. Rather, they compare groups that already exist (e.g., children in one school to children in another school) using various types of design and/or statistical controls to try to ensure that those groups are as comparable as possible in every respect except for receiving the experimental treatment(s). Here again, we infer that what happened to the units that did not receive the treatment—the comparison group—reflects what would have happened to the other group(s) had they not received the treatment.

Experimental Causes and Experimental Effects

The purpose of conducting an experiment is to determine whether or not a given treatment caused a given effect. Shadish et al. (2002) suggest that experiments are well suited to studying *cause* and *effect* relationships because they (1) ensure that a presumed cause is deliberately manipulated and, thereby, precedes the observed effect; (2) incorporate procedures that help determine whether the cause is related to the effect; and (3) incorporate procedures to minimize and/or assess the influence of extraneous factors that could produce the effect presumed to be attributed to the cause. In contrast, nonexperimental, correlational studies are not as well suited to studying causal relationships because, although they may allow one to determine whether two variables are related to each other, they cannot establish which of the two is the cause and which is the effect, and they cannot rule out alternative explanations for observed relationships, often called *confounds*.

The experimental paradigm can be conceptualized into two parts: experimental causes (treatments) and experimental effects. In the study of literacy development, a treatment might consist of an instructional program designed to facilitate acquisition of reading and writing skills, implemented either with individual children or with entire classrooms of children. However, for the sake of illustration, let us suppose that the treatment consists of a remedial intervention program designed to improve reading skills in struggling readers (e.g., daily one-to-one tutoring using a theoretically motivated approach to intervention). Outcome measures to assess the effects of the intervention might include tests evaluating word-level skills such as phonological awareness, phonological decoding, and word identification; tests evaluating reading comprehension; or different combinations of these measures. The investigator is, of course, interested in determining whether the intervention, as the putative cause, had any effect on the children's reading skills, as assessed by the outcome measures. Yet, establishing cause–effect relationships in any given experiment turns out to be a complicated undertaking. Consider the concept *experimental cause* in this context. It might be inferred that any positive change on a reading outcome measure used to assess the effect of the intervention was due to the particular type of intervention administered in the study. However, this inference may or may not be warranted. For example, positive change on the outcome measure could have been due to the fact that the children who received the intervention were also receiving classroom instruction that would have produced such change, even in the absence of the intervention. Or the change could have been produced simply by the fact that the children were receiving daily one-to-one tutoring (perhaps any kind of tutoring could have produced the effect), or even by the fact that some of the worst readers dropped out of the study, thereby increasing the probability that the remaining children would show gains on postintervention outcome measures. In short, there are many possible causes of a given effect. Thus, to the extent possible, the investigator must endeavor to control for and/or evaluate factors that could influence results on an outcome measure, other than the treatment under study.

Consider now the concept *experimental effect*. Shadish et al. (2002) define an effect produced by an experimental treatment as a hypothetical difference between what did happen when individuals received a treatment and what would have happened if the same individuals had not received the treatment. This entails a comparison of the treatment group with the hypothetical counterfactual. To correctly estimate a treatment effect, one must have two things: (1) one must have a reasonable and defensible hypothetical counterfactual that is as similar as possible to the treatment group; and (2) one must be able to compare this group to the group that received treatment. For example, in the case of the intervention study example given previously, the investigator could randomly assign struggling readers to intervention and nonintervention (control) groups, take steps to ensure the fidelity of the intervention program, control and/or assess extraneous factors that could produce the desired outcome, and compare the performance of the two groups on appropriate postintervention outcome measures. If random assignment to treatment and control groups is not possible, then other procedures could be employed to help the investigator establish cause–effect relationships, some of which we discuss later. In either case, the use of a control group provides a basis for making a claim for the existence of a treatment effect because it allows the investigator to approximate the magnitude and direction of change on the outcome measure(s), in the children who received the intervention, under (the hypothetical) conditions where the same children had not received the intervention. Thus, as pointed out by Shadish et al. (2002), "two central tasks in experimental design are creating a high-quality but necessarily imperfect source of counterfactual inference and understanding how this source differs from the treatment condition" (p. 6).

THE CONCEPT OF VALIDITY IN EXPERIMENTATION

In the present context, the term *validity* can be defined as "the approximate truth of an inference" about given aspects of an experiment (Shadish et al., 2002, p. 34). When discussing causal relationships between treatment and outcome measures, the term *validity* refers to inferences about whether a given treatment actually produced an observed effect. When discussing results associated with experimental treatments, the term *validity* refers to inferences about causal relationships based on the statistical analyses used to evaluate the size and direction of treatment effects. When discussing the operations involved in implementing an experiment, the term *validity* refers to inferences about whether the particular units (individuals, classrooms etc.), treatments, assessment instruments, and settings used in the experiment are representative examples of the higher order constructs defining these operations. When discussing generalization of experimental outcomes, the term *validity* refers to inferences about whether specific cause–effect relationships can be observed across variations in units, treatments, outcome measures, and settings. These different types of inferences correspond with what Shadish et al. (2002), respectively, call *internal validity, statistical conclusion validity, construct validity,* and *external validity.* We briefly describe each in the sections that follow.

Internal Validity

The validity of inferences about cause–effect relationships is dependent on the degree to which the researcher demonstrates that (1) a treatment preceded an observed effect, (2) the treatment is related to the effect, and (3) there are no other plausible explanations for the effect. The first of these criteria is guaranteed by experiments because they require that treatments be implemented before the effects of the treatments are measured. The second criterion is dependent on the degree to which the statistical procedures used for data analysis are able to detect treatment effects (discussed later), and the third depends on the degree to which the investigator takes into account plausible threats to internal validity—that is, circumstances that may compromise the accuracy of inferences about causal relationships. Examples of common threats to internal validity discussed by

Shadish et al. (2002) include *selection bias, history, regression to the mean, attrition, testing,* and *instrumentation.*

Selection bias occurs when individuals assigned to given treatments happen to be different at the outset of the experiment in ways that might erroneously be attributed to the treatment—for example, having different levels of ability in word recognition prior to being assigned to experimental conditions that are hypothesized to have differential effects on outcome measures of word recognition. *History* refers to differential experiences of individuals in comparison groups that might affect experimental outcomes—for example, having treatment and control groups (inadvertently) come from classrooms characterized by strong and weak literacy instruction, respectively. *Regression to the mean* refers to the tendency of individuals with extreme scores on one assessment to obtain scores that are closer to the population mean on a subsequent assessment. So whereas individuals with high scores on a pretreatment assessment will tend to have lower scores on a posttreatment assessment, individuals with low scores on the pretreatment assessment will tend to have higher scores on the posttreatment assessment, even in the absence of treatment effects. Such propensities could present a spurious account of any bonafide treatment effects that might have been observed. *Attrition* refers to unanticipated reduction in the number of participants completing the experiment. If those who drop out of the experiment differ, in important ways, from those who completed the experiment (e.g., they may be the worst readers), then the accuracy of causal inferences may be compromised.

Finally, *testing* threats to internal validity occur when taking a test creates practice effects or other reactive biases that could be mistaken for treatment effects. *Instrumentation* threats occur when the scaling properties of an assessment instrument change over time in ways that could influence test scores. For example, scoring 1 year below grade level in second grade does not imply the same degree of reading skills deficiency as scoring 1 year below grade level in seventh grade.

Statistical Conclusion Validity

Statistical conclusion validity is concerned with two major dimensions of causal inference: (1) the degree to which the cause is related to the observed effect, and (2) the magnitude and direction of the effect. In regard to the first, the investigator might erroneously conclude from the use of faulty statistical procedures that the cause is related to the effect (*type I error*) or he or she might erroneously conclude that the cause is unrelated to the effect (*type II error*). In regard to the second, it is possible to either overestimate or underestimate both the magnitude of an effect and the degree of confidence in the effect. Therefore, the quality of causal inferences is directly dependent on the use of appropriate statistical procedures that take into account the unique sampling and measurement problems associated with an experiment.

Examples of the most common threats to statistical conclusion validity include *low power, violation of assumptions of statistical tests, unreliability of measurement, restriction of range*, and *fidelity of treatment problems. Low power* is the inability of an outcome measure to detect an experimental effect and is caused by small sample sizes, unreliability of measurement, range restriction, and diffusion of treatment(s), among other circumstances. *Violation of statistical assumptions* refers to the failure to take into account theoretical assumptions associated with given statistical tests (e.g., assumptions about population distributions, freedom from sampling biases, independence of measurement, and equivalent variability in comparison groups, among others). A typical consequence of such violation is to underestimate error of measurement while overestimating treatment effects. *Unreliability of measurement* refers to erroneous estimation of causal relationships owing to low reliability in one or more of the measuring instruments evaluating these relationships. *Restriction of range* refers to low variability in test scores manifested either in *ceiling effects* (too many high scores) or in *floor effects* (too many low scores). Range restriction increases the probability that treatment effects will not be detected and can occur, either because treatments being compared are highly similar or because measuring instruments do not adequately sample the full range of abilities being evaluated in an experiment.

Construct Validity

Constructs are category labels for theoretical entities. In experimental research, constructs refer to the sampling components of an experiment (i.e., units, treatments, assessment instruments, and settings). Construct inferences are judgments about the degree to which a sampling component is a representative example of the construct it instantiates. In literacy research, a *unit* may consist of individuals or aggregates of individuals such as classrooms or schools. Construct inferences about units are concerned with whether a particular type of unit is representative of the population from which the experimental sample was drawn. For example, the construct label *struggling readers* may be overinclusive and inaccurately represent the population, if the sample included second-language learners or participants coming from classrooms servicing emotionally handicapped children. In contrast, there is less ambiguity about construct labels such as *males or females*. Similarly, a treatment in a literacy experiment may be a certain type of reading instruction which the investigator calls *comprehension strategy instruction*, and the question that needs to be addressed, in drawing conclusions about results generated by the experiment, is whether or not the instruction employed in the experiment is a representative example of comprehension strategy instruction as it has been defined in literacy research. Inferences as to the construct validity of assessment instruments used as outcome measures are concerned with the question of whether such instruments are valid measures of change in capabilities hypothesized to be causally related to an experimental treatment. For example, a test of word-recognition skills as a measure of the theoretical construct called *reading ability* would have inadequate construct validity, if this test were used as a proxy measure of reading comprehension ability. Finally, inferences as to the construct validity of the settings in which an experiment is carried out are concerned with the question of whether these settings are representative examples of the population of settings to which the investigator wishes to generalize results from the experiment. Consider, for example, the construct *second-grade classrooms in public schools located in densely populated urban areas*. If even a small number of children in the sample came from schools located in suburban and/or rural areas, then the research sample would not adequately represent children being educated in the settings of special interest to the investigator and the construct validity of both the participants in the experiment and the experimental settings could be questioned.

Perhaps the most common threat to construct validity is the failure to fully explicate and define a given construct. All the examples given earlier, to some extent, have this problem in common. For example, the category label *struggling readers from disadvantaged backgrounds* implies a set of descriptors defining children from a population that is different, in many important ways, from the population of children defined by the set of descriptors implied in the category label *struggling readers from advantaged backgrounds*, in terms of factors that might differentially influence response to experimental treatments in these two groups (knowledge of print concepts, vocabulary knowledge, phonological awareness, etc.). Such distinctions are not adequately reflected in the more general category label *struggling readers* exemplified previously. Thus, in describing the research sample being studied, the experimenter must take pains to use descriptors and category labels that clearly define the population from which the sample was drawn and that distinguish it from other populations, both to ensure that causal inferences about treatment effects observed in this sample are valid and to ensure that such effects are generalized only to individuals in the population represented by the sample.

Another common threat to construct validity is confounding of constructs. A good illustration of such confounding is provided by the construct labeled *second-grade classrooms in public schools located in densely populated urban areas*, which we discussed earlier. It is worth reiterating in this context that including even a small number of children from second-grade classrooms located in rural areas in the sample defined by this construct confounds the construct with one that might be labeled *second-grade classrooms located in sparsely populated rural areas* and, thereby, limits the experimenter's ability to generalize research findings to the populations represented by either construct.

Using only one implementation of a given construct is yet another common threat to construct validity (called *mono-operation bias* by Shadish et al., 2002)—for example, using only word-level intervention to improve reading comprehension skills or only a single measure of reading comprehension to evaluate the effects of word-level intervention on growth in reading comprehension. A similar threat is *mono-method bias*—that is, the use of a single method of operationalizing a given construct—for example, using only the *cloze method* of evaluating reading comprehension. One other threat to construct validity in experimentation worth mentioning is *treatment diffusion*, Treatment diffusion is handily exemplified in a situation in which the effects of an experimental classroom reading program are distilled when teachers in control classrooms advertently or inadvertently import and implement materials and/or procedures implemented by teachers in experimental classrooms. There are other threats to construct validity discussed by Shadish et al. (2002) that will not be discussed here, and the reader who is interested in a more comprehensive treatment of this topic would be well advised to consult that text.

External Validity

As we indicated in an earlier section, external validity is concerned with inferences about the degree to which experimental effects can be generalized across variations in units, treatments, assessment instruments, and settings. In the rare instances in which random sampling of given study operations employed in an experiment is possible, there is some degree of certainty that treatment effects obtained with the particular study operations can be generalized to the larger populations from which they were drawn—for example, to children having demographic characteristics similar to those who participated in the experiment (units); to reading intervention activities comparable to but different from those used as the treatment(s) in the experiment (treatments); to word recognition and/or reading comprehension measures comparable to but different from those used to evaluate treatment effects (assessment instruments); and to schools having demographic characteristics similar to those participating in the experiment (settings). But, under the more common circumstance where random sampling from given populations is not possible, the investigator must either provide documentation that the research sample consists of representative exemplars from those populations or make it clear, in reporting research findings, that experimental results may not readily be generalized to the populations, because there is no certainty that research samples were drawn from the populations. For example, if the researcher uses an experimental test of reading comprehension to evaluate the effects of a reading intervention program, he or she might justify the use of the test for this purpose by demonstrating that the operations used to evaluate reading comprehension are essentially the same as those used in existing, well-established comprehension tests (content validity); that these operations are theoretically well grounded (construct validity); and that correlations between performance on the experimental reading comprehension test and performance on existing, well-established tests of skills that underlie reading comprehension (e.g., word recognition and language comprehension) are comparable to correlations between such tests and existing tests of reading comprehension (empirical validity). Without such documentation, the investigator is obliged to limit generalizations about experimental effects to results produced by the experimental test.

Similarly, it is often the case that researchers wish to generalize from an experimental sample drawn from a well-defined population to broader or different populations, for example, from children being educated in suburban schools to children being educated in inner-city schools; or from implementation of a particular type of reading intervention program outside the classroom to implementation of essentially the same program in the classroom. The investigator may even wish to generalize experimental effects more narrowly, for example, from the children in the research sample, who, by virtue of sampling criteria, did not have general language impediments to children who do have general language impediments. The external validity question raised in each of these instances is whether experimental effects observed with given units, treatments, assessment instruments, and settings employed in an experiment will generalize in the various ways exemplified (among others of interest). It will suffice to reiterate that without evidence that results can be generalized to populations other than the one from which the research sample was drawn, the investigator is constrained to generalize experimental effects to the intended population and must conduct additional research to address the question of whether such effects can be generalized to other populations.

All of the foregoing examples illustrate variations in sampling particulars that were not included in a given experiment, but the external validity question also arises in the case of some that may have been included in the experiment. For example, more fine-grained analyses of results from a reading intervention study may show that children with at least average-level language abilities were more responsive to reading intervention than were children with below-average language abilities. Or such analyses may show that change on outcome measures was greater with reading intervention *A* than with reading intervention *B* or that intervention effects were more strongly observed on outcome measure *A* than on outcome measure *B*. Such circumstances call for qualification of experimental results in any forum or document where statements about the degree to which these results will generalize to target populations are presented to the research community.

Inherent in the examples given previously are common threats to external validity. One of the most common is that effects obtained with one type of unit (persons, schools, etc.) may not be obtained with different types of units. For example, intervention in small groups might be more effective with moderately impaired readers having at least average language abilities than with severely impaired readers having below-average language abilities, who may require more individualized and more intensive intervention. The latter example underscores a related threat to external validity, specifically that an effect obtained with one variation in treatment (e.g., one-to-one tutoring) may not be obtained with another variation in treatment (e.g., small group instruction). Another such threat is that an experimental effect observed with one type of outcome measure may not be observed with different outcome measures. For example, instruction to improve alphabetic coding skills may have a salutary effect on measures of word recognition and phonological decoding skills but not on measures of reading comprehension skills. Still another threat to external validity is one where an effect observed in one kind of setting may not be observed in a different kind of setting, as exemplified in the question of whether significant progress made by struggling readers in a reading intervention experiment involving one-to one daily tutoring implemented by experimental personnel outside the classroom would have been observed if the same type of intervention was implemented by the same experimental personnel in the children's classrooms, given the different types of potentially influential environments provided by the two venues.

Finally, in instances in which the investigator has clearly delineated populations of units, treatments, assessment instruments, or settings from which to obtain experimental samples, and can sample from each of these populations with known probability, *random sampling* from these populations, when feasible, is highly desirable. Random sampling from a population entails sampling in a way that ensures that given members of that population can be selected with equal probability, for example, by using tables of random numbers (provided by most statistical texts). When attrition is low, random sampling allows the investigator to generalize causal inferences to the population from which a given sample was drawn, within the limits of sampling error. However, because of practical and logistical problems, especially in terms of such barriers as theoretically constrained choice of treatments and/or availability of appropriate assessment instruments or settings, random sampling is not often feasible in field research and is much less frequently used in such research than what has been called *purposive sampling* (Shadish et al., 2002), that is, nonrandom, deliberate sampling from specific populations of interest. Purposive sampling of diverse exemplars, such as members of different ethnic groups and/or different genders, may enhance external validity by allowing the investigator to assess the degree to which causal inferences can be generalized across these diverse populations. Similarly, purposive sampling of typical exemplars, such as poor versus normal readers, domain-specific assessment instruments with well-known statistical properties, or different settings with demographic properties of special interest (e.g., urban vs. suburban schools), may enhance external validity by allowing the investigator to assess the degree to which different units, instruments, or settings produce essentially the same pattern of results under given experimental circumstances. And, of course, purposive rather than random sampling is necessary when the investigator wishes to generalize experimental results to and compare specific populations of interest that are not represented in sufficient numbers in available populations to allow random sampling from those populations, for example, impaired readers equated with younger, normally developing readers on measures of word recognition and spelling ability.

However, in view of the limited applicability of generalizations from single experiments, the external validity of given causal inferences will probably depend, in the long run, on programmatic research, across many research settings, that produces reliable results over wide variations in units, treatments, assessment instruments, and settings.

Interrelationships among Different Types of Validity

It may be useful to point out that although we discussed the different types of validity separately, some degree of reflection will make it clear that they are functionally interdependent. For example, inferences about causal relationships (internal validity) are dependent, in large measure, on the nature and quality of the statistical analyses documenting the relationship between a hypothesized cause and an observed effect (statistical conclusion validity). Similarly, the nature and quality of statistical analyses performed for purposes of documenting cause–effect relationships and the quality of causal inferences based on those analyses depend significantly on theoretically grounded explication and generalization of the construct inferences associated with the units, treatments, assessment instruments, and settings employed in an experiment (construct validity). And, the quality of the target generalizations presented in forums and documents reporting results of an experiment, regarding units, treatments, assessment instruments, and settings employed in the experiment (external validity), depend significantly on the quality of inferences about causal relationships, the quality of statistical analyses leading to those inferences, and the quality of the theoretical constructs underlying the operations that define the experiment.

Before leaving the topic of validity, it might be worthwhile to note that no design perfectly controls all threats to validity. All have potential weaknesses and flaws. Oftentimes, strengthening a design against a particular threat to validity may increase the threats to other types of validity. For example, trying to control many aspects of a study to increase its internal validity may have the consequence of decreasing its external validity. That is, as we incorporate more controls in an experimental design, we increase the likelihood of introducing artificial elements that would not generalize to the target population. This is not an argument for less controlled studies, but the researcher is urged to be mindful of all the threats to validity in order to make sound judgments about experimental design.

EXPERIMENTAL AND QUASI-EXPERIMENTAL DESIGNS

As we indicated earlier, the central distinction between experimental and quasi-experimental designs is how the units being observed are assigned to conditions. Experimental designs assign units (persons, classrooms, schools, etc.) to experimental conditions (e.g., treatment or control groups) via random assignment. Random assignment ensures that every unit has the same probability of being assigned to given conditions, because assignment to each condition is based purely on chance. Thus, in an experiment with only two conditions, random assignment to each could be accomplished by repeated tossing of a (fair) coin, which has a 50% chance of coming up heads or tails on each toss. Units designated as "heads" would then be assigned to one experimental condition whenever heads came up on given tosses and units designated as "tails" would be assigned to the other condition whenever tails came up. In a randomized experiment with six conditions, there is a 16.7% chance that a given unit will be assigned to one of the six conditions and random assignment could be accomplished by repeated rolling of a (fair) die that has the numbers 1 through 6 on its sides. In most cases, however, investigators tend to use more formal methods of random assignment such as tables of random numbers, but these simple examples should serve to illustrate the concept of randomization (see Shadish et al., 2002, for other examples).

There are several advantages in using random assignment to experimental conditions when this procedure is feasible. If implemented correctly, it creates two or more experimental groups that will be similar to each other on relevant variables (on average) before any treatment is administered, barring pretreatment differences among given groups that may occur by chance, which become increasingly less probable as sample sizes increase. As a result, any observed differences between (or among) groups on outcome measures are likely to be due to the experimental treatments rather than to group differences that existed before the experiment was initiated. Randomization also makes alternative explanations of treatment effects that constitute threats to internal validity less plausible by distributing these threats randomly over experimental conditions. This means that extraneous factors that could influence performance on outcome measures should occur with equal probability among experimental groups, thereby increasing the probability that the only systematic differences that occur between and among groups should be due to experimental treatments. Finally, randomized designs also provide the best chance of creating adequate hypothetical counterfactuals that are so important in estimating treatment effects.

However, random assignment of units to conditions is oftentimes impossible or prohibitive. But just because some situations are not conducive to random assignment and experimentation does not mean that we are left without recourse. Studies can be designed to investigate cause and effect that do not employ random assignment. These types of studies make use of what have come to be called quasi-experimental designs (Campbell & Stanley, 1963). These designs are similar to experimental designs in every respect except one—the assignment of units to conditions is not random because random assignment is precluded by practical problems. For example in literacy research, it is often not possible to randomly assign schools or classrooms to receive a particular kind of curriculum or intervention. Most school administrators have definite ideas about which programs are better than others and it may not be possible, in given instances, to convince them to agree to implement a different literacy program. If the design also calls for randomization of interventions within schools, it is also sometimes difficult to persuade teachers to comply with the dictates of the randomization procedure (especially when they have been designated to be in the control group). Oftentimes, these limitations will compel a researcher to employ a quasi-experimental design, where groups are assigned nonrandomly. In such cases, the groups may be assigned by an administrator or perhaps via a joint decision of the researcher and a school official.

Yet, quasi-experimental designs do not have the advantages that come with random assignment. In instances in which random assignment is not employed, the adequacy of the hypothetical counterfactual is called into question. Without random assignment, we have no way of distributing potential confounds equally across all groups. For example, suppose that those administrators inclined toward one intervention over another assign more effective teachers to that condition and the overall effectiveness of those teachers causes differences in student growth. How do we know that observed differences are the result of the intervention or the result of the influence of the administrator? And, without an adequate counterfactual, any attempt to estimate treatment effects could be confounded with other causes that were not evenly distributed among the preexisting groups. Nevertheless, when random assignment to experimental conditions is not feasible, important information can still be obtained regarding potential causal effects, as we suggested earlier. While (randomized) experiments rely on random assignment to make other explanations for treatment effects implausible, Shadish et al. (2002) argue that researchers can use other techniques to make the same case. Specifically, they cite three related principles to follow in an attempt to make other plausible explanations of treatment effects implausible: (1) *identification and evaluation of plausible threats to internal validity*, (2) *primacy of control by design*, and (3) *coherent pattern matching*.

Identification and Evaluation of Plausible Threats to Internal Validity

What would make the groups different at the outset, or during treatment, and would this difference affect the estimation of a treatment effect? These are the questions that need to be asked when assessing potential threats to internal validity. One major problem could occur if treatment and control groups differ on variables thought to affect treatment. This would be a form of *selection bias*. Another problem could occur if the groups were treated differently during implementation of the treatment and this difference was not a part of the treatment. An example of this circumstance would be one in which one group of schools agrees to implement a particular treatment program and another group of schools agrees to act as a control, and some of the treatment schools decide to implement a pullout tutoring program outside the scope of the research project. This would mean that any differences found in comparisons of treatment and control schools are potentially confounded with the effects of the pullout tutoring program that was not included in the original treatment protocol. This is an example of a *history* effect.

Another potential threat to validity can occur when the groups are differentially identified based on their performance on preselected variables. For example, one technique employed in literacy research is the "matched reading-level" design (Backman, Mamen, & Ferguson, 1984; Bryant & Goswami, 1986; Vellutino & Scanlon, 1989). This design entails matching children who have reading problems with younger children who are reading at the same overall skill level but are developing normally in relation to their peers. In this case, the older group of children, who, in relation to their peers, are at the lower end of the reading ability distribution, may show an increased *regression to the mean* in comparison to the group of younger children who were selected to be in the average range of their reading ability distribution. This effect can be substantially reduced by using multiple measures at multiple time points in order to place children into groups.

Primacy of Control by Design

Once threats to validity have been identified, attempts to minimize their effects can be implemented. Shadish et al. (2002) suggest ways in which threats to internal validity can be minimized by adding design controls such as administering more measurements at pretest and employing additional control groups. The overall goal is to prevent the confounding of treatment effects with other effects, while investigating whether given confounds could plausibly influence the treatment effects. These confounds are best controlled by adding design elements that address the particular threats to validity. For example, adding multiple control groups would have the benefit of increasing the chance that one of them would be suitable as a hypothetical counterfactual. Actively controlling what happens to the control group can also help reduce threats to validity. Adding multiple pretests would help identify preexisting differences among the groups and would also reduce the chances of a regression to the mean effect being confounded with a treatment effect. That is, children shown to be consistently below average on an ability using multiple measures of that ability administered over time will manifest less regression to the mean than will children identified as below average using only one measure at one time point.

The alternative to using design elements to control for these threats is to use statistical controls to try to remove potential confounding influences on the treatment effects through statistical adjustments. The main tool in this strategy is to use covariates to control for preexisting differences among the groups that may relate to treatment outcome. The thinking behind this strategy is that groups can be made to be equivalent statistically at baseline on variables thought to affect treatment. Groups are made to be statistically equivalent by adding or subtracting a statistically determined value to everyone's predicted score on the dependent variable. For example, the researcher may discover that his or her treatment groups differed significantly on an important pretest measure and may use that measure to statistically control for pretest differences.

Statistical control of confounds is seen as an inferior method of controlling for threats to validity as compared to the use of design elements. It is impossible to statistically control for all the possible ways that groups can differ on variables that relate to outcome—often called the *hidden bias* (Shadish et al., 2002). Unmeasured variables cannot be controlled statistically. This is the main reason why experimental designs hold the advantage over quasi-experimental designs. While unmeasured effects cannot be controlled, they can be randomly distributed across the groups when assignment to experimental conditions is randomized. Also, statistical controls are often employed incorrectly. One assumption of using statistical controls is that the variable being covaried has an equal (and linear) relationship with the dependent variable across all levels of other independent variables. That is, one of the assumptions of using a covariate (such as in an analysis of covariance) is that it does not interact with other variables. Another is that it does not have a curvilinear relationship with the dependent variable. If either of these assumptions were violated, it would render the statistical adjustments invalid. There are, of course, a number of ways to adjust an analysis to reflect these situations, but it is all too common to leave these potential violations unexplored.

This is not to say that there is no place for statistical controls. However, these controls should be used *after* design controls have already been employed to control for minimal differences that may remain and they should be used as a "method of last resort." Winship and Morgan (1999) provide an excellent review of the use of statistical controls in experimental design.

Coherent Pattern Matching

This principle involves making a complex prediction about a particular causal hypothesis that would leave few viable alternative explanations. The logic behind coherent pattern matching is that the more complex the prediction, the less likely a given alternative could generate the same results. One example of this principle in literacy research would be a study evaluating a reading curriculum designed to increase reading achievement that emphasized working on phonological awareness and decoding skills but not on reading fluency or comprehension skills. In this instance, the experimenter could assess the efficacy of the curriculum by investigating whether increases in reading achievement were related to greater gains in phonological awareness and decoding skills and lesser gains in fluency and reading comprehension. The drawback of this approach is that we still cannot know with certainty that an increase in these skills caused an increase in reading achievement. However, as more complex predictions become confirmed, alternative explanations become less likely.

Another example would be a study examining whether hypothesized treatment effects had an impact on the constructs it was supposed to affect, and had little or no impact on constructs that are unrelated to outcome. The experimenter might hypothesize, for example, that treatments that affect reading skills would have minimal effects on mathematical computational skills. But, if it were discovered that a reading treatment had comparable rather than distinctly different effects on reading and mathematical computational skills, then the causal mechanisms of the treatment effects would be called into question. This type of hypothesis testing is commonly referred to as testing for *discriminant validity*.

With all these techniques, it is useful to keep in mind that the goal is to minimize threats to validity that are introduced by the inability to randomly assign units to conditions. Yet, all else being equal, a randomized experimental design will always be a more powerful mechanism for causal explanation than a quasi-experimental design. Researchers are encouraged to employ randomized experimental designs whenever possible. It is often the case that the researcher may employ a quasi-experimental design because it is easier than trying to randomize units to treatments. We want to make it clear that this choice does come at the cost of a loss of causal information.

STANDARDS OF QUALITY FOR EXPERIMENTAL AND QUASI-EXPERIMENTAL DESIGNS

We propose that experiments and quasi-experiments can be evaluated on the basis of two related criteria: The adequacy of the hypothetical counterfactual and how well a design addresses the four types of validity we described earlier in this chapter (from Shadish et al., 2002). These criteria provide benchmarks by which standards of quality could be assessed.

Adequacy of the Hypothetical Counterfactual

As stated earlier in this chapter, treatment effects are evaluated against what the investigator thinks would have happened had the treatment not been given. In this regard, the adequacy of the hypothetical counterfactual is of paramount importance. Accordingly, the control group must be comparable to the treatment group in all respects except for the experimental treatment in order for post-treatment differences between the groups to have any meaning. It is also possible to construct a control group that would help control for peripheral effects of the treatment. That is, a good control group need not only be one where the experimenter passively observes what is happening to the group. Control groups can also be actively constructed so that effects due to treatment can become less ambiguous. One example of this circumstance would be a study in which a researcher was interested in assessing a particular small-group remedial program designed to increase reading ability. The researcher could design an experiment that identified children who might benefit from remedial reading and then randomly assign them to small groups that received either the remedial reading program (treatment) or extra help in math. The math group would serve as a control group that is specifically designed to assess the effects of receiving extra attention in small groups, which, in this example, is confounded in the experimental condition. One could then argue that any differences between these groups could be attributed to the effects of the content of the remedial reading program and not to the extra attention each student receives during small group instruction, regardless of the nature of that instruction. Thus, inadequate control groups would be defined as contrast groups that are not comparable to the treatment groups on important pretreatment variables.

Control groups that differ from the treatment group in uncontrolled ways can introduce other possible causes for the observed treatment effect. Unfortunately, this will always be true in the case of quasi-experimental designs and statements about treatment effects will be less powerful when they emanate from quasi-experimental designs. This is because we are less confident that mechanisms that could affect treatments are accounted for in the quasi-experimental design. However, as we indicated earlier, these designs can still provide some useful information. The degree to which any such design can do so depends largely on its ability to account for plausible alternative explanations for the treatment effects and should be judged accordingly.

Threats to Validity

Quality studies that employ experimental and quasi-experimental designs must also be able to adequately address threats to validity. Studies employing these designs can be evaluated in terms of how well they have addressed these threats. The experimenter's ability to account for threats to validity directly constrains his or her ability to draw causal inferences from a study employing a particular design. In the next section, we summarize two literacy studies—one experimental and one quasi-experimental—and attempt to evaluate them against the criteria presented previously. To protect the innocent, we have decided to evaluate two studies of our own (Vellutino & Scanlon, 1987; Foorman, Francis, Fletcher, Schatschneider, & Mehta, 1998).

EXPERIMENTAL DESIGN EXEMPLAR

A study that exemplifies several of the advantages and disadvantages of implementing an experimental design was conducted by one of us some years ago (Vellutino & Scanlon, 1987). A major objective of this study, among others, was to evaluate the relative merits of using a whole (sight) word-meaning-based approach to teaching word identification compared with a code-based (phonics) approach singly or in combination. In accord with the view that children must have ready access to both the names and meanings of printed words as integrated wholes and the sounds associated with their component letters (or combinations of their letters) in order to learn to identify them, the investigators hypothesized that a treatment condition that facilitated the complementary use of both approaches would facilitate better performance on an experimental task that simulated beginning reading than would treatment conditions that facilitated the use of one without the other. Participants (units) in the study were poor and normally developing readers in second and sixth grade. Each was initially selected on the basis of performance on an oral reading test and, thereafter, on the basis of intellectual and exclusionary criteria typically used to distinguish between children with and without specific reading disability. Participants in each reader group at each grade level were also assessed on pretreatment measures of phonemic segmentation and letter–sound (pseudoword) decoding ability before being randomly assigned to one of five experimental conditions: three treatment and two control conditions. Thus, the fully crossed design was a $2 \times 2 \times 5$ randomized block design (2 reader groups by 2 grade levels by 5 experimental conditions) with 20 possible cells (i.e., groups assigned to given conditions). Note that the poor readers at each grade level performed significantly below the normal readers on both of the pretreatment tests of phoneme segmentation and letter–sound decoding, which indicated that they had deficient phonological skills. This was of interest because one objective of the study was to evaluate differential response to treatments in the poor and normal reader groups.

One of the treatment conditions (phonemic segmentation training [PST]) was designed to foster an analytic disposition to search for letter–sound invariance in printed words and it simulated the code-oriented approach to reading instruction. It consisted of an ordered series of training activities designed to foster phoneme segmentation of spoken and written words and pseudowords followed by activities designed to facilitate functional use of an alphabetic coding strategy to mediate word identification. The alphabetic coding activities initially entailed practice (15 trials) in learning to identify four printed trigraphs comprised of novel alphabetic characters (*sij, suf, dij, duf*), using letter–sound strategies to do so. This task was followed by a transfer of learning task in which permuted forms of the initial training set (*jid, juf, sif, dus*) were presented to assess the child's ability to generalize letter–sound knowledge acquired during initial learning (15 to 20 trials). The children were encouraged, on both tasks, to search for letter–sound invariance to aid word identification. The training activities for the PST condition were completed in 5 or 6 days, and after no more than a 2-day hiatus, the children were presented with a new set of printed trigraphs comprised of novel alphabetic characters (*gov, goz, vab, zab*), and were given 20-paired associates (whole word) learning trials to assess their ability to use a code-oriented (analytic) strategy to learn to identify these trigraphs (code acquisition training). The very next day, they were given reversed derivatives of these stimuli (*vog, zog, bav, baz*) to learn to identify (code acquisition transfer), using the same paired-associates format. Because the experimenters were interested in whether the children could independently implement the (hypothesized) disposition to search for letter–sound invariance the PST condition was designed to foster, they were not told of the alphabetic properties of the novel trigraphs on either the initial learning or the transfer learning tasks. The code acquisition training and transfer tasks were the primary outcome measures used to assess treatment effects in this study and were administered to participants exposed to the three treatment conditions and one of the two control conditions. Participants in the other control condition were presented only with the code acquisition transfer task (see later).

The second treatment condition (response acquisition [RA]), was our analogue of the whole word/meaning-based approach to word identification (often called "sight word" learning). The initial phase of the training implemented in this condition consisted of a phonological memory task designed to familiarize the children with the oral counterparts (names) of the trigraphs they would encounter on the initial learning task used as one of the outcome measures (code acquisition training). It involved 20 free recall trials using an alternating presentation/test format. Thus, on a given trial, the experimenter presented all four nonsense syllables, then had the child recite digits backwards and after a 6-second hiatus asked the child to recall these stimuli in any order. After a short break, the child learned to associate these same stimuli with pictures of novel cartoon animals so as to imbue them with meaning. The intent of this training was to help ensure that the children in this condition would have ready access to the verbal response counterparts of the trigraphs they would encounter on the code acquisition training task and that they would be learning to read "words" that were meaningful to them. RA training was followed by presentation of the same code acquisition training and transfer tasks administered to the PST group no more than two days after training was completed.

Children in the third treatment condition (PSTRA) received both phoneme segmentation/alphabetic coding and RA training, followed by presentation of the same initial learning and transfer learning tasks administered to the PST and RA groups 1 or 2 days after training was completed. Of the two control conditions, one (C-1) entailed exposure to both the initial learning and transfer learning tasks and the other (C-2) entailed exposure to only the transfer learning task. The C-1 condition allowed the investigators to evaluate the differential effects of the three types of training on the child's ability to learn to identify (read) printed words derived from an alphabet, and, thereafter, capitalize on their alphabetic properties in learning new words. Because it controlled for generalization and intrusion (reversal) errors that might be caused by previous exposure to words presented on the initial learning task (e.g., calling *zog* /*zob*/ or calling *bav* /*vab*/ *as in* calling *was* /*saw*/), the C-2 condition allowed the investigators to evaluate the effects of the three treatment and the C-1 control conditions on the child's tendency to make such errors. In all instances, assessments on pre- and posttreatment measures and implementation of experimental conditions took place in a quiet room outside a participants' classroom. Note also that for all five experimental conditions, time spent with an examiner was equated through "filler" activities unrelated to the experimental tasks.

Finally, to further evaluate the differential effects of the treatment conditions, an alternate form of the phoneme segmentation test administered to all participants before they were exposed to given experimental conditions was administered to each participant approximately 2 weeks after administration of the paired associates task used as the primary outcome measure (see Figure 7.1 for a summary of the design).

Space limitations preclude a detailed account of results from this study. It will suffice to point out that the data were consistent with the hypothesis that the whole-word/meaning-based and code-oriented approaches to word identification are both important components of reading instruction insofar as the children exposed to the treatment conditions that simulated these approaches (RA and PST, respectively) performed significantly better on the initial learning

Experimental Conditions	Phonemic segmentation training	Response acquisition		Code acquisition	
		Free recall	Picture syllable association	Symbol syllable training	Symbol syllable transfer
PST	X	N.A.	N.A.	X	X
RA	N.A.	X	X	X	X
PSTRA	X	X	X	X	X
CONTROL-1	N.A.	N.A.	N.A.	X	X
CONTROL-2	N.A.	N.A.	N.A.	N.A.	X

FIGURE 7.1. Order of tasks administered to subjects in each experimental condition of the study of the effects of phonemic segmentation training and response acquisition training on code acquisition. N.A., not administered; filler activities unrelated to the experiment were substituted in order to control for time spent with the examiner outside of the classroom; PST, phonemic segmentation training; RA, response acquisition; PSTRA, phonemic segmentation training and response acquisition; CONTROL-1, received both symbol syllable training and symbol syllable transfer tasks; CONTROL-2, received only symbol syllable transfer task.

task (code acquisition training) used as the primary outcome measure than did the control children exposed to this task (C-1). Moreover, the children exposed to the condition that incorporated both approaches (PSTRA) performed significantly better on the code acquisition training task than did those exposed to the other three conditions. This pattern of results was observed in all reader groups at all grades levels, with the exception of the second grade poor readers. The second grade poor readers who were exposed to the PST condition performed as well as those in the group exposed to the PSTRA condition and both of these groups performed better on the initial learning task than did the second grade poor readers exposed to the RA and C-1 conditions. However, on the transfer learning task (code acquisition transfer), the children in all the reader groups exposed to conditions that facilitated the use of letter sounds to mediate word identification (PST and PSTRA) performed significantly better than did children in any of the other groups, and made fewer generalization and intrusion errors (e.g., *was/saw* types of reversals) from the initial learning task than did children in all other groups, save for the C-2 control children who had not been exposed to the initial learning task. Finally, children in the PST and PSTRA groups performed better on the posttreatment phoneme segmentation test than did children in all other groups.

The study just described provides a reasonable illustration of the relative merits of randomized designs in general and randomized factorial designs in particular. In regard to the validity of causal inferences about given treatment effects, the fact that children in each reader group at each grade level were randomly assigned to each of the five experimental conditions, and that sample sizes were adequate for the contrasts of interest, minimized most of the various threats to internal validity discussed (e.g., selection bias, history, testing, instrumentation, and regression to the mean), except for attrition and exposure to pretreatment testing. Attrition was not a problem in this study because the experimental itinerary was implemented very soon after participants were identified, which resulted in an attrition rate of zero. Pretreatment testing effects (e.g., test–retest) were minimized by the use of an alternate form, at posttest, of the phoneme segmentation test administered at pretest and by the fact that the primary outcome measures were experimental tasks that the participants had not previously encountered. Moreover, given that the experimental design incorporated different treatments tied directly to different predicted effects on different outcome measures, in addition to two control groups allowing evaluation of these predicted effects, there were several complementary sources of counterfactual inference provided by this design. Thus, by most standards, this study had a high degree of internal validity. This conclusion is buttressed by the finding that treatments effects were replicated across different groups of participants.

That statistical conclusion validity was reasonably high in this study is suggested by the finding that treatment effects were generally robust (p values typically $< .001$), implying adequate power, and by the finding that the pattern of results was replicated across participant groups using different outcome measures, implying adequate reliability of assessment instruments and experimental results. Similarly, the construct validity and external validity of the participants in this study seems assured by (1) the fact that poor and normal reader groups were selected in accord with psychometric and exclusionary criteria typically used to distinguish these groups; (2) the finding that group differences were observed on independent measures that typically distinguish the groups (e.g., phoneme segmentation and pseudoword decoding) as well as on experimental measures that should (theoretically) distinguish between them; and (3) the fact that results can be generalized to both typical and diverse samples of participants (i.e., poor and normal readers in second and sixth grades). One can also have confidence in the construct validity of the treatment and outcome measures insofar as each was defined on the basis of theoretical analyses of word-recognition processes in developing readers grounded in a great deal of empirical research. Moreover, typical threats to construct validity of treatments, such as treatment diffusion, mono-operation bias, and monomethod bias were minimized by the use of a factorial design, by the use of different outcome measures tied to different predicted outcomes, and by the finding that hypothesized outcomes on these measures were observed in different populations of participants. Little can be said of the construct validity of the settings in which the experiment was conducted, except that they constituted a random sampling of "quiet rooms outside the child's classroom" and, therefore, could be considered representative examples of such settings.

Perhaps the major problem with the Vellutino and Scanlon (1987) study is the external validity of the treatment effects observed in the study under the conditions in which these effects were observed. It will suffice to point out that because reading instruction is carried out in classrooms rather than in restricted laboratory-like settings, such as those used in the study, with instruction implemented with an entire class (or small groups), rather than with one child at a time, and because the different treatments were "capsule versions" of the different approaches to reading instruction that used novel materials to control for previous learning and were implemented over restricted periods of time, it was not clear at the time the study was conducted that obtained results would generalize to more natural settings. To be more specific, it must be acknowledged that children do not normally acquire new vocabulary words by associating them with cartoon characters, which was our method of imbuing the nonsense words used in certain of the experimental conditions with meaning. Moreover, many of the measures used on the simulated reading tasks involved reading of nonsense words, and nonsense words are not in children's listening vocabularies. Similarly, children do not normally acquire different reading strategies and learn to read new words over the 1- to 8-day time period that encompassed the different experimental conditions compared in this study. Thus, the simulated reading tasks presented to the children who participated in this study were clearly artificial, as were the experimental conditions under which they were presented, and the external validity of this study can justifiably be questioned. Yet, despite this weakness of the study, recent intervention research has provided independent confirmation that both meaning-based and code-oriented approaches to instruction are important ingredients in facilitating the acquisition of functional literacy skills (e.g., Hiebert & Taylor, 2000; Foorman et al., 1998; Torgesen, 2000; Vellutino et al., 1996), thereby lending additional support for one of the central hypotheses the study was designed to evaluate. Indeed, the fact that this hypothesis has been cross validated in classroom, small-group, and one-to-one tutoring studies, as well as in a randomized experiment designed to simulate beginning reading, is rather compelling and reinforces our assertion that conducting programmatic research and multiple experiments across many venues is a critically important ingredient in validating causal inferences in literacy research.

AN EXEMPLAR OF A QUASI-EXPERIMENTAL DESIGN

One example of a literacy research study that employed a quasi-experimental design was conducted by a group of literacy researchers of which one of us was a member (Foorman et al., 1998). This year-long study was designed to compare the effects of three types of literacy instruction on a group of children receiving Title 1 services. Two hundred eighty-five first- and second-grade students received one of three types of classroom reading programs. The programs differed in the amount of direct instruction in alphabetic coding that the children in each classroom received. The *direct code* group received explicit instruction in letter–sound correspondences and practiced using them in decodable text. The *embedded code* group received less direct instruction but practiced with systematic sound–spelling patterns that were embedded in text. The *implicit code* group received implicit instruction in the alphabetic code within the context of text reading. A fourth group was identified in the study as a *control group* that received the school district's standard form of reading instruction, which was similar to the type of implicit instruction that the children in the implicit code group received, except that the teachers in the control group did not receive supplementary assistance in implementing the instruction (see discussion later).

Randomly selected children from each classroom were assessed five times a year to evaluate growth in reading and reading related skills. To assess fidelity of treatments, reading instruction in experimental classrooms was either audiotaped or was observed by trained observers to assess whether the teacher was adhering to the reading program. Teacher ratings of child performance and behavior were also obtained, along with school records of attendance. Achievement data from this study were analyzed using hierarchical linear modeling to assess growth in reading and end-of-year outcomes. The results of the study indicated that children who received direct code instruction improved significantly faster in the acquisition of word-identification skills than did children who received implicit code instruction, with the embedded code groups not differing significantly from either the direct code or implicit code groups. The impact of direct code instruction was moderated by initial level of phonological processing skills in that those children with the lowest levels of phonological processing skills benefited the most from direct code instruction.

Unfortunately, the experimental and control groups were constituted based on the willingness of teachers and other school officials to participate in the study and not via random assignment. This meant that other strategies had to be employed to ensure that treatment effects were due to the experimental treatments and not to extraneous or confounding variables. A combination of strategies was employed to achieve this objective. First, the study employed two comparison groups. We wanted to know whether explicit instruction was better than implicit instruction in helping children from disadvantaged backgrounds to learn how to read. The school district in which the study was conducted had already been using implicit instruction in all its schools. In most cases, allowing classroom teachers to implement the type of reading instruction they would normally implement would provide a natural instance of a hypothetical counterfactual. However, in this case, we were concerned that the mere implementation of any new program might have an effect, which would be a concern for both experimental and quasi-experimental research designs. The teachers in the experimental conditions were slated to receive extensive training over the summer and support throughout the year to implement the new treatments. This presented the possibility that attending reading workshops (for any program) over the summer and receiving supplemental support might themselves cause reading scores to improve. So we constituted another group (the implicit code group) that received implicit instruction that was essentially the same as that implemented in control classrooms, but the teachers from these classrooms also received extensive training during the summer and support throughout the year, just like the direct code and embedded code groups. Thus, any differences between the two implicit code groups could be attributed to the differential training they received in providing implicit instruction.

Because random assignment was not possible in this study, serious threats to internal validity had to be addressed. Our first concern was that the groups would not be comparable at the beginning of the year on variables that we thought would impact reading. To address these concerns, we analyzed pretest data and found that the four groups did not significantly differ on word reading and phonological awareness. Although these groups were still vulnerable to a hidden unobserved bias, we tried to provide evidence that the groups were comparable on variables that were important to reading. We also examined variables that might have had an impact on children throughout the year. Specifically, there were no differences among the groups in rates of attrition or in school attendance. Moreover, teachers across all conditions were reported as implementing their respective reading programs with a high level of fidelity. Because we tested children five times throughout the year, practice effects were highly probable. With this type of design, the experimenter has no way of knowing how much of the growth during the year might be due to practice effects. However, it seemed reasonable to assume that practice effects would affect all groups equally, and that the impact of test practice on differences between group means would be minimal.

Statistical conclusion validity was addressed in a number of ways. First, we took into account the fact that these students were not statistically independent of each other because some of the children in the study came from the same classroom. One assumption common to all inferential statistical procedures is that each observation is independent of each other. This assumption, called the *independence assumption*, is one of the most important assumptions in statistics. Indeed, even small violations of independence can lead to a large increase in type I error rate (Scariano & Davenport, 1987; Stevens, 1992). In this study, we could not assume that children in the same classroom were independent of each other. That is, we had to account for the possibility that teachers influence the children in their classrooms in ways that might make them more similar to each other than students in other classrooms. This is why we employed hierarchical linear modeling (HLM) as our main statistical tool. HLM allows for the estimation of treatment effects while accounting for the fact that children may not be statistically independent of each other.

Other statistical techniques were employed to provide additional control over extraneous influences. We had originally planned to use initial levels of phonological awareness measured at pretest as a covariate in the analyses, but while examining the assumption of homogeneity of regression, we discovered that phonological awareness at pretest interacted with the treatment to produce differential results. We explored this interaction and found that the effects of the treatment groups were more pronounced for children who had lower initial levels of phonological awareness skill. So, in this instance, the effects of initial levels of phonological awareness were more adequately accounted for in the model and we would have lost important information about causal relationships of interest in this study, if we had not evaluated the moderating effects of phonological awareness and simply used this measure as a pretest covariate.

We also tried to control for type I error by using the Bonferroni correction to adjust the alpha level for the group-wise mean comparisons. A more stringent approach would have been to also correct for the number of different dependent variables that were analyzed. When considering ways to limit type I error, there is a balance that must be struck between statistical power (the ability to detect an effect if it exists) and controlling type I error. All else being equal, the power of a particular test will decrease as the control for type I error increases (Maxwell & Delaney, 1990). We decided that we would lose too much statistical power to correct for the total number of comparisons being made. However, we did leave ourselves open to the criticism that type I error was not adequately controlled.

We also addressed concerns about construct validity and mono-method bias by making multiple assessments of the variables thought to be important in studying the impacts of the treatment. We assessed phonological awareness using seven different tests and reading using two tests of word identification and two tests of reading comprehension. Some constructs, however, were only measured by one test (such as IQ and vocabulary). When designing studies, it is difficult to balance the amount of assessment time with the number of constructs that the researcher would like to measure.

Finally, the evidence for the external validity of results from this study is less clear. While the study was conducted in a school-based setting, there are some weaknesses to the design of the study that could mitigate generalizations to the target population. First, this was not a random sample from a population of all children receiving benefits from Title I funds. Thus, it is not possible to estimate how this sample might be different from the population of Title I students at large (e.g., those outside the geographic area where we conducted the study). In this sense, it was a sample of convenience. So, it is difficult to say how these results would replicate in another Title I sample. Also, the teachers who implemented the experimental reading programs that were administered to the various classrooms received support and training throughout the school year. Thus, it is possible that these same effects may not be observed in another sample if the level of support provided were to change. This underscores the importance of multiple studies that employ different designs that possess different strengths and weaknesses to attempt to triangulate on the existence and strength of a particular effect. In fact, the results from this study are consistent with the findings from an increasingly large body of studies demonstrating that explicit training to facilitate functional use of the alphabetic principle does have positive effects (e.g., Ball & Blachman, 1991; Bradley & Bryant, 1983; Blachman, 1997; Torgesen, 2000; Vellutino et al., 1996).

SUMMARY

Because of significant methodological advances in the basic and applied sciences, especially during the 20th century, literacy researchers now have access to a multitude of methods for addressing important questions in research concerned with literacy development and how best to facilitate adequate literacy development. The method(s) employed in conducting any piece of research in this area of inquiry, will, of course, depend on the nature of the questions addressed, but, for purposes of establishing causal relationships that will generalize across units, treatments, outcome measures, and settings, the experimental method is the method of choice. In this chapter, we discussed the two most general and widely used experimental methods for establishing causal relationships: the experimental design and the quasi-experimental design. We discussed these designs within the context of a validity typology forwarded by Shadish et al. (2002) and pointed out that they are similar in that both entail deliberate manipulation of treatments for the purpose of observing hypothesized effects; both ensure that hypothesized causes precede hypothesized effects; both are based on the principle of counterfactual inferencing, insofar as both incorporate procedures (e.g., control groups) that allow the experimenter to approximate effects on outcome measures under the hypothetical circumstance where treatments had and had not been administered to the same units; and both incorporate procedures that allow the experimenter to minimize and/or assess the influence of extraneous factors that could produce the effect(s) hypothesized to be attributed to the treatment(s). But, whereas in experimental designs, units are assigned to experimental conditions randomly, in quasi-experimental designs, units are assigned to treatments nonrandomly, typically for practical reasons. In discussing the advantages and disadvantages of both designs, we pointed out that randomized experimental designs are better able to create adequate hypothetical counterfactuals than are quasi-experimental designs because they create experimental groups that are (on average) similar to one another on relevant variables before treatments are administered; they decrease the plausibility of most threats to internal validity (save for attrition) by distributing them randomly across experimental conditions and, thereby, increase the probability that systematic differences that occur between treatment and control groups are due to experimental treatments rather to extraneous factors. In contrast, quasi-experimental designs must rely more heavily on additional design features (pretreatment assessment, additional control groups, coherent pattern matching, etc.) and statistical controls to identify and control plausible threats to internal validity and ensure adequacy of counterfactual inferencing.

Finally, to concretize methodological issues we discussed concerning threats to validity and standards of quality in experimental design, we described, in some detail, two studies that have appeared in the literacy research literature in recent years, one exemplifying a randomized experimental design and a second exemplifying a quasi-experimental design. We underscored the strengths and weaknesses of each, vis-à-vis the threats to validity and standards of quality we outlined earlier. In so doing, we hope that we have made it clear that no experimental design perfectly controls all threats to validity and all have flaws and weaknesses that limit their contribution to the research community and to the knowledge base. Indeed, a causal relationship that is detected in a single experiment must be independently replicated in programmatic research and across variations in units, treatments, outcome measures, and settings before the research community can have any faith in that relationship. This is one reason why the knowledge base in a given area of inquiry tends to accumulate slowly. That said, each individual experiment, in its own way, contributes incrementally to programs of research that can eventually offer clear and reasonably coherent conclusions about literacy education.

ACKNOWLEDGMENTS

Much of the work discussed in this paper was supported by grants from the National Institute of Child Health and Human Development. The data for the experimental study reported in Vellutino and Scanlon (1987) were collected under the auspices ofNICHD grant RO1 HD 09658, awarded to Vellutino. Other NICHD grants involving Vellutino contributed to the creation of this chapter, specifically RO1 HD34598 and RO1 HD42350. The data for the quasi-experimental study reported in Foorman et al. (1998) was supported by NICHD grants HD 30995 and HD 28172, awarded to Barbara Foorman.

REFERENCES

Backman, J. E., Mamen, M., & Ferguson, H. B. (1984). Reading level design: Conceptual and methodological issues in reading research. *Psychological Bulletin, 96,* 560–568.

Ball, E. W., & Blachman, B. A. (1991). Does phoneme awareness training in kindergarten make a difference in early word recognition and developmental spelling? *Reading Research Quarterly, 26,* 49–66.

Blachman, B. A. (1997). Early intervention and phonological awareness: A cautionary tale. In B. A. Blachman (Ed.) *Foundations of reading acquisition and dyslexia: Implications for early intervention* (pp. 409–430). Mahwah, NJ: Erlbaum.

Bradley, L., & Bryant, P. E. (1983). Categorizing sounds and learning to read—A causal connection. *Nature, 301,* 419–421.

Bryant, P., & Goswami, U. (1986). Strengths and weaknesses of the reading level design: A comment on Backman, Mamen, and Ferguson. *Psychological Bulletin, 100,* 101–103.

Campbell, D. T., & Stanley, J. C. (1963). *Experimental and quasi-experimental designs for research.* Chicago: Rand McNally.

Dawes, R. M. (1994). *House of cards: Psychology and psychotherapy built on myth.* New York: Free Press.

Drake, S. (1981). *Cause, experiment, and science.* Chicago: University of Chicago Press.

Fisher, R. A. (1925). *Statistical methods for research workers.* Edinburg, Scotland: Oliver & Boyd.

Fisher, R. A. (1935). *The design of experiments.* Edinburg, Scotland: Oliver & Boyd.

Foorman, B. R., Francis, D. J., Fletcher, J. M., Schatschneider, C., & Mehta, P. (1998). The role of instruction in learning to read: Preventing reading failure in at-risk children. *Journal of Educational Psychology, 90,* 37–55.

Hume, D. (1999). In T. Brauchamp (Ed.), *An enquiry concerning human understanding* (Oxford Philosophical Texts). Oxford, UK: Oxford University Press. (Original work published 1748)

Lewis, D. (1973). Causation. *Journal of Philosophy, 70,* 556–567.

Maxwell, S. E., & Delaney, H. D. (1990). *Designing experiments and analyzing data: A model comparison approach.* Belmont, CA: Wadsworth.

Mill, J. S. (1843). A system of logic: Ratiocinative and inductive. In J. S. Mill, J. Bentham, & R. Ryan (Eds.), *Utilitarianism and other essays.* New York: Viking.

Scariano, S. M., & Davenport, J. M. (1987). The effects of violations of the independence assumption in the one way ANOVA. *The American Statistician, 41,* 123–129.

Shadish, W. R., Cook, T. D., & Campbell, D. T. (2002). *Experimental and quasi-experimental designs for general causal inference.* Boston: Houghton Mifflin.

Stevens, J. (1992). *Applied multivariate statistics for the social sciences* (2nd ed.). Hillsdale, NJ: Erlbaum.

Torgesen, J. K. (2000). Individual differences in response to early interventions in reading: The lingering problem of treatment resisters. *Learning Disabilities Research and Practice 15*(1),55–64.

Vellutino, F. R., & Scanlon, D. M. (1987). Phonological coding, phonological awareness, and reading ability: Evidence from a longitudinal and experimental study. *Merrill–Palmer Quarterly, 33,* 321–363.

Vellutino, F. R., & Scanlon, D. M. (1989). Some prerequisites for interpreting results from reading level matched designs. *Journal of Reading Behavior, 21*(4), 361–385.

Vellutino, F. R., Scanlon, D. M., Sipay, E., Small, S., Pratt, A., Chen, R., & Denckla, M. (1996). Cognitive profiles of difficult-to-remediate and readily remediated poor readers: Early intervention as a vehicle for distinguishing between cognitive and experiential deficits as basic causes of specific reading disability. *Journal of Educational Psychology, 88,* 601–638.

Winship, C., & Morgan, S. L. (1999). The estimation of causal effects from observational data. *Annual Review of Sociology, 25,* 659–707.

CHAPTER 8

Connecting Research and Practice Using Formative and Design Experiments

David Reinking
Barbara A. Bradley

There has always been a great divide between education research and practice.

—COLLINS (1999, p. 289)

How can and how should literacy research inform instructional practice? These questions are central to the rationale for formative, or design, experiments, the research methodology we present in this chapter. Educational researchers who have gravitated toward this methodology have typically done so because they are dissatisfied with more established and widely used experimental or naturalistic methodologies. The warrant for that dissatisfaction can be found in considering the relation between conventional research methodologies and instructional practice. Thus, that is where we begin.

For example, at the time we are writing this chapter, the U.S. government is vigorously promoting the view that experimental methods should be the gold standard for implementing scientifically based reading instruction (National Reading Panel Report, 2000). Those who hold this view believe that practitioners should design and implement literacy instruction to be consistent with generalizations derived across carefully controlled experiments. They see the role of literacy research as a systematic winnowing to determine which among many alternative instructional interventions or approaches work best on average. What works best is typically defined narrowly as instruction that results in statistically superior student achievement based on quantifiable measures. Determining what works best on average to promote educational achievement is useful information, but it does not inherently provide guidance about what factors might be relevant to successful implementation in a particular context.

Researchers who employ naturalistic methodologies, on the other hand, also, generate useful information, but of a different kind. Because such methodologies are suited to a deep examination of particular instructional contexts, they produce data that are perhaps more useful in helping practitioners understand the complexities and subtleties of instructional practice. When studying classroom instruction, these researchers often aim to reveal aspects of instructional practice that might otherwise go unnoticed by practitioners or that might help them better understand and reflect on their practice. Strong generalizations about practice or conclusions about best methods are not typically the goal of such studies, although they may be guided by and interpreted in light of pedagogical theories, educational philosophies, or ideologies designed to provide a broad frame for instruction. The topics investigated typically are not related to conventional measures of achievement but, instead, tend to focus on dimensions of literacy such as developing motivation to read, acquiring personal agency through texts, and promoting sociocultural awareness.

For some researchers, the best of all worlds would be one in which these two broad methodological options would be complementary, perhaps creating a synergy that would guide teachers and improve instructional practice toward realizing a wide range of valued goals for literacy instruction. However, that has not often been the case. Not only have literacy researchers employing these different methodologies been unlikely to collaborate in gathering data or synthesizing their respective findings (see Oldfather & Wigfield, 1996, for a notable exception), they typically work in distinctly separate research communities sometimes characterized by competition, if not animosity. Further, as many writers have noted, educational research in general, whether it be experimental or naturalistic, has not had a pervasive influence on classroom practice (e.g., Collins, 1999; Eisenhart & Borko, 1993; Lagemann, 2000). One commentator has characterized educational research as a "lesser form of knowledge" and consequently suggests that the field should lower its expectations about the extent to which research should guide instructional practice (Labaree, 1998, p. 4).

The explanation for the gap between research and practice is surely a complicated one. However, we agree with those who have pointed out that a major reason this gap exists is that the work of educational researchers and the work of teachers are often disconnected. For example, Eisenhart and Borko (1993) have stated, "Researchers see the significance of research in terms of its implications for understanding far-ranging repercussions, predicting and improving the future, information policy, or getting tenure, whereas teachers usually want research results to bear directly on their classroom practice" (p. 79).

What is missing, we argue, is a research methodology that addresses specifically how promising instructional interventions might be implemented in classrooms to achieve valued pedagogical goals. Such a methodology would acknowledge the complexities of classroom teaching and be aligned with the day-to-day management of that complexity. It not only would enlighten practitioners about research-based pedagogies to enhance literacy, but would provide them with specific insights about how they might effectively implement instructional interventions. In short, it would narrow the gap between research and practice, serving as an intermediary between the findings generated by other methodologies and the realities of teaching. Formative, or design, experiments aim to fill that gap, and they may contribute to synthesizing in action the work of researchers who hold diverse methodological perspectives (McCandliss, Kachman, & Bryant, 2003). In the remainder of this chapter we explain this methodology in relation to other methodologies, trace its roots, offer general guidelines for those who wish to employ it, and provide one example of its use in literacy research.

WHAT ARE FORMATIVE EXPERIMENTS AND DESIGN EXPERIMENTS?

> Classroom life, in my judgment, is too complex an affair
> to be viewed or talked about from any single perspective.
> —JACKSON (1990, pp. xxi–xxii)

A Note about Terminology

Before addressing the question central to this section, we want to simplify the terminology we use in the remainder of this chapter. If there are differences between formative experiments and design experiments, those differences are subtle and have not been clearly delineated in the literature. Design experiments perhaps focus on broader educational goals and theory development (Design-Based Research Collective, 2003) and less specifically on a particular intervention, whereas the emphasis may be somewhat reversed for those who prefer the term *formative experiments*. Nonetheless, we believe that formative and design experiments are more closely related to each other than they are to other approaches that have similar goals and use similar approaches to data collection such as formative evaluation (Flagg, 1990), situated evaluation (Bruce & Rubin, 1993), rapid prototyping (Tripp & Bichelmeyer, 1990), and developmental work research (Engstrom, Miettinen, & Punamäki, 1998). Thus, for the sake of economy, we use both terms interchangeably but in most cases use *formative experiment*. We choose the term *formative experiment* over *design experiment* for no other reason than we have adopted that term in our own work and it has been used by other literacy researchers (e.g., Jimènez, 1997; Neuman, 1999). However, we wish to emphasize that one of the earliest references to the methodology underlying both terms was referred to as a "design experiment" (Brown, 1992, p. 141) and that term continues to be used by some researchers (Cobb, Confrey, diSessa, Lehrer, & Schauble, 2003). Both terms, *formative* and *design*, as we will explain in subsequent sections of this chapter, highlight important dimensions of this methodology.

Conceptualizing Formative Experiments in Relation to Other Methodologies

> The study of how educational interventions work can never be far removed from the task of engineering them to work better.
> —NEWMAN, GRIFFIN, AND COLE (1989, p. 147)

> Educational research often sits in the uneasy intersection between science and engineering.
> —FEURER, TOWNE, AND SHAVELSON (2002, p. 28)

Formative experiments fill a neglected gap in research aimed at guiding instruction, because they address more directly the questions and issues that practitioners face and that are not addressed by other research methodologies. That is, scientific inquiry comparing the effectiveness of alternative instructional interventions provide useful generalizations across diverse contexts. However, experimental studies of classroom interventions must simplify and control the wide range of variation that is inherent in classrooms and schools and that often influences the effectiveness of an intervention in a particular classroom (Labbo & Reinking, 1999). Further, for experimental research to be valid, an instructional intervention must be implemented in a standard fashion, not adapted to unique or changing conditions (see Reinking & Pickle, 1993, for an example of how this is problematic). Ignoring the panoply of variables that are continually fluctuating in classrooms and failing to adapt instruction to those variables are contrary to the essence of teaching. Naturalistic studies, on the other hand, may document the complexity and subtleties of implementing an intervention, but they do not typically address how that complexity might be managed by a practitioner working to accomplish specific pedagogical goals. Formative experiments, unlike experimental or naturalistic studies of instructional interventions, accommodate both the variation inherent in classrooms and the need to adapt interventions in response to relevant variation.

To oversimplify for the sake of comparison, a controlled experiment might ask: "Which intervention is better on average, X or Y?" (What is best?) A naturalistic study might ask: "When implementing intervention X (or Y), what happens?" (What is?) A formative experiment, on the other hand, is best suited for the following type of question: "Given that intervention X (or pedagogical theory Y) shows promise to bring about a valued pedagogical goal, can it be implemented to accomplish that goal, and, if so, how?" (What could be?) Two other key questions are important to understanding a formative experiment: What factors enhance or inhibit an intervention's effectiveness in moving toward the pedagogical goal? How might the intervention or its implementation be modified, in light of these factors, to be more effective? It is these latter two questions that make a formative experiment formative. That is, formative experiments entail an iterative process of data collection to determine what is or is not working followed by carefully reasoned modifications, as needed, to enhance the effectiveness of the intervention. (Or, in terms of the *design* in design experiments, how can instruction be designed to realize a pedagogical goal?)

A formative experiment is also an experiment, but in a sense broader than the formal hypothesis testing that guides a controlled experiment. Schön (1987) in his seminal book on reflective practice argued that several forms of experimentation are useful and that three forms are used simultaneously by reflective practitioners: (1) *exploratory experimentation*, which is action just to see what happens; (2) *move-testing experimentation*, which is aimed at determining whether an action is affirmed or negated toward a desired end, and to note any unintended consequences; and (3) *hypothesis testing*, which is formal experimentation to see whether alternative hypotheses are affirmed or negated. Formative experiments employ all three types of experimentation, just as reflective teachers do, but formative experiments entail a more systematic record of this experimentation and typically include collegial discussions and overt reflections based on careful data collection. Thus, formative experiments, because they address questions clearly relevant to practitioners, and because they employ forms of experimentation similar to practitioners, are more directly related to practice than to other forms of research and are more likely to appeal to practitioners. A further advantage of formative experiments, when compared to more dominant research methodologies, is that they draw on and acknowledge the importance of intuitive professional knowledge, incorporating that knowledge within a systematic framework for practice-oriented research.

Engineering might be a useful analogy for conceptualizing formative experiments in relation to other education research methodologies, and here the term *design experiment* might be more apt. Engineers make use of theoretical and empirical research to design something of practical value. Their work builds bridges (sometimes literally) between theory, research, and practical application. But, workability in the real world is the essence of their work, where sometime relevant variables only emerge in the real-world application of theoretical or laboratory research. Wind tunnels are clearly useful in designing airplanes consistent with the principles of aerodynamics, but wind tunnels may not easily simulate the sustained wear some parts experience during thousands of hours of real flying conditions. Further, the work of engineers in the real world of practical application can sometimes clarify or stimulate the need for more theoretical and laboratory investigations. In fact, Stokes (1997) has argued that often the most important theoretical concepts in science emerge when scientists focus their attention on achieving practical goals. He highlights Louis Pasteur's work in seeking ways to preserve food as a classic example of how the distinction between basic and applied research is often an unfortunate dichotomy.

Likewise, knowledge of what has or has not worked under a variety of practical conditions allows engineers and mechanics to acquire useful intuitive knowledge that may lead them occasionally to work outside or beyond accepted theory and research. Duffy (1994) has acknowledged that such intuitive knowledge is necessary for teaching. He stated, "Viewing research findings as something to be handed down as technical information ignores the reality that teachers must make strategic decisions about when to apply findings, how to adapt them to certain situations and even when it might be appropriate to ignore the findings altogether" (p. 19). Thus, formative experiments value and systematically identify how the intuitive knowledge of experienced practitioners might elucidate and refine, and perhaps occasionally negate, the findings generated by other research methodologies. In that sense formative experiments focus on what has been referred to as conditional knowledge (Paris, Lipson, & Wixson, 1983) and the knowledge that is necessary to be a successful practitioner in ill-structured domains such as teaching (Spiro, Feltovich, Jacobson, & Coulson, 1992).

A formative experiment then, with its emphasis on workability or achievability, is a methodological parallel to a science of engineering that tests theory and empirical research in the real world of practice. It employs systematic and rigorous data collection, qualitative and quantitative, toward achieving a desired pedagogical goal while valuing intuitive knowledge and engaging in experimentation beyond formal hypotheses testing. Further, formative experiments are aimed toward generating research that not only is more directly relevant to practice but can inform theory development and identify variables that might be investigated through conventional experimental or naturalistic approaches. Nonetheless, despite our use of engineering as a metaphor to understand formative experiments, like most metaphors, it has its limits. We do not wish to suggest that formative experiments should be associated with the concept of social engineering, which suggests that human interactions can be or ought to be controlled or manipulated to accomplish a researcher's vision of the world. The pedagogical goals that drive formative experiments do not exist in a vacuum, but exist, like all educational research, within a web of sometime conflicting values, ideologies, and epistemologies.

HISTORICAL AND PARADIGMATIC ROOTS

> Ignorance is a better starting place than truth for assessing the usefulness of educational research ... some research projects are of little use to researchers or practitioners even though they reflect our highest ideals of truthfulness in data collection and analysis.
> —WAGNER (1993, p. 15)

Tracing the origin of formative experiments as a research methodology is akin to identifying the headwaters of a river. There seems to be no single, clearly identifiable source for the concept or for the term.

Instead, formative experiments have emerged from and been supported by the ideas of diverse researchers and writers in the late 1980s and early 1990s who shared a dissatisfaction with experimental methods as a means for informing instructional practice. Many of these writers also saw improving education as the critical goal of educational research (see Moll & Diaz, 1987). However, formative experiments, or related methodologies, have not emerged strictly among researchers interested in conventional school learning. They have been employed by researchers in other fields interested in implementing effective interventions in a variety of areas (e.g., health care—see Gittleson et al., 1998, for an example and a review; communication design—see Atkin & Freimuth, 1991; and work environments—see Engeström et al., 1998).

Jacob (1992), who discussed formative experiments in her chapter in the *The Handbook of Qualitative Research in Education,* traced the roots of formative experiments to neo-Vygotskian scholars (e.g., Davydov, 1988) and to cognitive psychologists who became interested in the social construction of psychological tasks. Newman, Griffin, and Cole (1989) articulated some of the tenets of this view, and subsequently Newman (1990) used the term *formative experiment* to describe his study of how computer technology might be used to enhance scientific thinking among middle school students. That study was important because it was the first to outline and illustrate a specific methodological framework for conducting a formative experiment. Brown (1992) contributed an often-cited article that described her own turn as a classical theorist to *design experiments*, a term she attributed to Collins (1992). Brown stated, "As a design scientist in my field, I attempt to engineer innovative educational environments and simultaneously conduct experimental studies on those innovations" (p. 141). Her article was particularly important in familiarizing literacy researchers with this methodology because of her well-known and highly regarded work on the metacognitive aspects of reading.

Since the mid-1990s, several literacy researchers have published work employing the methodology of formative experiments. Several of these studies (Jimènez, 1997; Neuman, 1999; Reinking & Watkins, 2000), have been published in *Reading Research Quarterly*, a highly regarded outlet for literacy research. Contemporary with our own research using this methodology, we have attempted to articulate the basis and need for formative experiments, and more important how methodology might be translated into specific methods for conducting a formative experiment (Baumann, Dillon, Shockley, Alvermann, & Reinking, 1996; Reinking & Pickle, 1993; Reinking &

Watkins, 2000). However, it is clear to us, particularly after participating in a symposium on formative experiments at the annual meeting of National Reading Conference in 1997, that literacy researchers
employing formative experiments, while they may share many fundamental assumptions about methodology, do not have a consensus
about its procedural and interpretive dimensions (see Neuman,
Jimènez, Reinking, & Au, 1997).

As we have noted previously in this chapter, formative experiments share many conceptual and methodological characteristics
with related approaches referred to by different terms. Perhaps most
closely related to formative experiments is Bruce and Rubin's (1993)
work, which they describe as *situated evaluation*. The need for situated
evaluation emerged from their discovery that teachers did not necessarily implement innovative instructional interventions, in this case a
computer-based intervention to enhance purposeful reading and
writing, in ways consistent with the intent of the developers. We believe that such an insight is a critical but neglected one in other educational research methodologies and a key advantage of formative experiments. Their work also points to another aspect of formative
experiments. They have been used frequently to investigate instructional innovations, particularly the use of new computer-based technologies. The belief that new technologies have the potential to
transform instruction has led several researchers who share this belief
to employ formative experiments in their research. It also explains
why those in the field of instructional technology have developed
and used related concepts such as formative evaluation (Flagg, 1990)
and rapid prototyping (Tripp & Bichelmeyer, 1990). This plethora of
terms and interpretations gives testimony to the conceptual power of
formative experiments but at the same time illustrates the muddiness
of the waters concerning precisely what they are conceptually and
procedurally.

To our knowledge, no one has proposed an explicit theoretical,
paradigmatic, or philosophical foundation for formative experiments
as a research methodology. However, we believe that such a foundation operates implicitly among those who have used formative experiments and might be articulated more explicitly within the existing
literature. For example, activity theory (Engeström et al., 1998) has
explicitly guided developmental work research, a methodology similar to formative experiments. Activity theory suggests that change in
work environments can only be brought about by acknowledging the
relation between sociohistorical context, the objects and tools that
are integral to the work environment, and the social interactions that
mediate their use. However, we believe that formative experiments

and related methodologies fit most naturally with the philosophical tenets of pragmatism, which has been associated with education and education research since John Dewey and which has been revived as a paradigm useful to educational research in general (Cherryholmes, 1993) and to literacy research in particular (Dillon, O'Brien, & Heilman, 2000). Pragmatism seems especially well suited to the aims and methods of formative experiments. For example, it allows for more epistemological flexibility in method and analysis, focuses on useful ends, and encourages a democratic involvement of multiple stakeholders, which is illustrated in the example that follows subsequently in this chapter.

DISTINGUISHING METHODOLOGICAL CHARACTERISTICS

> Educational research is evolving; its designs and
> procedures are not cast in stone. Conscientious
> researchers are continually trying out new methods . . .
> to make their work stronger, more compelling, and more
> useful.
> —EISENHART AND BORKO (1993, p. 11)

Given the diverse origins of formative experiments and related methodologies, and the lack of a well-articulated paradigmatic frame, it is understandable that there is no consensual, authoritative source explicitly identifying their essential characteristics or procedural components. That is, there is no equivalent to Campbell and Stanley (1963) in designing and conducting experimental studies or, for example, to Strauss and Corbin (1990) for naturalistic studies. In fact, given the emphasis on educational outcomes in formative experiments, such specificity may actually work against the flexibility and fluidity that are necessary for researchers who employ this methodology and that have been argued to be necessary to moving the field of literacy research forward (Dillon et al., 2000). This lack of specificity might even be considered one of a formative experiment's distinguishing characteristics. However, it adds a burden to researchers who wish to conduct a formative experiment. As Eisenhart and Borko (1993) stated subsequent to the quote introducing this section, "[using alternative methodologies of classroom research] demands more thought and explanation than might be necessary if conventional procedures were used" (p. 11).

Nonetheless, several general characteristics establish the appropriateness, rigor, and validity of formative experiments and together distinguish them from other related methodologies. We offer the following characteristics adapting and extending the work of Cobb et al. (2003):

1. *Theoretical.* Theory plays a predominant role in a formative experiment, which distinguishes it from related data collection methodologies such as formative evaluation (Flagg, 1990) and rapid prototyping (Tripp & Bichelmeyer, 1990) that are often atheoretical in seeking ways to reach a particular goal. As is the case with other research methodologies, theory in a formative experiment is used to justify the importance of the inquiry, to provide a rationale for the intervention, interpret findings, contextualize conclusions, and so forth. However, as Cobb et al. (2003) state, the purpose of design experiments is "to develop a class of theories about both the *process* of learning and the *means* that are designed to support learning" [italics in the original]. Further, they state that in developing theories "design experiments create conditions . . . [that] place these theories in harm's way" and that theory "must do real work" by being "*accountable to the activity of design*" (italics in original, p. 10). That is, theories that do not directly inform practice are at best tangential to a formative experiment.

2. *Interventionist and goal oriented.* Formative experiments investigate how to improve education and learning toward well-specified goals that are explicitly justified in relation to theory and practice. Thus, researchers conducting formative experiments must explicitly identify and justify a goal accompanied by a scholarly explanation of why it is worthy of investigation. Moreover, a researcher must specify a planned intervention believed to have promise in making progress toward that goal. The intervention, too, must be justified in terms of theory and practice. In most formative experiments the intervention is innovative; however, in our view, it need not be. That is, a formative experiment might examine an intervention that is well established in the literature and/or practice and that has perhaps been investigated using more conventional research methods.

3. *Iterative.* The initial intervention is implemented within a continuous cycle of data collection and analysis aimed at determining what contextual factors enhance or inhibit the intervention's effectiveness. These data are used to modify the intervention and how it is implemented, as needed. Cycles of implementation and revision may be fluid, but a researcher must provide evidence of rigorous data

collection and analysis to guide this iterative process. Because a researcher engages in an ongoing determination of progress toward a pedagogical goal, establishing a baseline of conditions and/or performance is a procedural necessity. That formative experiments are iterative and involve fine-tuning instructional interventions also requires that they be conducted across a reasonable amount of time, at least many weeks, if not months.

4. *Transformational.* There is an assumption that the intervention may transform the educational environment in some way. This assumption is based on the fact that the intervention was most likely selected for its strong potential to further a worthy educational goal that has been difficult to attain. However, formative experiments are also guided by the realization that the intervention and its implementation within the context of a formative experiment may produce important unintended consequences. This aspect of formative experiments is important because it may contribute to building theory, and perhaps to suggesting ideas for further research.

5. *Methodologically inclusive and flexible.* Conceptualizing and conducting a formative experiment are not driven mainly by a particular method of collecting and analyzing data. Any approach to data collection and analysis may be appropriate to formative experiments if a researcher can justify how it furthers understanding about the effects of the intervention and how it might be implemented more effectively. Likewise, approaches to data collection and analysis may be adapted in response to developments during an investigation. Baseline data may be quantitative using standardized or experimenter-developed instruments, and statistical comparisons might be made between pre- and postexperiment performance. However, because formative experiments clearly fall into what Salomon (1991) has termed *systemic*, as opposed to *analytic*, research, collecting and analyzing qualitative data are essential to conducting a formative experiment. Thus, formative experiments are likely to involve mixed methods with all the attendant concerns, advantages, and standards of rigor associated with that research methodology (see Tashakori & Teddlie, 1998).

6. *Pragmatic.* This characteristic refers more broadly to the tenets of pragmatism than to simply a focus on what works. For example, pragmatism encompasses the broader view of experimentation to which we alluded in a previous section of this chapter, a valuing of intuitive knowledge, and an investment in democratic ideals, including the involvement of practitioners and students in setting research agendas and modifying interventions (see Dillon et al., 2000). Thus, formative experiments are typically collaborative efforts that involve

not only a researcher or research team, but also practitioners. There is also precedent for teachers to conduct formative experiments involving their own practice, in which formative experiments overlap with models of action research (Duffy-Hester, 1999; Garfield, 2000).

AN EXEMPLAR OF A FORMATIVE EXPERIMENT

Relatively few formative experiments have been conducted and few have been published in mainstream educational research journals. In selecting an illustrative example for this section, we chose our own work (Reinking & Watkins, 2000), because (1) it focuses on literacy, (2) it was rigorously peer reviewed and published in a highly regarded journal, (3) it involved extensive data collection and analysis in three schools and eight classrooms during 2 years, and (4) it illustrates the characteristics of formative experiments as presented previously in this chapter. Of course, it is also a study about which we have first-hand knowledge. However, because formative experiments represent an evolving methodology that accommodates flexibility, we emphasize that our example is not meant to be definitive. For readers who wish to consider a range of possible options for using this methodology in relation to literacy research, we recommend the following: Baumann (2003), Duffy-Hester, (1999), Garfield (2000), Jimènez (1997), Neuman (1999), and Newman (1990).

Our study investigated how engaging teachers and students in creating multimedia book reviews as an alternative to conventional book reports could increase elementary students' independent reading. We addressed six questions that provided a framework for conceptualizing, designing, and reporting our study. These six questions, which follow here, parallel the distinguishing characteristics of formative experiments introduced previously in this chapter, and we believe that these questions may be a useful guide for others interested in conducting formative experiments.

What Is the Pedagogical Goal and What Theory Establishes Its Value?

Our pedagogical goal was to increase the independent reading of elementary school students. We justified that goal on the basis of theoretical and empirical support for the importance of independent reading in enhancing literacy development among elementary school students. For example, on the theoretical side was the work of Stanovich (1986), who argued that discrepancies in reading performance widens among young readers as poor students read less and good students read more (what he called "Matthew effects," after the biblical passage about the rich becoming richer and the poor becoming poorer). On the empirical side, we cited evidence that the amount of reading and positive attitudes toward reading decrease as students move through the elementary grades (e.g., see McKenna, Kear, & Ellsworth, 1995). Initially, our goal was twofold. That is, we aimed to increase both the amount and diversity of independent reading. However, for various reasons, during the study we abandoned the goal of diversity because it seemed less relevant to the teachers and students we worked with and less connected to the potential benefits of independent reading. This reformulating of goals illustrates the flexibility of formative experiments and how implementing theory in practice may lead to reshaping pedagogical theory.

What Classroom Intervention Has Potential to Achieve the Pedagogical Goal?

In conceptualizing the study, we believed that an innovative use of computer technology might further the pedagogical goal. Specifically, we engaged teachers and students in creating a multimedia database about the books individual students were reading toward stimulating more interesting and creative responses to books and more interactions about independent reading among students. Our stance was supported by the often-cited limitations of widely used activities such as book reports and, more recently, computer-based activities such as the Accelerated Reader program based on extrinsic rewards and low-level, factual responses to texts (most recently supported by the work of Biggers, 2001). We believed that this innovative, technology-based intervention had potential to transform the dynamics of how teachers and students interacted about independent reading, although its implementation presented some formidable logistical obstacles, as is the case with many technology-based instructional activities. This emphasis on transforming instruction through innovative, often technology-based, interventions is consistent with how formative experiments have often been used.

What Factors Enhance of Inhibit the Effectiveness of the Intervention in Achieving the Pedagogical Goal?

Members of the research team collected various data to determine progress toward our pedagogical goal and what factors were enhancing or inhibiting progress. Data collection began by recording our experiences in several meetings with teachers before the school year began to acquaint them with our proposed intervention, our rationale, their investment in and ideas about it, and so forth. Before implementing a first draft of the intervention early in the school year, we gathered detailed observational data to characterize the schools and classrooms in which we worked. We also collected data to establish a baseline of independent reading and attitudes about reading in and out of school. These data included observational and interview data, a standardized measure of reading attitudes, and a survey completed by students' teachers and parents. Thus, we gathered both qualitative and quantitative data guided by principles underlying mixed-methods research (see Tashakori & Teddlie, 1998). When the intervention was implemented, we gathered primarily qualitative data comprised mainly of classroom observations two to three times a week to determine what aspects of the intervention were working or not, and why. However, data also included interviews with teachers, parents, and students, as well as an analysis of instructional artifacts produced in conjunction with the intervention. We also scheduled regular meetings with the teachers, typically after school, to discuss our mutual observations and plan accordingly.

How Can the Intervention Be Modified to Achieve the Pedagogical Goal More Effectively?

A distinguishing characteristic of formative experiments is that the instructional intervention of interest is modified as needed during the experiment toward more effectively or efficiently attaining the pedagogical goal that drives the investigation. Some modifications are in response to everyday variation in the instructional context, and are typical of the adaptations that practitioners must continuously address. For example, the number of computers available in the schools and whether they were placed in classrooms or a computer lab required modifications in the way the intervention was implemented. However, the systematic collection of data as described under the previous question also led to insights suggesting sometimes more subtle modifications. For example, in one classroom with a relatively high proportion of struggling readers, few students seemed interested in entering book reviews. Analyzing our observational data and interviews with students and teachers, we hypothesized that the struggling readers were reluctant to enter into the database the below-grade-level books they were reading, because it drew attention to their difficulties. That dynamic was easily changed after discussing our theories with the teacher who subsequently announced to the class that she hoped some students would enter easier books because the database would be eventually used by students in lower grades.

What Unanticipated Positive or Negative Effects Does the Intervention Produce?

This question is consistent with the rationale for a formative experiment because it acknowledges that instructional interventions are never implemented in a vacuum and that complex interacting variables with multiple effects operate in any instructional context. Thus, as we gathered and analyzed data focused on the intervention, we also noted how engaging teachers and students in creating multimedia book reviews had effects not directly related to our specified pedagogical goal. For example, we noted that the intervention heightened concern for the mechanics of writing, because the database for book reviews was designed to be used publicly beyond the classroom; that teachers became more involved in professional development activities and that their involvement became more supported by central administration, more or less as a consequence of their involvement with a research project; that parents become more involved in classroom activities as they became needed helpers in the computer lab of one school, although this effect was not always positive; and that special education students seemed to take on a different persona in the computer lab than they did in other school contexts. Some of the more positive unintended effects relate to other valued pedagogical goals and may become the grist for further studies involving different goals and interventions.

Has the Instructional Environment Changed as a Result of the Intervention?

This question is closely related to the previous one and is founded on the assumption that interventions most worthy of investigation are not only those that have potential to accomplish a pedagogical goal but also those that have strong potential to transform positively the teaching and learning environment. In our study, for example, we saw the intervention as having potential to transform teachers' and students' orientation to independent reading and particularly teachers' orientation to integrating technology into their instruction. Thus, our data collection and analysis attended to these and other possible transformations. We found evidence of such transformations in some of the classrooms. For example, several teachers abandoned activities that relied more on extrinsic motivation to promote independent reading and they began to integrate some more creative and engaging computer-based activities in other curricular areas. Such transformations did not occur in other classrooms, but our data revealed possible explanations. For example, in one school a top-down and heavy-handed administrative environment seemed to stifle creativity and experimentation among the teaching staff. Thus, in addressing this question and the previous one, a formative experiment involves an expansive examination of all aspects of an intervention's effects.

THE NEED FOR FORMATIVE EXPERIMENTS

> Education is not in need of research to find out how it works. It is in need of creative invention to make it work better.
> —EBEL (1982, p. 18)

We believe that Ebel's words are more poignant today than they were more than 20 years ago when he issued this challenge as President of the American Educational Research Association. His challenge, as stated in these few words, perhaps best represents the imperative underlying all the quotes presented in this chapter suggesting that research play a unique and more active and direct role in improving teaching and learning toward furthering valued pedagogical goals. Further, during the intervening years, there has been little evidence that educational research has provided strong guidance for practitioners who wish to implement interventions that have theoretical grounding and that have received empirical support through experimental methods. Neither has the turn toward naturalistic methodologies, which has occurred since his remarks, produced specific guidance about how practitioners might act on the important insights such methodologies provide. Not only have established research methodologies not addressed Ebel's challenge, it is clear today that researchers are increasingly being held accountable to demonstrate the fruits of their labors, often from the narrow perspective of quantifiable, experimental data that are far removed from the realities of classroom practice.

Thus, we believe formative experiments fill an important, indeed vital and neglected, niche within the diverse methodologies that might be employed within the educational research community. That is not to argue that formative experiments are superior to more established and more widely used methodologies or that they should replace them, only that those methodologies are decidedly incomplete without the insights formative experiments are aimed at providing. We believe that there must be a balance between understanding how education works or might work and conducting research aimed specifically at determining how it might work better through methods firmly grounded in the realities faced by practitioners. We believe that formative experiments provide a rigorous methodology that fills a gap between other research methodologies and instructional practice and that they do so by valuing both quantitative and qualitative data involving processes and toward ends that are readily accepted and understood by practitioners and the general public. We hope that this chapter serves to advance awareness of what we believe to be an exceptionally useful and timely methodology and that more researchers will consider employing this methodology to address important issues related to instructional practice.

REFERENCES

Atkin, C. K., & Freimuth, V. (1991). Formative evaluation research in campaign design. In R. E. Rice & C. K. Atkin (Eds.), *Public communication campaigns* (2nd ed.). Newbury Park, CA: Sage.

Baumann, J. F., Dillon, D. R., Shockley, B., Alvermann, D. E., & Reinking, D. (1996). Perspectives for literacy research. In L. Baker, P. Afflerbach, & D. Reinking (Eds.), *Developing engaged readers in school and home communities* (pp. 247–270). Mahwah, NJ: Erlbaum.

Baumann, J. F., Ware, D., Edwards, E. C. (2003, December). *Teaching vocabulary in fifth-grade: A year-long formative experiment.* Paper presented at the annual meeting of the National Reading Conference, Scottsdale, AZ.

Biggers, D. (2001). The argument against Accelerated Reader. *Journal of Adolescent and Adult Literacy, 45,* 72–75.

Brown, A. L. (1992). Design experiments: Theoretical and methodological challenges in creating complex interventions in classroom settings. *Journal of Learning Sciences, 2*(2), 141–178.

Bruce, B. C., & Rubin, A. (1993). Electronic quills: A situated evaluation of using computers for classroom writing. Hillsdale, NJ: Erlbaum.

Campbell, D. T., & Stanley, J. C. (1963). *Experimental and quasi experimental designs for research.* Chicago: Rand McNally.

Cherryholmes, C. H. (1993). Reading research. *Journal of Curriculum Studies, 25,* 1–32.

Cobb, P., Confrey, J., diSessa, A., Lehrer, R., & Schauble, L. (2003). Design experiments in education research. *Educational Researcher, 32*(1), 9–13.

Collins, A. (1992). Toward a design science of education. In E. Scanlon & T. O'Shea (Eds.), *New directions in educational technology* (pp. 83–103). New York: Springer-Verlag.

Collins, A. (1999). The changing infrastructure of education research. In E. C. Lagemann & L. B. Shulman (Eds.), *Issues in educational research: Problems and possibilities* (pp. 289–298). San Francisco: Jossey-Bass.

Davydov, V. V. (1988). Problems of developmental teaching: The experience of theoretical and experimental psychological research. Part 2. *Soviet Education, 30*(9).

Design-Based Research Collective. (2003). Design-based research: An emerging paradigm for educational inquiry. *Educational Researcher, 32*(1), 5–8.

Dillon, D. R., O'Brien, D. G., & Heilman, E. E. (2000). Literacy research in the next millennium: From paradigms to pragmatism and practicality. *Reading Research Quarterly, 35*, 10–26.

Duffy, G. G. (1994). How teachers think of themselves: A key to mindfulness. In J. N. Mangieri & C. Collins (Eds.), *Creating powerful thinking in teachers and students: Diverse perspectives* (pp. 3–25). Fort Worth, TX: HarperCollins.

Duffy-Hester, A. M. (1999). *The effects of a balanced accelerated and responsive literacy program on the reading of elementary school struggling readers.* Unpublished doctoral dissertation, University of Georgia, Athens.

Ebel, R. (1982). The future of educational research. *Educational Researcher, 22*(7), 5–11.

Eisenhart, M., & Borko, H. (1993). *Designing classroom research: Themes, issues, and struggles.* Boston: Allyn & Bacon.

Engeström, Y., Miettinen, R., & Punamäki, R.-L. (Eds.). (1998). *Perspectives on activity theory.* Cambridge, UK: Cambridge University Press.

Feuer, M. J., Towne, L., & Shavelson, R. J. (2002). Reply to commentators on "Scientific Culture and Educational Research." *Educational Researcher, 31*(8), 28–29.

Flagg, G. N. (1990). Formative evaluation for educational technologies. Hillsdale, NJ: Erlbaum.

Garfield, V. (2000). *A formative experiment investigating the use of electronic portfolios as a means of improving elementary students' perceptions of themselves as readers.* Unpublished doctoral dissertation, University of Georgia, Athens.

Gittleson, J., Evans, M, Helitzer, D, Anliker, J, Story, M, Metcalfe, L., Davis, S., & Cloud, P. I. (1998). Formative research in a school-based obesity program for Native American school children (pathways). *Health Education Research, 13*, 251–265.

Jackson, P. W. (1990). *Life in classrooms.* New York: Teachers College Press.

Jacob, E. (1992). Culture, context, and cognition. In M. D. Lecompte, W. L. Millroy, & J. Preissle (Eds.), *The handbook of qualitative research in education* (pp. 293–335). San Diego: Academic Press.

Jimènez, R. T. (1997). The strategic reading abilities and potential of five low-literacy Latina/o readers in middle school. *Reading Research Quarterly, 32*, 224–243.

Labaree, D. (1998). Educational researchers: Living with a lesser form of knowledge. *Educational Researcher, 27*(8), 4–12.

Labbo, L. D., & Reinking, D. (1999). Negotiating the multiple realities of technology in literacy research and instruction. *Reading Research Quarterly, 34*(4), 478–492.

Lagemann, E. C. (2000). *An elusive science: The troubling history of education research.* Chicago: University of Chicago Press.

McCandliss, B. D., Kachman, M., & Bryant, P. (2003). Design experiments and laboratory approaches to learning: Steps toward collaborative exchange. *Educational Researcher, 32*(1), 14–16.

McKenna, M. C., Kear, D. J., & Ellsworth, R. A. (1995). Children's attitudes toward reading: A national survey. *Reading Research Quarterly,30,* 934–957.

Moll, L., & Diaz, S. (1987). Change as the goal of educational research. *Anthropology and Education Quarterly, 18,* 300–311.

National Reading Panel Report. (2000, April). Retrieved January 25, 2003, from http://www.nichd.nih.gov/publications/nrp/smallbook.htm

Neuman, S., Jimènez, R., Reinking, D., & Au, K. (1997, December). *A formative view of formative experiments in classrooms using technology to promote independent reading.* Symposium at the annual meeting of the National Reading Conference, Scottsdale, AZ.

Neuman, S. B. (1999). Books make a difference: A study of access to literacy. *Reading Research Quarterly, 34,* 286–311.

Newman, D. (1990). Opportunities for research on the organizational impact of school computers. *Educational Researcher, 19,* 8–13.

Newman, D., Griffin, P., & Cole, M. (1989). *The construction zone: Working for cognitive change in school.* Cambridge, UK: Cambridge University Press

Oldfather, P., & Wigfield, A. (1996). Children's motivation for literacy learning. In L. Baker, P. Afflerbach, & D. Reinking (Eds.), *Developing engaged readers in school and home communities* (pp. 89–114). Mahwah, NJ: Erlbaum.

Paris, S. G., Lipson, M. Y., & Wixson, K. K. (1983). Becoming a strategic reader. *Contemporary Educational Psychology, 8,* 293–316.

Reinking, D., & Pickle M. (1993). Using a formative experiment to study how computers affect reading and writing in classrooms. In D. J. Leu & C. K. Kinzer (Eds.), *Examining central issues in literacy research, theory, and practice* (pp. 263–270). Chicago: National Reading Conference.

Reinking, D., & Watkins, J. (2000). A formative experiment investigating the use of multimedia book reviews to increase elementary students independent reading. *Reading Research Quarterly, 35*(3), 384–419.

Salomon, G. (1991). Transcending the qualitative-quantitative debate: The analytic and systemic approaches to educational research. *Educational Researcher, 20*(6), 10–18.

Spiro, R. J., Feltovich, P. J., Jacobson, M. J., & Coulson, R. L. (1992). Cognitive flexibility, constructivism, and hypertext: Random access instruction for advanced knowledge acquisition in ill-structured domains. In T. M. Duffy, & D. H. Jonassen (Eds.), *Constructivism and technology of instruction: A conversation* (pp. 57–75). Hillsdale, NJ: Erlbaum.

Strauss, A., & Corbin, J. (1990). *Basics of qualitative research: Grounded theory procedures and techniques.* Newbury Park, CA: Sage.

Stokes, D. E. (1997). *Pasteurs's quadrant.* Washington, DC: Brookings Institution Press.

Tashakkori, A., & Teddlie, C. (1998). *Mixed methodology: Combining qualitative and quantitative approaches.* Thousand Oaks, CA: Sage.

Tripp, S. D., & Bichelmeyer, B. (1990). Rapid prototyping: An alternative instructional design strategy. *Educational Technology Research and Development, 38*(1), 31–44.

Wagner, J. (1993). Ignorance in educational research: Or how can you *not* know that? *Educational Researcher, 22*(5), 15–23.

CHAPTER 9

Doing Historical Research on Literacy

Norman A. Stahl
Douglas K. Hartman

Everything has a history. Everything that exists in the present comes out of the past. Indeed, as Benjamin (2001) so wisely counsels, "The house of the present is filled with windows into the past" (p. 2). The purpose of this chapter is to strengthen the way we look through these windows. For example, an individual who grew up attending an elementary school in the United States or Canada is probably familiar with the basal readers used for formal reading instruction. These comprehensive, leveled anthologies of stories, skills, activities, and worksheets have been the prevailing instrument for teaching reading throughout North America. A publishing house carefully designs each new edition of these materials. Even though one probably used the newest basal series on the market at the time, each series has a history that is several hundred years old reaching back through the "Dick and Jane" readers of the mid-20th century to the *McGuffey* readers of the latter 19th century to Webster's "Blueback Spellers," and even back to the *New England Primer* and beyond. The lines linking past basal readers to present ones never break.

Looking for historical signs in these readers is like being an archeologist or geologist. But instead of digging into the earth to uncover the past, the historical researcher digs into the visible, everyday elements of reading materials to find the historical roots from which they sprang. The features, layout, and content of the current basal readers are just the uppermost layer of history. From these readers we can make inferences about reading curriculum in the last few years, but what about the historical roots of the previous generations of readers? How far into the past can we see through the pages of current readers?

If we study the passage of time between *McGuffey's* rural farm ditties to Dick and Jane's suburban neighborhood happenings to today's tales from urban and global communities, we come to understand some of the cultural, political, demographic, technological, and economic movements that shaped each successive generation of readers and the history of U.S. reading instruction. The more we understand the changes made in the readers, when they were made, who made them, and why, the better equipped we will be to see into the kind of future we as literacy professionals may be heading.

To look through windows into the past requires that we also be able to look *at* the windows too. To do this requires a kind of double, double vision, where we look not only at the historical artifact (such as a textbook, journal, photo, or letter) but at ourselves analyzing the artifact, as well as the historical profession as it discusses its collective analyzing of artifacts. We can almost see the rough outlines of three concentric circles in this description, with the artifact in the inner circle, us in the middle circle, and the profession in the outer one. To acquire this vision, we begin by focusing on the outer circle, the profession. The questions and conversations that occupy historians' lives have a history of their own. In our mind's eye, the windows in this house are the logical starting place for learning to look through any window into the past—whether it be reading instruction, basal readers, the Cold War, or the French Revolution. The fundamental questions for anyone embarking on historical work in any area are *What is history?* and *Why should we do it?*

WHAT IS HISTORY?

There is no single answer to the first question, What is history? But there are answers that mark the terrain better than others. Wood Gray (1991) suggests that three features are essential to any response: history as happening, record, and a field of study.

History Is Happening

First and foremost *history is a happening*, everything that has ever occurred or been thought about from the beginning of time right up to the last elapsed moment is history. To bring this concept directly back to us as readers, our very identity is as much or more historical as it is present or future oriented: our having learned to read with a "Dick and Jane" reader or with an SRA kit is history. Our moment in the present is but fleeting, as it quickly becomes our contribution, meaningful or not, to history. It is only the future that is infinite and beyond the scope of history until it too will become history—something that is assured to happen.

History Is the Record

Second, *history is the record* of things past. This is the record we studied as part of a fifth-grade social studies unit on the Civil War with Miss Jameson or in our foray into 10-grade world history at Abraham Lincoln High School. The locations of these happenings for each of us are different as were the times, but the experience was likely to have been much the same. We studied the record of important events and the thoughts and actions of those of great minds (i.e., the elite) as selected for us by the elders of our society. Yet for most of us, history as a record of world literacy or reading instruction never received more than passing attention in our professional training either at the undergraduate or graduate levels.

Unlike history as a happening, history as a record has quite finite parameters. About 5,000 years ago, with the growing complexity of economic and political activity throughout ancient Mesopotamia and Egypt, writing was invented—and the record of history began. For an excellent text on the history of writing see Fischer (2001). It is the period since then that the great preponderance of the Western historical record is focused on. With the development of printing in the West, the documentary record was more likely to survive. Furthermore, with each new technology for capturing the present, there is less and less that cannot be preserved for the historical record if there is an archive, whether physical or digital, to preserve the documentary evidence.

In the field of literacy we may propose that there are three areas of history as record: the history of reading instruction (e.g., Mathews, 1966; Smith, 2002), the history of literacy (e.g., Cavallo & Charter, 1999; Fischer, 2003; Manguel, 1996), and the history of the book or print culture (e.g., Darnton, 1990; Johns, 1996). As such we have the opportunity to learn of literacy history, but we must be careful as Leedy and Ormrod (2001) warn us not to confuse the study of history with the conduct of the historical method.

History Is a Field of Study

Finally, *history is a field of study* where the practice of historical method—known as historiography—is undertaken by institutionally trained academics or self-trained amateurs. In its earliest practice history was written in the form of chronicles that praised a monarch or glorified a city or state. It was with the coming of Herdotus and Thucydides that the writing of history began to seek the "truth" and examine relationships between cause and effect. With the arrival of the Middle Ages and the decline of classical civilization in the West, the historical method also slipped into the dark ages. Not until the philosophy of the rationalists evolved during the Enlightenment of the 18th century did a comprehensive study of history once again emerge. It was in Germany at the University of Berlin in the 1820s that Leopold von Ranke advocated to his students the systematic approach to evaluating documents and the practice of presenting the past "as it actually happened" (*wie es eigentlich gewesen ist*). As this perspective spread through the academic community, the foundation for history as an academic discipline based on scientific principles was set in place for the modern era.

Throughout the next two centuries various theoretical constructs and, hence, research agendas evolved so that historians interpret our past through different lenses (Brundage, 2002; Gilderhus, 2003). The social historians influenced by Thomas Malthus and Karl Marx among others lead us to examine the roles ordinary peopled played in history along with the impact of the conflict between classes in and across each era. Rather than having a focus on the great men, the noble conflicts, and the nation states, the focus changed to what has been regularly described as history from below. W. E. B. Dubois's work in the latter 1800s can be viewed as the beginnings of another theoretical stance associated with the struggles for economic, civil, and social equity by African Americans, Hispanics, Asians, Native Americans, and, more recently, the social and political movements associated with gender and sexual orientation. Such historians seek each group's proper place in history so as to escape from marginalization if not invisibility.

During the latter 1920s and the 1930s there evolved in France a form of historiography based on the research methods from the social sciences. The followers of what is called the Annales School employed a historical thoughtway concerned with the regular and ongoing flow of life and the everyday values of society that carry forward regardless of the major economic, political, or military events. More recently the work of the proponents of cliometrics use quantitative research based on social science modeling theory and powered my new technological applications. These researchers are less likely to use documentary sources as such analysis leads to impressionistic analysis of data.

Another school of historians influenced by Sigmund Freud follows the precepts of psychoanalysis through clinical or case evidence, often reported as biography, to unearth the actual reasons or policies for an event as opposed to the visible and alleged reasons. Finally, the proponents of postmodernism as pioneered by Michel Foucault and Jacques Lacan question whether reason and scientific thought have promoted a humane and reasoned society. They purport that the texts and the discourse forms of society have been constructed to consolidate the power of the elites and lead to social, economic, cultural, and political marginalization and oppression of the nonelite. Through deconstruction they strive to remove the surface level from the dominant discourse, endeavoring to show the true reflection of society and the impact of events.

Thus there are different theories powering research and, hence, different ways of knowing the past. The one thing we may be sure of is that history is not a single interpretation of events that is carved in stone for future generations—although there may be a political or pedagogical agenda (often one and the same) that values one interpretation over another. History is a dynamic field of study, and it is forever changing through the process of revisionism. Each generation and each group selects and integrates the data (facts) and the artifacts of the past with the current cultural, social, economic, and political interpretations of the world, the new tools and approaches to inquiry, and the newly discovered historical sources and data to recreate and understand the past. As such, history is more than the simple story of the chronological march of time. For a more in-depth discussion on historiography across the years see Gilderhus (2003) and Tosh (2002).

A WORKING DEFINITION FOR THE HISTORY OF LITERACY

With Gray's (1991) three features in mind, we propose a working definition of history, akin to that of Borg, Gall, and Gall (1993): history *is the interpretative reconstruction of the known past*. This definition highlights three elements of historical analysis.

1. History is an *interpretation* of the past. It involves the careful weighing and sorting of evidence into patterns, arguments, and narratives based on judgment. It is more than marshaling a chronology of acts. History is the production of meanings for an audience relative to a purpose.
2. History is *reconstruction* of the past. It is a refabricating of something that once was. It is not the same thing as the actual event or episode. History is a "making again" of an account or explanation that re-presents that which already happened.

3. History is about the *known* past. There is much in the past that was and happened, but we can only know pieces and parts of it because of the evidence that remains. That which can be known, then, is that which has been saved or survived into the present for interpretation and reconstruction.

As a whole, we think this working definition offers considerable flexibility. The focus can be on an individual, a group, a movement, an institution, a place, or an era (Best & Kahn, 1989; Skager & Weinberg, 1971). In the literacy field this activity might entail the investigation of the impact of educational policies, legislation, and laws (Right to Read, Goals 2000, No Child Left Behind), curriculum models and movements (basal systems, whole-language philosophy, Initial Teaching Alphabet, Direct Instruction), instructional methods and materials (KWL, phonics workbooks, Dolch word materials), or assessment practices (informal reading inventories, miscue analysis, standardized testing) across time or within defined eras. The focus could also be on the lives and contributions of distinguished literacy educators or researchers, such as Edmund Burke Huey, William S. Gray, Noah Webster, or Arthur I. Gates, or the literative lives of the nonelites, be they teachers, administrators, or former students.

The historical process might be used to study the development and influence of specific educational institutions either in higher education (e.g., the Center for the Study of Reading and the college reading programs in Georgia throughout the 1980s) or in the pre-K–12 environment (e.g., the Benchmark School and University of Chicago Laboratory School). Finally, the literacy historian can delve into the roots of current literacy practices, techniques, or strategies to discover whether they were developed to meet instructional parameters that no longer exist today or to learn whether they have fallen victim to the "confusions of time" such that application and delivery no longer resemble the original constructs (Skager & Weinberg, 1971). Conversely, the literacy historian can identify instructional activities or movements that were lost to the times (Stahl, King, & Eilers, 1996) but would have practical application for the current educational scene.

As an interpretive and reconstructive process, historical topics are not considered in isolation. Each builds on, borrows from, and gives to the philosophies, thoughts, and movements of institutions within a particular era or an identified setting/locale. In addition, the researcher must be cognizant of the historical events beyond the literacy field that might have influenced the issue or event. For instance, the growth of postsecondary reading programs in the early 1950s as well as the birth of both the National Reading Conference

(NRC) and the College Reading Association would not likely have happened if the Congress had not passed the "G.I. Bill" leading to enrollment of thousands of returning service personnel in post-secondary education and in college reading courses.

A working definition of history, such as the one we have proposed, is rooted in two broad categories of historical research: (1) *document/artifact analysis*, which requires the researcher to examine documents objects such as birth records, census data, photographs, contracts, commission reports, newspapers, periodicals, manuscripts, diaries and journals, videotapes, and speech transcripts (McDowell, 2002), and (2) *oral history analysis*, where individuals who lived through an event or era or knew individuals of importance to the research are interviewed. The oral history project, also recognized as oral biography, oral chronicles, and life history, produces the oral evidence that is preserved through the process of transcription (Baum, 1987; Caunce, 1994; Kyvig & Marty, 2000; Sitton, Mehaffy, & Davis, 1983; Thompson, 1988).

WHY UNDERTAKE HISTORICAL RESEARCH IN LITERACY?

The second question fundamental to those embarking on historical research in literacy is, Why do it? Not surprisingly, there are several answers to this question. One is that we conduct historical research to form the reading field into a profession or community of scholars with a history that is known, valued, and disseminated through the professoriate and our professional associations to the current and future generations of literacy specialists. History provides us with a sense of honor as a profession all the while focusing us on the unique onus we bear as reading educators and researchers.

We may draw on five additional reasons for doing historical research in literacy from Cohen and Manion (1994). Historical research in literacy (1) yields insights into some pedagogical problems that could not be achieved by other means, (2) informs us how our current system came about and to how to build a sound basis for future directions, (3) permits us to use past practices to evaluate emerging and current practices, (4) allows us to identify and evaluate recurrent trends in literacy education, and (5) assists us in understanding the relationship between politics and literacy education, school and society, local and central governments, and teachers and students.

Good (1966) perceptively points out that through the historical process, we gain a greater understanding about the dynamics of change in education. Finally, Stahl (2002) notes that history is our first and best teacher, for through the study of literacy's history we learn that variations of even the most protracted problems of our day have been tackled in one manner or another by previous generations of literacy specialists.

THE RESEARCH PROCESSES FOR THE HISTORICAL ANALYSIS OF LITERATE PRACTICE

We now turn from the larger questions of historical methodology to the specific skills, strategies, and procedures that will mark the path through an historical inquiry in literacy. As with any research endeavor, there is a process that outlines the general flow of historical research, allowing for false starts, recursions, digressions, and revisions. The outline that follows suggests this flow and allowances. We begin with the all-important first step, choosing a topic.

Choosing the Topic

When selecting a topic we should heed Gray's (1991) advice that the researcher needs to consider the topic's (1) value, (2) originality, (3) practicality, and (4) unity of theme. Nailing down the topic enables us to focus on those things that will help us tell our story. Conversely, it helps us set aside things that are not useful to our storytelling. Experience shows us that the beginning researcher often proposes a topic that is too broad in nature. A topic's focus may be delimited chronologically, spatially, thematically, or by a combination of these three parameters. Hence, we may need to focus—and refocus—the investigation through a continuous narrowing process. Often this action includes the formulation of at least a tentative working hypothesis or a set of guiding questions. Yet with a working hypothesis, it may be revised through new questions, new foci, or new goals after the collection, evaluation, and initial analysis of appropriate data.

Collecting Evidence

Unlike with other forms of research, an historian does not create evidence: Rather, the historian uses that which is available. In collecting evidence the researcher is likely to examine both primary sources and secondary sources. *Primary sources* are original documents, artifacts, remains, or relics associated with the topic under investigation. Documents and artifacts are records of eyewitnesses or direct outcomes of incidents. These items are intentionally or unintentionally left in order to provide a firsthand record of the event. As Ary, Jacobs, and Razavich (2002) notes, "Only the mind of the observer intrudes between the original event and the investigator" (p. 450).

Examples of primary sources for literacy education would include those works of (1) a personal nature (e.g., manuscripts, personal journals, memoirs, diaries, blogs, autobiographies, private and public letters, memos, and e-mails), (2) a public nature (e.g., written transcriptions and oral testimonies from participants and observers, photographs, films, and audio, video digital recordings), (3) a professional nature (e.g., community and school newspapers, magazines, journals, school bulletins, curriculum guides, courses of study/units, textbooks/workbooks, children's books, software, student work, portfolios, report cards, record books, and examinations), and (4) an official nature (e.g., official records, minutes and reports of legislatures, school boards, state and county offices of education, specific schools, postsecondary institutions, or special task forces; certificates, licenses, and credentials; evaluation and research data/reports to local, state, and federal agencies, and census reports, immigration records, and laws).

Remains or relics associated with a particular person, group, institution, or periods in time were not meant to transmit information across time as part of the record, but, nonetheless, they can shed light on a research question. In literacy education these may include school buildings and specific rooms (e.g., reading clinics and resource rooms), classroom furniture (e.g., language centers), period technology (e.g., tashistoscopes, controlled readers, and language masters), tools (e.g., handwriting implements), teaching materials (e.g., basals and software), student work samples (e.g., completed handwriting manuals, spelling books, and portfolios), and so on.

Secondary sources do not have a direct relationship to the case under study. The individual writing or talking about the event was not present as the incident unfolded. This narrator obtained the description of the event or era from another source, which may or may not have been a primary source (e.g., Wyatt, 1992). Examples of secondary sources covering literacy history include textbooks (Anderson & Dearborn, 1952), history books (Balmuth, 1982), articles in an encyclopedia (Monaghan, Hartman, & Monaghan, 2002; Rose, 2002), reviews of research (Stahl & Henk, 1986), reproductions of materials (Gorn, 1998), or prints of originals (Nolin, Swan, & West, 1991). The literacy historian may find an extensive list of secondary sources by consulting the books reviewed in the *History of Reading News* found on the History of Reading Special Interest Group web site at *http://www.historyliteracy.org*. Another valuable source would be the annotated bibliography *Historical Sources in U.S. Reading Education 1900–1970* (Robinson, 2000).

Secondary source materials will be of interest as they present a particular vantage on primary sources and the topic itself, and secondary sources may also review previously unread bibliographic information that should be read on the topic of interest. Nevertheless, it must always be understood that with secondary sources there is a chance of error as information is conveyed from person to person or from text to text. In addition, such works generally include the prejudices and the assumptions of the authors. The final point to be made is that each secondary source should be used with great care, with accurate citation, and with appropriate critique of the perspectives and biases found within the work. The reality is that most historical work in literacy will use a combination of primary and secondary sources in developing the report.

With most historical investigations the primary sources are available in the rare book rooms of public and academic libraries or in archives associated with learned societies, religious groups, museums, and other archival sites across the continent. Archives that include artifacts needed for research in the history of literacy can be difficult to locate so Sears, Hartman, and Monaghan (2003b) have authored an extensive e-book of archives with respective listings of holdings and URLs for direct contact.

More recently the field of historiography has been able to draw on a greater number of sources that can be classified as reproductions of primary sources (e.g., *New England Primer Enlarged*, 1800/1975; Stickney, 1885/1985; Webster, 1866/n.d.). Monaghan and Hartman (2000) note that printed copies reproduced with "scrupulous care" can be acceptable substitutes for actual primary sources if the reproduction of the material fits the purpose of the research.

As we move more fully into the digital age, many primary sources are being preserved via digital technologies such as CD-ROMs and Internet sites. Such practices make the use of primary sources accessible to all historians (trained or amateur), but these technologies require that the literacy historian become knowledgeable about and competent with online catalogs, online networks, search engines, and CD-ROM-based systems (see Benjamin, 2001; Greenstein, 1994; Reiff, 1991). When such materials are used in the research process, it is quite imperative that citations note the actual source of the evidence. While printed or digtialized reproductions may be acceptable for research purposes, the review of a document over the Internet will never replace the sensual experience or the being at one with the author through the holding and perusing of the primary source.

Regardless of one's use of primary sources or secondary sources, or originals or reproductions, the historian must understand from the onset of the study that one can only investigate those topics (whether about events or people) for which either public or private documents and artifacts were preserved by official action or by happenstance for posterity, or those events or people for which there are available and cognizant witnesses willing to discuss them for the record. As such, an historian should strive to review conscientiously the available data, and then within the report discuss the depth and the breadth of the existing pool of documents (and as possible, the degree to which historical traces have been lost over the years). Unfortunately, many historical narratives published in the education journals fail to provide information about the location, selection, and evaluation of both primary and secondary sources. Willis (2002) in her work on the Calhoun Colored School presents such a valuable discussion in the text of the article.

Evaluating Evidence

While there is a degree of thrill in the hunt for materials, the responsibility of the historian does not end there. Indeed, potential problems may arise with the documents that have survived for the historian's review. In his seminal work on educational historiography, Kaestle (1988) poses four questions that must be considered when dealing with any documents:

- How conscientiously were the data reported in the first place?
- What individuals and institutional biases may have affected the results?
- What are the contradictions between different sources that claim to measure the same variables in the same population?
- Are items defined differently in different eras or omitted altogether?

These concerns call for us to evaluate critically the information under review. Historical criticism is the underlying foundation of historiography. Every time a historian accepts a piece of evidence or rejects another source and then interprets data in a research report, the act of historical criticism either external or internal is taking place (Issac & Michael, 1976). Careful and ordered evaluation of evidence in historical research leads the process to be more demanding than experimental methods. The analysis is not a one-time procedure that is run to "crunch" data but an ongoing vigilance to the questioning of data across the life of the project. Kaestle's (1988) four questions serve as a kind of analytic mantra to be repeated and answered of all data gathered in historical research.

When we say that evidence is evaluated critically, we mean that it is evaluated through a two-step process of external and internal criticism. With *external criticism* (sometimes referred to as lower criticism) the question is asked as to whether the evidence under consideration is authentic and genuine. There is a focus on the textual integrity of the document or source rather than the message it carries. In other words, the historian asks four questions: Who wrote the work? Where was the work authored? When was the document developed? Under what conditions was the work authored?

All the while the historian is looking for frauds, distortions, or ghostwritten works. For documents this process may include several steps: (1) the authentication of authorship through signatures, script, handwriting, and spelling style by comparison to known signatures, script, handwriting, and spelling from a particular person and historical period; (2) the verification through physical and chemical tests that the document's paper, parchment, cloth content, or inks were available in the period the document was purported to have been written; and (3) the matching of writing style and the point of view as evidenced in the document with texts previously verified as written by the individual. For relics, external criticism might include chemical analysis of paints and inks or even carbon dating of relics and remains.

Internal criticism (sometimes referred to as higher criticism) is the act of evaluating the accuracy and worth of the evidence that has been unearthed. This is the case for both document analysis and also oral history interviews. The historian seeks to establish the credibility of the informant by asking whether the individual was a trained or untrained observer/recorder of the event. One also asks whether there were any motives that might have induced the informant to overstate, misconstrue, or overlook information. Indeed, the historian looks for forms of bias whether these are sympathetic or antagonistic about the topic. For instance, one would ask whether there is a bias to the information based on the social, cultural, economic, or educational values and backgrounds of the individual(s) who authored the documents or provided the testimonies of the events of interest. One must query whether the informant's participation in the event influenced the reporting of the event and whether there is agreement in the report with other descriptions and reports of the event. Finally, if there are quantitative data, the historian must question whether it seems to be reasonable?

Internal criticism also requires that the historian turn inward to assess whether there is an implicit or explicit personal bias demonstrated through the selection of either documents/artifacts or quantitative data to support the hypothesis and thus slant the interpretation of the evidence in the report. With oral history the researcher must ask whether there is a form of bias from the interaction of the interviewee and the interviewer. Authors of literacy-oriented histories do not tend to describe explicitly how they undertook either external criticism or internal criticism. Still such information is often hinted at within the footnotes for each article or chapter of a book.

Some scholars think that the distinction between external criticism and internal criticism is somewhat artificial (Gray, 1991). Instead, Gray suggests a set of heuristic questions that deal with opportunity, objectivity, transmission, and meaning. Whether one engages in formal criticism or follows Gray's (1991) informal approach, his or her historical study should report the processes of criticism used as well as his or her evaluation of the adequacy of the data used in support of the hypothesis.

Working with Evidence

The activity of taking notes when reviewing a document is as individualistic as is each historian, and in some cases, it depends on the era in which the individual was trained. A time-honored tradition is the development of a manual note card system for both bibliographic notes and content notes.

Bibliographic cards contain standard reference information including the name of the library or archive, specific cataloguing information for the document, and information about the source, the author, or the site. It is important to include complete documentation because reference styles for different scholarly journals and book publishers require different degrees of completeness for a referenced source.

Content cards contain the working material or facts that are extracted from the particular piece of evidence. In taking notes one should be generous in the use of cards, as this action will promote ease with the organization of the research report. The page number for the information's bibliographic source should be written down, verbatim quotes must be so noted but used sparingly on cards and in the report, and summarization of ideas and data should be used rather than simple copying of words (prevents plagiarism). Personal inferences or ideas about the documents must be recorded so that they will not be confused with facts from the document when both are reviewed at a later date. While photocopying or scanning of documents might be desired, many archives will not permit such activities as the process damages the primary sources.

There are, however, traditions and inventions other than note cards for recordkeeping. We have colleagues who prefer to take notes in a composition book or journal and then reorganize the notes at a later date on note cards or in a digital data file. Others have recommended the use of an audiorecorder with which they dictate notes for future transcriptions and organization. Still others choose to use a laptop computer so digital note cards are taken at the time the source is reviewed, and then each saved digital note card is organized in a file corresponding to each source in a database. Through the use of a find feature, recurring words and phrases permit the location of text which can be moved into appropriate files.

Regardless of the process or medium used, it is imperative that one always match the information recorded to the source and the actual placement of the information in the source. This is particularly important when the archive is not immediately available so that reviewing the primary sources would not be possible for a second time.

Analyzing and Interpreting Evidence

In analyzing data the first task is to make sure it is dependable and relevant to the topic. Then the evidence is synthesized into a pattern that tests the hypothesis or answers questions guiding the work. This synthesis first requires that one employ a systematic plan for the organization, storage, and retrieval of the data collected. When Leedy (1958) undertook his expansive history of postsecondary reading he organized data by cross-filing the bibliographic and factual data (cards or files) in triplicate by three general categories: (1) chronological order, (2) author or informant, and (3) subject of theme. Through such a scheme he was able to cross reference, or link, common subject data separated by the intervention of other events and the passage of time. More recently he advocated (Leedy & Ormrod, 2001) the use of a fourth classification, geography of event. The preparation and then use of multiple files is facilitated through the use of index cards color-coded to the classification category.

The actual process of constructing history is directed by three factors: the philosophical stance held by the writer, the evidence that was discovered in the available primary and secondary sources, and the researcher's interpretation of the data. The facts that are uncovered by the historian say little in and of themselves. It is the interpretation of those facts that leads to understanding the hypothesis that was posed and the answering of the questions driving the study. The process of interpreting the facts individually or in sets constructed through induction depends on having both mastery of the data and an understanding of the significance of that material.

Best and Kahn (1989) point out a work can fall short because of oversimplification and illogical analysis when there are multiple and complex causes of events. On the other hand, the presentation of overgeneralizations based on insufficient evidence or false analogies when there are only superficial similarities is an equally serious problem. Kaestle (1988) follows the same track as he cautions that one must be careful not to confuse correlation with causality. Just because two events occurred simultaneously does not mean that one event caused the other.

While it is expected that one will build an interpretive stance based on one's philosophy, politics, or even pedagogy of literacy as well as prior knowledge of the historical era and practice of historiography, the interpretation must be the result of acceptable and ethical scholarship. Making a case based on the selection of facts that are in agreement with the hypothesis while ignoring data that are not in accordance with a preferred outcome is not acceptable. The context of quoted ideas and passages must be honored, people and ideas must be treated in a just and scholarly manner, and both criticism and admiration will be tempered through professional ethics. Best and Kahn (1989) offer sage advice when they state that impartiality and not neutrality is the aim of systematic research presentation in history.

Kaestle (1988) suggests that historians consider two potentially overlooked issues when interpreting the evidence. First, we must distinguish between the evidence of ideas about how people should behave as opposed to the evidence about how people actually behaved during an era. Most of us are quite familiar with oft quoted statement that regardless of the policies and curriculum adopted by a school district, when a teacher closes the classroom door, literacy instruction becomes that with which there is the greatest comfort. Simply put, people may be told that they need to act in a particular way, but the actual behavior either explicitly or covertly may be different.

Second, it is necessary to distinguish between intent and consequence, because the consequences of an event or a movement do not provide evidence of the participants' intent in undertaking the action under study. Intent must be based on specific evidence and not an inference from the consequences of the event. An historian has a great advantage in having the power of hindsight. However, the participant in an event in history most likely did not have the clairvoyant powers to predict the future.

Writing the Article or Book

Finally, the research article or book should be written to present the information in an understandable and interesting manner. We should be careful not to be overly sentimental, didactic, or persuasive. Generally the work is presented in a form of a narrative, with a chronological discourse pattern. Yet with the evolvement of discourse patterns associated with the theoretical perspectives of historiography presented earlier in the chapter, there is no hard and fast structure for the report. Still, we would be remiss if we did not put forward several recommendations for writing the report that have been accepted by literacy historians over the years.

First, the argument as driven by one's hypothesis should be explicitly stated in the initial stages of the work. Then as each position is put forth, it should be followed by examples for support and explication. Equally important is the provision for general historical context in the report as literacy events and personalities were intertwined with the greater cultural and societal events of the times. For instance, the impact of the Emergency School Education Act on the nation's literacy instruction during the presidency of Lyndon Johnson cannot be examined without attention to the administration's War on Poverty or the civil rights movement.

As writers we must also be concerned with how we use specific terms within the research report. Kaestle (1988) in his seminal work describes two potential problems with language use in the research report. First there is *vagueness* or the use of umbrella/overarching terms that do not carry the necessary degree of specificity when precision of language is essential. Many terms such as *literacy* itself have lost the precision and focus that was once associated with the term. Second, there is *presentism* or the act of applying current-era terms that did not exist in the past or that have since evolved etymologically to carry different denotations or connotations to past events, movements, and so on. For instance, we would need to consider carefully our era-appropriate use of terms such as work-type skills, work-study skills, study skills, study strategies, and learning strategies as the underlying concept evolved across the 20th century.

Should there be points in our work that are still open to conjecture or yet to be validated, such a condition should be treated openly, or, in other words, these unresolved points should not be glossed over or hidden. Footnotes or endnotes may need to be included for explication.

The act of disseminating a historical report in the field of literacy requires that we know both the audience and the disciplinary medium that best fits our work. Historical works in literacy are welcomed in the literacy journals sponsored by the International Reading Association, the National Reading Conference, the College Reading Association, and the College Reading and Learning Association among others. Such works may also find homes in other education journals, history journals, and as books or monographs put out by university and scholarly presses. We suggest that any new author to the field review Monaghan and Hartman (2000) and Sears and Hartman (2003) before selecting a potential vehicle for publication.

Finally we wish to make a point that comes from our shared experiences in reviewing research reports for journals, book publishers, and yearbooks over several decades. A manuscript that has problems with the presentation can often be revised to find an academic home and make a contribution to the scholarship of the profession. A manuscript, no matter how elegant either the presentation of the case or the statistical model used to analyze the data, will be doomed from the start if investigator did not employ appropriate research methods/design. In other words, there is truth in the old adage that an ounce of prevention is worth a pound of cure.

ORAL HISTORY

The oral history project accepts the responsibility of saving the most fragile and irreplaceable form of historical trace, which is the human memory. Indeed, we are ever cognizant of the old African adage used by Zimmerman (1982) that states that whenever an elder member of a community dies, an entire library is lost. This wisdom has led Stahl and King (2000b) to argue that our legacy as members of the literacy community must be preserved through gathering transcriptions of personal and professional recollections and life stories of our senior colleagues. Stahl, King, Dillon, and Walker (1994) suggest that oral history projects such as being undertaken by the National Reading Conference (NRC) and by the learning assistance program at National Louis University will allow us to (1) learn about the impact of both educational events and individuals through the saving of participants' and observers' recollections, which are unlikely to be saved in documents or the public record; (2) gain a more holistic vantage of our entire reading community by studying the observations of pre-K–12 literacy teachers; and (3) know the lineage of each succeeding academic generation to understand the impact our professional ancestors have had on each of us. We believe that oral histories for literacy can be taken one step further as did Brandt (2001) as she interviewed of community members about the role of literacy experiences within their school years and across the lifespan. Hence, our primary duty as potential oral historians in literacy is to save the record of individual's contributions to the profession as well as individual's views on pedagogical movements or literacy experiences as encountered across the lifespan. Furthermore, we will have the opportunity to identify and record the underlining reasons, motivations, policies, and experiences behind individuals' life actions and scholarly endeavors.

As with all historical endeavors part of the groundwork for undertaking an oral history interview is developing a working knowledge of the era the interviewee observed or participated in the event of interest. Individuals serving as interviewers in the NRC project will consult era-appropriate primary sources or historically accurate secondary sources before conducting an interview and then again in seeking clarification of points raised during an interview. These works may include those authored by or of influence on the interviewee. Should the project focus on the nonelite, one might consider visiting a state or local historical society's archive for regional data, a school district's or state educational agency's repository for district records and curriculum materials, or a postsecondary institution such as the University of Pittsburgh or Northern Illinois University for a textbook collection. Review of such documents should help in the development of a purpose statement and the preparation of the questions to appear in the interview guide. In addition, gaining local color is possible through initial interviews of community members or family members.

The first step in undertaking the NRC project has been the selection of individuals to be interviewed. Interviewees in the NRC project are from the category of the elite as they are likely to have left a visual or auditory legacy through presentations at reading conferences, publication of professional articles, chapters and books, or service activities for organizations such as the NRC. The individuals participating in other projects may be classified as the nonelite because they are not as likely to leave a written legacy of their careers or experiences. It may be even more important to capture the perspectives of the nonelite on the role literacy played within their personal or professional lives. Brandt (2001) shows with her exemplary study of literacy in the lives of typical Americans the importance of selecting participants across varied professional status groups, their residence in different economic and geographical communities, and their diversity in culture.

Once a potential interviewee has agreed to be interviewed, that person must be informed of the project's focus and the type nature of questions to be asked. The greater the fit between the interviewer and the interviewee, the more apt that cooperation will be achieved and the interview process will be completed, particularly if there is a need for multiple interviews. The interviewee must be comfortable with the interview process and the recording of recollections through either audio or video technology.

Three cautionary notes need to be considered at this point in our discussion. Obviously, it is very important that any participant have the physical and mental capabilities to participate in the oral history interview. Within the NRC project one colleague planned to conduct an oral history with an elder member of our field's elite only to arrive at the interview site to discover that the individual's failing memory prevented the undertaking of the interview. Second, unlike with other historical investigations that do not focus on the personal element, the consent of the interviewee to participate in the study and to permit archiving and future research use of the transcription is standard procedure. (At the time of writing this chapter, the federal policy for institutional review of research involving human subjects dropped the requirement for the oral historian to obtain human subjects' approval. We suggest that each literacy historian check with the office of research compliance at his or her institution to learn of local requirements.) Finally, it is imperative that one be fully competent with the technology to be used during the interview process. Practice sessions are appropriate with each recording device to guarantee mastery with the technology and to evaluate its working condition.

An interview guide composed of open-ended questions will informally direct the interview process. While not every oral historian uses such a guide, these are helpful for the less experienced interviewer, and guides assist an interviewer with the obtaining of data for cross-case analysis. Participants in the NRC project are given an 11-stage lifespan guide with multiple subcategories (Stahl & King, 2000b) for interviewing members of the literacy profession. Brandt (2001) includes an excellent guide that should be consulted in designing a protocol for interviewing individuals from the general public about literacy lives. As important as an interview guide might be, Stahl and King (2000b) do note that one should not be a slave to the interview guide as the guide is but a starting point for the interview process.

The heart of the oral history process is the interview. Yet given our experiences we recommend undertaking several preparatory steps before the interview begins. First, the interviewer should share four or five topical statements about the subject matter of the interview with the respondent to activate prior knowledge. Next, he or she must visit the site of the interview to discover the likelihood that distractions or background noises will interfere with the interview. The interviewer must be sure that he or she and the interviewee will be seated comfortably and that the recorder will not be in direct view of the subject. In addition, the initial dialogue should be conversational to both break the ice and also make sure that the recorder or video camera can be checked for proper functioning. The preliminary step of the interview is the recording of identification information including the participants' names, the date, the time, the location, and the subject matter.

As the actual interview is undertaken, the questions in the guide provide a basic street map of the process. We are influenced by the seminal work of Baum (1987) in suggesting that guidelines for an oral history interview would include:

- Be careful not to dominate the interaction but, rather, draw out clear responses from the interviewee.
- Use open-ended questions (e.g., Can you tell me more about basal readers used in Catholic schools during the 1950s? What were your feelings about your attendance at your first International Reading Association convention?) rather than simple questions that elicit yes/no-type responses.
- Ask a single question at a time and make each question direct and to the point.
- Do not begin with more controversial topics such as the government's role in promoting high-stakes testing. Save these queries for when appropriate levels of trust and rapport have been developed. Be careful not to contradict the respondent.
- Listen carefully and provide for wait time.
- Do not interrupt the respondent. Gently move the person back on topic should digressions occur. Revisit the question at another time if necessary for clarity.
- Use questions that ask the respondent to describe individuals (i.e., personality, appearance, character, and actions) or the specific locations (e.g., classrooms, clinics, and schools) by drawing on the senses.
- Ask about the individual's specific role in each event (e.g., the founding of the College Reading Association or participation on the National Reading Panel). Was the interviewee an observer or an active participant?
- Encourage the respondent's answers to questions with the use of artifacts, documents, and photographs pertaining to the individual's literacy life.

- Avoid comments that are off the record. You can always "seal" the record for a period of time if necessary.
- Write down important points in a notebook. Ask for correct spellings (particularly names and locations) to promote accuracy.
- Do not allow fatigue to become a factor in the interview. It is better to schedule a second interview session if necessary.

Once the interview(s) are complete, the same identifying information as noted previously is once again read into the recording. Shortly after the session is over, an initial review of the recording should be made so that any problems with the recording can be identified and self-notes can be taken while information is still fresh in one's mind. A copy of the recording should be produced and stored in an alternative setting for safe keeping.

The transcription process should be undertaken within a short time of the interview session. Transcriptions are developed directly from the tape in a verbatim manner. The transcript must be a true accounting of the verbal dialogue between the interviewee and the interviewer. At a later date the interviewer would ask the respondent to review the tape for accuracy as well as personal comfort with the information included in the transcript.

The dissemination stage of a project is composed of two parts: immediate dissemination and long-term archival and dissemination functions. Immediate dissemination may take the form of presentation as done with the NRC project at the annual conference or the publication of either a report of an individual oral history (e.g., Dillon, 1985) or a report of thematically categorized oral histories (e.g., Clegg, 1997; King, 1991). Long-term archival functions require that the researcher find a depository for the transcripts and the tapes so that future generations of researchers might be able to review these materials in the years ahead. In some cases local or state historical societies or university libraries will undertake the archival responsibilities for a project, or as with the NRC project, an organization's historian or archivist will maintain the project's data.

OPPORTUNITIES FOR HISTORICAL RESEARCH

The opportunities for individuals to raise and then answer questions through the historical method are numerous and certainly needed at the cross-national, national, and nearby levels. Topics that have been studied in the past are also always open for revisionist interpretations based on new and overlooked evidence as well as different philosophical perspectives. Hence, rather than offering specific topics for potential research we integrate a number of broadly defined avenues for historical research as originally put forward by Stahl and King (2000a) for the field of postsecondary reading and by Skager and Weinberg (1971) for the general field of education:

- *Judging the impact of historical events* examines how pedagogical, sociological, political, and economic events and trends at the either the nearby, national, and cross-national levels affected the literacy field.
- *Focusing on an era* such as the "cognitive era" as promoted by the Center for the Study of Reading examines the impact of influential theories, philosophies, research findings, individuals, texts, institutions, and so on. within a demarcated era.
- *Assessing the impact of influential individuals* (the elite) examines the major contributions of leaders in the field such as William S. Gray, Helen Robinson, or George Spache and *tracing the literacy experiences of the nonelite* examines how teachers of reading and their learners were influenced by literacy practices and personalities through out their careers.
- *Consulting the experienced* examines what can be learned about the history of the literacy field and literacy practices by conducting interviews and archiving transcripts of the elite as with the NRC project and as with nonelite informants as undertaken by Brandt (2001) and King (1991).
- *Noting trends in literacy programs* examines changes in programs at schools, literacy centers, and colleges through collecting, summarizing, and analyzing program descriptions, evaluation-research data and reports, and field surveys over the years.
- *Tracing changes in materials* examines how published reading materials such as basal systems have changed or evolved based on theory, research, and pedagogical trends.
- *Observing changes across multiple editions* of targeted methods textbooks, worktexts, basal series, and so on leads to examining how theory, research, and best practice influenced the field through focus on long-lived texts with multiple editions such as Harris and Sipay's *How to Increase Reading Ability* (1991) or Pauk's *How to Study in College* (2001).
- *Judging innovation and movements* examines how instructional methods and curricular models such as Reading Recovery, the directed-reading thinking activity, or Direct Instruction have compared in effectiveness to their precursors and how well they have stood the test of time.
- *Appraising elements of instrumentation* examines how informal as-

sessment measures such as informal reading inventories and formal testing instruments such as the Stanford Diagnostic Reading Test have evolved and influenced literacy practice historically.

- *Comparing instruction, curriculum, and practice* examines programs across time and national boundaries through the comparative approach.

- *Focusing on an institution or a locale* examines literacy instruction or research that took place in a particular school, community, city, region, and nation and its impact on the field.

- *Tracking and evaluating an idea or a problem* examines the roots of a particular issue (e.g., schema theory or the literacy wars of the 1990s) and follows its evolvement or its impact across the years.

- *Creating archives and preserving a legacy* examines the processes of historiography for the profession and the practices of preserving primary sources such documents, relics, and oral transcriptions for future generations of professionals.

Such avenues for research are only suggestions for consideration. The final selection of a topic will be based in part on one's inherent interests in the topic. The final decision of the use of methodology—whether document analysis or oral history or a mixed method—will rest on the questions driving the research. Certainly an individual should have the degree of interest in the topic and the competence with the method(s) that will drive the research endeavors forward through a multitude of tasks and across what is often a lengthy period of time. Second, the decision should be based on an understanding of the standards and the parameters described throughout this chapter.

A still evolving mastery of the historical method should not stop an individual from undertaking historical research or from becoming a literacy historiographer. As Butchart (1986) counsels, "There is no need to be intimidated. You need not know all the methods or even most of them. The work of the historian has more in common with old craft traditions than with modern professions. . . . Native intelligence, careful work, and a willingness to learn are the only prerequisites" (p. 9). Still, we counsel the new literacy historian that there is value in reading texts on historiography (Tosh, 2002), on pedagogical historiography (Butchart, 1986; Goodson & Sikes, 2001; McCulloch & Richardson, 2000), and on literacy historiography (Gilstad, 1981; Monaghan & Hartman, 2000; Moore, Monaghan, & Hartman, 1997).

Furthermore, one should not feel that the first steps of being a literacy historian need be taken in monastic solitude as the new historiographer will find support through membership in the International Reading Association's History of Reading Special Interest Group. The online site for the SIG (*www.historyliteracy.org*) contains several "e-books" on resources for the conduct of literacy research. One of the works, titled *Connecting to Others Who Do Research on the History of Literacy* (Sears, Hartman, & Monaghan, 2003a), provides information on over 50 organizations supporting the work of individuals who study the history of literacy.

In closing we note that there has never been a better time to undertake historical research in the field of literacy. Moreover, there has never been a time where there was greater need for such research to be conducted.

REFERENCES

Anderson, I. H., & Dearborn, W. F. (1952). *The psychology of teaching reading*. New York: Roland Press.

Ary, D., Jacobs, L. C., & Razavich, A. (2002). *Introduction to research in education* (6th ed.) Belmont, CA: Wadsworth/Thompson Learning.

Balmuth, M. (1982). *The roots of phonics*. New York: McGraw-Hill.

Baum, W. K. (1987). *Oral history for the local historical society*. Nashville: American Association for State and Local History.

Benjamin, J. R. (2001). *A student's guide to history* (8th ed.). New York: Bedford/St. Martin's.

Best, J. W., & Kahn, J. V. (1989). *Research in education* (6th ed.). Englewood Cliffs, NJ: Prentice-Hall.

Borg, W. R., Gall, J. P., & Gall, M. D. (1993). *Applying educational research: A practical guide* (3rd ed.). New York: Longman.

Brandt, D. (2001). *Literacy in American lives*. Cambridge, UK: Cambridge University Press.

Brundage, A. (2002). *Going to the sources: A guide to historical research and writing* (3rd ed.). Wheeling, IL: Davidson.

Butchart, R. E. (1986). *Local schools: Exploring their history*. Nashville: American Association for State and Local History.

Caunce, S. (1994). *Oral history and the local historian*. London: Longman.

Cavallo, G., & Charter, R. (1999). *A History of Reading in the West*. Amherst: University of Massachusetts Press.

Clegg, L. B. (1997). *The empty schoolhouse: Memories of one-room Texas schools*. College Station: Texas A&M University Press.

Cohen, L., & Manion, L. (1994). *Research methods in education* (4th ed.). London: Routledge.

Darnton, R. (1990). What is the history of the books? In R. Darnton (Ed.),

The kiss of Lamourette: Reflections in cultural history (pp. 107–135). New York: Norton.

Dillon, D. (1985). Ira E. Aaron: A qualitative case study of a career history. *Georgia Journal of Reading, 11*(1), 18–25.

Fischer, S. R. (2001). *A history of writing*. London: Reaktion Books.

Fischer, S. R. (2003). *A history of reading*. London: Reaktion Books.

Gilderhus, M. T. (20031996). *History and historians: A historiographical introduction* (3rd ed.). Englewood Cliffs, NJ: Prentice-Hall.

Gilstad, J. R. (1981). Methodology of historical research of reading instruction: Principles and criteria. *Reading World, 20*, 185–196.

Good, C. V. (1966). *Essentials of educational research*. New York: Meredith.

Goodson, I., & Sikes, P. (2001). *Life history research in educational settings*. Buckingham, UK: Open University Press.

Gorn, E. J. (Ed.). (1998). *The McGuffey readers: Selections from the 1879 edition*. Boston: Bedford/St. Martin's.

Gray, W. (1991). *Historian's handbook: A key to the study and writing of history* (2nd ed. reissued). Prospect Heights, IL: Waveland Press.

Greenstein, D. I. (1994). *A historian's guide to computing*. New York: Oxford University Press.

Harris, A. J., & Sipay, E. R. (1990). *How to increase reading ability: A guide to developmental and remedial reading* (9th ed.). New York: Longman.

Issac, S., & Michael, W. B. (1976). *Handbook in research and evaluation*. San Diego: EdITS.

Johns, A. (1996). *The nature of the book: Print and knowledge in the making*. Chicago: University of Chicago Press.

Kaestle, C. F. (1988). Recent methodological developments in the history of American education. In R. M. Jaeger (Ed.), *Complementary methods for research in education* (pp. 61– 71). Washington, DC: American Educational Research Association.

King, J. R. (1991). Collaborative life history narratives: Heroes in reading teachers' tales. *Qualitative Studies in Education, 4*(1) 45–60.

Kyvig, D. E., & Marty, M. A. (2000). *Nearby history* (2nd ed.). Walnut Creek, CA: Alta Mira.

Leedy, P. D. (1958). *A history of the origin and development of instruction in reading improvement at the college level*. Unpublished doctoral dissertation, New York University. (University Microfilms No. 59–01016)

Leedy, P. D., & Ormrod, J. E. (2001). *Practical research—Planning and design*. Upper Saddle River, NJ: Merrill Prentice-Hall.

Manguel, A. (1996). *A History of Reading*. New York: Viking-Penguin Books.

Mathews, M. (1966). *Teaching to read: Historically considered*. Chicago: University of Chicago Press.

McCulloch, G., & Richardson, W. (2000). *Historical research in educational settings*. Buckingham, UK: Open University Press.

McDowell, W. H. (2002). *Historical research: A guide for writers of dissertations, theses, articles and books*. New York: Longman.

Monaghan, E. J., & Hartman, D. K. (2000). Undertaking historical research in literacy. In M. Kamil, P. Mosenthal, P. D. Pearson, & R. Barr (Eds.),

Handbook of reading research (Vol. III, pp. 109–121). Mahwah, NJ: Erlbaum.

Monaghan, E. J., Hartman, D. K., & Monaghan, C. (2002). History of reading instruction. In *Literacy in America: An encyclopedia of history, theory, and practice* (Vol. 1, pp. 224–231). Santa Barbara, CA: ABC/CLIO.

Moore, D. W., Monaghan, E. J., & Hartman, D. K. (1997). Values of literacy history. *Reading Research Quarterly, 32*(1), 90–102.

New England Primer Enlarged. (1975). Highland Park, NJ: Drier Educational Systems. (Original work published 1800)

Nolin, L., Swan, H. A., & West, P. C. (1991). *Historical images of education: Prints from the Blackwell history of education research collection.* DeKalb: Northern Illinois University.

Pauk, W. (2001). *How to study in college* (7th ed.). Boston: Houghton Mifflin.

Reiff, J. L. (1991). *Structuring the past: The uses of computers in history.* Washington, DC: American Historical Association.

Robinson, R. D. (2000). *Historical sources in U. S. Reading Education 1900–1970: An annotated bibliography.* Newark, DE: International Reading Association.

Rose, J. (2002). History of the Book. In *Literacy in America: An encyclopedia of history, theory, and practice* (Vol. 1, pp. 231–233). Santa Barbara, CA: ABC/CLIO.

Sears, L. A., & Hartman, D. K. (2003). *Disseminating research on the history of literacy.* History of Reading Special Interest Group (*http://www.historyliteracy.org/publications.html*).

Sears, L. A., Hartman, D. K., & Monaghan, E. J. (2003a). *Connecting to others who do research on the history of literacy.* History of Reading Special Interest Group (*http://www.historyliteracy.org/publications.html*).

Sears, L. A., Hartman, D. K., & Monaghan, E. J. (2003b). *Locating data for research on the history of literacy.* History of Reading Special Interest Group (http://www.historyliteracy.org/publications.html).

Sitton, T., Mehaffy, G. L., & Davis, O. L. (1983). *Oral history: A guide for teachers (and others).* Austin: University of Texas Press.

Skager, R. W., & Weinberg, C. (1971). *Fundamentals of educational research: An introductory approach.* Glenview, IL: Scott Foresman.

Smith, N. B. (2002). *American reading instruction* (spec. ed.). Newark, DE: International Reading Association.

Stahl, N. A. (2002). Epilogue. In N. B. Smith, *American reading instruction* (Special Edition) (pp. 413–418). Newark, DE: International Reading Association.

Stahl, N. A., & Henk, W. A. (1986). Tracing the roots of textbook-study systems: An extended historical perspective. In J. A. Niles & R. V. Lalik (Eds.), *Solving problems in literacy: Learners, teachers, and researchers. 35th yearbook of the National Reading Conference* (pp. 366–374). Rochester, NY: National Reading Conference.

Stahl, N. A., & King, J. R. (2000a). A history of college reading. In R. F. Flippo & D. C. Caverly (Eds.), *Handbook of college reading and study strategy research* (pp. 1–23). Mahwah, NJ: Erlbaum.

Stahl, N. A., & King, J. R. (2000b). Preserving the heritage of a profession through California Reading Association oral history projects. *The California Reader, 34*(1), 14–19.

Stahl, N. A., King, J. R., Dillon, D., & Walker, J. (1994). The roots of reading: Preserving the heritage of a profession through oral history projects. In E. G. Sturtevant & W. Linek (Eds.), *Pathways for literacy: 16th Yearbook of the College Reading Association*. Commerce: East Texas State University and the College Reading Association.

Stahl, N. A., King, J. R., & Eilers, V. (1996). Postsecondary reading strategies: Rediscovered. *Journal of Adolescent and Adult Literacy, 39*(5), 368–379.

Stickney, J. (1985). *Classics for children: A primer*. Boston: Ginn & Co. (Original work published 1885)

Thompson, P. (1988). *The voice of the past: Oral history* (2nd ed.). Oxford, UK: Oxford University Press.

Tosh, J. (2002). *The pursuit of history* (3rd ed.). New York: Pearson.

Webster, N. (n.d.). *The elementary spelling book, being an improvement on the American spelling book*. New York: American Book Company. (Original work published 1866)

Willis, A. I. (2002). Literacy at Calhoun Colored School 1892–1945. *Reading Research Quarterly, 37*(1), 8–44.

Wyatt, M. (1992). The past, present, and future need for college reading courses in the U. S. *Journal of Reading, 36*(1), 10–20.

Zimmerman, W. Z. (1982). *Instant oral biographies*. New York: Guarionex.

CHAPTER 10

Developing Affective Instrumentation for Use in Literacy Research

William A. Henk
Michael C. McKenna

The value of most literacy research depends on the integrity of the means used to assess the phenomena under study. Surely, the creation of valid and reliable *cognitive* measurements for reading, writing, and other language processes presents its share of noteworthy challenges (Gronlund, 1993). It is no small feat to generate higher-level achievement items and to identify authentic literacy tasks that measure not only what they purport (i.e., validity) but that do so in a genuinely dependable manner (i.e., reliability). Even so, as complicated as cognitive assessments can be to produce for use in literacy contexts, the development of *affective* indices represents an even more formidable task. As Athey (1985) has suggested, the affective aspects of literacy tend to be ill-defined and involve "shadowy variables" that are difficult to conceptualize, measure, and address.

Indeed, we believe that the special challenges inherent in the development of affective instruments make their consideration particularly instructive relative to the broader issues of instrument development in literacy research. Understanding the nature of these challenges and arriving at creative ways of meeting them can enhance one's understanding and appreciation of the issues entailed in cognitive instrument development.

In this chapter, we attempt to lay the groundwork for improving the current state of affective-related literacy measurement. To do so, we discuss the importance of rigorous affective instrument development, note the challenges inherent in creating such measures, and outline the attributes of desirable affective research tools. The heart of the chapter then describes specific procedures for developing these tools. We conclude by sharing our personal experiences with the instrument development process, highlighting the insights we have gained through our work on measuring reading and writing attitudes and self-perceptions.

Interestingly, a fair amount of literacy research involves the assessing of affective constructs of varying type and scope despite their elusive nature and attendant measurement obstacles. These measures can be self-report instruments, or they can be used either to guide observations or to note behavioral or physiological markers. They can be forced-choice or open-ended in nature and can occur in experimental, descriptive, qualitative, longitudinal, and even case-study research. The measures can inform both large-scale and small-scale investigations. From a developmental standpoint, affective measures can be found in studies whose emphasis ranges from emergent through adult and even family literacies. Within these studies, topics might range from literacy instruction and assessment to cultural and linguistic diversity, electronic technologies, urban education, task engagement, and preservice and in-service teachers' professional growth, to name just a few (Henk, 1999).

The respective affective constructs might be broadly defined (e.g., motivation for reading) or quite narrowly designed for a very specific purpose within a particular study (e.g., confidence about decoding a specific list of unfamiliar words, attitude toward reading a certain type of poetry, and teacher beliefs about the need for precise spelling in a particular writing genre). In the case of broadly defined affective constructs, the development of the instrument itself is often the whole purpose of the research effort. By specifying the development process and reporting the instrument's psychometric properties, authors who are engaged in this kind of research hold the expectation or hope that the tool will be used widely (Henk & Melnick, 1995; McKenna, Kear, & Ellsworth, 1995a). Despite the importance of these kinds of efforts, they are not overly plentiful in the professional literature, in all probability because they represent exhaustive undertakings. More frequently, instrument development is done to target the narrower affective measurement goals of an investigation, and the creation of the tools may not need to be quite as intensive. In either case, for the research to truly be of value, it is critical that both broadly and narrowly defined instruments be held to very high standards.

Unfortunately, regardless of the type and scope of this research and regardless of its diversity of topics, constructs, and developmental parameters, the affective measures in many literacy-oriented studies lack genuine psychometric integrity (Henk & Melnick, 1992). As a result, the findings cannot be regarded as altogether truthful or trustworthy, and the merit and usefulness of the work, which might otherwise be exemplary, can be called into question. In other words, literacy studies will only be as strong as their weakest links, and the measurement of affective elements seems to achieve this dubious distinction with considerable frequency.

Our twofold hope in presenting this information is (1) to help literacy professionals of all types become more informed consumers of research involving affective measures and (2) to provide a working knowledge of the instrument development process for individuals who may either want or need to fashion such tools. In the latter case, we recommend that readers seek knowledge and expertise beyond the scope of this chapter by consulting books devoted to affective instrument development (e.g., de Vaus, 2002; Gable & Wolf, 1993) and by collaborating with a measurement specialist.

Also, it should be noted that our treatment of affective instrument development in this chapter focuses on larger scale, broadly based measures. We think that this focus provides ample coverage of key concepts that can and should be applied to more narrow affective measures, also. That is, essentially the same procedures should be followed in the development of narrow, smaller-scale measures, although to a somewhat lesser extent. Whether large-scale or small-scale measures are to be created, we maintain that it is important for readers to have a solid sense of the nature and scope of the process, particularly the rigor necessary to ensure quality. Likewise, we focus on forced-choice types of instruments, rather than open-ended approaches to gathering affective data, such as interview protocols and questionnaires (see Baumann & Bason, Chapter 13, this volume, for discussion of interview and survey research). At the same time, however, we believe that our sections on desirable attributes of affective items and on the steps of the instrument development process itself are extremely instructive for those types of measures as well.

WHY AFFECTIVE INSTRUMENT DEVELOPMENT IS IMPORTANT

Achievement and Affect

The importance of developing high-quality affective instrumentation derives from the critical link between achievement and affect in literacy learning (Purves & Beach, 1972; Walberg & Tsai, 1985). Clearly, the attitudes, values, expectations, and beliefs that individuals possess will play a vital role in shaping their engagement with reading, writing, and other literacy processes. We know, for instance, that children who believe they are competent readers outperform those who fail to hold such beliefs and that children who perceive reading as valuable and personally relevant will approach reading in a more deliberate and engaged way (Ames & Archer, 1988; Dweck & Elliott, 1983; Paris & Oka, 1986; Schunk, 1985). In effect, we know that children who report positive associations with literacy will tend to read and write more often, for greater periods of time, and with heightened intensity. Accordingly, this deeper engagement translates to superior reading and writing ability (Anderson, Fielding, & Wilson, 1988; Foertsch, 1992). By the same token, we know that when children feel negatively about literacy, their achievement tends to suffer (Spaulding, 1992). These disaffected children, and similarly afflicted adults for that matter, will either avoid literacy tasks at nearly every opportunity or read and write with little passion, commitment, or intensity.

In some ways, of course, a circular, chicken-and-egg causality exists between achievement and affect. Just as negative attitudes can curtail achievement, problems in learning to read can lead to negative attitudes, and so forth. A dismal downward spiral can result (McKenna, 2001), and research has documented a Matthew effect over time as the attitudes of the best and worst readers diverge (McKenna et al., 1995a). In his classic study of avid adult readers (whom he described as "ludic"), Nell (1988) could find only one characteristic that all of them shared—proficiency. Reading ability does not ensure positive attitudes, but it is almost certainly a prerequisite. The complex relationship between achievement and affect makes it imperative for teachers and researchers to monitor affective dimensions of reading growth and for instrument developers to provide them with the tools they need to do it.

Gaps in the Field

Not surprisingly, then, the affective domain remains an area of keen interest for both literacy educators and researchers (Cramer & Castle, 1994; Henk & Melnick, 1998; Mathewson, 1985; Turner & Paris, 1995). Regrettably, despite the significant role played by affective variables influencing literacy-related motivation (attitudes, self-perceptions, beliefs, etc.), there is a striking lack of truly valid and reliable instrumentation to tap these constructs. This dearth is particularly acute in terms of quantitative group surveys that can function as a natural complement to individually administered qualitative instruments (McKenna & Kear, 1990). Moreover, the scarcity serves as an ongoing obstacle to the assessment of the reading and writing profiles of individual children as well as to the more expansive goal of evaluating affective aspects of literacy interventions and programs. The lamentable result is that our instructional practices in literacy have not fully benefited from this potentially useful information.

The history of affective instrument development in literacy pales in comparison to the rich tradition enjoyed by cognitive measurements (Henk & Melnick, 1995). Because constructs in the affective domain are more difficult to operationalize and measure, researchers have been unwilling or unable to embrace the profound challenges that empirically sound literacy instrumentation demands. Put another way, high-quality affective instruments require adherence to an intense multistage validation process that many developers intentionally or unintentionally circumvent. As a result, most instruments exhibit weak psychological grounding, small and idiosyncratic samples, and psychometric inadequacies (McKenna et al., 1995a). These conditions compromise construct validity and internal scale reliabilities and surely threaten external generalizability. Such drawbacks are especially problematic in studies whose affective measures lack appropriate theoretical grounding or are so vaguely defined that they seem to be more a function of intuition than disciplined inquiry.

OUR WORK BRIEFLY NOTED

Despite the many barriers to developing high-caliber affective measurements, the past decade or so has witnessed some noteworthy progress in assessing these aspects of literacy. For instance, McKenna and Kear (1990) developed the Elementary Reading Attitude Survey (ERAS), a very popular and useful instrument that taps elementary children's attitudes toward both academic and recreational forms of reading. Another affective instrument that has emerged, the Reader Self-Perception Scale (RSPS), measures how children in grades 4 through 6 feel about themselves as readers (Henk & Melnick, 1992, 1995), and more recently, the Writer Self-Perception Scale (WSPS) has been used to assess how children at these upper elementary levels feel about themselves as writers (Bottomley, Henk, & Melnick, 1997). Still more recently, Kear, Coffman, McKenna, and Ambrosio

(2000) introduced the Writing Attitude Survey (WAS), an instrument for use in grades K–12. All four of these self-report instruments have been validated systematically, and each gauges dimensions of affect that clearly influence literacy engagement. Most important, they allow for a richer appraisal to be made of an individual's literacy orientation and permit various approaches to reading and writing instruction to be compared along key affective lines.

Our work in developing these multifactor, forced-choice, self-report instruments served as true learning experiences for us. While both of us were well versed in assessing the cognitive domain, the affective domain represented somewhat of a stretch. Neither of us possessed a firm understanding of the steps involved in the affective instrument development process, nor did we possess *a priori* direct experience with sophisticated statistical tools such as factor analysis that are used to evaluate affective scales. Among many lessons learned, we came to know that affective literacy constructs do indeed tend to defy operationalization and are otherwise resistant to capture.

In comparing our respective bodies of work in the affective domain, we also learned that our approaches, while quite similar, were not identical. For example, the ERAS built on a rather long history of moderately successful attempts to measure attitude toward reading, but its unique contributions centered on differentiating between academic and recreational forms of reading and on invoking large-scale norming. The WAS expanded on earlier work by Knudson (1991, 1992, 1993), whose three scales covered grades K–12. The WAS represented a consolidated and expanded version of Knudson's item sets and, equally important, served to establish norms. The RSPS and WSPS broke new ground by adapting Bandura's (1977, 1982) theory of self-efficacy to reading and writing and by adhering to rigorous standards for factor analysis. For the purposes of illustration, we use the RSPS as our exemplar for large-scale affective instrument development in this chapter.

The Motivation to Read Profile (MRP) by Gambrell, Palmer, Codling, and Mazzoni (1996), another well-developed, larger-scale affective literacy instrument, deals with self-concept and reading task value. It followed yet another development pathway centered on expert ratings of content validity and internal consistency estimates. Likewise, the Motivation for Reading Questionnaire by Wigfield and Guthrie (1997) took still another route. This latter instrument was predicated on an earlier study involving interviews and classroom observations, and its item writing corresponded to three major categories of motivation: self-efficacy, intrinsic and extrinsic motivation and learning goals, and social aspects of motivation. In turn, these categories were further divided into a total of 11 aspects of motivation, and these aspects were analyzed using internal consistency estimates, item-to-total correlations, interscale correlations, and factor analysis. We regard this work as one of the better examples of smaller-scale affective instrumentation specifically developed for an explicit purpose within a single literacy study, although there may be some question about the factor-analytic procedures that were used. While we do not discuss the study at length here, we encourage readers who are interested in consuming or conducting this kind of research to consult the work and judge its value themselves.

Across all the aforementioned instruments, differences in the nature of the affective constructs themselves and their respective foundations allowed for varied yet equally defensible approaches to instrument development. This assertion drives our current thinking that there is simply no one lockstep method for creating sound affective literacy measurements. The model we describe later in this chapter, then, represents a flexible prototype that will lend itself to both large- and small-scale applications. The key point, however, is that meticulous affective instrument development—and meticulous development for instruments of any kind—leads to higher quality in the literacy studies that deploy them.

CONSIDERATIONS FOR AFFECTIVE LITERACY INSTRUMENTS

Appropriate Purposes and Uses of Affective Instruments

Affective literacy instruments can be used for a wide range of research purposes. In *experimental* research, these tools and their component scales can yield scores that function as primary or secondary dependent variables. Employed properly, they are particularly well suited to serving as final outcome measures in studies comparing different methods of reading and writing instruction (e.g., Bottomley, Truscott, Marinak, Henk, & Melnick, 1999; McKenna, Stratton, Grindler, & Jenkins, 1995b). Some interesting situations could emerge from this type of research, especially when literacy achievement is considered simultaneously. That is, it is enlightening to note instances in which dramatic affective changes occur, yet literacy achievement remains equivalent between groups. In such cases, a method might still be defensible on its affective merits alone. Conversely, an intervention might enhance literacy achievement but fail to exert a significant affective impact, or even have a negative impact? While growth in achievement would commend the approach, the likelihood of its promoting lifelong literacy learning would be debatable.

Scores from affective instruments can also be used as blocking variables and covariates in experimental literacy research. In the former case, subjects can be grouped for investigation in terms of having high or low levels of a particular affective construct such as attitude toward writing. These differentiations would enable researchers to explore interactions between degrees of the affective construct and various treatments such as Balanced Literacy (Blair-Larsen & Williams, 1999), Four Blocks (Cunningham & Allington, 1999), Reading Recovery (Clay, 1985), or Reciprocal Teaching (Palinscar & Brown, 1984, 1985; Rosenshine & Meister, 1994). As covariates, however, affective measures taken either before or at the outset of an experiment can be used to adjust both cognitive and affective posttest measures statistically. For example, if one group of subjects held an initial affective advantage of some kind, an analysis of covariance procedure could be used to adjust posttest measures accordingly. In turn, this adjustment would help to ensure the fairness and merit of the comparison. Using covariation as a statistical control is important when the researcher suspects a logical relationship, often causal, between the affective construct and posttreatment indices of the intervention's effectiveness.

In *descriptive* research, an affective instrument might serve the role of trait indicator or as a predictor or criterion variable in regression analyses. As a trait indicator, it would function much like a blocking variable. As a case in point, classroom observations might be made more meaningful when the findings are viewed in light of children having been classified as possessing high or low levels of an affective construct such as literacy self-esteem or perceived locus of control. When applied to regression analyses, the construct and its scale scores could be used, singularly or among a list of factors, to predict some outcome. Applied this way, they could possibly be correlated with various other affective or achievement measures or included among several predictor variables aimed at explaining some criterion. For that matter, the affective scores might also serve as the very criterion variables that the researcher is trying to predict. Regrettably, precious few examples of appropriately developed affective instruments for descriptive literacy research exist.

Although the present volume focuses on literacy *research*, it bears mentioning that affective instruments are often used by educators to inform instructional *practice*. Data yielded by affective scales such as the ERAS, the WAS, the RSPS, the WSPS, and the MRP's Reading Survey and Conversational Interview can be used for diagnostic purposes with individual children (McKenna & Stahl, 2003). Often this information helps to explain why certain children fail to achieve their literacy potentials. For example, a child with average or higher intelligence might not be performing as expected because her literacy attitudes, self-perceptions, or motivation might be below par. Likewise, a teacher can create a class profile using tools of this type to give strategic direction to enhancing the affective climate for literacy learning (see Bottomley et al., 1997, for an explanation). In this instance, the data would indicate whether the classroom environment contributes positively or negatively to various aspects of children's affective literacy perceptions.

Desirable Attributes of Affective Literacy Instruments

Appropriate Wording of Items

If an instrument is to elicit responses that accurately reflect an individual's feelings, beliefs, or behaviors, the clarity of items is essential. Items that do not clearly communicate what the researcher wishes to know pose threats to reliability and validity alike. The six guidelines that follow may help refine an instrument prior to field testing by improving the clarity and precision of items. We base these guidelines loosely on questions posed by de Vaus (2002).

1. *Keep the language simple.* Be mindful of the age of the participants you intend to target. Avoid words and expressions they are unlikely to know. Aim for simple grammatical structures and shorten overall length of items where feasible. If you find it impossible to simplify an item to the point at which intended participants are likely to understand it, it may be better to eliminate the item than to risk its being misunderstood.

2. *Avoid items that ask two questions in one.* The question, "How often do you read to your children?," for example, assumes that the respondent has children. One technique for avoiding this pitfall is to use filter questions. In this instance, the respondent would first be asked, "Do you have young children?" Only if the answer is "yes" would the question about read-alouds be raised. Filter questions have long been used in print instruments but are also well suited to computer contexts.

3. *Avoid leading items.* The way an item is worded can bias responses in a particular direction. Consider: "Do you agree with the large body of scientific research proving that the method of repeated readings contributes to oral reading fluency?" Incorporating such biases may occasionally be deliberate (e.g., in political polling), but they can prevent a researcher from discovering the true perspectives of participants. Better would be: "Do you agree with research indicating that the method of repeated readings may contribute to oral reading fluency?"

4. *Avoid negatively worded items.* These can be difficult to understand, especially for children. Consider a statement such as this: "If I do not read my assignments, I may not graduate." In this case, the double negative may confuse students, who may assume that by agreeing to the statement they are somehow indicating that it is desirable not to read one's assignments. A related problem involves items that have an orientation that is the reverse of the others. In the ERAS, for example, a positive response to each item involves the broadly grinning Garfield at the far left. In developing the instrument, however, items such as the following were initially considered: "How would you feel if there were no books?" To respond to this item by circling the grinning Garfield would reflect a negative attitude, unlike all the other items. Researchers occasionally embed items such as this one, with reverse directionality, in order to detect a response set (i.e., a tendency to respond in like manner to every item without deliberation). But reversing the order of the response categories can be confusing, especially to young children, and some researchers deliberately avoid this practice (e.g., Ragheb & Beard, 1982). Besides, there is other evidence that a response set may be present, as when a child renders uniformly positive or negative responses.

5. *Use words that have similar meanings for everyone.* This is not always possible, of course, but you should attempt to anticipate how the terms you use are likely to be interpreted. In a survey of struggling secondary students (McKenna, 1986), participants were asked to rate various reading topics. They rated "science" low even though their ratings of several science-related topics was much higher. It appears likely that they associated the term *science* with a school subject and summarily dismissed it as boring.

6. *Make sure the frame of reference is clear.* Respondents may find it difficult to answer unless certain parameters are clarified. Consider: "How many hours per week do you spend reading?" A student may well wonder if the questioner intends to include assigned reading or just leisure reading.

Ease of Responding

In open-ended instruments requiring written responses, the chief factor to consider is an appropriate amount of space in which to write. The amount provided must be adequate for the responses sought. It may also convey a subtle message about the extent of elaboration expected. In forced-choice instruments, requiring the respondent to select from among several options, the mechanics of responding should be as simple as possible (checking, circling, bubbling, etc.). Experienced examinees should have no problem with response columns, where the categories appear only once per page at the top of each column or in a legend at the beginning of the instrument. For young children, however, it is imperative to repeat the categories *for each item*, whether they are words, pictures, or numbers. Looking elsewhere for reference points and keeping one's bearings on the page while doing so are sophisticated skills that young children may lack.

Another consideration is whether the respondent is expected to read the items. When the target group comprises mature readers, this expectation is usually realistic. However, when the instrument targets young children or older struggling readers (often the case in reading-related assessments), the examiner must take into account possible decoding deficits of the target group. If these difficulties are likely to interfere with comprehension of items, then the items must be read aloud by the examiner while the children respond in tandem.

Clear Directions

Respondents must understand exactly what is requested of them. Mature individuals, with experience in responding to affective instruments, may need little other than a straightforward, directive sentence. In the case of children, however, more may be required. A sample item might be included so that the task is fully exemplified. The examiner might be instructed to make a transparency of the response categories and to explain them carefully. In the case of the ERAS, for example, pilot testing revealed that younger students tended to confuse the second and third pictures of Garfield, which differ only around the mouth. In one, Garfield is slightly smiling; in the other, he wears a slight frown. By pointing out this distinction, the ambiguity was eliminated. It is important to try to anticipate such problems, or at least to address them during the piloting process.

Length

Generally speaking, the longer the instrument, the more reliable it is. This is why piloting generally begins with an overabundance of items and then pares them down to a manageable number that is still high enough for adequate reliability. A balance must be sought between too few items (resulting in low reliability) and too many (resulting in fatigue and distraction). Some authorities (e.g., de Vaus, 2002) recommend arranging the instrument so that it progresses from conceptually simpler items to those requiring more thought and striving for a logical "flow" from item to item.

Steps for Validating Affective Literacy Instruments

Our recommended process for developing valid and reliable affective literacy instrumentation is adapted from Gable (1986). The process involves several related steps, all of which contribute to the caliber of the final affective instrument (see Table 10.1). In general, as adherence to the process increases, one can expect a higher standard of quality. We present a preferred order of steps, but the actual sequencing can be varied somewhat. Because the instruments can be scaled in different ways, it may make sense to diverge from the prescribed format.

Identify the Constructs and Conceptual Definitions

Every meaningful affective instrument, like any cognitive instrument, begins with an exhaustive review of the relevant literature. The

---

TABLE 10.1. Steps in the Affective Instrument Development Process

1. Identify the constructs and conceptual definitions.
2. Develop operational definitions and generate the potential item pool.
3. Select a scaling technique.
4. Conduct a judgmental review of items.
5. Identify a response format.
6. Prepare draft and final instruments.
7. Gather and analyze pilot data from appropriate samples.
8. Revise the instrument.
9. Conduct a final pilot study.
10. Produce the final instrument.
11. Conduct additional validity and reliability analyses.
12. Consider social desirability.
13. Prepare documentation for the instrument.

---

literature review allows the developer to determine the specific constructs to study, and to create conceptual and operational definitions of the constructs. This step ensures that the instrument receives appropriate theoretical grounding, and it reveals the full history of the construct's treatment in the field. The developer learns how the construct or related constructs have been conceived, how they have been defined, and how they have been measured. In turn, this knowledge assists the researcher in refining the construct and its measurement by pointing to the breaking of new ground. Basically, the review enables the developer to build on the sum total of previous work related to the literacy phenomena under study.

With regard to the RSPS, Henk and Melnick (1992) originally sought a theoretical framework that would undergird the instrument. The review of the literature suggested that Bandura's theory of self-efficacy (1977, 1982) held excellent promise as a model to apply to the construct of reader self-perceptions. These researchers noted Bandura's four major categories of self-efficacy (i.e., performance, observational comparison, social feedback, and physiological states) and began thinking seriously about how to define each of these concepts as a prelude to drafting the items themselves.

Develop Operational Definitions and Generate the Potential Item Pool

Once the literature has been properly reviewed and the conceptual definitions established, operational definitions must be developed. This notion of jumping the gap between the conceptual variable and the operational definition is so important that it has been noted as perhaps the essence of science (Forsyth, n.d.). The operational definitions drive the writing of the items and result in the belief statements to be used in the instruments. Depending on the type of scaling, the developer might purposely create statements (or adjectives) that (1) collectively span favorable, neutral, and unfavorable aspects of the construct's continuum; (2) can be judged to be either favorable or unfavorable, but not neutral; or (3) form the extremes of the favorable or unfavorable continuum. In any event, the items must be written with the greatest of care if the construct is to be assessed effectively.

Select a Scaling Technique

There are multiple techniques available to scale affective characteristics including equal-appearing intervals (Thurstone, 1931), latent trait analysis (Lazarsfeld & Henry, 1968), summated ratings (Likert,

1932), and the semantic differential (Osgood, Suci, & Tannenbaum, 1957). As Gable and Wolf (1993) suggest, all the techniques attempt to locate an individual's response on a bipolar evaluative dimension with respect to a given target object. Each scaling technique results in a single affective score derived on the basis of responses to a set of belief statements.

The most popular scaling technique is Likert's summated rating. A Likert scale allows for the summation and averaging of scaled responses—that is, attaching numbers to levels of meaning. Likert scales typically involve using statements that span the construct's continuum, but this is not always the case. With the RSPS, a Likert type scale was used, but to some extent, with its focus on factor analysis, the interpretation resembled latent trait analyses. That is, Likert response choices, which typically span a continuum (such as "strongly agree, somewhat agree, neither agree nor disagree, somewhat disagree, and strongly disagree"), were used, and the factor analysis used these response patterns to designate items as belonging to one of the principal RSPS scales.

Osgood's semantic differential, another type of scaling, involves the use of bipolar adjectives (e.g., valuable/worthless and excitable/calm). Respondents are asked to rate the object along the line between the two anchoring antonyms. The semantic differential centers on a person's subjective understanding of the connotative meanings of words: *evaluation*, *power*, and *activity*. These three measurable, underlying dimensions of attitude are used by individuals to evaluate everything in their social environment, regardless of language or culture. A discussion of differentiated intensity, which typically accompanies any description of the semantic differential (i.e., evaluative, potency, and activity dimensions), is beyond the scope of this chapter; however, suffice it to say that these types of scales typically comprise evaluative adjectives, with only a few adjectives from the potency and activity dimensions included as anchors to clarify the interpretation of a later factor analysis (Gable, 1986). The problem with the semantic differential is that it does not distinguish beyond a single evaluative continuum, with positive attitude at one end of the scale and negative attitude at the other end. That is, it does not actually identify any individual emotions.

Still another scaling technique is Thurstone's equal-appearing interval. Here, a large number of statements pertaining to the attitude topic are generated, and judges rate them in terms of whether they are positive, negative, or neutral. Items are then selected to create a scale that has several items for each gradation of attitude toward the topic, ranging from some very positive items, some less positive items, and so on. In responding to the final scale, subjects choose only those items that reflect their attitudes.

Conduct a Judgmental Review of Items

One of the most important steps in the affective instrument development process involves the rating of proposed statements or items by content experts (de Vaus, 2002). Again, this step will vary somewhat depending on the scaling technique, but in all cases, the judges must review and evaluate the statements or adjectives in terms of how well they relate to the conceptual definitions of the affective construct. The review might also involve rating the assignment of items to scale categories as well as how favorable or unfavorable they are (as with equal-appearing intervals), how well they relate to the conceptual definitions and categories (latent traits), or their relative positivity or negativity and the extent to which the statements reflect the conceptual definition and categories (summated ratings).

With the RSPS, the developers asked content experts to rate items in terms of which categories the statements best represented and the strength of the association to the category. The original content validity rating scale appears in Figure 10.1. Note that the adult judges were asked to assign each of the proposed 49 items to one of Bandura's self-efficacy dimensions (or a default "Other" category) and to rate how strongly they felt the statement fit the category. In effect, the judgmental review examines the degree of fit of items within categories. Beyond the actual rating of the items, the judgmental review provides insight into the clarity of the directions and the operational definitions of the categories. It is essential that these aspects of the task are clear so that the fit of the items is the only factor being measured. The developer hopes not only that the items are placed in the intended categories but also that the placements are robust ones.

Making subjective judgments about items is intended to help ensure that they in fact gauge the constructs we intend to measure. Put another way, such judgments can be effective in establishing the instrument's validity. It is important, however, to note that this attribute can never be absolutely established. It is rather a case to be made, and the greater the variety of evidence one can offer, the more persuasive that case becomes. To expert judgment of items, for example, we might compare the scores on a newly developed instrument with those of an established measure, thus producing evidence of concurrent validity. We might demonstrate that scores on the new instrument correlate with future outcomes' evidence of predictive validity.

Content Validity Rating Form
Self as Reader Scale

Instructions

1. Read the conceptual definitions for each category listed below. For each item stem, please fill in the category letter (A, B, C, D, E) that you believe each statement best fits. (Statements not fitting any category should be placed in Category E.)
2. Please indicate **how strongly you feel about your placement of the statement into the category** by filling in the appropriate rating number as follows:

   3—no question about it
   2—strongly
   1—not very sure

Categories	Conceptual Definitions
A. Performance	An individual's self-perception of ability based upon any of the following: —*past success or failure* with the task —the amount of *effort* necessary to be successful —the *ease or difficulty* of the task —task *persistence* —the *need for assistance* with the task —*patterns of progress* with the task —*seeking* or *avoiding* the task —belief in the *effectiveness of task-related instruction*
B. Observational Comparison	An individual's self-perception of ability based on observations of *how similar others (especially peers) perform the task*
C. Social Feedback	An individual's self-perception of ability based on *direct and indirect feedback from others*
D. Physiological States	An individual's self-perception of ability based on *bodily feedback* (such as comfort, calmness, trembling, and sweating) while engaged in the task
E. Other	Statement does not fit into any of the above categories

FIGURE 10.1. Original content validity rating form for the Reader Self-Perception Scale.

We might document that scores are related to present circumstances in logical ways. Higher reading attitude scores should, in theory, be related to public library visits or the likelihood of having a library card—evidence of construct validity. The best affective instruments offer more than a single source of validation as the developers make their case to prospective users and to consumers of research employing those instruments.

Identify a Response Format

The scaling technique selected will largely determine the response format. When using the latent trait and Likert techniques, the format must allow the respondent to indicate relative degrees of agreeing, importance, or frequency, most often using a 5-point scale. The equal-appearing-intervals technique requires a format that enables respondents to select statements that describe the target being rated, whereas the semantic differential uses bipolar adjectives (antonyms) that appear at the ends of the response continuum.

Develop Directions for Responding

As noted previously, clear directions for responding to the instrument are critical, and precise wording becomes even more vital when young children represent the target group. Vague, incomplete, or overly complex directions can literally ruin the instrument. Just as the items should be written at an appropriate readability level for all respondents, the directions must be equally comprehensible. Respondents need to know exactly what they are supposed to do. To achieve this goal, it is useful to provide a supplementary oral script or set of guidelines for the administrator to follow. These instructions often go well beyond the written directions provided on the instrument. They might explain the purpose of the instrument, help put respondents at ease, elaborate on response options, elucidate sample items, encourage honesty and completeness, note any time limits, or describe what to do when problems occur during the task as well as when they have finished their work. As a crosscheck, directions should be reviewed by colleagues and tested on members of the target group.

Prepare Draft and Final Instruments

Considerable care should be taken in formatting the instrument. The layout should make appropriate use of spacing and should be designed not only to be attractive but also to be fully functional. The size and color of the paper as well as the style and size of font can give the instrument a professional appearance. The arrangement of print on the page should lead the respondent effortlessly through the instrument. Directions should be clearly marked, and the scaling information should stand out visually and be stated in explicit terms. The focal point of any sample items should be completely familiar to the respondents, and an explanation linked to the response choices should be given. Again, a small number of colleagues should be consulted regarding the clarity of the directions, the readability of the items, and the ease of responding. A well-designed, easily read protocol signals to the respondent that the task is a serious one.

Gather and Analyze Pilot Data from Appropriate Samples

A major criticism of many existing affective measures is that they have not been tested with large enough samples to ensure stability. It is recommended that there be 6 to 10 times as many respondents as there are statements in the instrument in order to conduct a factor analysis (Gable, 1986). While this number may seem large for a pilot study, these data represent crucial determinants of the validity, reliability, and scoring scheme of the instrument. The pivotal issue here, though, is not so much the size of the pilot sample but rather the variability and representativeness of its response patterns compared with the target population. When the response patterns do not match the larger population, both the factor structure and internal consistency of the scales will be compromised. A mismatch can occur if the heterogeneity of the target population is not adequately reflected in the sample. For example, an instrument designed to assess the reading attitudes of inner-city children at risk should not be piloted with a sample of affluent suburban children. Therefore, it is suggested that the sample vary with regard to ability, gender, curriculum track, school type, and the like. By the same token, once the results are finalized, they should not be generalized to other populations because the factor structure of the affective construct is likely to vary across different ages and grade levels. We suspect that the challenges of large-scale sampling represent a prevalent disincentive for developing high-quality affective measures, particularly for small-scale applications.

There are three key analyses associated with pilot data: item analysis, factor analysis, and reliability analysis. Item analyses involve response frequencies, percentages, measures of central tendency and variation, and correlations. Typically, items exhibiting unusually high or low means and small standard deviations warrant closer inspection and should be considered for elimination or revision. The items should also be significantly related to the scale score that represents all the valid items defining the scale. In turn, the categories or scales comprising the affective construct should probably be correlated with one another, but only moderately so. If the correlations are too high, it would indicate that the scales share so much variance as to be essentially measuring the same factor.

Factor analysis is a sophisticated statistical procedure that specifies which items are being responded to on a similar basis. The analysis presumes that there is a psychological reality to likenesses in response patterns that signal the presence of construct validity. Consequently, a factor analysis can tell the researcher which specific items belong to particular scales.

The output of a factor analysis resembles a matrix in which the columns equal the number of significant factors revealed by the procedure, and each item is represented by a unique row. For each item, a weight is calculated under each significant factor, and the researcher pays special attention to the largest positive coefficient in the row, assuming that the item is most related to, or loads on, this factor (see Table 10.2). Ideally, all the items presupposed to represent a particular scale will load most on that factor.

In the case of the RSPS, the hope was that there would be four significant factors corresponding to Bandura's self-efficacy dimensions. For the ERAS, it was hoped that two significant factors would emerge corresponding to attitudes toward academic and recreational reading. Within each of these scales, the desired result was that all the items revealed by the judgmental review as being strongly associated with a particular scale or category would, in fact, show the highest factor loadings on the same factor. When the items cluster in this manner, the assumption is that the instrument has psychometric integrity. Achieving a desirable factor structure is an extremely difficult task, and this fact coupled with the numerous conceptual complexities associated with factor-analytic techniques (multivariate mathematical modeling, extraction methods, assumptions of models, rotational patterns, etc.) drives our recommendation to seek the services of an expert consultant when engaged in affective literacy instrument development.

Pilot data also need to be examined in terms of scale reliabilities. A reliability coefficient is calculated for each item cluster indicated by the factor analysis. The coefficient indicates the extent to which the items making up the scale are internally consistent. Cronbach's

TABLE 10.2. Factor Analysis of Reader Self-Perception Scale Items

Item	1	2	3	4
R10	.706	.103	.179	.152
R13	.563	.201	.205	.198
R15	.705	.131	.170	3-780E-02
R18	.809	8.943E-02	7.719E-02	.147
R19	.706	.109	.186	.196
R23	.670	.300	.194	−1.061E-02
R24	.699	.323	.189	.138
R27	.657	.308	.154	8.778E-02
R28	.601	.294	.239	6.449E-02
R4	.160	.211	.695	.290
R6	.230	2.594E-02	.670	7.633E-.02
R11	.265	5.502E-02	.741	.245
R14	.402	.129	.497	8.898E-02
R20	.300	.109	.790	.161
R22	.172	.380	.663	.229
R2	6.099E-02	.208	6.468E-02	.780
R3	.248	.123	.298	.626
R7	9.430E-02	.255	.301	.568
R9	.183	.220	.327	.405
R12	.368	9.111E-02	.225	.597
R17	.201	.177	.181	.776
R30	.141	.255	.303	.527
R31	.259	.198	.211	.681
R33	7.227E-02	.369	6.030E-02	.605
R5	3.554E-02	.284	.101	.477
R8	.246	.581	4.009E-02	.277
R16	.275	.708	6.126E-02	.309
R21	.177	.682	.211	1.412E-02
R25	.234	.671	.171	.124
R26	.262	.754	.119	.168
R29	.215	.800	9.396E-02	.205
R32	.176	.768	9.880E-02	.215

Note. Principal component analysis with varimax rotation. **Boldface** indicates the highest factor loading for each item. Factor 1 = Progress; Factor 2 = Observational Comparison; Factor 3 = Social Feedback; Factor 4 = Physiological States.

alpha is the statistic most commonly used for this computation (Cronbach, 1951). For affective measures, reliability coefficients of .70 or higher are considered to be acceptable (Gable, 1986), whereas coefficients of .90 are required for cognitive measures. Computer programs such as *SPSS* (*Statistical Package for the Social Sciences*) can indicate the alpha coefficient that would exist when a particular item is removed from the scale. As a general rule, the discarding of items with low item-to-scale correlations should increase the reliability for the remaining items, especially when the number of items per scale is limited.

Revise the Instrument

The analysis of the pilot data will point the developer to ways that the instrument could or should be modified. Usually this process involves deleting, adding, refocusing, or rewording items. These changes should improve the clarity of the items while increasing the validity and reliability of the instrument as a whole.

Conduct a Final Pilot Study

When the revisions to the instrument are extensive, it will be necessary to collect and analyze additional pilot data. Fortunately, careful attention to previous steps often precludes the need for a final pilot study. However, if any doubt remains, it is advisable to conduct the "extra" pilot because unstable factor structures and reliabilities will undermine the future usefulness of both large- and small-scale affective measures.

Produce the Final Instrument

Steps should again be taken to produce a fully functional, professional-looking final instrument. Most important, it should be reinspected for physical layout and ease of reading.

Conduct Additional Validity and Reliability Analyses

Once the factor structure appears to be stable and the items have been refined, the examination of validity should be extended by correlating the instrument with other known related measures and conducting additional factor analyses. For instance, the concurrent validity of the RSPS was established by correlating each of its subscales with the subscales of the ERAS. Moreover, various types of factor rotations can be undertaken to ensure that the factor structure will hold up in the future. Likewise, additional types of reliability evidence could be sought, such as stability–reliability, to check that the affective construct and its scales are constant over time. All this extended information contributes to a meaningful understanding of scores derived from the new affective instrument.

Consider Social Desirability

The term *social desirability* (SD) generally refers to the tendency to re-spond in a manner inconsistent with one's true feelings but, rather, with what the respondent believes the examiner wishes. For example, an individual may harbor negative feelings toward reading but re-spond to the contrary on a written survey. SD poses a threat to the internal validity of affective instruments, and it behooves investiga-tors to acknowledge the extent to which the tendency to produce SD responses may have influenced results. As an illustration of the SD tendency to portray one's feelings more positively than they truly are, consider the fourth item of the ERAS (McKenna & Kear, 1990, p. 630):

4. How do you feel about getting a book for a present?

Some students who know they would, in fact, be disappointed at this prospect may nevertheless respond affirmatively in order to please the teacher. Does this mean that ERAS scores are always inflated? Is the problem likely to occur more frequently at some grade levels? Most important, are there precautions an investigator can employ to mitigate the difficulty?

Screening for SD Bias

A quick way of screening for such bias is to identify children who have provided the most positive response to every item. Such a pat-tern does not, of course, confirm that they were dissembling (i.e., cre-ating a false appearance), but it would be consistent with an SD ten-dency. Other evidence may support or refute the suspicion of false appearances, such as an individual child's classroom behavior with respect to reading.

From the standpoint of instrument development, it is important to consider first whether such a scale should be used at all. There is some evidence that the use of open-ended projective techniques, in which children respond to incomplete sentences, may reduce the ef-fects of social desirability (Patnaik & Puhan, 1988). It may be more difficult for children to generate an SD response without the prompt that is available in a scale format. Projective instruments are more difficult to evaluate, however, and their results are not easy to aggre-gate for quantitative analysis. Moreover, because SD research has been mainly conducted in the field of clinical psychology with older, abnormal populations, it is difficult to infer much about the SD bias of instruments designed to measure literacy affect with normal children in classrooms.

Correlation with an SD Scale

An SD scale measures the tendency of an individual to produce socially desirable responses. If a literacy scale is being developed, one method of detecting an SD bias is to administer the new instrument together with an SD scale and to measure the degree to which the two are correlated. An investigator hopes for a zero correlation between the SD measure and the scale being developed.

In theory, the extent to which children may produce socially desirable responses on a newly developed measure of literacy affect can be determined by simultaneously administering the new instrument with the Children's Social Desirability Questionnaire (CSDQ) (Crandall, Crandall, & Katkovsky, 1965). If a significant Pearson product-moment correlation coefficient were obtained, then (1) the new instrument could be revised to reduce the correlation, (2) the coefficient could be reported as a limitation of subsequent investigations, or (3) a multiple regression analysis could be computed in order to remove the effects of social desirability. We suspect, however, that the SD bias among children tends to be overestimated by instruments like the CSDQ. Consider the following item:

3. Do you always enjoy yourself at a party?

The correct answer to this question is supposed to be "no." That is, the instrument developers assumed that to respond affirmatively means that the child is dissembling. The reasoning is that no one has fun at every party one attends. While this may be true for adults, whose more extensive experiences tend to include a boring party or two, the experiences of young children are likely to be quite different, so that it is clearly possible to provide an honest positive response. This unintended artifact may explain findings suggesting that SD bias tends to decline as children get older (Cruse, 1963; Walsh, Tomlinson-Keasey, & Klieger, 1974). The slight SD bias found in ERAS scores (McKenna, Stratton, & Grindler, 1992) can probably be safely discounted for this reason.

Prepare Documentation for the Instrument

If the affective instrument is intended for large-scale use, documentation for administration, scoring, and interpretation should be made available to colleagues through a test manual, website, or professional publication of some sort. The documentation should explain the pragmatic and theoretical rationale for the instrument, describe the instrument development process in sufficient detail to allow for replication, report validity and reliability data, and provide tables to enable score interpretation.

INSIGHTS AND LESSONS LEARNED

There is no question that we learned many valuable lessons as a result of our experiences developing affective literacy instruments. We realized very quickly, for instance, that when the wording of an item is not ideal, all manner of outcomes can occur and none of them are good. It has amazed us how a single less-than-perfect word choice can utterly compromise the measurement characteristics of an otherwise reasonable item. Without a doubt, the developer of an affective literacy measure must strive for explicitness because anything less will engender flawed response patterns. Beyond precision, the developer must carefully anticipate how items are going to be interpreted by respondents. The intent of an item must be absolutely straightforward, because any lack of clarity, any potential ambiguity, any unexpected word connotation, or any deviance from the nature of the construct will invariably cause the item to perform poorly.

We also learned that one of the greatest challenges in affective instrument development involves getting the factor-analytic model to converge and the individual items to load properly. It is not uncommon for the factor structure to contain either fewer or more factors than the intended model, and there are often items that simply do not load on the expected scales. In the development of both the ERAS and the RSPS, the original factor structures did not manifest as originally hoped, and there were individual items whose factor loadings were undesirable. For instance, the ERAS factor structure indicated three factors, when the model called for two factors that represented attitudes toward academic and recreational reading, respectively.

The initial RSPS factor structure was even more problematic. Three factors came together as predicted (i.e., observational comparison, social feedback, and physiological states); however, the items identified in the judgmental review as belonging to the performance category failed to coalesce in anything even remotely close to a meaningful way. In this case, it was not a simple matter of some less-than-ideal word choice in the items. Something was fundamentally wrong with the category from a measurement standpoint. The developers struggled intensely with this psychometric dilemma, trying to find a solution that would galvanize the category. They came to realize that the problem stemmed from the multifaceted way that the performance dimension had been operationalized initially by Bandura (i.e., success, effort, ease, persistence, need for assistance, avoidance, progress, and instructional effectiveness), and later in the instrument's judgmental review. The items reflected dimensions that were simply too disparate to allow for the scale to converge. Clearly, a unifying concept was needed to align as many of those dimensions as possible. Fortunately, an insightful graduate student who assisted with the project, Sylvia Rosen, commented informally that most of the dimensions might fall under the single aspect of progress. That conclusion proved to be invaluable. The performance items were rewritten to force the progress dimension by contrasting past reading status with current reading status (e.g., "I can figure out words better than I could before." Or, "When I read, I don't have to try as hard as I used to."). Once these changes were made, a second piloting was conducted, and a new factor structure emerged. Four scales were indicated whose respective items clustered tightly within them, as hoped. This new structure occurred because the revamped progress scale finally converged.

Interestingly, using the concept of progress, as opposed to performance, made the development of the subsequent WSPS much easier (Henk, Bottomley, & Melnick, 1996; Henk et al., 1997). In that instance, though, the factor structure took an unexpected turn, namely, two distinct dimensions of writing progress resulted—general progress (e.g., "My writing has improved.") and specific progress (e.g., "The order of my sentences makes better sense now."). Without advance planning on the developers' part, a second scale whose characteristics were extremely desirable literally presented itself. The key point here is that it takes considerable time and energy, and sometimes good fortune, to achieve the desired factor structure and individual item factor loadings.

As we reflect on our experiences, we understand why it might be that high-quality affective literacy measures have tended to be in short supply. Certainly, the complexities of factor-analysis techniques alone represent a deterrent; however, assuming that researchers are aware of the formal instrument development process, we believe that its intensity discourages interested researchers from embracing such a formidable challenge. Not only does faithfulness to the process require extensive labor, but it also requires an abundance of time. For researchers who want to use a specialized affective measure as only one narrow aspect of their work, the cost of time and energy might seem particularly exorbitant relative to the outcome. The seduction here would be to dilute the meticulous technical development of the measures in the interest of generating results in a more timely fashion. We think that, in the interest of true disciplined inquiry, the additional quality assurances are more than worth the price; they are essential.

Our primary goal in writing this chapter has centered on advancing the field of literacy as it pertains to measuring affect. To that end, we have attempted to inform all readers about proper procedures for developing affective instruments. And, more specifically, we hope that at one important level our treatment of the topic here directly enhances the caliber of affective indicators literacy researchers will use in doing their work. At another level, we hope to sharpen the critiques of literacy professionals when they consume research literature involving affective measurement. And, at an intervening level, we hope to encourage the gatekeepers of the professional discourse on literacy to exercise the highest standards of evaluation when reviewing research whose findings have affective implications. Editors, reviewers, newsletter editors, webmasters, and executive board members of professional organizations alike should insist that all affective claims are ultimately grounded in defensible measurement paradigms. In sum, by trying to raise the bar for affective measurement at all these levels, our fondest wish is that the field of literacy, and all its numerous stakeholders, will be better served.

REFERENCES

Ames, C., & Archer, J. (1988). Achievement goals in the classroom: Students' learning strategies and motivation processes. *Journal of Educational Psychology, 80*, 260–267.

Anderson, R. C., Fielding, L. G., & Wilson, P. T. (1988). Growth in reading and how children spend their time outside of school, *Reading Research Quarterly, 23*, 285–303.

Athey, I. (1985). Reading research in the affective domain. In H. Singer & R. B. Ruddell (Eds.), *Theoretical models and processes of reading* (3rd ed., pp. 527–557). Newark, DE: International Reading Association.

Bandura, A. (1977). Self-efficacy: Toward a unifying theory of behavioral change. *Psychological Review, 84*, 191–215.

Bandura, A. (1982). Self-efficacy mechanism and human agency. *American Psychologist, 37*, 122–147.

Blair-Larsen, S., & Williams, K. (Eds.). (1999). *Working together to provide a balanced reading program*. Newark, DE: International Reading Association.

Bottomley, D. M., Henk, W. A., & Melnick, S. A. (1997). Assessing children's views about themselves as writers using the Writer Self-Perception Scale. *The Reading Teacher, 51*, 286–296.

Bottomley, D. M., Truscott, D. M., Marinak, B. A., Henk, W. A., & Melnick, S. A. (1999). An affective comparison of whole language, literature-based, and basal literacy instruction. *Reading Research and Instruction, 38*(2), 115–129.

Clay, M. M. (1985). *The early detection of reading difficulties* (3rd ed.). Portsmouth, NH: Heinemann.

Cramer, E. H., & Castle, M. (Eds.). (1994). *Fostering the love of reading: The affective domain in reading education*. Newark, DE: International Reading Association.

Crandall, V. C., Crandall, V. J., & Katkovsky, W. (1965). A children's social desirability questionnaire. *Journal of Consulting Psychology, 29*, 27–36.

Cronbach, L. J. (1951). Coefficient alpha and the internal structure of tests. *Psychometrika, 16*, 297–334.

Cruse, D. B. (1963). Socially desirable responses in relation to grade level. *Child Development, 34*, 777–789.

Cunningham, P. M., & Allington, R. L. (1999). *Classrooms that work: They can all read and write* (2nd ed.). New York: HarperCollins.

de Vaus, D. A. (2002). *Surveys in social research* (5th ed.). New York: Routledge.

Dweck, C., & Elliot, E. (1983). Achievement motivation. In P. Mussen (Ed.), *Handbook of child psychology, Vol. 4: Socialization, personality, and social development* (pp. 643–691). New York: Wiley.

Foertsch, M. A. (1992). *Reading in and out of school: Factors influencing the literacy achievement of American students in grades 4, 8, and 12 in 1988 and 1990* (Vol. 2). Washington, DC: National Center for Education Statistics.

Forsyth, D. R. (n.d.) *Measurement in social psychological research*. Retrieved from http://www.people.vcu.edu/~jforsyth/methods/measure.htm

Gable, R. K. (1986). *Instrument development in the affective domain*. Boston, MA: Kluwer-Nijhoff.

Gable, R. K., & Wolf, M. B. (1993). *Instrument development in the affective domain: Measuring attitudes and values in corporate and school settings* (2nd ed.). Boston, MA: Kluwer-Nijhoff.

Gambrell, L. B., Palmer, B. M., Codling, R. M., & Mazzoni, S. A. (1996). Assessing motivation to read. *The Reading Teacher, 49*, 518–533.

Gronlund, N. (1993). *How to make achievement tests and assessments* (5th ed.). New York: Allyn & Bacon.

Henk, W. A. (1999). *Exploring how kids feel about themselves as readers and writers*. Paper presented at the annual meeting of the Keystone State Reading Association, Hershey, PA.

Henk, W. A., Bottomley, D. M., & Melnick, S. A. (1996). Preliminary validation of the Writer Self-Perception Scale. In E. G. Sturtevant & W. M. Linek (Eds.), *Growing literacy: Eighteenth yearbook of the College Reading Association* (pp. 188–199). Harrisonburg, VA: College Reading Association.

Henk, W. A., Bottomley, D. M., Melnick, S. A., Truscott, D. M., Finke, J. A., Rickelman, R. G., Marinak, B. A., & Helfeldt, J. P. (1997). The Writer-Self Perception Scale: A cumulative validation update. In C. K. Kinzer, K. A. Hinchman, & D. J. Leu (Eds.), *Inquiries in literacy theory and practice: Forty-sixth yearbook of the National Reading Conference* (pp. 555–563). Chicago: National Reading Conference.

Henk, W. A., & Melnick, S. A. (1992). The initial development of a scale to measure "perception of self as reader." In C. Kinzer & D. Leu (Eds.), *Literacy research, theory, and practice: Views from many perspectives: Forty-first yearbook of the National Reading Conference* (pp. 111–117). Chicago: National Reading Conference.

Henk, W. A., & Melnick, S. A. (1995). The Reader Self-Perception Scale (RSPS): A new tool for measuring how children feel about themselves as readers. *The Reading Teacher, 48,* 470–482.

Henk, W. A., & Melnick, S. A. (1998). Upper elementary-aged children's reported perceptions about good readers: A self-efficacy influenced update in transitional literacy contexts. *Reading Research and Instruction, 38,* 57–80.

Kear, D. J., Coffman, G. A., McKenna, M. C., & Ambrosio, A. L. (2000). Measuring attitude toward writing: A new tool for teachers. *The Reading Teacher, 54,* 10–23.

Knudson, R. E. (1991). Development and use of a writing attitude survey in grades 4 and 8. *Psychological Reports, 68,* 807–816.

Knudson, R. E. (1992). Development and application of a writing attitude survey for grades 1 to 3. *Psychological Reports, 70,* 711–720.

Knudson, R. E. (1993). Development of a writing attitude survey for grades 9 to 12: Effects of gender, grade, and ethnicity. *Psychological Reports, 73,* 587–594.

Lazarsfeld, P. F., & Henry, N. W. (1968). *Latent structure analysis.* Boston: Houghton Mifflin.

Likert, R. (1932). A technique for the measurement of attitudes. *Archives of Psychology, 140,* 152.

Mathewson, G. C. (1985). Toward a comprehensive model of affect in the reading process. In H. Singer & R. B. Ruddell (Eds.), *Theoretical models and processes of reading* (3rd ed., pp. 841–856). Newark, DE: International Reading Association.

McKenna, M. C. (1986). Reading interests of remedial secondary school students. *Journal of Reading, 29,* 346–351.

McKenna, M. C. (2001). Development of reading attitudes. In L. Verhoeven & C. Snow (Eds.), *Literacy and motivation: Reading engagement in individuals and groups* (pp. 135–158). Mahwah, NJ: Erlbaum.

McKenna, M. C., & Kear, D. J. (1990). Measuring attitude toward reading: A new tool for teachers. *The Reading Teacher, 43,* 626–639.

McKenna, M. C., Kear, D. J., & Ellsworth, R. E. (1995a). Children's attitudes toward reading: A national survey. *Reading Research Quarterly, 30*, 934–956.

McKenna, M. C., & Stahl, S. A. (2003). *Assessment for reading instruction*. New York: Guilford Press.

McKenna, M. C., Stratton, B. D., & Grindler, M. C. (1992, November). *Social desirability of children's responses to a reading attitude survey*. Paper presented at the annual meeting of the College Reading Association, St. Louis, MO.

McKenna, M. C., Stratton, B. D., Grindler, M. C., & Jenkins, S. (1995b). Differential effects of whole language and traditional instruction on reading attitudes. *Journal of Reading Behavior, 27*, 19–44.

Nell, V. (1988). *Lost in a book: The psychology of reading for pleasure*. New Haven: Yale University Press.

Osgood, C. E., Suci, C. J., & Tannenbaum, P. H. (1957). *The measurement of meaning*. Urbana: University of Illinois Press.

Palinscar, A. S., & Brown, A. L. (1984). Reciprocal teaching of comprehension fostering and comprehension monitoring activities. *Cognition and Instruction, 1*(2), 117–175.

Palincsar, A. S., & Brown, A. L. (1985). Reciprocal teaching: Activities to promote reading with your mind. In T. L. Harris & E. J. Cooper (Eds.), *Reading, thinking and concept development: Strategies for the classroom*. New York: College Board.

Paris, S. G., & Oka, E. R. (1986). Children's reading strategies, metacognition, and motivation. *Developmental Review, 6*, 25–56.

Patnaik, S., & Puhan, B. N. (1988). Immunity of projective-inventories to social desirability. *Psychological Studies, 33*(2), 132–136.

Purves, A. C., & Beach, R. (1972). *Literature and the reader: Research in response to literature, reading interests, and the teaching of literature*. Urbana, IL: National Council of Teachers of English.

Ragheb, M. G., & Beard, J. G. (1982). Measuring leisure attitude. *Journal of Leisure Research, 14*, 155–167.

Rosenshine, B., & Meister, C. C. (1994). Reciprocal teaching: A review of the research. *Review of Educational Research, 64*, 479–530.

Schunk, D. H. (1985) Self-efficacy and classroom learning. *Psychology in the Schools, 22*, 208–223.

Spaulding, V. (1992). The motivation to read and write. In J. W. Irwin & M. A. Doyle (Eds.), *Reading/writing connections: Learning from research* (pp. 177–201). Newark, DE: International Reading Association.

Thurstone, L. L. (1931). The measurement of attitudes. *Journal of Abnormal and Social Psychology, 26*, 249–269.

Turner, J. C., & Paris, S. G. (1995). How literacy tasks influence children's motivation for literacy. *The Reading Teacher, 48*, 662–673.

Walberg, H. J., & Tsai, S. (1985). Correlates of reading achievement and attitude: A national assessment study. *Journal of Educational Research, 78*, 159–167.

Walsh, J. A., Tomlinson-Keasey, C., & Klieger, D. M. (1974). Acquisition of the social desirability response. *Genetic Psychology Monographs, 89,* 241–272.

Wigfield, A., & Guthrie, J. T. (1997). Relations of children's motivation for reading to the amount and breadth of their reading. *Journal of Educational Psychology, 89,* 430–432.

CHAPTER 11

Meta-Analysis in Reading Research

Adriana G. Bus
Marinus H. van IJzendoorn

WHAT IS META-ANALYSIS?

Meta-analysis is the empirical analysis of empirical studies—that is, the quantitative analysis and synthesis of a set of related empirical studies in a well-defined domain. Similar to narrative reviews of extant literature on a specific hypothesis or theory, meta-analysis tests hypotheses and aims at uncovering trends and gaps in a field of inquiry. Different from narrative reviews, meta-analysis uses rigid replicable analytic procedures. A common and defining characteristic of all meta-analytic approaches is the use of a specific set of statistical methods compared to the methods used in primary research. The reason is simple: In primary research the unit of analysis is the individual participant (or class, or other group), whereas the unit of meta-analysis is the study result. Study results are usually based on different numbers of participants, and they are, therefore, point estimates with different precision and confidence boundaries (Mullen, 1989). It would be incorrect to give a significant correlation of .30 in a sample of 50 participants (confidence interval: .02 ~ .53) the same weight as a correlation of .30 in a sample of 500 participants (confidence interval: .22 ~ .38). Basically, however, meta-analytic research follows the same steps and standards as empirical research.

Meta-Analysis as a Step in a Research Program

Meta-analysis can be applied most fruitfully within research programs in which studies with similar designs or measures accumulate over the years. In the spiral of research efforts, primary studies, secondary analyses, replications, and meta-analyses each play their crucial roles in promoting our understanding (see van IJzendoorn, 1994, for further details). In primary studies, data are collected to test a hypothesis derived from a well-articulated theory; the hypothesis often will be stated in the form: variable X is associated with variable Y, or X is causally related to Y. In correlational or experimental designs, measures prototypical to assess X and Y are being used, and the results are therefore comparable across studies. If the results of the first empirical study on the association between X and Y are remarkable because of their effect size or direction, the next step in the spiral of research may be the secondary analysis of this first study. The secondary analysis uses the data as collected in the primary study, and through recoding with a different coding system and reanalyzing these data with different statistical methods, the original outcome is scrutinized.

The reanalysis may lead to falsification of the original outcome, as in Kamin's (1974) reanalysis of some of Burt's data on the heredity of intelligence in twins. In some cases it may be difficult, however, to make the original data available for further study (Wolins, 1962). In any case, replication studies should then be performed to test the same hypothesis with new data that are collected in a different sample, and with different designs or measures. If the number of replications increases, and if characteristics of replication studies vary, the meta-analytic approach is feasible to synthesize the literature and to test the effects of variations in study characteristics on the outcome of the studies.

Because meta-analyses are based on numerous decisions about collecting, coding, and analyzing the pertinent studies, meta-analytic results, in their turn, need to be replicated as well (Lytton, 1994). Even if replications of meta-analyses yield the same results, they will never constitute the final argument in the spiral of scientific research. On the contrary, the most fruitful meta-analyses will lead to new hypotheses for further primary study (Eagly & Wood, 1994).

Figure 11.1 presents a process model of progress in research programs through different methodologies. Meta-analyses have not been positioned in a more crucial role than any other systematic form of inquiry. Meta-analyses are part of a series of connected steps in the description and explanation of human behavior that never reaches a final point (van IJzendoorn, 1994).

A BRIEF HISTORY OF META-ANALYSIS

A century ago Karl Pearson (1904) reported on one of the first meta-analytic combinations of the outcomes of a set of medical studies, and during the past few decades the approach became extremely pop-

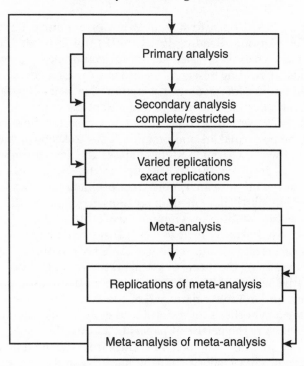

FIGURE 11.1. A process model of different types of replications. Adapted from van IJzendoorn (2002). Copyright 2002 by Bohn Stafleu Van Loghum. Adapted by permission.

ular in the so-called evidence-based medical science. It was the educational researcher Glass (1976) who coined the concept "meta-analysis" some 25 years ago and introduced it into the educational and behavioral science. He provided one of the most controversial examples of its application on psychotherapy studies, arguing that, in general, psychotherapy had considerable effect, but that no specific treatment modality stood out (Smith & Glass, 1977).

To our knowledge, one of the first meta-analyses in reading was conducted by Kavale on correlates of reading: visual perceptual skills, auditory perceptual skills, and auditory–visual integration. He simply provided average correlations across studies between these predictors and success or failure in reading (Kavale, 1980, 1981, 1982; Kavale & Forness, 2000). During the past 15 years, meta-analysis has become widely used and hotly disputed in educational science. In fact, it seems that is has been applied on a much wider scale in education than in any other social or behavioral science. The reason may be that educational policy decisions (like medical decisions) are supposed to be based on a firm foundation of empirical data (Slavin, 2002). The National Reading Panel (NRP), for example, decided to conduct meta-analyses in their search for commonalities and important trends in reading research, in order to present evidence-based recommendations for reading instruction (National Reading Panel, 2000). Every decade the number of scientific papers is doubling (Garfield, 1979), and it becomes impossible even for the specialists—let alone the policymakers and practitioners—to keep track of the literature in their own field. Meta-analyses are increasingly used to monitor new developments in any area of the social and behavioral sciences. In reading research more than 30 meta-analyses have been conducted, in particular on interventions to enhance the development of reading abilities in children (see Table 11.1).

In the past, narrative reviews were considered the royal road to the synthesis of literature, and some narrative reviews indeed were very powerful in shaping the future of a field of enquiry (e.g., Adams, 1990). In a narrative review of high standards, the author tries to make sense of the literature in a systematic and at the same time creative way. In formulating a hypothesis for review in a precise manner, and in collecting systematically the pertinent papers to address the issue, the narrative reviewer does not act much differently from the meta-analyst. It is in the stage of data analysis that the narrative and meta-analytic reviewer go separate ways. Narrative reviewers may have the focus of telling readers what the field has and has not investigated more than what has been found. Insofar as they focus on conceptual analysis of studies these might not include numerical results at all—as in a review of ethnographies of home literacy practices in different communities. The meta-analysts, on the contrary, proceed in a statistically rigorous way analyzing studies that include numerical results.

Cooper and Rosenthal (1980) showed experimentally that narrative reviewers are more inclined to commit type II errors (i.e., they tend to not reject the null hypothesis although it should be rejected on statistical grounds). Cooper and Rosenthal asked 41 graduate students and senior researchers to review a set of seven studies on the association between sex and persistence in performing rather dull tasks. Half of the reviewers were randomly assigned to a course on meta-analysis. Seventy-three percent of the untrained, narrative reviewers found no association; only 32% of the meta-analysts came to this conclusion. The correct outcome was that female participants are significantly more persistent in performing boring tasks than are males. In particular, in cases in which studies show insignificant trends, the accumulated effect size across these studies tends to be underestimated. It should be noted that despite this potential bias,

TABLE 11.1. Focal Questions in Meta-Analyses in the Domain of Reading

Beginning reading methods

- Are whole language or language experience approaches more effective than basal readers? (Stahl & Miller, 1989)
- Is whole language instruction effective compared to basal instruction for kindergarten to third-grade pupils with low SES? (Jeynes & Littell, 2000)
- Is systematic phonics more effective than unsystematic phonics? (Ehri et al., 2001a)

Phonemic awareness instruction

- Does phonemic awareness training affect learning-to-read processes in a positive and substantial way and are programs combining phonemic awareness training with letters and words more effective? (Bus & van IJzendoorn, 1999)
- Is phonemic awareness instruction effective in helping children learn to read? Under what circumstances and for what children? (Ehri et al., 2001b)

Book reading

- Is there a relation between parent-preschooler book-reading and emergent and conventional reading? (Bus et al., 1995)
- Does book reading in schools affect oral language and reading skills? (Blok, 1999)

Preschool intervention

- Do preschool intervention programs cause a positive effect on reading achievement? (Goldring & Pressbey, 1986)

Reading comprehension instruction

- Does vocabulary instruction affect reading comprehension? (Stahl & Fairbanks, 1986)
- Does sentence-combining promote reading comprehension? (Fusaro, 1992)
- Does instruction in question asking affect reading comprehension? (Rosenshine, Meister, & Chapman, 1996)
- Which forms of comprehension instruction improve reading comprehension? (National Reading Panel, 2000)

Acquiring vocabulary through reading

- Does instruction in deriving meaning from context improve skills to derive meaning from context? (Fukkink & de Glopper, 1998)
- Do children incidentally derive new words from texts? (Swanborn & de Glopper, 1999)

Other aspects of reading instruction

- Does some form of guided oral reading stimulate reading achievement? (National Reading Panel, 2000)
- Does the Lightspan program (computer games to improve school-based achievement) improve reading comprehension, reading vocabulary, sounds/letters, word reading? (Blanchard & Stock, 1999)

(continued)

TABLE 11.1 *(continued)*

Effects of grouping and tutoring

- Does one-to one tutoring on reading promote reading skills? (Elbaum et al., 2000b)
- Is effect size of reading instruction related to grouping format (pairing, small groups, etc.)? (Elbaum et al., 1999; Elbaum et al., 2000a)

Effects of school organization

- Do second graders who have received 2 years of instruction in smaller classes score significantly higher in reading than do second graders who have experienced no project classes? (McGiverin et al., 1989)
- Does reading achievement decline over summer holiday? (Cooper, Nye, Charlton, & Lindsay, 1996)

Instruction of children with reading disabilities

- What is the overall effectiveness of sight word teaching for individuals with moderate and severe disabilities? (Browder & Xin, 1998)
- Does direct instruction yield higher effect sizes than strategy instruction in groups with learning disabilities? (Swanson & Hoskyn, 1998; Swanson, 1999)
- Do studies using strategy instruction or direct instruction yield higher effect size estimates than studies using competing models? (Swanson & Sachse-Lee, 1999)
- Do instructional components predict positive outcomes for adolescents with learning disabilities on measures of higher-order processing? (Swanson, 2001)

Bilingual education

- Is bilingual education more effective than submersion? (Willig, 1985)

Characteristics of children with learning disabilities

- Are auditory perception skills related to reading? (Kavale, 1980, 1981)
- Is visual perception an important correlate of reading achievement? (Kavale, 1982)
- Which of six variables (language, sensory skills, behavioral-emotional, soft neurological, IQ, and teacher ratings) provide the best early prediction of later reading difficulties? (Horn & Packard, 1985)
- Do dyslexics and normal readers differ in terms of phonological skill despite equivalent word recognition abilities? (van IJzendoorn & Bus, 1994)
- Do measures that tax the processing as well as the storage resources of working memory predict comprehension better than do measures that tax only the storage resources? (Daneman & Merikle, 1996)
- Is a regularity effect also present in a group with learning disabilities? (Metsala et al., 1998)
- Do children with learning disabilities differ from normal achieving children in immediate memory performance and does this difference continue? (O'Shaughnessy & Swanson, 1998)
- Do underachieving students with and without learning disabilities label differ? (Fuchs, Fuchs, Mathes, & Lipsey, 2000)
- What is the relative importance of auditory and visual perception in predicting reading achievement? (Kavale & Forness, 2000)

narrative reviews remain indispensable, in particular in those areas in which a restricted number of empirical studies have been conducted or in the absence of strong research programs that unify the empirical approaches and make them comparable for meta-analytic purposes.

STAGES AND QUALITY STANDARDS IN META-ANALYSIS

Meta-analysis and primary studies are structured in similar ways. In fact, meta-analysts should proceed through the same stages as the primary researchers (Cooper, 1982). The meta-analysis should start with the formulation of a specific and theoretically relevant hypothesis. Its domain should be clearly defined, and the central meta-analytic question should be theoretically derived and meaningful ("precise and relevant hypothesis").

In the next stage, the meta-analyst should systematically collect the relevant published as well as unpublished literature from at least three different sources. The "snowball" method (using references lists from key papers in the field), the "invisible college" approach (using key figures in the field to collect recent or unpublished materials), and computer searches of subject indexes such as ERIC, PsychLit, Medline, Dissertation Abstracts, or citation indexes such as SSCI or SCI may be used in a multimethod combination.

In some meta-analytic approaches selection of studies is based on the idea that only randomized experimental designs produce valid findings to be taken seriously. The Cochrane consortium in medical science, for example, uses this selection criterion in their worldwide efforts to generate evidence-based medical recommendations (website: Cochrane.org). The NRP applies a similar criterion, in their case accepting findings based on experimental or quasi-experimental designs; they object to inclusion of all studies regardless of design features. Restrictions of the type of papers to be included, however, may imply an untenable reduction of the available evidence. For instance, the NRP discards the many correlational investigations in the area of reading research (National Reading Panel, 2000; Williams, 2001) which means a loss of potentially important information. It should also be noted, that in this respect the meta-analytic method is basically indifferent: The central hypothesis should decide about the feasibility of selection criteria, and when this hypothesis is not stated in strictly causal terms there is no reason to leave correlational studies aside. Effects of the quality of research on effect sizes can be tested. In this respect, the exhaustive search for pertinent literature is preferred compared to the best evidence approach (Slavin, 1986), in which only the qualitatively sound studies would be allowed to enter a meta-analysis. Because of their emphasis on explanation of variability in effect sizes, in recent meta-analytic approaches it is preferred to test whether quality of research (which always is a matter of degree, and a matter of different strengths and weaknesses) explains variation in study results, in order to make the process of study selection and evaluation transparent, and to maximize the power of the analyses.

The basic problem to be faced in this stage of the meta-analysis is the "file-drawer" problem (Rosenthal, 1991). Primary researchers know that it is easier to get papers published in which they report significant results than to guide papers into print with null results—regardless of the quality of the study (Begg, 1994). This publication bias may even lead to the unfortunate situation that the majority of papers remain in the file drawers of disappointed researchers, whereas only a minority of papers with significant results is published (Cohen, 1990). Average or combined effect sizes of published papers may therefore present an inflated picture of the real state of the art in a specific field. The number of unpublished papers with null findings can be estimated that are needed to make the meta-analytic outcome insignificant (the "fail-safe number"; Rosenthal, 1991). The "file-drawer" problem may suggest that *a priori* selection of only published papers is not always warranted. Although published studies have been subjected to more or less thorough reviewing procedures and therefore seem to carry more quality weight than unpublished studies, the reasons for remaining unpublished may be unrelated to quality. In many cases it is therefore better to collect all studies regardless of origin or status, and to analyze *post hoc* whether publication status makes a difference in combining effect sizes ("unbiased and exhaustive set of papers").

Studies may report effects on several dependent measures for similar outcome measures. To avoid a situation in which studies with more results have a greater impact, the effect sizes should be aggregated within studies and domains. Experiments may include two or more interventions but only one control group. Effect sizes are dependent if the same control group is used to calculate the effect sizes for each treatment (e.g., Ehri et al., 2001b). Gleser and Olkin (1994) state that in multiple-treatment studies, "the treatments may all be regarded as instances or aspects of a common treatment construct." Furthermore they state that "there is strong reason a priori to believe that a composite effect size of treatment obtained by combining the end point effect sizes would adequately summarize the effect of treatment" (p. 351). Another, more pragmatic solution of the multiple-interventions problem is to divide the control group in the same number of subgroups as there are interventions, in order to avoid the situation in which control subjects count for more than one unit of analysis.

Studies may use a variety of outcome measures to test effects, which makes outcomes hard to interpret. For instance, Stahl, McKenna, and Pagnucco (1994) noted that whole-language researchers increasingly preferred to use attitude toward reading rather than direct measures of performance assessment. Whole-language advocates assert that the key to learning language well rests in enjoying the learning process. They state that because whole language constitutes a more natural way of learning language, students will enjoy learning more and hence learn more. For instance, the study by Jeynes and Littell (2000) includes various attitude measures, and it is unclear what nonattitudinal effects are measured. The lower effect sizes for reading achievement measures indicates that measures such as attitude toward reading produce larger effect sizes than direct measures of performance.

The retrieved papers, dissertations, and unpublished documents are considered to be the raw data to which a coding system is applied to produce the variables to be used in the analysis. The application of the coding system should be tested for intercoder reliability. The coding system contains potential moderator variables that can be used to explain the variability of the effect sizes in the specific set of studies. The variables in the coding system should therefore be theoretically relevant and constitute pertinent moderator hypotheses. In view of the relatively small number of studies included in most meta-analyses, the coding system should not be too extended. If potential moderators exceed the number of studies, inflated meta-analytic outcomes may be the nonreplicable result ("reliable and concise coding system").

Data analysis often consists of three steps (Mullen, 1989): First, the central tendency of the study results is computed (i.e., the combined effect size). Because p values heavily depend on the number of observations, recent meta-analyses focus on the combined standardized differences between the means of the experimental and control group. The statistic used to assess the effectiveness of a treatment or other variable is the effect size, d, which measures how much the mean of the treatment group exceeds the mean of the control group in standard deviation units. Effect size expresses how many standard deviation units treatment groups differ from control groups without treatment. An effect size of 1.0 indicates that the treatment group mean is one standard deviation higher than the control group mean while an effect size of 0 indicates that treatment and control group mean are identical. According to Cohen (1988), an effect size of .20 is considered small, an effect size of .50 moderate, and an effect size of .80 or above large. Translated into percentiles, $d = .20$ indicates that the treatment has moved the average child from the 50th to the 58th percentile; $d = .50$ indicates that the treatment has moved the child on average to the 69th percentile; $d = .80$ indicates that the treatment has moved the child on average to the 79th percentile. As an alternative, Rosenthal and Rubin (1982) suggested the binominal effect size display (BESD), which indicates the change in predictive accuracy attributable to the relationship in question and is computed from the formula .50 ± $(r/2)$. The BESD shows the extent to which prediction is enhanced (i.e., the percentage increase in prediction) with the use of intervention X to predict reading skill Y (for details, see later).

A weighted effect size is mostly used to adjust for the bias due to small sample sizes (i.e., the tendency of studies with small samples to overestimate effects). Unweighted d's are sometimes presented to provide information about the direction of biases related to sample size. The effect size can be computed on the basis of the standard deviations of the control group (Glass, 1976), the pooled standard deviations (Rosenthal, 1991), or the pooled variance (Hedges & Olkin, 1985). Cohen's d, for instance, is calculated as the difference between control and experimental treatment posttest mean scores (partialed for the influence of pretest scores if information is available) divided by the pooled standard deviation. Alternatively, the test statistics (F, t, χ^2) can be transformed into an effect size (Rosenthal, 1991). In practice, different strategies do not seem to make a substantial difference (Johnson, Mullen, & Salas, 1995).

Second, the variability of the results around this central tendency is assessed, and outliers as well as homogeneous subsets of studies are identified. To determine whether a set of d's shares a common effect size, a homogeneity statistic—Q—which approximates chi-square distribution with $k - 1$ degrees of freedom, where k is the number of effect sizes, can be computed. Homogeneity analysis compares the amount of variance exhibited by a set of effect sizes with the amount of variance expected if only sampling error is operating. If sets of study results remain heterogeneous, combined effect size computed on the basis of the fixed model may be biased estimates, that is, it cannot be concluded that they are a sample from the same population, and a random model should be preferred (Hedges, 1994). If a distribution of study results is extremely skewed and shows several outlying values, the average effect size does not adequately represent the central tendency. Inflated meta-analytic findings may result from ignoring heterogeneity in study outcomes, and the random model may lead to lower estimates for the combined effect size as well as larger confidence boundaries (Hedges, 1994).

Third, through a moderator analysis, the meta-analysts try to explain the variability on the basis of study characteristics. A significant chi square indicates that the study features significantly moderate the magnitude of effect sizes. For example, intervention studies with randomized designs may, on average, yield smaller effects than studies without randomization. Mostly the analyses do not include tests of interactions between moderator variables because the number of comparisons is insufficient in many cases. It should be noted that in meta-analytic as well as in primary studies every subject or sample should be counted independently from each other and only once. That is, if a study presents more than one effect size for the same hypothesis, these effect sizes should be combined within the study before it is included in the overall meta-analysis ("independent and homogeneous effect sizes").

The interpretation of the size of the combined effects is a matter of much debate (Rosenthal & McCartney, 2000). In a meta-analysis, Bus, van IJzendoorn, and Pellegrini (1995) showed that the association between early storybook reading and later literacy was about $d = .59$, which explains about 8% of the variance in children's literacy skills. In an earlier meta-analysis, van IJzendoorn and Bus (1994) showed that the phonological deficit explains only 6% of the variance in dyslexia ($d = .48$) which is about half a standard deviation difference between the experimental and control group. A correlation of .28 between book reading and reading may seem a rather modest outcome. However, in terms of the BESD (Rosenthal, 1991), this effect is sizable. The BESD is defined as the change in success ratio because of an intervention. The BESD shows the extent to which prediction is enhanced (i.e., the percentage increase in prediction) with the use of intervention X to predict reading skill Y. If we equal the combined effect size $d = .59$ with an $r = .28$, the success ratio in the experimental group would be: $.50 + (.28/2) = .64$; the success ratio in the control group would be $.50 - (.28/2) = .36$. It should be noted, therefore, that it certainly can make a tremendous difference in the lives of young children whether or not they are read to. The difference between the experimental and control group would amount to a substantial difference if we translate this outcome to the millions of children who may profit from book reading (Rosenthal, 1991). Taking into account that experimental studies revealed outcomes similar to correlational/longitudinal/retrospective studies, this meta-analysis provides a clear and affirmative answer to the question of whether or not storybook reading is one of the most important activities for developing the knowledge required for eventual success in reading. Therefore, parental storybook reading should be recommended because in terms of BESD it makes a difference for many thousands of preschoolers ("BESD interpretation of effect size"). In the same vein, phonological deficit is correctly considered as a main cause of dyslexia.

The basic stages and quality standards of a meta-analysis may be summarized as follows:

1. Hypothesis formulation
   - *Precise and relevant hypothesis*

2. Retrieval and coding of studies
   - *Unbiased and exhaustive set of papers*
   - *Reliable and concise coding system*

3. Analysis of study results and characteristics
   a. Central tendency
   b. Variability
   c. Moderators
   - *Independent and homogeneous effect sizes*

4. Interpretation of meta-analytic outcomes
   - *BESD interpretation of effect size*

WHAT KINDS OF QUESTIONS ARE APPROPRIATE FOR META-ANALYSIS?

Review of Meta-Analyses in Reading Research

In Table 11.1, 34 meta-analyses in the various domains of reading have been listed. We used a computer search of PsychInfo and ISI, with the key words *literacy and meta-analysis* and *reading and meta-analysis* to trace the relevant meta-analyses. A set of about 40 meta-analyses on reading since 1982 resulted from this search (see Table 11.1 for a summary of the reviews we could trace). Assuming that since 1966 approximately 100,000 research studies on reading have been conducted, with perhaps another 15,000 appearing before that time (National Reading Panel, 2000), only a small part of all available studies is meta-analyzed. The 34 meta-analyses cover at most 5% of all available studies on reading.

Meta-analysis appears a useful tool to test theories of reading problems as Metsala, Stanovich, and Brown (1998) showed. Their synthesis of research counters a prediction based on classic dual-route models of word recognition that children with reading disabilities show an absent or reduced regularity effect even though separate studies support this hypothesis. The regularity effect in reading has been defined as the observation of superior performance in recognition of regular versus exception words. It is assumed that if the phonological route is less available as a result of impairment, the advantage for regular words should be eliminated or reduced. Children with learning disabilities should prefer a direct visual route without phonological mediation above an indirect route through phonological processsing that involves stored spelling–sound correspondences in order to circumvent phonological coding. The synthesis of a series of small-scale studies is not in line with the dual-route model. It shows that both individuals with reading disabilities and normally achieving readers show a regularity effect and that effect sizes indicating higher scores on regularly spelled words were not related to reading level. Regardless of the reading level, regularly spelled words are easier to read than irregularly spelled words. Metsala et al. (1998) report heterogeneity in effect sizes that cannot be explained as an effect of reading level. Carrying out secondary analyses on this data set with Comprehensive Meta-Analysis (Statistical Solutions Limited) the effect sizes appear to be homogeneous within the groups of normally developing and children with learning disabilities.

Even though not all individual studies report a regularity effect for children with reading problems, the results combined across the studies revealed a regularity effect. This finding is similar to results from the van IJzendoorn and Bus (1994) meta-analysis on the pseudoword deficit of individuals with reading problems. That is, even when individual studies did not report a significant pseudoword reading deficit for participants with reading disabilities relative to reading-level-matched participants the studies overall did show this pattern when the results were combined across studies. The synthesis of studies on the regularity effect does not harmonize with the available theoretical models and thus new models and further research are required to understand reading problems. The finding that both groups are susceptible to the regularity effect is inconsistent with the dual-route models of word reading but consistent with emerging connectionist models and their empirical findings on reading disability.

Most meta-analyses on reading synthesize the results of intervention studies. In an attempt to settle an ongoing debate on the best method to teach beginning reading skills studies contrast whole language with basals (Stahl & Miller, 1989) or systematic phonics instruction with none or incidental instruction in phonics (Ehri & Willows, 2001a; Jeynes & Littell, 2000). Other studies synthesize effects of special measures: programs to instruct phonemic awareness (Bus & van IJzendoorn, 1999; Ehri et al., 2001b), guided oral reading (National Reading Panel, 2000), book reading in groups (Blok, 1999), question generation (National Reading Panel, 2000), or learning to derive word meaning from context (Fukkink & De Glopper, 1998). Furthermore, it is evaluated how direct and strategy instructions support groups with learning disabilities (Swanson & Sachse-Lee, 1999) and whether one-to-one tutoring in reading (Elbaum, Vaughn, Tejero-Hughes, & Watson-Moody, 2000b) or instruction in small groups especially stimulates these children's reading development (Elbaum, Vaughn, Hughes, & Moody, 1999; Elbaum, Vaughn, Hughes, Moody, & Schumm, 2000a). Few studies test effects of school organization on reading achievement: class size (McGiverin, Gilman, & Tillitski, 1989) or summer holiday (Cooper et al., 1996). Only a few studies focus on interventions in preschool age and test effects of book reading in the family (Bus et al., 1995) or preschool intervention programs (Goldring & Pressbey, 1986). Not all research domains are ready for meta-analysis despite of numerous studies. The NRP did not succeed in finding sufficient studies to meta-analyze effects of all formal efforts to increase the amounts of independent or recreational reading that children engage in, including sustained silent reading programs, due to a lack of studies that meet NRP standards such as experimental or quasi-experimental designs, including a control group (National Reading Panel, 2000). They conclude that it would be difficult to interpret the small collection of studies that remained as representing clear evidence that encouraging students to read more actually improves reading achievement. Only three of the remaining studies reported any clear reading gains from encouraging students to read. However, one may wonder to what extent the selection criteria were responsible for this (counterintuitive) result. The selection of studies did not include a screening of studies in order to ensure that the participants needed what the treatment was designed to influence. The NRP routinely selected and analyzed studies that experimentally tested the efficacy of encouraging students to read more without ensuring that the participants in the selected studies indeed did not have the ability and opportunity outside of school to read independently (cf. Cunningham, 2001).

Meta-Analyses about Meta-Analyses

The set of meta-analyses reports effects of instruction on reading comprehension ($n = 13$) and on word recognition ($n = 9$). From the stem-and-leaf-display (Figure 11.2), it appears that both word recog-

Word recognition		Reading comprehension
	1.00	
	.9	5
2	.8	
	.7	2
	.6	7
7554	.5	
10	.4	13
2	.3	0245666
7	.2	8
	.1	
	0	

FIGURE 11.2. Stem-and-leaf display of *d* indexes for effects of interventions on achievement test scores in word recognition and reading comprehension. Combine the stem (.1, .2, .3, etc.) with the leaves to the left and to the right to find *d* values. Stem combined with leaves to the right represents reading comprehension and stem combined with leaves to the left word recognition. For instance, in the range .2 to .3 one intervention caused an ES of .28 on reading comprehension and another caused an ES of .27 on word recognition. Note that many *d*'s for reading comprehension concentrate between .3 and .4 and *d*'s for word recognition between .5 and .6.

nition and reading comprehension are susceptible to forms of instruction. Insofar as several dependent measures were available we selected tests with established (by the experimenter or someone else) construct validity and reliability (using multiple measures of reliability) above experimenter tests.

When a series of word-recognition outcomes were reported we left out outcomes for selected words (e.g., pseudo- or only regularly spelled words). For both word recognition and reading comprehension, outcomes are homogeneous according to an analysis on this data set with Comprehensive Meta-Analysis (Statistical Solutions Limited) even though the interventions cover a range of instructions varying in form (group vs. one-to-one tutoring) and ranging from phonemic awareness to deriving meaning from context. Only a meta-analysis on single-subject studies revealed outlying results for both dependent measures, word recognition ($d = .82$) and reading comprehension ($d = .95$) (Swanson & Sachse-Lee, 1999). To explain this finding we may assume that any special measure to improve word recognition or text comprehension supports those skills directly or indirectly whatever the exact nature of the instruction. Another explanation might be that interventions share the same effective component. For instance, whatever the nature of the intervention a common experience of the experimental children might be that an adult shows interest in how they solve a task.

Another notable result is that effect sizes for word-recognition skills exceed those for reading comprehension. With word recognition as a dependent variable the median effect size of interventions is about half a standard deviation. With reading comprehension being the dependent measure it is about a third of a standard deviation. These outcomes are similar whatever the focus of the study: improving word recognition, practicing comprehension skills, or one-to-one tutoring. In other words, word recognition is more susceptible to instruction than text comprehension. Reading comprehension is more strategic and based on higher-level skills and may therefore be less trainable than decoding that is based on low-level skills. Interventions that include strategic and other higher-level processes promise progress in comprehension (Pressley & Harris, 1994), but not to the same extent as a training of lower-level skills warrants progress in word recognition. Because the interventions varied so much we were unable to test characteristics of instruction. For instance, assuming that instruction on comprehension supports skills beyond those stimulated by word recognition one may expect that the effect of comprehension instruction on comprehension is quite a bit higher than the effect of word-recognition instruction on comprehension, particularly after the early grades.

Quality of Meta-Analyses in Reading

Most syntheses of research satisfy the criterion that effect sizes across comparisons are independent (68%). Intercoder reliability for coding the studies on this and hereafter discussed measures was satisfactory. Reliabilities of moderator variables are not always reported (36%) and neither do meta-analysts always make an estimate of a publishing bias (21%). To prevent independence of effect sizes various strategies may be used. Some adjust n for significance tests so that a single subject's data did not count more than once. In other studies a combined effect is estimated and subsequent contrasts between two or more kinds of interventions are not tested (Bus & van IJzendoorn, 1999). Some studies ignore the problem and use the same control group more than once (e.g., Ehri et al., 2001b).

In most cases, Q-statistics are reported (74%), but most studies applied a fixed model even though the populations did not involve a common effect size estimate as is indicated by the tests of homogeneity (e.g., Bus et al., 1995; Elbaum et al., 2000b). Sometimes authors may draw strong conclusions and bold implications for practice from a combined effect size even though the point estimate is not representative of the central tendency in the total set of studies. In that case, conclusions are at least premature. Large variation in effect sizes requires a random-effects model which implies a broader confidence interval and a higher chance that the effect size is not significantly different from zero. This scenario, however, not always holds, as can be illustrated for the book-reading study. We reanalyzed the data of the book-reading meta-analysis with a random-effects model because the overall point estimate of effect size was not based on a homogeneous set of studies (Bus et al., 1995). Reanalyzing the combined effects for book-reading outcomes with a random-effects model, we found outcomes that were very similar to those resulting from a fixed model. A point estimate of $r = .27$ for the overall effect of book reading on emergent literacy, reading achievement in school age, and language skills remains significant as is indicated by a 95% confidence interval ranging from .21 to .32.

META-ANALYTIC EXEMPLAR

Numerous studies relate phonemic awareness and reading achievement, but various questions remain unresolved because characteristics of replication studies vary. As the number of studies replicating the relationship between reading and phonemic awareness increases, quantitative synthesis of the research is warranted to test the effects of variations in study characteristics on the outcome of the studies (Bus & van IJzendoorn, 1999).

Precise and Relevant Hypotheses

First, we wondered whether phonemic awareness indeed is the single strongest predictor of reading development, as is often suggested (e.g., Elbro, 1996), and whether effects of alternative experiences as book reading are minor compared to a training of phonemic awareness. Another aim of this meta-analysis was to test whether children learn about the phonemic structure of words more easily when they learn to interpret spellings as maps for pronunciations. Therefore, we tested effects of characteristics of training programs making a distinction between purely phonetic training, embedded in letter training, or embedded in reading and writing practice.

A Homogeneous Set of Studies

Several meta-analyses have been subjected to thorough and sometimes harsh criticism because of the heterogeneity of independent variables across intervention studies, and the heterogeneity of the interventions themselves (Dunst & Snyder, 1986; but see Casto & Mastropieri, 1986). Dunst and Snyder (1986), for example, conclude that the Casto and Mastropieri (1986) findings cannot be the basis for policy: It would be both dangerous and unwarranted to develop policy about early intervention based on their flawed meta-analyses. We circumvented this problem by carefully selecting studies that test effects of training phonological awareness. We put considerable effort into excluding reading instruction programs that focus on the instruction of reading skills.

Reliable and Concise Coding System

As we have shown earlier, the heterogeneity of the studies can be productively used to explain variation between study outcomes. The meta-analysts should pay systematic attention to the discrimination of relevant subsets of more homogeneous studies, using quantitative approaches based on expert ratings. In the synthesis of phonemic awareness research we therefore coded characteristics of the training program (purely phonetic, embedded in a letter training, or embedded in reading and writing practice), setting (training with a group or individual), number of training sessions, and the person who implemented the training (teacher vs. examiner). Quality of study designs is never an easy all-or-nothing decision; in the meta-analysis of training phonological awareness quality dimensions were tested by coding design characteristics (randomized, matched, or not) and kind of control group (no treatment, dummy treatment, or some related training). Two coders coded all relevant studies separately and succeeded in reaching agreement on these characteristics of the phonemic awareness interventions.

The synthesis of phonemic awareness training studies revealed that a purely phonemic training such as the thoroughly replicated Lundberg program is less effective than a program such as Sound

Foundations that includes letter training in addition to phonological awareness. This meta-analytic finding is in line with Ehri's (1979) assumption that letters appear to function as an intermediary, because they may facilitate the discrimination of phonemes. The results support a theory with important practical implications, that is, letters draw the child's attention to the sounds in spoken words, and a distinct visual symbol for each phoneme may anchor the phonemes perceptually (Adams, Treiman, & Pressley, 1998).

Independent and Homogeneous Effect Sizes

An important criticism concerns the dependence of effect sizes within a study, thus violating crucial assumptions of independence of observations. To prevent studies with more than one training group and only one control group from inflating the number of participants, we combined the effect sizes of the interventions within the study. This practice is now recommended in standard introductions to meta-analysis (Cooper & Hedges, 1994), and it would be important to replicate the contaminated meta-analyses following this guideline.

Diffuse comparisons of effect sizes within phonemic awareness training studies showed considerable heterogeneity of results which led to a search for a more homogeneous subset of studies. The training experiments with randomized or matched groups of participants from the United States met this criterion, and we computed a point estimate of the effect size for this subset of studies separately. In this homogeneous set of experimental studies with more than 700 children, experimentally manipulated phonological awareness explains about 12% of the variance in word-identification skills. The combined effect with controlled designs is $d = .70, r = .33$ ($p < .001$) for reading.

New Insights and New Hypotheses to Be Tested

From a meta-analysis of 36 studies we concluded that experimentally manipulated phonological awareness is a substantial predictor of reading but not the single strongest predictor. Compared with the outcome for phonemic awareness, early storybook reading leading to emergent literacy skills predicts reading skills somewhat less strongly than experimentally manipulated phonological awareness, but the difference is only marginal. Bus et al. (1995) showed that the association between early storybook reading and later literacy was about $d = .59$, which explains about 8% of the variance (combined $r = .27$) in children's literacy skills. In other words, it is not only direct training of phonemic awareness that supports emergent literacy and thus later literacy. Emergent literacy supported by phonological awareness training as well as book reading appears to be important in shaping the early reading process. Thus, these meta-analyses may mark a new stage in the systematic study of reading development with emphasis on both "outside-in" as well as "inside-out" factors that stimulate emergent literacy (cf. Whitehurst & Lonigan, 1998). Future research should test the specific additive or interactive effects of formal and informal experiences with aspects of written language and how they promote reading development.

CONCLUSION

Meta-analysis not only provides a summary of research but also produces new insights and facts. Through meta-analysis we use the combined power of the primary studies to address issues that otherwise would require hundreds of participants and many different interventions within the same study. Only a meta-analysis could show that the teacher expectancy effect works better when the teachers do not know their pupils for more than a few weeks (Raudenbush, 1984).

Combining the results of several meta-analyses, researchers are able to construct models of associations between theoretically important variables which are not yet combined in any separate empirical study, and to show at what point the model still is incomplete. For instance, we combined meta-analyses on the associations between book reading and literacy and phonemic training and reading to show that not just formal training but informal experiences are relevant to becoming literate. New meta-analytic approaches for creating and testing causal and multilevel models have been proposed (Cook et al., 1992), and will continue to develop in decades to come.

REFERENCES

Adams, M. J. (1990). *Beginning to read. Thinking and learning about print*. Cambridge, MA: MIT Press.

Adams, M. J., Treiman, R., & Pressley, M. (1998). Reading, writing, and literacy. In I. E. Sigel & K. A. Renninger (Eds.), *Handbook of child psychology: Child psychology in practice* (Vol. 4, pp. 275–355). New York: Wiley.

Blanchard, J., & Stock, W. (1999). Meta-analysis of research on a multimedia elementary school curriculum using personal and video-game computers. *Perceptual and Motor Skills, 88*, 329–336.

Blok, H. (1999). Reading to young children in educational settings: A meta-analysis of recent research. *Language Learning, 49,* 343–371.

Browder, D. M., & Xin, Y. P. (1998). A meta-analysis and review of sight word research and its implications for teaching functional reading to individuals with moderate and severe disabilities. *Journal of Special Education, 32,* 130–153.

Bus, A. G., & van IJzendoorn, M. H. (1999). Phonological awareness and early reading: A meta-analysis of experimental training studies. *Journal of Educational Psychology, 91,* 403–414.

Bus, A. G., van IJzendoorn, M. H., & Pellegrini, A. D. (1995). Joint book reading makes for success in learning to read: A meta-analysis on intergenerational transmission of literacy. *Review of Educational Research, 65,* 1–21.

Casto, G., & Mastropieri, M. A. (1986). The efficacy of early intervention programs: A meta-analysis. *Exceptional Children, 52,* 417–424.

Cohen, J. (1988). *Statistical power analysis for the behavioral sciences.* Hillsdale, NJ: Erlbaum.

Cohen, J. (1990). Things I have learned (so far). *American Psychologist, 45,* 1304–1312.

Cook, T. D., Cooper, H., Cordray, D. F., Hartman, H., Hedges, L. V., Light, R., Louis, T. A., & Mosteller, F. (1992). *Meta-analysis for explanation: A casebook.* New York: Russell Sage.

Cooper, H., & Hedges, L. V. (1994). *The handbook of research synthesis.* New York: Russell Sage.

Cooper, H., Nye, B., Charlton, K., & Lindsay, J. (1996). The effects of summer vacation on achievement test scores: A narrative and meta-analytic review. *Review of Educational Research, 66,* 227–268.

Cooper, H. M. (1982). Scientific guidelines for conducting integrative research reviews. *Review of Educational Research, 52,* 291–302.

Cooper, H. M., & Rosenthal, R. (1980). Statistical versus traditional procedures for summarizing research findings. *Psychological Bulletin, 87,* 442–449.

Cunningham, J. W. (2001). The National Reading Panel report. *Reading Research Quarterly, 36,* 326–335.

Daneman, M., & Merikle, P. M. (1996). Working memory and language comprehension: A meta-analysis. *Psychonomic Bulletin and Review, 3,* 422–433.

Dunst, C. J., & Snyder, S. W. (1986). A critique of the Utah State University early intervention meta-analysis research. *Exceptional Children, 53,* 269–276.

Eagly, A. H., & Wood, W. (1994). Tying research synthesis to substantive issues. In H. Cooper & L. V. Hedges (Eds.), *The handbook of research synthesis* (pp. 485–502). New York: Russell Sage.

Ehri, L. C. (1979). Linguistic insight: Treshold of reading acquisition. In G. Waller & G. MacKinnon (Eds.), *Reading Research: Advances in Theory and practice* (Vol 1, pp. 63–111). New York: Academic Press.

Ehri, L. C., Nunes, S. R., Stahl, S. A., & Willows, D. M. (2001a). Systematic phonics instruction helps students learn to read: Evidence from the National Reading Panel's meta-analysis. *Review of Educational Research, 71,* 393–447.

Ehri, L. C., Nunes, S. R., Willows, D. M., Schuster, B. V., Yaghoub-Zadeh, Z., & Shanahan, T. (2001b). Phonemic awareness instruction helps children learn to read: Evidence from the National Reading Panel's meta-analysis. *Reading Research Quarterly, 36,* 250–287.

Elbaum, B., Vaughn, S., Hughes, M., & Moody, S. W. (1999). Grouping practices and reading outcomes for students with disabilities. *Exceptional Children, 65,* 399–415.

Elbaum, B., Vaughn, S., Hughes, M. T., Moody, S. W., & Schumm, J. S. (2000a). How reading outcomes of students with disabilities are related to instructional grouping formats: A meta-analytic review. In R. M. Gersten & E. P. Schiller (Eds.), *Contemporary special education research: Syntheses of the knowledge base on critical instructional issues. The LEA series on special education and disability* (pp. 105–135). Mahwah, NJ: Erlbaum.

Elbaum, B., Vaughn, S., Tejero-Hughes, M., & Watson-Moody, S. (2000b). How effective are one-to-one tutoring programs in reading for elementary students at risk for reading failure? A meta-analysis of the intervention research. *Journal of Educational Psychology, 92,* 605–619.

Fuchs, D., Fuchs, L. S., Mathes, P. G., & Lipsey, M. W. (2000). Reading differences between low-achieving students with and without learning disabilities: A meta-analysis. In R. M. Gersten & E. P. Schiller (Eds.), *Contemporary special education research: Syntheses of the knowledge base on critical instructional issues* (pp. 81–104). Mahwah, NJ: Erlbaum.

Fukkink, R. G., & de Glopper, K. (1998). Effects of instruction in deriving word meaning from context: A meta-analysis. *Review of Educational Research, 68,* 450–469.

Fusaro, J. A. (1992). Meta-analysis of the effect of sentence-combining on reading comprehension when the criterion measure is the test of reading comprehension. *Perceptual and Motor Skills, 74,* 331–333.

Garfield, E. (1979). *Citation indexing. Its theory and application in science, technology, and humanities.* New York: Wiley.

Glass, G. V. (1976). Primary, secondary and meta-analysis of research. *Educational Research, 5,* 3–8.

Gleser, L. J., & Olkin, I. (1994). Stochastically dependent effect sizes. In H. Cooper & L. V. Hedges (Eds.), *The handbook of research synthesis* (pp. 339–355). New York: Russell Sage.

Goldring, E. B., & Pressbrey, L. S. (1986). Evaluating preschool programs: A meta-analytic approach. *Educational Evaluation and Policy Analysis, 8,* 179–188.

Hedges, L. V. (1994). Statistical considerations. In H. Cooper & L. V. Hedges (Eds.), *The handbook of research synthesis* (pp. 29–38). New York: Russell Sage.

Hedges, L. V., & Olkin, I. (1985). *Statistical methods for meta-analysis.* New York: Academic Press.

Horn, W. F., & Packard, T. (1985). Early identification of learning problems: A meta-analysis. *Journal of Educational Psychology, 77*, 597–607.

Jeynes, W. H., & Littell, S. W. (2000). A meta-analysis of studies examining the effect of whole language instruction on the literacy of low-SES students. *The Elementary School Journal, 101*, 21–33.

Johnson, B. T., Mullen, B., & Salas, E. (1995). Comparison of three meta-analytic approaches. *Journal of Applied Psychology, 80*, 94–106.

Kamin, L. J. (1974). *The science and politics of I.Q.* New York: Wiley.

Kavale, K. A. (1980). Auditory-visual integration and its relationship to reading achievement: A meta-analysis. *Perceptual and Motor Skills, 51*, 947–955.

Kavale, K. A. (1981). The relationship between auditory perceptual skills and reading ability: A meta-analysis. *Journal of Learning Disabilities, 14*, 539–546.

Kavale, K. A. (1982). Meta-analysis of the relationship between visual perceptual skills and reading achievement. *Journal of Learning Disabilities, 15*, 42–51.

Kavale, K. A., & Forness, S. R. (2000). Auditory and visual perception processes and reading ability: A quantitative reanalysis and historical reinterpretation. *Learning Disability Quarterly, 23*, 253–270.

Lytton, H. (1994). Replication and meta-analysis: The story of a meta-analysis of parents' socialization practices. In R. van der Veer, M. H. van IJzendoorn, & J. Valsiner (Eds.), *Reconstructing the mind: Replicability in research on human development* (pp. 117–150). Norwood, NJ: Ablex.

McCartney, K., & Rosenthal, R. (2003). Effect Size, practical Importance, and social policy for children. *Child Development, 71*, 173–180.

McGiverin, J., Gilman, D., & Tillitski, C. (1989). A meta-analysis of the relation between class size and achievement. *Elementary School Journal, 90*, 47–56.

Metsala, J. L., Stanovich, K. E., & Brown, G. D. A. (1998). Regularity effects and the phonological deficit model of reading disabilities: A meta-analytic review. *Journal of Educational Psychology, 90*, 279–293.

Mullen, B. (1989). *Advanced basic meta-analysis.* Hillsdale, NJ: Erlbaum.

National Reading Panel. (2000). *Report of the National Reading Panel: Teaching children to read: An evidence-based assessment of the scientific research literature on reading and its implications for reading instruction: Reports of the subgroups.* Rockville, MD: NICHD Clearinghouse.

O'Shaughnessy, T. E., & Swanson, H. L. (1998). Do immediate memory deficits in students with learning disabilities in reading reflect a developmental lag or deficit?: A selective meta-analysis of the literature. *Learning Disability Quarterly, 21*, 123–148.

Pearson, K. (1904). Report on certain enteric fever inoculation statistics. *British Medical Journal, 3*, 1243–1246.

Pressley, M., & Harris, K. R. (1994). Increasing the quality of educational intervention research. *Educational Psychology Review, 6*, 191–208.

Raudenbush, S. W. (1984). Magnitude of teacher expectancy effects on pupil IQ as a function of the credibility of expectancy induction: A synthesis of findings from 18 experiments. *Journal of Educational Psychology, 76,* 85–97.

Rosenshine, B., Meister, C., & Chapman, S. (1996). Teaching students to generate questions: A review of the intervention studies. *Review of Educational Research, 66,* 181–221.

Rosenthal, R. (1991). *Meta-analytic procedures for social research* (rev. ed.). Newbury Park, CA: Sage.

Rosenthal, R., & Rubin, D. B. (1982). Further meta-analytic procedures for assessing cognitive gender differences. *Journal of Educational Psychology, 74,* 708–712.

Slavin, R. E. (1986). Best-evidence synthesis: An alternative to meta-analytic and traditional reviews. *Educational Researcher, 15,* 5–11.

Slavin, R. E. (2002). Evidence-based education policies: Transforming educational practice and research. *Educational Researcher, 31,* 15–21.

Smith, M. L., & Glass, G. V. (1977). Meta-analysis of psychotherapy outcome studies. *American Psychologist, 32,* 752–760.

Stahl, S. A., & Fairbanks, M. M. (1986). The effects of vocabulary instruction: A model-based meta-analysis. *Review of Educational Research, 56,* 72–110.

Stahl, S. A., McKenna, M. C., & Pagnucco, J. R. (1994). The effects of whole-language instruction: An update and a reappraisal. *Educational Psychologist, 29,* 175–185.

Stahl, S. A., & Miller, P. D. (1989). Whole language and language experience approaches for beginning reading: A quantitative research synthesis. *Review of Educational Research, 59,* 87–116.

Swanborn, M.-S. L., & De Glopper, K. (1999). Incidental word learning while reading: A meta-analysis. *Review of Educational Research, 69,* 261–285.

Swanson, H. L. (1999). Reading research for students with LD: A meta-analysis in intervention outcomes. *Journal of Learning Disabilities, 32,* 504–532.

Swanson, H. L. (2001). Research on interventions for adolescents with learning disabilities: A meta-analysis of outcomes related to higher-order processing. *Elementary School Journal, 101,* 331–348.

Swanson, H. L., & Hoskyn, M. (1998). Experimental intervention research on students with learning disabilities: A meta-analysis of treatment outcomes. *Review of Educational Research, 68,* 277–321.

Swanson, H. L., & Sachse-Lee, C. (2000). A meta-analysis of single-subject-design intervention research for students with LD. *Journal of Learning Disabilities, 33,* 114–136.

van IJzendoorn, M. H. (1994). Process model of replication studies: on the relations between different types of replication. In R. van der Veer, M. H. van IJzendoorn, & J. Valsiner (Eds.), *Reconstructing the mind: Replicability in research on human development* (pp. 57–70). Norwood, NJ: Ablex.

van IJzendoorn, M. H. (2002). Methodologie: Kennis door veranderen, de empirische benadering in de pedagogiek. In M. H. van IJzendoorn & H. de Frankrijker (Eds.), *Pedagogiek in beeld* (pp. 2–35). Houten, The Netherlands: Bohn Stafleu Van Loghum.

van IJzendoorn, M. H., & Bus, A. G. (1994). Meta-analytic confirmation of the nonword reading deficit in developmental dyslexia. *Reading Research Quarterly, 29,* 266–275.

Whitehurst, G. J., & Lonigan, C. J. (1998). Child development and emergent literacy. *Child Development, 69,* 848–872.

Williams, J. (2001). Commentary: Four meta-analyses and some general observations. *The Elementary School Journal, 101,* 349–354.

Willig, A. C. (1985). A meta-analysis of selected studies on the effectiveness of bilingual education. *Review of Educational Research, 55,* 269–317.

Wolins, L. (1962). Responsibility for raw data. *American Psychologist, 17,* 657–658.

CHAPTER 12

Neuroimaging in Reading Research

Jack M. Fletcher
Panagiotis G. Simos
Andrew C. Papanicolaou
Carolyn Denton

Neuroimaging studies involving reading are receiving considerable attention in scientific circles and from the media. Although many of these studies involve children and adults identified with reading difficulties, studies involving functional neuroimaging are emerging that examine a range of children in the process of learning to read. These studies are beginning to address fundamental questions about how the brain participates in reading development. In this chapter, we examine neuroimaging as an example of the application of technology to the study of reading. We begin with a brief explanation of different methods for structural and functional neuroimaging, focusing especially on the latter as these methods are seeing more widespread application. Then we examine results of studies applying these technologies to a variety of questions involving the neural correlates of reading and language development. We conclude with a recent study from our group in which functional neuroimaging was conducted as part of an intervention study of first graders at risk for reading difficulties, but which also involved first graders not at risk for reading difficulties.

HISTORICAL FOUNDATIONS OF NEUROIMAGING

Neuroimaging represents an attempt to directly measure the structure and/or function of the brain. At the simplest level, there are two types of neuroimaging methods. One method involves an examination of the anatomy of the brain, or *structural* neuroimaging. The other involves an examination of brain function, or *functional* neuroimaging. The two methods are closely related. Functional neuroimaging is an extension of structural neuroimaging as it depends on careful specification of brain anatomy. One of the goals of functional neuroimaging can be the localization of function to specific areas of the brain, though it is a simplification to define any form of neuroimaging just in terms of this goal. As illustrated in this chapter, it is also a simplification to simply view neuroimaging as an extrapolation of the "medical model" to social and behavioral research, or to see the application to reading as a technology looking for a home. As with any method or technology, the key issues involve the questions that lead to the application of the method, the theory behind the application, and the integration of the results of studies using these methods with the broader area under investigation, in this instance reading.

ORIGINS

Both structural and functional neuroimaging have their origins in the need for noninvasive methods for examining the brain in clinical populations characterized by some form of injury or disease to the brain. Prior to the advent of computed cerebral tomography scanning (CT scan) in the 1970s, methods for identifying brain abnormalities in patient populations were often invasive and based on attempts to trace radioactive isotopes in the vascular system of the brain (angiography) or the injection of air into the ventricular system (pneumoencephalography). For patients undergoing neurosurgery, functional mapping methods that involved selective anesthesia of one of the cerebral hemispheres to lateralize language or memory, known as the Wada technique (Wada & Rasmussen, 1960), are still used as part of neurosurgical planning, especially for epilepsy. Such methods are essential for ensuring that the surgical procedure does not further debilitate the patient by removing an area of the brain critical for cognitive or motor function. For similar purposes, direct electrical stimulation of the cortex to map function in patients undergoing surgical ablation for control of epilepsy dates back to the seminal studies of Penfield and Roberts (1959). Finally, neurophysiological methods, such as electroencephalography (EEG) and evoked potentials, have also been used as noninvasive methods for identifying abnormal brain function.

None of these methods has been terribly satisfactory as they are either imprecise because of poor resolution for visualizing brain anat-

omy and/or very invasive. Yet the results of studies of patient populations with brain injury have long been used to advance hypotheses
about relations of brain and behavior. The limits of inferences from
injury or disease are well-known. Damage to the brain does not necessarily indicate that the area would mediate function in a non-brain-
injured person and certainly does not indicate how the behavior was
acquired (Benton, 1962; Fletcher & Taylor, 1984). Thus, methods
for the noninvasive study of the brain in clinical populations and in
samples with no acquired neurological disorder have long been desired by researchers interested in questions concerning how the brain
mediates behavior.

CURRENT METHODS

With the development of CT scanning in the 1970s, modern neuroimaging began to take advantage of the growing availability of computer technologies. CT, like all other contemporary neuroimaging
methods, is a computer-enhanced technology. It is based on X-ray
methods. Simply conducting an X-ray examination of the skull is not
very revealing of the underlying anatomy. In a CT scan, X-ray technology is used to take successive pictures (slices) of the brain and
then reconstructed by computer technologies, thus revealing brain
anatomy with much greater resolution. However, while CT scans
were a significant advance over older methods, the skull remained a
significant source of artifacts and better resolution was desired.

The development of magnetic resonance imaging (MRI) in the
mid-1980s has largely superseded CT scans, though the latter continues to have some clinical application. For research, MRI is preferred
because it is not invasive. No radiation is used and children as young
as 6 years of age are usually able to participate in a study. The primary limitation is that all neuroimaging methods require the child to
sit still to avoid artifact due to motion, so children have to be able to
understand this requirement and cooperate.

MRI scanning is an application of physics (Krasuski, Horowitz,
& Rumsey, 1996). A simplified explanation revolves around the spin-
ning of protons and neutrons in atoms. The spin results in the generation of magnetic energy. In an MRI machine, this magnetic spin is
greatly magnified by applying a strong pulsating magnetic field, so
that small differences in the magnetic energy can be detected. By manipulating magnetic pulse sequences, the MRI scanner is able to assess the effects of these sequences on the magnetic energy generated
by different brain tissues. It can therefore contrast the brain's gray

matter, white matter, and cerebrospinal fluid and the skull, dura, and other components of the brain. With the use of special software the origin of these magnetic signals can be calculated precisely, so that an actual image of the brain can be constructed in three dimensions. The results of a MRI scan can also be digitized into a computer and actually measured to assess the volume of selected brain regions. In addition, the image can be resliced in different planes depending on the question of interest (Krasuski et al., 1996; Papanicolaou, 1998).

Functional imaging methods include older techniques, such as regional cerebral blood flow, in which radioactive isotopes are introduced into the body. The decay of these isotopes in the brain's vascular system can be measured as an index of blood flow. When different areas of the brain are engaged in a mental operation, the shifts in blood flow can be measured as an indicator of what areas of the brain are involved in the operation.

Regional cerebral blood flow has been superseded by other methods, such as single positron emission computed tomography (SPECT) and positron emission tomography (PET). Like regional cerebral blood flow, these methods involve attempts to image brain metabolism through assessments of glucose consumption or blood flow. They also involve the use of some type of radioisotope, typically assessing different properties of decay to reconstruct pictures representative of changes in brain function.

More recently, the development of methods for rapid acquisition of MRI slices in the 1990s has largely been proven to be more sensitive to brain function, with much better resolution. These methods essentially use conventional MRI scanners with software that permits fast image acquisition to detect alterations in blood flow and volume. No radiation is involved and like a structural MRI, there is no need for injection of any contrast material. Functional MRI (fMRI) has generally superior temporal and spatial resolution compared to PET, SPECT, and other such methods. These methods are probably less sensitive to changes in blood flow than PET or SPECT, and the assessment of neuronal activity is indirect (Krasuski et al., 1996; Papanicolaou, 1998).

Direct assessments of neural activity also take place with neurophysiological methods, such as electrocephalography and evoked potentials, or magnetoencephalography, also known as magnetic source imaging (MSI). The latter represents the newest method for functional brain imaging. It is unique in that it assesses neural activity in real time. All the functional imaging methods are discussed in more detail later.

THE NEUROSCIENCE OF READING

Researchers who use neuroimaging represent many disciplines, including physicians in specialties such as neurology and neurosurgery, behavioral scientists in neurophysiology, neuropsychology, and cognitive neuroscience, speech pathologists, and more recently, educational researchers. Prior to the development of modern neuroimaging, research on behavior–brain relations relied on the interpretation of behavioral performance relative to what was known about injury to the brain or from animal studies. As animals do not read, the latter extrapolation was rare, though many early theories of reading acquisition that invoked the brain made ample use of research on adults with brain injury (Benton, 1975). Studies of the effects of brain lesions on reading, language, and other cognitive functions are still very important (Heilman & Watson, 2003). Now the hypotheses that emanate from this work can be directly tested with neuroimaging methods in patient groups and in people with no acquired brain disorder. The technology continues to evolve, and growth in the knowledge base is expanding in many areas, including reading.

There has also been great interest in brain structure and function in children and adults with unexpected reading difficulties. The earliest observations of unexpected reading failure led to hypotheses about the neural underpinnings of these severe disabilities (Hinschelwood, 1902). These observations were fueled by studies of clinical populations who lost some aspect of reading and subsequently underwent postmortem examination. By identifying the areas of the brain that had been damaged, and linking findings across patients, theories of language and reading evolved that usually found their way to children with reading difficulties and no brain injury (Benton, 1975). These theories led to the conviction that these reading difficulties were intrinsic to the child and not due to environmental causes (Orton, 1927; Critchley, 1970). However, despite the tenacity of these convictions, the hypotheses were not really testable until the advent of modern neuroimaging.

Application of neuroimaging to children and adults with unexpected reading difficulties has supported the idea that the brain is involved in critical ways but also has shown that how the brain is involved is closely linked with how typically achieving children learn to read (Lyon, Fletcher, & Barnes, 2003). Instruction and other experiential factors also play a critical role, with the most recent neuroimaging studies implying that instruction is critical to helping many brains learn to read. Thus, neuroimaging has moved research from simple questions such as "is the brain related to reading disability" or "what areas of the brain "cause" reading disability" to much more complex questions involving the interplay of experience, instruction, and the brain in learning to read.

STRUCTURAL NEUROIMAGING

As mentioned previously, the advent of CT was a revolution in the neurosciences. However, CT has limited spatial (anatomical) resolution and cannot be used for research purposes with healthy volunteers because of the use of radiation. Thus, the advent of MRI in the later part of the 1980s was a significant advance as this method is not invasive and is approved for use with children.

The initial structural MRI studies were significantly influenced by autopsy studies of a few adults with a history of reading difficulties. These studies involved a total of 10 brains that had been accumulated over several years. The reports indicated that individuals with reading disabilities are anatomically different from normative expectations, although no control brains were employed. The differences involved the size of specific brain structures, focusing on an area of the temporal lobes, the planum temporale, known to be important for mediating language. Specific microscopic neuroanatomical anomalies were also reported (Filipek, 1996; Galaburda, 1993; Shaywitz et al., 2000). A detailed report of these findings is beyond the scope of this chapter. Briefly, the most influential findings were that the planum temporale was comparable in size in the left and the right hemispheres in adults with reading difficulties, in contrast to the normative expectation that it would be larger in the left than right hemisphere. This initial report prompted an intensive search for anatomical correlates of reading disability.

The autopsy studies have not been without controversy (Filipek, 1996; Shaywitz et al., 2000). People do not usually succumb to reading problems, so it is a small, unusual sample of brains. In addition to concerns about the nature and definition of reading difficulties after the fact, it is not possible to relate the findings of an autopsy study to actual reading performance. Thus, when structural MRI became available, it was almost immediately used to study brain structure in children and adults with reading difficulties. Structural MRI scans can be examined for anomalies, though the resolution is probably not adequate to visualize some of the microscopic abnormalities seen in the autopsy studies. Indeed, the MRI scans of virtually all persons with a reading disability are visibly normal. However, detailed measurements of different brain structures and regions of interest can be performed on a digital version of high-resolution MRIs. These measurements can then be correlated with actual reading performance.

Structural Neuroimaging Studies of Reading Disability

The initial structural neuroimaging studies used CT scans and anatomical MRI. As CT scans did not prove particularly useful, and were done largely on a few adults and children who required an examination for clinical purposes, these studies are not discussed here (reviewed by Hynd & Semrud-Clikeman, 1989).

Many MRI studies of brain anatomy have now been completed with children and adults who experience reading difficulties. These studies implicate several structures and regions of the brain (Filipek, 1996; Shaywitz et al., 2000). However, the results are inconsistent across studies. On a normative basis the planum temporale is usually larger in the left hemisphere than in the right hemisphere, reflecting its important role in language processing. Some comparisons of the planum temporale in children and adults who vary in reading proficiency do not find the expected asymmetry (Hynd, Semrud-Clikeman, Lorys, Novey, & Eliopulos, 1990; Larsen, Hoien, Lundberg, & Ödegarrd, 1990). Others find reversals in the expected patterns of asymmetry so that the planum temporale is larger in the right hemisphere of individuals with reading disability (Hynd et al., 1990). A third set of studies fails to identify differences in the size or symmetry of the planum temporale in people with reading disabilities (Rumsey et al., 1997; Schultz et al., 1994).

If the region of interest is expanded simply to represent the temporoparietal areas of the left hemisphere known to mediate language, results are more consistent, tending to show that these areas are smaller in people with reading disabilities (Filipek, 1996; Shaywitz et al., 2000). However, results are still mixed, with some studies reporting differences (Duara et al., 1991; Kushch et al., 1993) and others not finding differences (Hynd et al., 1990; Jernigan, Hesselink, Sowell, & Tallal, 1991). Similarly, studies of the corpus callosum, the great commissure connecting the two hemispheres of the brain, have been mixed. Some studies report differences in the size and/or shape (Duara et al., 1991; Hynd et al., 1995), whereas others have not found differences (Larsen et al., 1990; Schultz et al., 1994).

These studies involved selection of specific brain regions for analysis, partly because early technologies made it difficult to acquire images in a manner that would permit three-dimensional reconstruction and measurement. In a more recent study using newer technolo-

gies (Filipek, 1996), Pennington et al. (1999) performed morpho-
metric analysis of the entire brain in a sample of twins. They found a
bilateral reduction in the size of the insula and frontal cortex in the
more anterior parts of the brain in twins with dyslexia. In addition,
posterior brain regions, including posterior temporal, parietal, and
occipital cortex, were larger in both hemispheres in twins with dyslexia. These differences were small, occurring in a sample with large
differences between the IQ of the dyslexic and nondyslexic twin
pairs. The results held up when age, gender, and IQ were statistically
controlled.

Few studies find consistent correlations between measurements
of brain structure and reading performance. For example, Leonard et
al. (1996) reported that better reading performance was correlated
with greater degree of asymmetry of the planum temporale (left
larger than right). These results were apparent regardless of the presence of reading disability. This finding implies lack of specificity to
children with reading disability. However, Leonard et al. (2001) did
not replicate these findings.

Many of the differences across studies reflect variations in participant characteristics and imaging methods. This is technically
complicated and time-consuming research. Although acquiring the
images is relatively simple, the machines vary in technical characteristics and resolution. Methods for acquiring images vary and evolve
over time with improved technology. To do the measurements themselves is a tedious and time-consuming process as someone must digi-
tize the scans and often must manually outline the regions of interest. Thus, samples tend to be small and variable. Factors such as age,
gender, and handedness influence the anatomical organization of the
brain and these effects are magnified in small samples. Schultz et al.
(1994) found statistically significant differences on multiple measures in children with reading disabilities and age-matched controls.
However, when subject selection variables were statistically controlled, these differences disappeared and the only reliable finding
was that the left temporal lobe was smaller in children with reading
disabilities.

There are newer techniques for structural neuroimaging that are
emerging and will be very applicable to studies of reading. These
techniques move beyond measurement of brain regions and look at
other aspects of the integrity of the brain. For example, Klinkenberg
et al. (2000) used MRI for diffusion tensor imaging, a method for acquiring images that is sensitive to the white matter of the brain.
Comparisons of these measures in adults with and without a history
of reading difficulties showed less development of white matter in

language areas of the left hemisphere in those with reading disability. The authors interpreted the results as indicating that these language areas were less myelinated. In the future, it is likely that diffusion tensor imaging will be used in conjunction with the functional brain imaging methods used in the next section.

FUNCTIONAL NEUROIMAGING

Reflecting in part the dissatisfaction with the inconsistent results of structural neuroimaging studies, more recent research has emphasized the assessment of brain function. In these studies, changes in brain metabolism or neuronal signaling are assessed in relation to some type of challenge task. Thus, for example, a child might be asked to read words or sentences. As they read, changes in the rate of communication among brain cells in different regions take place, resulting in increased regional brain metabolism. As a result there are local increases in blood flow in order to supply the increased metabolic activity with oxygen and glucose.

In contrast to studies of brain structure, the results of research on brain function tend to converge across methods and laboratories in good and poor readers (Eden & Zeffiro, 1998). By way of overview, these studies indicate that a network of brain areas mediates different word-recognition processes, as well as other processes involved in language and reading. These networks, however, vary with proficiency, showing different patterns of activation in poor readers versus more skilled readers. The areas most consistently involved in these networks include the ventral temporo-occipital region in the base of the brain, the temporoparietal region (including the posterior portion of the superior temporal gyrus, the angular and supramarginal gyri), and inferior frontal regions, predominantly in the left hemisphere (Eden & Zeffiro, 1998; Papanicolaou, Pugh, Simos, & Mencl, 2004; Shaywitz et al., 2000). In this section, we review methods of functional neuroimaging and then turn to results of studies of brain function related to a variety of aspects of reading.

Functional Neuroimaging Methods

The four primary functional brain imaging methods used to study reading vary in how brain function is measured and the spatial and temporal resolution of the modality (Papanicolaou, 1998): (1) PET, (2) fMRI, (3) magnetoencephalography or MSI, and (4) magnetic resonance spectroscopy (MRS). Electrophysiological methods are also used to measure brain function. We do not discuss these latter methods as their capability for imaging of brain anatomy is not as developed as that of these four primary modalities (see Dool, Stelmack, & Rourke, 1993, for a review of research on reading difficulties using electrophysiological methods).

The rationale behind functional brain imaging is straightforward. When a person engages in a cognitive operation such as thinking, remembering, reading, or using language, changes occur in the brain. Oxygen is consumed, which can be reflected metabolically by glucose utilization or shifts in blood flow. These changes are the basis for PET and fMRI. Similarly, when a person engages in a cognitive operation, neurons discharge. These discharges are reflected in changes in the electrical activity of the brain, which can recorded with EEG. There are also changes that occur in the magnetic energy generated by the brain when neurons discharge, representing another form of neuronal signaling. MSI measures these changes and can therefore provide information about where and when the brain produced the changes in the magnetic signals. MRS noninvasively measures changes in brain chemistry, such as lactate or glutamine, in response to some type of challenge (Hunter & Wang, 2001).

The principles of functional neuroimaging are similar across methods (Shaywitz et al., 2000). When an individual performs a cognitive or motor task, the changes in glucose metabolism (PET), blood flow (PET and fMRI), electrical activity (EEG or evoked potentials), magnetic activity (MSI), or brain chemistry(MRS) are recorded. A structural MRI scan is usually obtained and the patterns of brain activation are superimposed on this MRI to identify the areas of the brain where changes are taking place. Most of these methods are safe, noninvasive, do not involve radiation, and therefore can be used with children. Methods involving PET, however, require use of a radioactive isotope that is ingested in order to measure changes in brain function. The exposure to small amounts of radioactivity precludes participation of children, unless they can directly benefit from PET due to a neurological condition. The radioactivity also limits the number of times an adult can participate in studies involving PET (Papanicolaou, 1998).

Despite these differences across methods, there are common methodological features to which all functional neuroimaging modalities can be compared (see Billingsley et al., 2003). One major consideration involves the selection of tasks. Good imaging studies carefully outline the rationale behind task selection, particularly if the study is based on hemodynamic methods and therefore uses across-task comparison to determine differences in patterns of regional activation. This issue is discussed in more detail later when specific methods are described, but it is clear that task selection must be analytic and guided by strong theory. If the purpose is to image some aspect of cognition, the underlying cognitive theory should be well established independently of applications to neuroimaging. Other desirable characteristics include the need for adequate spatial resolution to identifying brain areas activated by a particular task. Imaging modalities vary considerably in their spatial resolution, with PET much weaker than fMRI and MSI (in conjunction with structural MRI). The imaging modality should provide information on the temporal resolution of the task, but this is possible in real time only with neurophysiological procedures (e.g., MSI) as hemodynamic shifts take time to occur and are often "after the fact." The methods should permit images of individuals rather than requiring averages across groups, which can be done with MSI and is emerging with fMRI. The images should reasonably converge across modalities, externally validating the different methods. This is a strong feature of reading studies. The maps themselves should also be compared to those derived from direct anatomical verification, which is apparent for MSI and fMRI. In all these comparisons, differences will emerge that reflect characteristics of the method, but there should be significant overlap. Finally, the method should be easy to apply, especially in studies of children. As we shall see later, fMRI and MSI have more of these characteristics, which is why PET and electrophysiological methods are less desirable.

In evaluating an imaging study, the consumer must understand these issues and the strengths and weaknesses of different modalities. Consider, for example, the spatial resolution and temporal sensitivity of the four modalities. The metabolic activity recorded by PET and fMRI takes place after the actual shifts have occurred, so that the temporal resolution of these methods is weak. If a task requires long periods of activity, as with MRS, this is not a major problem. The chemical shifts occur in real time but require longer acquisitions to measure the shift (Hunter & Wang, 2001). The spatial resolution of MRS is poor, so the maps are aligned with a structural MRI scan to allow precise localization of brain activity associated with performance of a particular task. MSI, on the other hand, affords measurement of neurophysiological activity in real time and provides information on the actual time course of neuronal events. MSI scans, however, do not convey structural information for the brain being imaged, so MSI activation maps are also superimposed onto a structural MRI scan. PET also has weak spatial resolution and requires a structural MRI. However, fMRI uses very fast magnetic resonance images collected serially in order to measure the changes in blood flow associated with cognitive activity (Papanicolaou et al., 2004; Shaywitz et al., 2000). Thus, spatial resolution with fMRI is excellent despite weak temporal resolution as the changes in blood flow do not precisely co-occur with the event. In contrast to fMRI, MSI is weak in detecting subcortical brain activity and is largely sensitive to surface cortical activation. These strengths and weaknesses help the consumer evaluate the contribution of different imaging studies.

All four neuroimaging methods have been used in different studies of the organization of language and reading in children as well as the representation of language in monolingual adults and children and bilingual adults. Other cognitive processes have also been imaged, including attention, memory, problem solving, and other operations (Papanicolaou et al., 2002; Posner & Raichle, 1996; Thatcher, Lyon, Rumsey, & Krasnegor, 1996). Prior to applying these methods to populations of children and those with disabilities, the methods were extensively studied in normal adults. To illustrate, Figure 12.1 shows an activation map of language representation created by MSI in neurologically normal adult volunteers. The upper panel of Figure 12.1 shows the typical hemispheric asymmetry in the degree of neurophysiological activity in response to a task in which the adult was required to process spoken language. There is much more activation of the left hemisphere than the right hemisphere, especially for regions known to mediate receptive language functions (i.e., spoken word recognition and comprehension): the posterior portion of the superior, middle temporal gyri, and the supramarginal gyrus (Wernicke's area). This area is also involved in reading as will become evident in the paragraphs to follow. The lower panel shows activation of Wernicke's area in the left hemisphere of an individual with epilepsy who also underwent direct electrical stimulation prior to neurosurgical intervention for intractable seizures. The correspondence of the cortical stimulation study and the MSI study is clearly apparent.

In the next section, we review studies involving reading using all four functional imaging methods. The findings converge in suggesting that tasks involving different aspects of reading are associated with increased activation in ventral occipitotemporal (or basal) regions, the posterior portion of the superior and middle temporal gyri extending into inferior parietal areas (supramarginal and angular gyri), and the inferior frontal lobe areas, primarily in the left hemisphere (Eden & Zeffiro, 1998; Papanicolaou et al., 2004; Rumsey et al., 1997; Shaywitz et al., 2000). There are inconsistencies involving the involvement of a particular area (Poeppel, 1996), but it is apparent that a network of areas is common across methods, activated to a different degree depending on the modality and the reading task. The network is clearly apparent in Figure 12.2, which illustrates the regions of interest.

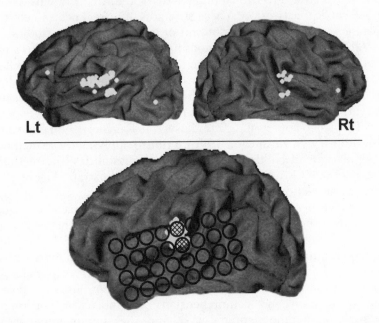

FIGURE 12.1. The upper panel shows a brain activation map from MSI involving a spoken-word-recognition task superimposed on an anatomical MRI scan (three-dimensional rendering). Note the significantly greater activation of the sites in the left hemisphere (Lt) versus the right hemisphere (Rt), especially in Wernicke's area. In the lower panel, the precise location of Wernicke's area is identified using MSI in the context of the same task in a patient before undergoing epilepsy surgery. During the operation, as the surface of the patient's temporal lobe was exposed, an array of electrodes was placed on brain. Electrical interference was then produced at different sites of the array as the patient attempted to recognize and respond to spoken words and simple commands. Observing the effects of focal, transient interference with normal neurophysiological function enables researchers to confirm the accuracy of MSI for localizing activation produced by Wernicke's area. In a similar manner, the accuracy of MSI has been established for activity originating in more anterior parts of the brain, predominantly involved in expressive language (Broca's area). The location of both areas on a model of the human brain is displayed in Figure 12.2.

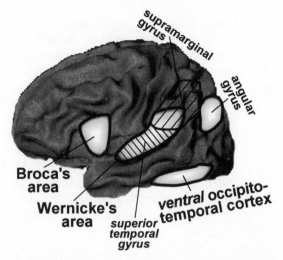

FIGURE 12.2. Model of a neural network for reading showing four major participating areas. Broca's area is responsible for phonological processing involving articulation mapping as in the pronunciation of words. Wernicke's area (which includes portions of the superior temporal and supramarginal gyri) is responsible for phonological processing involving letter–sound correspondence. The angular gyrus is a relay station that links information across modalities. The visual association cortex in the occipitotemporal region is responsible for graphemic analysis. Most of the empirical evidence that supports this model for the brain circuit that supports reading derives from the study of acquired reading difficulties secondary to brain damage (Damasio & Damasio, 1983; Henderson, 1986), although more recent studies of the effects of transient interference with normal function in certain areas, in the context of neurosurgical operations, generally corroborates earlier findings (e.g., Simos et al., 2000c).

Functional Neuroimaging Studies of Reading

The reading studies that we focus on involve different tasks that manipulate components of word recognition. This is partly because the studies have been oriented toward adults and children who have word-recognition difficulties, by far the most common form of reading disability (Shaywitz, 1996). Word-recognition tasks lend themselves to functional neuroimaging methods. Such tasks can closely link stimulus presentation and response, which helps interpret the time course of the cognitive operation. Word recognition tasks can be manipulated to address a variety of component processes that are common to both aural language function and reading, such as phonological and semantic analysis, and others that are specific to print (visual and orthographic processing). It is possible to image other more complex aspects of reading, such as fluency and comprehension. This goal is far more difficult to achieve, because fluency and comprehension involve several component processes, the contribution of which to the overall pattern of brain activity must be isolated experimentally. This requires the use of a series of activation tasks, each placing differential demands upon one or more of the components of the reading function. For example, the processes that support word recognition are also involved in a comprehension task; thus to understand operations specific to comprehension, such as semantic processing, there must be control tasks that separate out the influence of word recognition. As the goal of functional neuroimaging is to relate components of a task to specific patterns of brain activation, tasks that permit this type of decomposition in relation to brain activation are highly desirable.

PET

The activation patterns of adults who read poorly have been compared to those of adults who read well using PET. These studies were the earliest applications of functional imaging methods, reflecting the earlier emergence of PET compared with fMRI and MSI, the newest modality. They have been done in adults because PET is invasive, involving injection of radioactive isotopes. The participant receives a preparation containing the isotope, which has known properties of decay. The rate of decay in different brain regions is measured as the person performs a task, thus providing evidence of the involvement of these regions.

Studies of adults with reading disabilities using PET have found reduced blood flow in the left temporoparietal area during performance of word and sentence reading and phonological processing tasks (Rumsey et al., 1992, 1997). Activation in the left inferior frontal areas was similar in good and poor readers (Rumsey et al., 1994). In addition, whereas good readers showed more activation of the left than right hemisphere in reading, poor readers did not show this asymmetry (Gross-Glenn et al., 1991). By examining relationships among brain areas with respect to the relative degree of regional activity, Horwitz, Rumsey, and Donohue (1998) showed significant coactivation in good readers between the left angular gyrus and other brain areas during a phonological task. These measures of functional connectivity among reading areas in the left hemisphere were not as strong in poor readers. For reasons explained earlier, studies with PET, which has lower spatial resolution than fMRI, have rarely involved children.

fMRI Studies

The basis for fMRI involves changes in blood flow. If a set of neurons in the brain begins to participate in a particular cognitive operation, it increases the rate at which the set communicates with nearby neurons. Increased neurophysiological activity elevates the rate of metabolic processes that take place inside each neuron, which in turn causes increased consumption of oxygen. This results in a depletion of oxygenated blood (hemoglobin) in the region of these neurons. A change in oxygenated blood leads to a vascular reaction in which more blood is sent to this region, resulting in an oversupply of hemoglobin. The process takes several seconds and fMRI essentially detects these changes in oxygenation by measuring changes in the perturbation of the magnetic energy generated by changes in hemoglobin. To detect these changes, the distribution of hemoglobin is measured in resting states and then in response to activation and is depicted in the actual MRI images (Krasuski et al., 1996).

As with PET, a careful approach to task construction is necessary to identify areas activated by different cognitive operations. The changes in hemoglobin distribution must be measured before, during, and after engagement of the person in a cognitive task. However, these changes are small and are hidden by ongoing brain activation. To identify how different areas of the brain are engaged in a particular cognitive operation, metabolic changes related to overall brain function must be isolated so that the changes specific to a task can be identified. To accomplish this, tasks are designed that account for general features of activation and those that are specific to a task. Different images can be compared and the specific components of activation identified by "subtracting" across images to remove aspects of the activation that are not specific to the operation of interest (Papanicolaou et al., 2004).

To illustrate, consider the approach to task selection developed by the Yale Center for the Study of Learning and Attention Disorders (Shaywitz et al., 1998, 2000, 2002). In a series of experiments, word recognition was viewed as organized on a hierarchy of component processes (Pugh et al., 1996, 2000; Shaywitz et al., 1998). At the bottom of this hierarchy is visuospatial analysis, followed by orthographic analysis, simple and complex phonological analysis, and, finally, semantic analysis. A series of tasks was designed to engage an increasingly greater number of component processes. To engage solely visuospatial analysis a line orientation matching task was used. To engage both visuospatial and orthographic analysis, a case-matching task was employed. To create different degrees of difficulty

in phonological analysis, in addition to visuospatial and orthographic analysis, tasks involved letter–name matching and rhyming
of pseudowords. Finally, a semantic category judgment task was employed that requires visuospatial, orthographic, lexical/semantic and,
to some extent, phonological analysis. Then, a "subtraction" technique was used in which patterns of activation were compared across
tasks in order to tease apart activation associated with a particular
component process.

In a series of fMRI studies, this approach has led to consistent
results in proficient readers (Pugh et al., 1996), and it was successful
at producing brain activation profiles that differentiated good and
poor readers (Shaywitz et al., 1998, 2002). Prototypical results associated with the phonological analysis operation can be seen in Figure
12.3, in which good readers showed increased activation with increasing demands for phonological analysis in temporoparietal areas, including the superior temporal gyrus (which encompasses
Wernicke's area) and the angular gyrus. In contrast, poor readers did
not demonstrate this pattern but showed more activation of anterior

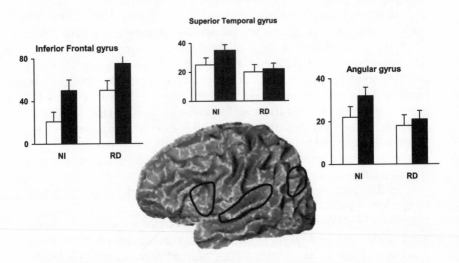

FIGURE 12.3. Relative degree of change in blood flow in response to an orthographic compared to a phonological task, using fMRI in nonimpaired readers
(NI) and poor readers (RD). The number of activated image elements (pix-
els) within each area serves as the dependent variable. In posterior regions,
such as the superior temporal and angular gyri, the change in activation is
large in nonimpaired readers but small in poor readers. In contrast, anterior
regions demonstrate increased activation in poor readers (inferior frontal
gyrus) relative to nonimpaired readers (Shaywitz et al., 1998).

portions of the brain (inferior frontal gyrus). In addition, the latter group showed reversed (right greater than left) hemispheric asymmetry in activation in posterior temporal regions as compared to the group of nonimpaired readers, a finding that corresponds with previous reports of atypical patterns of hemispheric asymmetry in regional metabolism in impaired readers (Rumsey et al., 1992). Pugh et al. (2000) also found evidence that the angular gyrus was poorly connected with other areas involving reading in adults who were poor readers. Compared to adults, children who are poor readers show a similar reduction in the activation of left-hemisphere temporoparietal regions and a similar increase in the activation of mirror areas in the right hemisphere (Shaywitz et al., 2002). It appears, however, that the increased engagement of inferior frontal region in children is not as pronounced as for adults. In the same large sample, Mencl et al. (in press) also found evidence that in children who were poor readers, these left-hemisphere regions were not as likely to become active in unison during performance of reading tasks, as it was in proficient readers.

MSI Studies

Studies using MSI, or magnetoencephalography, have also revealed reliable differences in activation patterns of children with reading disabilities and typically achieving children at group and individual levels. For these studies, activation maps are obtained while the children completed tasks in which they listen to or read real words or read pseudowords in which the children had to decide whether the pseudowords rhyme (Simos et al., 2000a, 2000b). Reading fluency and sentence comprehension tasks have also been developed, along with other experiments examining different aspects of spoken language processing, including word recognition and comprehension and phonological analysis (Billingsley et al., 2003).

Unlike PET and fMRI, MSI directly assesses neuronal signaling in real time (Papanicolaou, 1998; Papanicolaou et al., 2004). Its development for imaging higher cortical processes began with studies of people with epilepsy, a disorder characterized by abnormal electrical discharges that sometimes eventuate in seizures. When neurons signal, electricity is generated. In a state in which no cognitive process is engaged, these electrical discharges appear random. If a group of neurons that are not usually synchronized begins to discharge in unison, the combined electrical currents would deviate well beyond the apparent moment-by-moment fluctuations. This is what happens in people with epilepsy and MSI can identify where in the brain the abnormal discharges are occurring. However, the sources of these currents cannot be directly measured. In EEG, voltage changes associated with these currents can be measured at the surface of the scalp, but precise localization of cortical regions producing them is prevented by various forms of passive electrical interference. However, these sources also produce small amounts of electromagnetic energy that emanate around the source and travel outside the head. These minute magnetic signals can be captured by MSI in the form of a magnetic field (or magnetic flux) distributed along the head surface. Local, transient changes in magnetic flux are recorded by superconducting loops of wire that are contained in a helmet-like device covering the head. Based on the recorded changes in the surface distribution of electromagnetic energy, researchers obtain precise estimates of the location of the sets of active neurons using simple statistical modeling techniques (Papanicolaou, 1998).

Unlike PET and fMRI, MSI does not require subtraction methods. For example, the tasks in word-recognition experiments use actual words whose properties may be manipulated to require phonological, orthographic, or semantic processing. Like other neuroimaging techniques, MSI requires many trials and the results are averaged across trials, similar to evoked potential methods. But the phenomena of interest occur in real time as the basis is neuronal signaling, not metabolism.

In a series of studies of adults and children who vary in reading proficiency, good and poor readers have not been found to differ in activation patterns when they *listened* to words, showing patterns predominantly in the left hemisphere that would be expected for such a task (Simos et al., 2000a). However, on *printed* word-recognition tasks, striking differences in the activation patterns of good and poor readers occur (see Figure 12.4). In the children who were good readers, there was a characteristic pattern in which the occipital areas of the brain that support primary visual processing were initially activated (not shown in Figure 12.4). Then the ventral visual association cortices in both hemispheres were activated, followed by simultaneous activation of three areas in the *left* temporoparietal region (essentially the angular, supramarginal, and superior temporal gyri, encompassing Wernicke's area). In the children with reading problems, the same pattern and time course was apparent, but the temporoparietal areas of the *right* hemisphere were activated. On the whole, the findings are similar to those from the PET and fMRI studies, but the differences between good and poor readers are more strikingly lateralized, especially in areas associated with mapping of letters and sounds (see Figure 12.2).

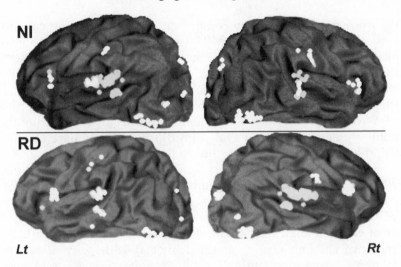

FIGURE 12.4. Three-dimensional renderings of MRI scans from a reader with impairment (lower set of images) and a nonimpaired reader (upper set of images) during a printed word-recognition task in an MSI study. Note the clear preponderance of activity sources in left (Lt) temporoparietal cortices in the proficient child and in homotopic right-hemisphere (Rt) areas in the poor reader. (Data adapted from Simos et al. (2000a).

Altogether, these findings suggest that in children with reading disabilities, it is the functional connections among brain areas that account for differences in brain activation as opposed to specific or general dysfunction of any single brain area. A critical question is whether the patterns seen in the poor readers are compensatory or reflect the failure of instruction to impact the brain in a manner necessary to form the neural networks that support word recognition. Thus, the pattern may be similar to that seen in a young child who has not learned to read and may change by virtue of development, instruction, or even intervention. These studies may provide an example of how brain and environment interact in forming the neural networks supporting word recognition.

Changes in Brain Activation in Relation to Intervention

The relationship of neuronal activation changes and response to intervention were evaluated in several recent studies (Richards et al., 2000; Simos et al., 2002c; Temple et al., 2003). In Richards et al. (2000), MRS was used to evaluate metabolic processes before and after a 3-week, 30-hour intervention focusing on phonological process-

ing, word decoding, reading comprehension, and listening comprehension. Children received a MRS examination of the left anterior
quadrant of the brain—known to be related to language processing—
before and after the intervention. Prior to intervention, the MRS
scans revealed a higher metabolic rate of lactate in this quadrant
when children with reading problems completed a task requiring
them to decide whether words and nonwords rhymed. After the
training program, lactate metabolism did not differentiate children
with dyslexia and controls on the reading task.

In a second study, Simos et al. (2002c) employed MSI before
and after children with severe reading disability participated in an intense phonologically based intervention. These children ranged in
age from 7 to 17 years and had severe word-recognition difficulties.
Six of eight children read at the third percentile or below, with the
other two children reading at the 13th and 18th percentiles. The
children received intervention for 2 hours a day, 5 days a week, over
an 8-week period, about 80 hours of intensive phonologically based
instruction per child. Before intervention, the eight children with
dyslexia uniformly displayed the aberrant pattern of activation in the
right hemisphere that has been reliably identified with MSI. After intervention, children's word reading accuracy scores improved into the
average range. In addition, in each case, there was significant activation of neural circuits in the left hemisphere commonly associated
with proficient word reading ability. There was also a tendency for reduction in right-hemisphere activity. Figure 12.5 provides a representative example of the changes before and after intervention. The
changes were statistically significant, though the sample size is small.
In addition, even with the improvement in word reading accuracy, latency data from MSI continued to show delays in the evoked fields
associated with the left-hemisphere response. These studies imply a
significant role for instruction in establishing the neural networks
that support reading development.

More recently, Aylward et al. (2003) evaluated changes in response to reading intervention in 10 children with reading difficulties
averaging about 11½ years of age and 11 age-matched controls. The
children with reading difficulties were less severely impaired than
those in the Simos et al. (2002c) study, with the basis for selection a
discrepancy in reading relative to verbal ability as indexed by an IQ
test. The participants engaged in a 3-week intervention addressing
the application of phonological and morphological strategies to
word recognition. On average, the children with reading difficulties
showed about one-half standard deviation improvement in word-
recognition ability (from a word reading quotient of about 87 to 93).
They were imaged before and after the instructional period with

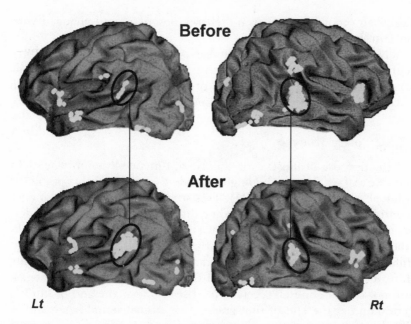

Before

After

Lt   *Rt*

FIGURE 12.5. Activation maps from a poor reader before and after intervention. Note the dramatic increase in left temporoparietal activation associated with the significant improvement in phonological decoding and word-recognition ability. Data adapted from Simos et al. (2002c).

fMRI, using a phoneme sound matching task and a morpheme mapping task. At baseline and compared to nonimpaired readers, the children with reading difficulties showed much less activation of areas in the left hemisphere that varied with the task. After intervention, comparisons with the controls were no longer statistically significant, with the authors concluding that the brain activation patterns were normalized as opposed to indicating a compensatory pattern. The areas of the brain that changed were different than in the Simos et al. (2002c) study, but the tasks and interventions were also different, and the poor readers in the Aylward et al. (2003) study were less impaired. In imaging research, slight differences in participant and task conditions can produce significant variations in activation patterns. What is similar in Simos et al. (2002c) and Aylward et al. (2003) is that the brain areas were largely in language areas of the left hemisphere and have been associated with the neural network supporting different aspects of word recognition. Moreover, neither study indicated compensatory patterns. More important, all three studies illustrate the potency of targeted instruction and its impact on brain function. The areas of the brain that do not perform adequately in poor readers can be reliably described and changed with instruction.

None of these studies addresses processes that might occur as part of typical reading development. What happens in the brain as younger children at varying levels of proficiency learn to read? The next section addresses this set of questions.

An Exemplary Study

For the purpose of illustrating the use of functional neuroimaging in the study of reading, we highlight a study that we recently completed using MSI (Simos et al., 2004). This study involved a group of children identified as at risk for reading difficulties at the end of kindergarten and a comparison group of children in the same classrooms who did not show risk characteristics. The at-risk children received different reading interventions in grade 1 designed to prevent reading difficulties in first grade. As part of this study, a subset of the at-risk and not-at-risk children received MSI scanning at the end of kindergarten and at the end of first grade. This study exemplifies many of the characteristics of a good neuroimaging study. The methods used to identify areas of regional brain activation, as described previously, have been subjected to direct anatomical verification. Individual maps can be constructed that are reliable and stable in the same individuals over time. The results agree with other established methods (i.e., have external validity). They are easily applied, in this instance to young children as part of a reading intervention study. Moreover, the study demonstrates how neuroimaging research can be integrated with more traditional studies of reading development and intervention. The children were recruited from schools and were ethnically, culturally, and economically diverse. The tasks themselves closely paralleled areas of potential difficulty for the children (letter–sound knowledge, word recognition). The two tasks were selected to take into account the major changes that occur in reading development early in school. Thus, all children were able to perform the sound knowledge task in kindergarten and development would be expected regardless of risk status from kindergarten to grade 1 on the word-recognition task. The neural correlates of these tasks are well established and replicated across imaging modalities.

Procedures: Intervention Study

The intervention study (Mathes et al., 2004) took place in six non-Title 1 schools in a large urban school district in Texas. These schools were selected because of evidence indicating that they had strong core reading programs. As we intended to evaluate the use of secondary interventions for children who were struggling to learn to read, we wanted to work in schools in which the core reading programs appeared strong.

Over each of 2 consecutive years, the risk status of all children in kindergarten in these schools were evaluated using the teacher administered Texas Primary Reading Inventory (TPRI; Fletcher et al., 2002). Those children who were identified as at risk based on the screening section from the TPRI received additional assessments of word recognition and text reading to eliminate potential false positives as the TPRI was designed to minimize the risk of missing children who might have reading problems, with the expected consequence of higher rates of false positives.

Those children who were identified as at risk were randomly assigned to one of three reading interventions. Two of these interventions involved small group instruction using two different approaches. Both of these interventions took place in groups of three with a certified teacher supervised by the researchers. The instruction took place on a daily basis for about 40 minutes per day for 30 weeks. One intervention (Proactive) was based on a direct instruction model that included explicit instruction in the alphabetic principle, fluency, and comprehension strategies. The other approach (Responsive) explicitly taught the alphabetic principle, along with fluency and comprehension strategies, but in the context of reading and writing. The programs differed largely in that the Proactive program had an explicit scope and sequence and used highly decodable text. In the Responsive program, teachers are expected to respond to the needs of the child in context of reading and writing, so there was no explicit scope and sequence. Texts with high-frequency words were used. Both approaches were comprehensive, well-integrated approaches to reading instruction that included an explicit emphasis on teaching the alphabetic principle. It should be noted that the purpose of these two interventions was not to contrast them but to look at how well they worked with students who varied in their learning characteristics. We expected both approaches to be effective. In addition to the two groups of students who received a pullout intervention, a third group of students remained in the classroom and did not receive a pullout intervention unless it was provided by the school. In addition to the district's enhanced professional development in reading instruction, we provided additional professional development for all teachers involving the use of assessment data for instructional purposes. We also ensured that teachers, principals, and parents had enhanced access to assessment data and the results of progress monitoring throughout the year. As such, this group is not a traditional untreated control group but rather a comparison group addressing the value-added impact of small-group instruction on top of enhanced classroom instruction.

Results: Intervention Study

The results of the intervention study are easily described (Mathes et al., 2004). Group averages across children who received the two pullout interventions generally did not differ significantly across a wide range of assessments of word recognition, fluency, and comprehension. There were some slight differences that would be expected on the basis of the program that was taught. For example, children who were in the Proactive intervention had significantly higher word attack skills. Children who received either pullout intervention performed at higher levels and showed greater growth than at-risk children who stayed in the classroom. At the end of the year, the number of children who were not reading in the average range was less than 1% for Proactive, 8% for Responsive, and 16% for children who stayed in the classroom.

Procedures: Imaging Study

Volunteers for the imaging study were recruited directly at the schools. The researchers attended different meetings of parents, including kindergarten graduation ceremonies, explaining the study and soliciting volunteers. Those who volunteered and whose children assented traveled to the Texas Medical Center to participate in the MSI study. This required written informed consent from the parents and written assent from the child. When the child arrived at the laboratory, considerable time was taken to acclimate the child to the procedure and help the child become as comfortable as possible. The actual recording required about 10 minutes per task; the entire session lasted about 2 hours.

Scans were initially obtained at the end of kindergarten or beginning of first grade. There were 28 children who were at risk (18 males, 10 females) and 17 participants who were not at risk (10 males, 7 females). The average age was about 6½ years. None of these children had been identified with any form of neurological, emotional, or other problem. At the end of first grade, we were able to reimage 33 of the 45 original participants. The Texas Medical Center experienced a major flood in the summer of 2001 that resulted in damage to the laboratory and an inability to reimage all the volunteers from the first year. We were unable to extend the study to the second intervention cohort. Seventeen of the children were not at risk and 13 were children from the initial at-risk group who responded to systematic classroom instruction and/or pullout intervention and read in the average range at the end of grade 1 (responders). There were also three children from the initial at-risk group who did not respond to the intervention and read below the 25th percentile (nonresponders).

During each of the two visits, each child completed two activation tasks. One task required the children to look at a letter of the alphabet and pronounce the most common sound associated with that letter. The second task required them to read aloud simple consonant-vowel-consonant pseudowords. To complete the tasks, the child was placed in a comfortable position lying down and looking at a screen projected on the roof. While the child completed each task, he or she was imaged with a whole head neuromagnetometer array that consists of 148 magnetic sensors, housed in a magnetically shielded chamber (see *cars.uth.tmc/project/ieri* for a short video showing a child participating in the study). The results are achieved by averaging across the responses for each task.

The specific methods that are used for signal processing, source localization, and co-registration with the anatomical MRI scan can be found in Papanicolaou et al. (2004). In essence, the machine measures the magnetic flux that is generated by the changes in neural signal. Each trial generates an evoked response field that is averaged over the stimulus presentations, with rejection of trials that might have eye movement or other magnetic artifacts. A mathematical model is applied to the averaged responses to identify the intracranial sources of activity that would represent sets of active neurons. The method provides an estimated location of strength of these sources during the temporal evolution of an averaged evoked response. The emergent location estimates are then superimposed on the brain using a coordinate system that is co-registered with a structural MRI scan.

Results: Imaging Study

The results of the initial assessment before intervention were reported in Simos et al. (2002a). Activity sources were consistently found in five regions of the brain: the posterior portion of the superior temporal gyrus, extending into the adjacent supramarginal gyrus (Wernicke's area), angular, and inferior frontal gyri, the *ventral* occipitotemporal (basal) region, and in the *lateral* occipitotemporal region. Both occipitotemporal regions contain complex visual processing areas. As MSI also provides information on when major events actually happen, two major components of the time course were identified. The early activity sources were largely in areas of the brain that are concerned with visual processing or print. The latest sources occurred largely after 150 milliseconds and involved the network of the brain regions listed above.

The major differences between the groups are displayed in Figure 12.6, which illustrates the significant group by hemisphere by area interaction, which was mainly due to regional differences in the direction of quasi-linear trends across groups. In posterior regions (angular gyrus and ventral occipitotemporal region, bilaterally, and Wernicke's area in the left hemisphere) there was greater activity for the not-at-risk group followed by the responders, and least activity for the nonresponders. This trend was reversed in the right-hemisphere homologue of Wernicke's area and in the inferior frontal gyrus, bilaterally. Hemispheric asymmetries in the degree of activity were found only in Wernicke's area but vary across groups: Not-at-risk children showed the expected L > R asymmetry, seen in older proficient children and adults, whereas responders displayed bilaterally symmetric activity. Nonresponders displayed a strikingly different pattern (R > L), which is typical of older children and adults with reading impairment. Group differences were also found with the respect to the relative timing of activity in certain areas, most prominent of which was the significant tendency for an early peak of activity in the left inferior frontal gyrus in the group of nonresponders, compared to the two groups of children who displayed typical reading achievement outcomes at the end of grade 1.

There were significant developmental changes during the 1-year study period. Not-at-risk and children in the responder group showed increased activation between Kindergarten and first grade in the inferior frontal region and lateral occipitotemporal areas bilaterally and for both tasks. Conversely, a significant reduction in the degree of activity was found in the superior temporal gyrus in both hemispheres and tasks. There were no changes in the degree or latency of activity in these areas for the group of nonresponders.

These findings demonstrate that in the majority of beginning readers, the general outline of the brain network that supports reading is already in place by the end of kindergarten. For a smaller proportion of children, this profile displays a less mature state, yet systematic classroom instruction is sufficient to help establish the "typical" network outline by the end of first grade. For a smaller pro-

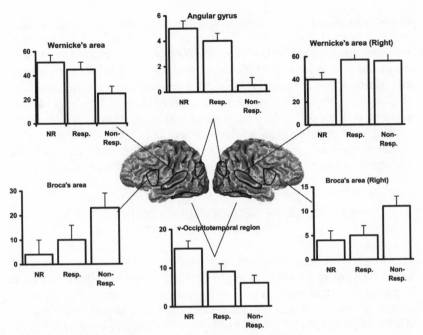

FIGURE 12.6. Group differences in the degree of brain activity in four major components of the reading circuit: temporoparietal cortex (posterior superior temporal and supramarginal gyrus, which includes Wernicke's area in the left hemisphere and the corresponding region in the right hemisphere), the angular gyrus, Broca's area (located in the inferior frontal gyrus), and ventral occipitotemporal cortex (located in the basal surface of the brain). Group differences were similar across tasks (letter sound and pseudoword reading) in all areas with the exception of the inferior frontal gyrus, where group differences were more pronounced for the more demanding pseudoword reading task. Estimates of the degree of brain activity were obtained with MSI at the end of kindergarten. NR, children not at risk for developing reading difficulties ($N = 17$); Resp., children who were deemed to be at risk for developing reading difficulties in kindergarten, but responded to systematic classroom instruction and scored within the average range 1 year later ($N = 13$); Non-Resp., at-risk children who could be classified as reading disabled at the end of first grade ($N = 3$).

portion of at-risk children, however, classroom instruction alone is not sufficient to promote the developmental changes required for the establishment of an efficient brain network to support fluent reading. These children show distinct activation profiles during the initial stages of reading acquisition, resembling the profile found in older poor readers (Simos et al., 2000a, 2000b, 2002a) even for tasks (letter–sound naming) that pose minimal demands for phonological decoding. Generally, changes in reading proficiency appear to parallel changes in neural activity, largely in the areas shown in Figure 12.3. For the majority of children, including those initially classified as at risk who responded to classroom instruction, these changes represent an initial strengthening of the brain network that involves regions in the frontal lobes and in more posterior regions of the brain, especially the angular gyrus. This network is largely bilateral but in proficient readers is lateralized in the temporoparietal areas especially concerned with phonological analysis. There is less lateralization in the at-risk responder group. The nonresponder group showed much less change and little development of the left-hemisphere network.

RELEVANCE OF NEUROIMAGING TECHNOLOGIES TO READING RESEARCH

Reading researchers commonly ask why neuroimaging studies are relevant to reading research. It might be better to phrase the question in terms of why reading research is relevant to neuroimaging. In many of the studies that have been described, the key has been theory-driven applications of the technology to different research questions. In other words, the application of the imaging modality and the interpretation of the results have been heavily dependent on theory and research in the cognitive sciences. This research has helped focus the lens of the technology so that appropriate questions are asked and tasks are designed that are linked to those that have been used in the cognitive sciences.

In addition, questions that would be of interest to reading educators have been asked because individuals interested in intervention have participated in the neuroimaging studies. Thus, the early focus of the imaging studies on the results of intervention studies has been critical for the development and enhancement of neuroimaging technologies. By the same token, using neuroimaging in reading research, particularly in the intervention studies, has helped advance understanding of how children learn to read and why some struggle. In this regard, the results can be integrated into the larger body of knowledge regarding the critical role of phonological processing and word recognition as a key phase in learning to read and as an obstacle for many children who do not develop adequate word-recognition strategies.

It is very important to carefully consider the results of the intervention studies. The fact that the neural systems can be shown to develop through interactions with the environment implies that they are not present at birth and that certain types of experiences are critical in developing these systems. Moreover, when children who are struggling to learn to read are examined, it becomes apparent that the systems are malleable and provide excellent examples of the plasticity and malleability of the brain for mediating different kinds of complex cognitive functions. In a word, the greatest relevance of neuroimaging studies is the clear indication that instructional approaches that are effective, whether they occur in the classroom or in a pullout program, in children who are at risk or not at risk for reading difficulties, or in children and adults who either good or poor readers, can modify aspects of brain function which are known to be critical for the cognitive operations targeted by instruction (such as phonological processing and word recognition). Teachers provide instruction. In the study examples that we have presented, the research provides excellent examples of how teachers provide effective instruction that alters brain function and supports critical areas of learning. Ultimately it is the teacher who has provided this instruction that has an impact on neural organization of the brain.

As the studies reviewed in this chapter demonstrate, not only is reading research relevant to neuroimaging studies but neuroimaging studies are very relevant to reading research. Historically, reading researchers are quick to denigrate a particular area of research, often on ideological grounds. Thus, neuroimaging studies are viewed as examples of the medical model or an attempt to reduce reading development to word recognition or to simplistic neural explanations. In this chapter, we have attempted to show that the application of neuroimaging methods in reading is a significant accomplishment. It is more than a technology looking for a home. Rather, these applications are dependent on other areas of reading research that lead to the imaging study and are critical for the interpretation of results, in turn suggesting modifications of theories of reading development. The task is not to decide whether any body of knowledge in reading (or other areas of education and science) is good or bad. Rather, the task is to integrate results across the different domains of inquiry that pertain to reading. Neuroimaging studies cut across multiple domains, including various age groups, levels of proficiency, and research on the brain; reading development; cognition; and instruction. These studies show that the brain is involved at all ages and levels of proficiency, but they do not indicate that the brain has a deterministic influence that can be separated from experience. Indeed, instruction and practice seems essential for developing and strengthening the neural networks that must be in place for the brain to support complex activities such as reading. Some of these appear to be specific to reading and are not simply activated by other language experiences or being exposed to written language. This type of knowledge must be integrated into the broader knowledge of research on reading. At the most dramatic level, neuroimaging research shows that teaching affects the brain in positive, long-term ways that are essential for the development of the reader.

ACKNOWLEDGMENTS

Work reported on in this chapter was supported in part by grants from the National Science Foundation (No. 9979968: "Early Development of Reading Skills: A Cognitive Neuroscience Approach") and the National Institute of Child Health and Human Development (No. HD38346: "Brain Activation Profiles in Dyslexia" and No. HD25802: "Center for Learning and Attention Disorders").

REFERENCES

Aylward, E. H., Richards, T. L., Berninger, V. W., Nagy, W. E., Field, K. M., Grimme A. C., Richards, A. L., Thomason, J. B., & Cramer, S. D. (2003). Instructional treatment associated with changes in brain activation in children with dyslexia. *Neurology, 22,* 212–219.

Benton, A. L. (1962). Behavioral indices of brain injury in school children. *Child Development, 33,* 199–208.

Benton, A. L. (1975). Developmental dyslexia: Neurological aspects. In W. J. Friedlander (Ed.), *Advances in neurology.* New York: Raven.

Billingsley, R. L., Simos, P. G., Castillo, E. M., Maestú, F., Sarkari, S., Breier, J. I., & Papanicolaou, A. C. (2003). Functional brain imaging of language: Criteria for scientific merit and supporting data from magnetic source imaging. *Journal of Neurolinguistics, 16,* 255–275.

Critchley, M. (1970). *The dyslexic child.* Springfield, IL: Charles C Thomas.

Damasio A. R., & Damasio H. (1983). The anatomic basis of pure alexia. *Neurology, 33,* 1573–1583.

Dool, C. B., Stelmack, R. M., & Rourke, B. P. (1993). Event-related potentials in children with learning disabilities. *Journal of Clinical Child Psychology, 22,* 387–398.

Duara, R., Kuslch, A., Gross-Glenn, K., Barker, W., Jallad, B., Pascal, S., Loewenstein, D. A., Sheldon, J., Rabin, M., Levin, B., & Lubs, H. (1991). Neuroanatomic differences between dyslexic and normal readers on magnetic resonance imaging scans. *Archives of Neurology, 48,* 410–416.

Eden, G. F., & Zeffiro, T. A. (1998). Neural systems affected in developmental dyslexia revealed by functional neuroimaging. *Neuron, 21,* 279–282.

Filipek, P. (1996). Structural variations in measures in the developmental disorders. In R. Thatcher, G. Lyon, J. Rumsey, & N. Krasnegor (Eds.),

Developmental neuroimaging: Mapping the development of brain and behavior (pp. 169–186). San Diego: Academic Press.

Fletcher, J. M., Foorman, B. R., Boudousquie, A. B., Barnes, M. A., Schatschneider, C., & Francis, D. J. (2002). Assessment of reading and learning disabilities: A research-based, intervention-oriented approach. *Journal of School Psychology, 40,* 27–63.

Fletcher, J. M., & Taylor, H. G. (1984). Neuropsychological approaches to children: Towards a developmental neuropsychology. *Journal of Clinical Neuropsychology, 6,* 39–56.

Galaburda, A. M. (1993). The planum temporale. *Archives of Neurology, 50,* 457.

Gross-Glenn, K., Duara, R., Barker, W. W., Lowenstein, D., Chang, J.-Y, Yoshii, F., Apicella, A. M., Pascal, S., Boothes, T., Seuush, S., Jallad, B. J., Novoa, L., & Lubs, H. A. (1991). Positron emission tomographic studies during serial word-reading by normal and dyslexic adults. *Journal of Clinical and Experimental Neuropsychology, 13,* 531–544.

Heilman, K., & Watson, R. (2003). *Clinical neuropsychology* (4th ed.). New York: Oxford.

Henderson V. (1986). Anatomy of posterior pathways in reading: A reassessment. *Brain and Language, 29,* 119–133.

Hinschelwood, J. (1902). Congenital word blindness, with reports of 10 cases. *Opthalmology Review, 21,* 91–99.

Horwitz, B., Rumsey, J. M., & Donohue, B. C. (1998). Functional connectivity of the angular gyrus in normal reading and dyslexia. *Proceedings of the National Academy of Sciences USA, 95,* 8939–8944.

Hunter, J. V., & Wang, Z. J. (2001). MR spectroscopy in pediatric neuroradiology. *MRI Clinics of North America, 9,* 165–189.

Hynd, G. W., Hall, J., Novey, E. S., Etiopulos, D., Black, K., Gonzales, J. J., Edmonds, J. E., Riccio, C., & Cohen, M. (1995). Dyslexia and corpus callosum morphology. *Archives of Neurology, 52,* 32–38.

Hynd, G. W., & Semrud-Clikeman, M. (1989). Dyslexia and brain morphology. *Psychological Bulletin, 106,* 447–482.

Hynd, G. W., Semrud-Clikeman, M., Lorys, A. R., Novey, E. S., & Eliopulos, D. (1990). Brain morphology in developmental dyslexia and attention deficit disorder/hyperactivity. *Archives of Neurology, 47,* 919–926.

Jernigan, T. L., Hesselink, J. R., Stowell, E., & Tallal, P. (1991). Cerebral structure on magnetic resonance imaging in language- and learning-impaired children. *Archives of Neurology, 48,* 539–545.

Klinkenberg, T., Hedehus, M., Temple, E., Salz, T., Gabrieli, J., Moseley, M., & Poldrack, R. (2000). Microstructure of temporo-parietal white matter as a basis for reading ability: Evidence from diffusion tensor magnetic resonance imaging. *Neuron, 25,* 493–500.

Krasuski, J., Horowitz, B., & Rumsey, J. M. (1996). A survey of functional and anatomical neuroimaging techniques. In G. R. Lyon & J. M. Rumsey (Eds.), *Neuroimaging: A window to neurological foundations of learning and behavior in children* (pp. 25–55). Baltimore: Brookes.

Kusch, A., Gross-Glenn, K., Jallad, B., Lubs, H., Rabin, M., Feldman, E., &

Duara, R. (1993). Temporal lobe surface area measurements on MRI in normal and dyslexic readers. *Neuropsychologia, 31*, 811–821.

Larson, J. P., Hoien, T., Lundberg, I., & Ödegaard, H. (1990). MRI evaluation of the size and symmetry of the planum temporale in adolescents with developmental dyslexia. *Brain and Language, 39*, 289–301.

Leonard, C. M., Eckert, M. A., Lombardino, L. J., Oakland, T., Franzier, J., Mohr, C. M., King, W. M., & Freeman, A. (2001). Anatomical risk factors for phonological dyslexia. *Cerebral Cortex, 11*, 148–157.

Leonard, C. M., Lombardino, L. J., Mercado, L. R., Browd, S. R., Breier, J. I., & Agee, O. F. (1996). Cerebral asymmetry and cognitive development in children: A magnetic resonance imaging study. *Psychological Science, 7*, 89–95.

Lyon, G. R., Fletcher, J. M., & Barnes, M. C. (2003). Learning disabilities. In E. J. Mash & R. A. Barkley (Eds.), *Child psychopathology* (2nd ed., pp. 520–586). New York: Guilford Press.

Mathes, P. G., Denton, C. A., Fletcher, J. M., Anthony, J. L., Francis, D. J., & Schatschneider, C. (2004). *An evaluation of two reading interventions derived from diverse models*. Manuscript under review.

Mencl, W. E., Shaywitz, B. A., Shaywitz, S. E., Pugh, K. R., Fulbright, R. K., Skudlarski, P., Constable, R. T., Marchione, K. E., Fletcher, J. M., & Gore, J. C. (2004). *Developmental changes in functional connectivity in nonimpaired and dyslexic readers*. Manuscript under review.

Orton, S. (1927). Specific reading disability—Strephosymbolia. *Journal of the American Medical Association, 90*, 1095–1099.

Papanicolaou, A. C. (1998). *Fundamentals of functional brain imaging*. Lisse, The Netherlands: Swets & Zetilinger.

Papanicolaou, A. C., Pugh, K., Simos, P. G., & Mencl, E. (2004). Functional brain imaging: An introduction to concepts and applications. In P. McCardle & V. Chabra (Eds.). *The voice of evidence: Bringing research to the classroom* (pp. 385–416). Baltimore: Brookes.

Papanicolaou, A. C., Simos, P. G., Castillo, E. M., Breier, J. I., Katz, J. S., & Wright, A. A. (2002). The hippocampus and memory of verbal and pictorial material. *Learning and Memory, 9*, 99–104.

Penfield, W., & Roberts, L. (1959). *Speech and brain mechanisms*. Princeton, NJ: Princeton University Press.

Pennington, B. F., Filipek, P. A., Churchwell, J., Kennedy, D. N., Lefley, D., Simon, J. H., Filley, C. M., Galaburda, A., Alarcon, M., & DeFries, J. C. (1999). Brain morphometry in reading-disabled twins. *Neurology, 53*, 723–729.

Poeppel, D. (1996). A critical review of PET studies of phonological processing. *Brain and Language, 55*, 317–351.

Posner, M. J., & Raichle, M. E. (1996). *Images of mind*. Washington, DC: APA Press.

Pugh, K. R., Mencl, W. E., Shaywitz, B. A., Shaywitz, S. E., Fulbright, R. K., Constable, R. T., Skudlarski, P., Marchione, K. E., Jenner, A. R., Fletcher, J. M., Liberman, A. M., Shankweiler, D. P., Katz, L., Lacadie, C., & Gore, J. C. (2000). The angular gyrus in developmental dyslexia:

Task-specific differences in functional connectivity within posterior cortex. *Psychological Science, 11*, 51–56.

Pugh, K. R., Shaywitz, B. A., Constable, R. T., Skudlarski, P., Fulbright, R. K., Bronen, R. A., Shankweiler, D. P., Katz, L., Fletcher, J. M., & Gore, J. C. (1996). Cerebral organization of component processes in reading. *Brain, 119*, 1221–1238.

Richards, T. L., Cornia, D., Serafini, S., Steury, K., Echelard, D. R., Dager, S. R., Marro, K., Abbott, R. D., Maravilla, K. R., & Berninger, V. W. (2000). The effects of a phonologically driven treatment for dyslexia on Lactate levels as measures by Proton MRSI. *American Journal of Neuroradiology, 21*, 916–922

Rumsey, J. M., Andreason, P., Zametkin, A. J., Aquino, T., King, A., Hamburger, S., Pileus, A., Rapport, J., & Cohen, R. (1992). Failure to activate the left temporoparietal cortex in dyslexia. An oxygen 15 positron emission tomographic study. *Archives of Neurology, 49*, 527–534.

Rumsey, J. M., Nace, K., Donohue, B., Wise, D., Maisog, J. M., & Andreason, P. (1997). A positron emission tomographic study of impaired word recognition and phonological processing in dyslexic men. *Archives of Neurology, 54*, 562–573.

Rumsey, J. M., Zametkin, A. J., Andreason, P., Hanchan, A. P., Hamburger, S. D., Aquino, T., King, C., Pikus, A., & Cohen, R. M. (1994). Normal activation of frontotemporal language cortex in dyslexia, as measured with oxygen 15 positron emission tomography. *Archives of Neurology, 51*, 27–38.

Schultz, R. T., Cho, N. K., Staib, L. H., Kier, L. E., Fletcher, J. M., Shaywitz, S. E., Shankweiler, D. P., Katz, L., Gore, J. C., Duncan, J. S., & Shaywitz, B. A. (1994). Brain morphology in normal and dyslexic children: The influence of sex and age. *Annals of Neurology, 35*, 732–742.

Shaywitz, B. A., Shaywitz, S. E., Pugh, K. R., Mencl, W. E., Fulbright, R. K., Constable, R. T., Skudlarski, P., Jenner, A., Fletcher, J. M., Marchione, K. E., Shankweiler, D., Katz, L., Lacadie, C., & Gore, J. C. (2002). Disruption of the neural circuitry for reading in children with developmental dyslexia. *Biological Psychiatry, 52*, 101–110.

Shaywitz, S. E. (1996). Dyslexia. *Scientific American*, pp. 98–104.

Shaywitz, S. E., Pugh, K. R., Jenner, A. R., Fulbright, R. K., Fletcher, J. M., Gore, J. C., & Shaywitz, B. A. (2000). The neurobiology of reading and reading disability (dyslexia). In M. L. Kamil, P. B. Mosenthal, P. D. Pearson, & R. Barr (Eds.), *Handbook of Reading Research* (Vol. III, pp. 229–249). Mahwah, New Jersey: Lawrence Erlbaum.

Shaywitz, S. E., Shaywitz, B. A., Pugh, K. R., Fulbright, R. K., Constable, R. T., Mencl, W. E., Shankweiler, D. P., Liberman, A. M., Skudlarski, P., Fletcher, J. M., Katz, L., Marchione, K. E., Lacadie, C., Gatenby, C., & Gore, J. C. (1998). Functional disruption in the organization of the brain for reading in dyslexia. *Proceedings of the National Academy of Sciences USA, 95*, 2636–2641.

Simos, P. G., Breier, J. I., Fletcher, J. M., Bergman, E., & Papanicolaou, A. C. (2000a). Cerebral mechanisms involved in word reading in dyslexic children: A magnetic source imaging approach. *Cerebral Cortex, 10,* 809–816.

Simos, P. G., Breier, J. I., Fletcher, J. M., Foorman, B. R., Bergman, E., Fishbeck, K., & Papanicolaou, A. C. (2000b). Brain activation profiles in dyslexic children during nonword reading: A magnetic source imaging study. *Neuroscience Reports, 290,* 61–65.

Simos, P. G., Breier, J. I., Wheless, J. W., Maggio, W. W., Fletcher, J. M., Castillo, E. M., & Papanicolaou, A. C. (2000c). Brain mechanisms for reading: The role of the superior temporal gyrus in word and pseudoword naming. *Neuroreport, 11,* 2443–2447.

Simos, P. G., Fletcher, J. M., Bergman, E., Breier, J. I., Foorman, B. R., Castillo, E. M., Davis, R. N., Davis, R. N., Fitzgerald, M., & Papanicolaou, A. C. (2002a). Dyslexia-specific brain activation profile becomes normal following successful remedial training. *Neurology, 58,* 1203–1213.

Simos, P. G., Fletcher, J. M., Foorman, B. R., Francis, D. J., Castillo, E. M., Davis, R. N., Fitzgerald, M., Mathes, P. G., Denton, C., & Papanicolaou, A. C. (2002b). Brain activation profiles during the early stages of reading acquisition. *Journal of Child Neurology, 17,* 159–163.

Simos, P. G., Fletcher, J. M., Sarkari, S., Billingsley, R. L., Francis, D. J., Castillo, E. M., Denton, C., & Papanicolaou, A. C. (2004). *Early development of neuropsychological processes involved in normal reading and reading disability.* Manuscript under review.

Simos, P. G., Papanicolaou, A. C., Breier, J. I., Wilmore, L. J., Wheless, J. W., Constantinou, J. C., Gormley, W., & Maggio, W. W. (1999). Localization of language-specific cortex using MEG and intraoperative stimulation mapping. *Journal of Neurosurgery, 91,* 787–796.

Temple, E., Deutsch, G. K., Poldrack, R. A., Miller, S. L., Tallal, P., Merzenich, M. M., & Gabrieli, J. D. (2003). Neural deficits in children with dyslexia ameliorated by behavioral remediation: Evidence from functional MRI. *Proceedings of the National Academy of Sciences USA, 100,* 2860–2865.

Thatcher, R. W., Lyon, G. R., Rumsey, J., & Krasnegor, N. (Eds.). (1996). *Developmental neuroimaging: Mapping the development of brain and behavior.* San Diego: Academic Press.

Wada, J., & Rasmussen, T. (1960). Intracarotid injection of sodium amytal for the lateralization of cerebral speech dominance: Experimental and clinical observations. *Journal of Neurosurgery, 17,* 266–282.

CHAPTER 13

Survey Research

James F. Baumann
James J. Bason

What are elementary students' attitudes toward reading in school? What do middle school students choose to read in their free time outside school? How do high school teachers accommodate students who struggle to read and understand content textbooks? How do parents support at home the reading instruction their children receive at school? What content do university teacher educators cover in their elementary reading methods courses? What are the teaching experiences and knowledge base about reading of upper-level school district administrators? Answers to questions such as these can be addressed through survey research.

It is the purpose of this chapter to describe how surveys can be used by literacy researchers to address a variety of questions about the characteristics of educational groups. We begin with a definition of survey research, followed by a brief history of literacy-related survey research. Next, we describe the various types of surveys, and then we address how survey researchers identify populations, draw samples, and make inferences from survey data. Next, we describe the process in which researchers engage when implementing a survey inquiry, followed by a discussion of quality standards for survey research. We conclude by presenting two exemplars of survey research projects and a summary of the chapter.

WHAT IS SURVEY RESEARCH?

According to the American Statistical Association, *survey* "is used most often to describe a method of gathering information from a sample of individuals" (*What Is a Survey?*, n.d., ¶ 3). Jaeger (1997) indicates that "the purpose of survey research is to describe specific characteristics of a large group of persons, objects, or institutions" (p. 449), which led him to the colloquial definition of *survey research* as a "study in which data are collected from part of a group, for the purpose of describing one or more characteristics of the whole group" (p. 450). Surveys are popular methods of collecting information from individuals and the preferred means to address a research question when it is most efficient to simply *ask* those who can inform the question. A survey typically involves the administration of a questionnaire or interview to a relevant group.

One way to describe surveys involves the degree of organization they entail. In this chapter, we focus on *structured surveys*, that is, research tools that involve having persons respond to a series of questions (and perhaps follow-up questions) through various media. Structured surveys generate numerical data directly or data that can be categorized and tabulated such that the data can be explored quantitatively through descriptive or inferential statistics.

In contrast, researchers can engage in *semistructured interviews* or *qualitative interviews*, in which the interviewer and interviewee engage in more of a conversation than in an interview. Qualitative interviews generate very rich and in-depth data as opposed to structured interviews, and hence they address different research questions. We confine our discussion to structured interviews in this chapter and refer readers to other sources for information about semistructured or qualitative interviews (Gubrium & Holstein, 2002; Seidman, 1998).

Finally, it should be understood that surveys are not limited to humans. For example, a researcher might survey objects such as instructional materials or achievement records. Most educational survey research, however, has involved questions about the attitudes, knowledge, experiences, and behaviors exhibited by *persons*: teachers, students, administrators, parents, policymakers, or others interested in education. Thus, we focus on survey research that has the potential to address research questions that describe human involvement in literacy education.

A BRIEF HISTORY OF SURVEY RESEARCH IN LITERACY

The beginnings of survey research can be traced back to the late 19th century, with the modern era of sample surveys beginning in earnest in the early 20th century (Weisberg, Krosnick, & Bowen, 1996). The first survey research in literacy occurred in the early 1900s and was tied to what Venezky (1984) referred to as "school surveys," in which U.S. school districts evaluated their entire educational programs, including reading instruction. For example, Venezky described a survey in Cleveland as involving "analyses of the goals of reading instruction, the training of teachers, the methods and materials and time used, and the achievements of students in different components of reading" (p. 18).

Survey research in the social, behavioral, and educational sciences gained widespread acceptance in the 1950s, becoming one of the most popular and efficient methods of collecting information from individuals (Weisberg et al., 1996). In 1961 Austin, Bush, and Huebner described in detail the process of "The Reading Survey" as a "survey method for getting a complete perspective on the reading program" (p. 131), and several significant reading survey studies were conducted during this period. Austin and Morrison (1961) published *The Torchlighters*, a mail survey of reading teacher education programs at 74 U.S. colleges and universities, which was replicated 13 years later (Morrison & Austin, 1977). As a follow-up to *The Torchlighters*, Austin and Morrison asked in 1963, "what guidance do teachers receive *after* they complete their baccalaureate education?" (p. ix). They addressed this question in *The First R* (Austin & Morrison, 1963) by conducting a mail survey of administrators in 1,023 U.S. school districts about the content and conduct of reading instruction and by conducting follow-up, on-site visits in 51 school districts. Barton and Wilder (1964) also reported an extensive study of reading that included face-to-face interviews with leading experts in reading education and mail surveys to university faculty, teachers and principals, and the general public.

Survey research has flourished from the 1970s to the present (Weisberg et al., 1996), with a number of recent surveys in the field of literacy education. For example, researchers have explored elementary students' attitudes toward reading (McKenna, Kear, & Ellsworth, 1995), middle school students' motivations for reading (Ivey & Broaddus, 2001), professional development for literacy educators (Commeyras & DeGroff, 1998; Hughes, Cash, Klingner, & Ahwee, 2001), reading experts' opinions of contemporary trends and practices (Baumann, Ro, Duffy-Hester, & Hoffman, 2000; Flippo, 1998), and educators' views of state-mandated, high-stakes testing (Hoffman, Assaf, & Paris, 2001), along with modified replications of Austin and Morrison's *The Torchlighters* (Hoffman & Roller, 2001) and *The First R* (Baumann, Hoffman, Duffy-Hester, & Ro, 2000).

TYPES OF SURVEYS

Surveys come in various forms and can be organized in different ways. The most common way to characterize surveys is by the method of data collection. Survey collection methods include face-to-face surveys, telephone surveys, mail surveys, and technology-enhanced survey methods. The decision regarding which method to use is typically based on the nature and size of the population under study, the content of the information to be collected, the length of the survey, or the difficulty of the task respondents are asked to complete.

Face-to-Face Surveys

Face-to-face surveys, or structured personal interviews, are preferred by many survey researchers because they afford the most flexibility, allowing a researcher to control the dynamics of the interview process considerably. Jaeger (1997) noted that "apart from their costs, face-to-face interview surveys have so many advantages that some survey researchers consider alternative methods to be totally unacceptable" (p. 459). Advantages of face-to-face surveys include the opportunity for the interviewer to ask for clarification, to ask follow-up or "branched" questions, and to observe and make note of surroundings. In addition, face-to-face surveys tend to result in high response rates. When depth of information and a flexible format are desired and feasible, a face-to-face survey may be the preferred method. When a researcher is interested in a rich, interactive description by a group of individuals on a specified topic, a *focus group* may be employed. However, given the unique purposes and requirements of focus groups, we do not pursue them further in this chapter and refer interested readers to other sources (Bloor, Frankland, Thomas, & Robson, 2001; Greenbaum, 1998; Krueger & Casey, 2000; *What Are Focus Groups?*, 1997).

Telephone Surveys

When many interviews need to be conducted or the sample of prospective respondents is geographically dispersed, the preferred method may be a *telephone survey*, which is administering a questionnaire during a phone conversation. Telephone surveys retain some of the advantages of face-to-face surveys—for example, the administrator can explain the purpose of a survey and ask follow-up or branched questions—while providing for a more economical way to gather information. In addition, a telephone survey researcher can inquire why an individual chooses to participate in a survey or not. Organizations such as the Harris Poll and the Gallup Poll conduct telephone interviews, as do marketing firms and researchers in the social, behavioral, and educational sciences.

A common approach to identifying telephone numbers and optimizing response rates is to employ the *list-assisted method*. In this approach, research firms combine published telephone directory information and random selection of numbers, resulting in telephone lists that have response rates between 50% and 85% (Kalton, 1983; Nachmias & Nachmias, 1981). The list-assisted method may be combined with *random digit dialing*, in which computers randomly generate telephone numbers such that every household in a given area (even those with unlisted numbers) has a known probability of being selected, resulting in highly accurate samples being drawn from specific populations (Tucker, Lepkwosksi, & Piekarski, 2002).

Telephone surveys are no panacea, however. Increasing use of telephone surveys among the general population and increased telemarketing and fundraising activities using the telephone have contributed to increasing refusal rates and growing concern about *nonresponse bias*, that is, failure to represent the views of those who choose not to participate (Groves, Dillman, Eltinge, & Little, 2002). The proliferation of cell phones, which are typically excluded from survey listings, and the use of telephone answering and caller ID devices used to screen incoming telephone calls raise additional concerns about bias using the telephone survey method (Link & Oldendick, 1999). In spite of these limitations, it is generally agreed that the telephone remains one of the most effective ways to collect data from large samples of individuals.

Mail Surveys

When it is not feasible to conduct face-to-face or telephone surveys, a *mail survey*, distributing a written questionnaire through the postal service, is a viable alternative. Advantages of mail surveys include relatively low cost, the ability to access a broad sample of potential respondents, and the possibility of obtaining a large number of responses. In addition, there is evidence that mail surveys tend to minimize *social desirability bias* (respondents answering in ways deemed to be socially acceptable or appropriate rather than reflecting their actual attitudes or behaviors) when compared to other survey methods (Hochstim, 1967; Wiseman, 1972).

Mail surveys are not without disadvantages, however. While economical, they may not produce as a high a response rate as other types of surveys, one must rely on the respondent to interpret questions properly (i.e., no opportunity for clarification), a researcher has no control over the actual administration of the survey, and one cannot determine why given sample members choose to participate or not participate. Most mail surveys employ the total design method (Dillman, 1978) to reduce nonresponse bias. The total design method uses an initial mail survey followed by one or more waves of follow-ups to nonresponders to enhance participation and minimize nonresponse bias. Typically, after the first survey is mailed, a postcard follow-up reminder is sent to all sample members, followed by the mailing of another questionnaire to nonresponders. Response rates to mail surveys vary widely depending on the amount and effort at follow-up.

In spite of their limitations, "mail surveys are a powerful, effective, and efficient alternative to their more expensive relatives—the telephone survey and the personal interview" (*More about mail surveys*, 1997, p. 1). Indeed, mail surveys have been (e.g., Austin & Morrison, 1961, 1963) and remain (e.g., Baumann, Hoffman, et al., 2000; Baumann, Ro, et al., 2000; Commeyras & DeGroff, 1998; Hoffman et al., 2001; Hoffman & Roller, 2001; Hughes et al., 2001) one of the most popular methods employed in literacy survey research.

Technology-Enhanced Survey Methods

A new set of data collection methods relying on technology include web- and Internet-based surveys. *Web surveys* require a respondent to visit a website, enter a password to access a survey instrument, and complete a survey online (Couper, 2002). *Internet surveys* involve sending an e-mail message to prospective respondents and inviting them to participate in a survey by completing a questionnaire in the body of the e-mail (Schaefer & Dillman, 1998).

Despite the advantages of low cost and speed provided by web- and Internet-based surveys, such surveys are limited to special populations known to have high rates of Internet access and thus tend not to represent broader populations. There currently is no known reliable means to access e-mail addresses, so it is difficult to obtain representative samples. These surveys are effective for known Internet users for whom e-mail addresses are readily accessible (e.g., literacy professors whose e-mail addresses are contained in university directories), but this requires the creation of specialized sample lists. With increasing Internet access in households and the growing availability of commercially available e-mail lists, however, it is likely that web-

and Internet-based survey use and credibility will increase in the future.

Technology is also enhancing the application of more conventional survey procedures. *Computer-assisted telephone interviews* are becoming increasingly common, in which the interviewer reads questions from a computer screen and uses a keyboard to enter an interviewee's responses directly, enhancing the speed and reliability of telephone interview data. Similarly, one finds face-to-face surveys being administered by interviewees who use notebook computers to conduct *computer-assisted personal interviews* (Couper et al., 1998)

With the advent of computer programs that can recognize speech, telephone surveys can be administered through *interactive voice recognition*, in which a respondent calls a toll-free number and communicates directly by saying prescribed responses. Similarly, using *touch-tone data entry*, interviewees proceed through a prerecorded interview in which they are asked to enter responses through their telephone touch-tone key pad. These approaches are most useful when factual information is required from the respondent, or when respondent–interviewer interaction is not a necessary requirement for completing an interview.

POPULATIONS, SAMPLES, AND INFERENCES

When a researcher's question requires responses from a small number of persons, for example, learning about the content area reading practices of subject-matter teachers at a particular high school, then it makes sense to interview all individuals. This would involve a census of the entire *population*, or surveying all persons who fit a particular classification. A *population parameter* is a value that describes an entire population, for example, the *mean*, or average, number of years of teaching experienced for the population of all full-time, public grade 10 English teachers in a specific school district.

When the population under study is large, however, for instance, when Phi Delta Kappa annually polls Americans about their attitudes toward public schools (Rose & Gallup, 2002), a census of the entire population is impractical, costly, or simply not possible. In this situation, other procedures are used to select a subset of the entire population. In fact, most surveys involve a subset of individuals, or *sample*, and most survey researchers wish to gather data on a sample in order to generalize to a broader group, that is, to estimate a population parameter.

To be able to make generalizations from a sample to a population, a survey researcher must begin by specifying a *sampling frame*, which includes all the members of a given population. Frames or populations might be small or large. For example, large populations would include all full-time, public school kindergarten teachers in the United States or all school district superintendents in the 50 states. Examples of smaller populations would be all parents of K–5 students in a small, rural school district or all students who have completed an academic assistance course in reading within the past year at a small state university.

Once a sampling frame is specified, a researcher must determine how to select a *probability sample*, or a subset of the specified population to interview and from which one can make generalizations. Two common probability samples are a simple random sample and a stratified random sample. A *simple random sample* is one in which everyone in the sampling frame has an equal chance of being selected through some random process, such as through the use of computer random sampling or a random table of numbers. For example, randomly selecting 1,000 names from all full-time K–5 classroom teachers in the state of Georgia would be a simple random sample. A *stratified random sample* involves selecting participants from certain subgroups, or strata, within a sample. For example, if there were smaller class sizes in the primary grades, there would be proportionally more teachers at those levels. In this situation, a researcher might identify each grade level as a stratum, or subgroup, and then randomly sample each grade level proportionate to its representation in the overall population. This would result in a sample that approximates the overall K–5 population better than a simple random sample.

When engaging in probability sampling research, any *sample statistic*, or value that describes the sample such as a sample mean, is not exact; there is some error associated with it. For instance, the average class size of a simple random sample of 1,000 full-time second-grade classroom teachers in South Carolina would be somewhat different from the actual population parameter should one be able to poll all teachers. If a researcher wishes to use sample statistics to estimate population parameters, the researcher needs to know and report the *sampling error*, or an estimate of the degree of error associated with a sample statistic. This estimate is commonly referred to simply as the "margin of error" (*What Is a Margin of Error?*, 1998).

The margin of error in a sample statistic is usually reported in plus or minus terms and at some degree of confidence. For example, Baumann, Hoffman, et al. (2000) reported that 1,207 responses to their teacher survey resulted in a 2.7% sampling error at the 95%

confidence level. This means that any sample statistic they reported for the full sample of teachers would represent the "true" or population parameter 95% of the time within plus or minus 2.7% of the reported score.

The sample margin of error is directly related to sample size. The larger the sample, the smaller the margin of error, the more the sample statistic approximates the population parameter, and the more confidence a consumer can have in the precision of survey results. For example, a simple random sample of 100 would result in about a 10% margin of error, a sample of 500 about 4.5%, and a sample of 1,000 about 3% (*What Is a Margin of Error?*, 1998, p. 6). A larger sample size is always preferable, but from a cost and efficiency perspective, there often comes a point at which collecting additional cases is not worth the per-case cost. Once sample sizes reach about 1,200, the reduction in sampling error becomes smaller as more and more cases are added, which is why one often finds sample sizes of around 1,000 for public opinion polls.

One final point: The margin of error as we have discussed it refers only to the sampling error. There are other possible errors in survey research, however. These *nonsampling errors* include poorly worded or confusing questions, nonresponse bias, and social desirability bias, to mention a few. Such nonsampling errors cannot be estimated mathematically, so a survey research consumer should be aware of these other sources of error (Fowler, 2002) and read an article critically to determine the degree to which the researcher has attempted to control for, or at least acknowledge, these additional sources of error.

SURVEY RESEARCH DESIGN PROCESS

Engaging in any scientific inquiry involves a careful, methodical process. Although there are no uniform, agreed-on number of steps in planning and conducting a survey research project, we present a six-step process that captures the essence of recommendations offered by other survey research methodologists (e.g., Jaeger, 1997).

1. *Formulate a research question and hypotheses.* If one accepts the notion that quality research begins not with methods but a carefully framed question (Shulman, 1997), then it follows that the selection of survey research as a method must depend on the formulation of a core research question that is amenable to being answered through a survey. Questions such as those we used to open this chapter are of

the type that would be appropriate for a survey study. Theory should be used to guide the development of the research question, and a thorough literature review of past and current research findings should be conducted to craft specific research hypotheses.

2. *Devise a measurement strategy.* In this step, a researcher must determine the type of survey and specific items that will best measure the features of the underlying psychological, behavioral, social, or educational topic or issue under consideration, or what is commonly referred to as *construct validity*. Special care also should be taken to ensure that measurement error is minimized. Although it is impossible to eliminate all measurement error, several sources of error can be reduced, including sampling, nonresponse, interviewer, and respondent error. Sampling error is probably the easiest source of error to control. If probability sampling procedures are used, the range of potential error is known by way of the sampling margin of error. Nonresponse error is more difficult to control. The lower the effective response rate in a survey, the greater the likelihood that nonresponders may be systematically different from responders. A researcher needs to obtain additional information about non-respondents in order to determine if responders and nonresponders differed in the way they answered survey items. Interviewer error occurs when interviewers fail to follow standardized procedures, for example, not reading survey questions exactly as written. Training survey interviewers thoroughly minimizes interviewer errors. Finally, respondent errors occur when survey items are unclear; when respondents engage in *satisficing*, or selecting an answer considered to be reasonable to the researcher (see Krosnick, 1999); or when respondents provide answers to survey questions even when they may not actually have an opinion on the topic (Converse, 1964). A researcher has responsibility for constructing clearly worded items and for being aware of, minimizing, or at least acknowledging, other respondent error.

3. *Determine the sampling frame and data-collection method.* The next step is to select the appropriate sampling frame, which will be determined, in large part, by the nature of the research question. If one wishes to seek information from teachers, for example, a researcher must determine which teachers to sample: their position type, the grade levels they teach, their subject specialization, the type of schools in which they work (e.g., public vs. private), and the like. A researcher can make generalizations only from the limits of the sampling frame, so identifying the appropriate group to survey is essential. Once the relevant population has been specified, the researcher must determine which method will be used to collect survey data—

that is, whether to choose a face-to-face, telephone, mail, or technology-based survey. Again, the research question, as well as pragmatics such as research budget and the availability of sampling sources (e.g., professional organization lists and marketing research lists), will generally guide a researcher in selecting the most suitable survey type.

4. *Establish sampling methodology and sample size.* The next step in the design process is to determine the method for sampling. If one is surveying a small population, it may be feasible to try to secure responses from all individuals in the population. If one is sampling a large population, which is typical in survey research, one must determine whether the sample will be a selective or a probability sample. If the sample is selective—for example, selecting parents who are members of a local parent–teacher organization—one cannot make generalizations to a broader population of parents. There may be times at which a selective sample is appropriate or when it is the only feasible option, but then a researcher must recognize that generalizing to a larger group is not possible. When a researcher employs a probability (i.e., random) sample, which is the typical standard in survey research, then the researcher should make a decision about sample size with the understanding of what the margin of error will be. When economically and pragmatically feasible, a sample should be sufficiently large in order to keep the margin of error reasonably low, so that statements about how a sample may represent the population under study can be made within appropriate confidence limits. When smaller random sample sizes must be selected, a researcher must understand the limits this imposes on generalization and acknowledge those in a research report.

5. *Collect and analyze data.* Data collection should be systematic, thorough, and consistent with the accepted procedures for the type of survey employed. For example, if a mail survey were used, the researcher should follow a series of phases in distributing, tracking, and monitoring surveys to promote an acceptable response rate and minimize nonresponse bias (Dillman, 1978). Likewise, data analysis procedures should be thoughtful, consistent with the research questions, and systematic. One must establish a data management and analyses plan prior to data collection, ideally when a study is conceived, so that analyses adequately test research hypotheses. In some cases, simple descriptive statistics such as cross-tabulations will be sufficient and appropriate to answer research questions. In other cases, particularly when a probability sample is obtained, inferential statistics may be appropriate in order to make generalizations from the data. Procedures such as factor or path analyses are commonly used in analyzing survey data. When inferential statistics are employed,

attention should be paid in advance to sample size to ensure that adequate statistical power will be present for the analysis method to be used (Kraemer, & Thiemann, 1987). In short, careful planning at the front end of the survey process will ensure that analysis requirements are met satisfactorily.

6. *Report findings*. Survey researchers ought to have an intended audience in mind as a study is conceived and planned, and this same audience should be considered and addressed as a report is written. The information contained in the following section and accompanying table can also guide a survey researcher in preparing a research report. Although the form, style, voice, and level of detail may vary depending on one's audience and intended publication outlet (e.g., a research journal vs. a more applied serial), basic standards for reporting an inquiry should be followed. The fifth edition of the *Publication Manual of the American Psychological Association* (2001) is a commonly used standard for writing for publication. And as usual, Strunk and White's (2000) classic "little book," *The Elements of Style* (4th ed.), is always a useful tool for a writer who wishes to be concise and precise.

QUALITY STANDARDS FOR SURVEY RESEARCH

Consumers of survey research should be able to examine key components of a data-collection effort to ensure that quality standards have been used, and it is the responsibility of survey researchers to ensure that they provide essential information to allow consumers to effectively evaluate a given survey effort. As a general rule, the methods and procedures used in a survey effort should allow for replication of the study by other researchers. To accomplish this, the population under study should be clearly defined, and the methods and procedures used to conduct the study should be clearly outlined. This includes how the sample was drawn, the exact question wording of the survey (which is often reproduced in an appendix to a report), the number of cases collected during the study, response rate information, and the sampling margin of error. Useful information about evaluating response rates, cooperation rates, and refusal rates for a study can be found through the American Association of Public Opinion Research (*http://www.aapor.org*) and the Council of Academic Survey Research Organizations (*http://www.casro.org*). Both of these professional associations provide valuable information on best practices for survey research, formulas to calculate response and refusal rates, and other helpful information to evaluate survey research quality.

As a further aide to evaluate survey research, we reproduce Jaeger's (1997) survey evaluation checklist in Table 13.1. Although Jaeger has prepared this as a means to help research consumers evaluate published studies, the checklist may also be useful to survey researchers as they conceive of and implement studies of their own.

LITERACY SURVEY RESEARCH EXEMPLARS

To illustrate the survey-research process in literacy, we have selected two exemplars: the McKenna et al. (1995) national survey of children's attitudes toward reading and the Baumann, Hoffman, et al. (2000) national survey of elementary reading instructional practices. Table 13.2 contains a consolidated version of Jaeger's (1997) survey evaluation criteria and presents a summary of how each of these literacy survey studies compares to these standards.

A Survey of Children's Attitudes toward Reading

McKenna et al. (1995) argued for the importance of understanding reading attitude in order to promote reading achievement and to combat aliteracy, and they asserted that research on reading attitudes had been plagued by ill-defined theories, the use of instruments with poor psychometric qualities, and inadequate samples (see Henk & McKenna, Chapter 10, this volume, for further discussion). They provided a detailed review of the theoretical literature on reading attitude and described the development of models by Matthewson (1994) and McKenna (1994), the latter of which was used to guide their investigation and which led them to pose three research questions:

1. What are the overall developmental trends in recreational and academic reading attitude across the elementary grades?
2. What is the developmental relationship between recreational and academic reading attitude, on the one hand, and (a) reading ability, (b) gender, and (c) ethnicity, on the other?
3. What effects on reading attitude can be ascribed to the use of basal reading materials? (McKenna et al., p. 942)

Participants were children in grades 1–6 U.S. classrooms. Their sampling frame was constructed by contacting officers of state and local councils of the professional organization, the International Reading Association, who identified potentially participating school

TABLE 13.1. A Short Checklist for Survey Evaluation

1. Does the report contain a list of specific research questions or issues the survey is intended to address?
2. Do the research questions posed by the investigators appropriately and adequately address the topic of the survey; e.g., in a survey on poverty in the United States, does the research include an examination of poverty as a function of race, level of education, and geographic location?
3. Are the research questions posed by the investigators well organized and well structured?
4. Does the report identify the target population to which generalization was desired?
5. Does the report describe available sampling frames?
6. Does the report indicate a close match between the target population and the operational population?
7. Does the report describe the sampling procedures used? Were probability sampling procedures used?
8. Are nonresponse rates reported for the entire survey and for individual questions?
9. Were nonresponse rates low enough to avoid substantial bias errors?
10. Are any analyses of potential sampling bias reported?
11. Are sample sizes sufficient to avoid substantial random errors? Are standard errors of estimate reported?
12. Is the primary mode of data collection (i.e., mailed questionnaires, telephone interviews, face-to-face interviews) consistent with the objectives, complexity, and operational population of the survey?
13. Are survey instruments provided in the report?
14. Are instructions for completing the survey clear and unambiguous?
15. Are questions on instruments clear and unambiguous?
16. Do questions on instruments encourage respondents' honesty in admitting lack of knowledge or uncertainty?
17. Are questions on instruments free from obvious bias, slanting, or "loading"?
18. Was the survey consistent with ethical research practice; e.g., was the anonymity and/or confidentiality of respondents protected?
19. Does the report contain a description of field procedures?
20. Are field procedures adequate and appropriate? Is it likely that major sources of bias error have been avoided?
21. Are data analyses clearly described?
22. Are data analyses appropriate to the purposes of the survey?
23. Did the survey provide answers to the research questions posed by the investigators?
24. Are the researchers' conclusions sound, or are alternative interpretations of findings equally plausible?
25. Does the survey report contain descriptions of deviations from plans for survey implementation and the likely consequences of such deviations?
26. Does the survey report contain an analysis of the quality of the survey?

Note. From Jaeger (1997, pp. 475–476). Copyright 1997 by the American Educational Research Association. Reproduced by permission.

TABLE 13.2. Evaluation Summary for the Survey Research Exemplars

Jaeger's (1997) criteria[a]	Studies critiqued	
	McKenna et al. (1995)	Baumann, Hoffman, et al. (2000)
Research questions (1–3)[b]	• Theoretically based, explicit research questions posed.	• Theoretically and empirically based research question.
Sampling and response rates (4–11)	• Large (18,000+) national, stratified sample. • Response rates and sampling biases analyses not discussed. • Sample margin of errors not reported, but survey reliabilities acceptable.	• Probability sample for primary (teacher) population, with linked samples for administrators. • Overall survey response rates provided but not item-by-item rates. • Sample margin of errors reported for each survey.
Instrumentation (12–18)	• Survey appended to article. • Reliability and validity data provided.	• Teacher survey appended to article; administrator surveys available from authors. • No reliability and validity data provided.
Data-gathering procedures (19–20)	• Data-gathering procedures summarized.	• Field procedures described in detail.
Analyses, conclusions, report (21–26)	• Descriptive statistics provided in tabular form. • Inferential analyses addressed research questions. • Detailed discussion with plausible interpretations of findings.	• Descriptive statistics integrated into article narrative. • Thorough discussion of findings and research limitations.

[a]Adapted from Jaeger's (1997) full survey evaluation checklist presented in Table 13.1.
[b]Numbers correspond to Jaeger's 26 questions presented in Table 13.1.

districts. The geographically diverse sample, stratified on the basis of gender and ethnicity, included 18,185 children from 229 schools in 95 school districts in 38 states. A table presented the breakdown of the sample according to reading ability, grade, gender, and ethnicity, and a figure presented a U.S. map that showed sampling by state.

The reading attitude instrument used was the McKenna and Kear (1990) Elementary Reading Attitude Survey, a "20-item, 4-

node, pictorial rating scale . . . based on the cartoon character Garfield . . . [that comprised] two 10-item subscales for recreational and academic (school-related) reading attitude" (McKenna et al., 1995, p. 943). Reliability data (coefficient alphas ranging from .74 to .89) and validity evidence (through factor analyses) were provided.

Surveys were mailed to participating teachers along with detailed administration instructions, which included making it clear to students that there were no correct answers. To preclude limited decoding ability from confounding attitude measurement, the teachers read each item aloud twice as students followed along. Teachers were asked to indicate the degree to which they relied on basal readers and to note each student's gender and ethnicity, along with their best professional judgment as to whether each student was above average, average, or below average in reading ability.

Descriptive statistics were presented through tables of means and standard deviations for the recreational and academic reading scales. Inferential statistics involved a series of one-way and factorial analyses of variance that were complemented by line graphs depicting data trends. The authors summarized their findings in five points that correspond to the research questions and subparts as follows:

1. Recreational and academic reading attitudes, on average, begin at a relatively positive point in Grade 1 and end in relative indifference by Grade 6.
2. Increasingly negative recreational attitude is clearly related to ability, and the trend is most rapid for least able readers. The attitudinal gap among ability levels widens with age. For academic reading attitude, however, the negative trend is similar regardless of ability.
3. Girls as a group possess more positive attitudes than boys at all grade levels, both toward recreational and academic reading. In the case of recreational attitude, this gap widens with age. In the case of academic attitude, it remains relatively constant. These gender differences appear to be unrelated to ability.
4. Ethnicity appears to play little role in the negative trend in either recreational or academic reading attitude.
5. The extent of a teacher's reliance on basal readers does not appear to be meaningfully related to recreational or academic reading attitude. (McKenna et al., 1995, pp. 951–952)

The authors interpreted these findings as general support for the McKenna (1994) model of reading attitude, noting that the strongest support came from data indicating that the relationship between reading attitude and reading ability strengthens across the elementary school years. According to McKenna et al. (1995), the results support "a model of reading in which social factors and expectations gradually shape attitudes over time" (p. 935). The authors call for further research on reading attitudes that employs observational rather than self-report methods and for studies that explore the impact instructional techniques have on students' reading attitudes.

A Survey of Reading Instruction Practices

Baumann, Hoffman, et al. (2000) conducted a modified replication of Austin and Morrison's 1963 *First R* study of U.S. public school elementary reading instruction. Noting that debate over the quality and status of elementary reading instruction preoccupied literacy professionals, policymakers, and the general populace in the late 1990s—just as it had in the early 1960s (Morrison, 1963)—the authors argued that a contemporary, empirical benchmark was needed to address the research question: "What is the nature of elementary reading instruction practices today" (Baumann, Hoffman, et al., 2000, p. 342). Following a search for and reconstruction of original survey instruments, the researchers constructed three forms of a mail survey (classroom teacher, building administrator, and district administrator form) that included multiple-choice, Likert, and open-response items that permitted cross-decade comparisons and allowed for querying educators about contemporary issues.

The primary sample was a probability sample of 3,199 elementary teachers drawn from a national listing of over 900,000 teachers. Modeling *First R* procedures, the building and district administrator samples were linked to the teacher sample, with teacher respondents identifying 623 building administrators, who, in turn, identified 91 district administrators for sampling. Employing the total design method (Dillman, 1978), surveys were distributed, collected, and analyzed by a university survey research facility. Response rates and sampling errors (at the 95% confidence level) were reported for the teacher (37.7% and 2.7%, respectively), building administrator (25.8% and 7.6%), and district administrator (52.7% and 14.1%) surveys.

Quantitative analyses involved the examination of descriptive statistics and selected cross-tabulations. A subset of teacher open-response items and all administrator open-response items were analyzed systematically for themes and trends. Results, reported as percentages of respondents, were juxtaposed to *First R* data by categories, permitting a historic and contemporary look at elementary reading education practices.

Results revealed similarities between teachers of the 1960s and 1990s in that both tended to teach self-contained, heterogeneous classes of students; provided significant time for reading instruction; taught phonics explicitly; were generally not satisfied with their university training in reading instruction; administered required standardized tests; and were challenged by teaching underachieving readers. Differences were noted in the areas of instructional philosophy (a balanced, eclectic view in the 1990s versus a skill orientation in the 1960s), instructional organization (more whole-class instruction in the 1990s vs. ability grouping in the 1960s), instructional materials (more use of trade books in the 1990s vs. primarily basal readers in the 1960s), early literacy instruction (the reading readiness perspective of the 1960s was supplanted by an emergent literacy orientation), and assessment (use of more nonstandardized, alternate assessments in the 1990s).

The authors noted that there were several parallel concerns expressed by teachers of the 1960s and 1990s—most significantly, an urgency to accommodate struggling readers—but they also commented that contemporary teachers and administrators were more likely to modify programs and explore alternate philosophical orientations than teachers and administrators of the past. They noted that reading instruction of the 1990s was "not some gussied-up version of the good old days," but instead they found "great energy," "a commitment to children, teaching, and learning," and "a sense of motivated urgency to adopt instructional principles, practices, and philosophies that will accommodate learners of today" (Baumann, Hoffman, et al., 2000, p. 361).

SUMMARY

The purpose of this chapter was to provide an overview of survey research methods employed in literacy research. Survey research is a method for gathering information from a sample of individuals in order to describe characteristics of a larger group. Survey research has been employed in education and social sciences for the past 100 years, with increasing activity in the past three decades. Commonly used survey methods involve collecting data through face-to-face, telephone, and mail surveys, with recent increase in the use of technology-enhanced methods. Most surveys involve probability samples from a specified population in order to make generalizations about the broader population. There is a generally accepted and implemented survey research design process that leads researchers from question and hypothesis formulation through sample description and data collection to data analyses and survey reporting. Quality standards can be applied to evaluate published surveys and to guide researchers in designing survey studies. The McKenna et al. (1995) survey of elementary children's reading attitudes and the Baumann, Hoffman, et al. (2000) survey of elementary reading instruction practices were presented as exemplars of sound literacy education survey research.

REFERENCES

Austin, M. C., Bush, C. L., & Huebner, M. H. (1961). *Reading evaluation: Appraisal techniques for school and classroom.* New York: Ronald Press.

Austin, M. C., & Morrison, C., with Kenney, H. J., Morrison, M. B., Gutmann, A. R., & Nystrom, J. W. (1961). *The torch lighters: Tomorrow's teachers of reading.* Cambridge, MA: Harvard Graduate School of Education/Harvard University Press.

Austin, M. C., & Morrison, C., with Morrison, M. B., Sipay, E. R., Gutmann, A. R., Torrant, K. E., & Woodbury, C. A. (1963). *The first R: The Harvard report on reading in elementary schools.* New York: Macmillan.

Barton, A. H., & Wilder, D. E. (1964). Research and practice in the teaching of reading: A progress report. In M. B. Miles (Ed.), *Innovation in education* (pp. 361–398). New York: Teachers College, Columbia University.

Baumann, J. F., Hoffman, J. V., Duffy-Hester, A. M., & Ro, J. M. (2000). *The first R* yesterday and today: U.S. elementary reading instruction practices reported by teachers and administrators. *Reading Research Quarterly, 35,* 338–377.

Baumann, J. F., Ro, J. M., Duffy-Hester, A. M., & Hoffman, J. V. (2000). Then and now: Perspectives on the status of elementary reading instruction by prominent reading educators. *Reading Research and Instruction, 39,* 236–264.

Bloor, M., Frankland, J., Thomas, M., & Robson, K. (2001). *Focus groups in social research.* Thousand Oaks, CA: Sage.

Commeyras, M., & DeGroff, L. (1998). Literacy professionals' perspectives on professional development and pedagogy: A United States survey. *Reading Research Quarterly, 33,* 434–472.

Converse, P. E. (1964). The nature of belief systems in mass publics. In D. E. Apter (Ed.), *Ideology and discontent* (pp. 207–261). New York: Free Press.

Couper, M. P. (2002). Web surveys: A review of issues and approaches. *Public Opinion Quarterly, 64,* 464–494.

Couper, M. P., Baker, R. P., Bethlehem, J., Clark, C. Z. F., Martin, J., Nicholls, W. L., & O'Reilly, J. M. (1998). *Computer assisted survey information collection.* New York: Wiley.

Dillman, D. A. (1978). *Mail and telephone surveys: The total design method.* New York: Wiley.

Flippo, R. F. (1998). Points of agreement: A display of professional unity in our field. *The Reading Teacher, 52,* 30–40.

Fowler, F. J. (2002). *Survey research methods* (3rd ed.). Thousand Oaks, CA: Sage.

Greenbaum, T. L. (1998). *The handbook of focus group research*. Thousand Oaks, CA: Sage.

Groves, R. M., Dillman, D. A., Eltinge, J. L., & Little, R. J. A. (Eds.). (2002) *Survey nonresponse*. New York: Wiley.

Gubrium, J. F., & Holstein, J. A. (Eds.). (2002). *Handbook of interview research: Context and method*. Thousand Oaks, CA: Sage.

Hochstim, J. R. (1967). A critical comparison of three strategies of collecting data from households. *Journal of the American Statistical Association, 62,* 976–989.

Hoffman, J. M., Assaf, L. C., & Paris, S. G. (2001). High-stakes testing in reading: Today in Texas, tomorrow? *The Reading Teacher, 54,* 482–492.

Hoffman, J. V., & Roller, C. M. (2001). The IRA Excellence in Reading Teacher Preparation Commission's report: Current practices in reading teacher education at the undergraduate level in the United States. In C. M. Roller (Ed.), *Learning to teach reading: Setting the research agenda* (pp. 32–79). Newark, DE: International Reading Association.

Hughes, M. T., Cash, M. M., Klingner, J., & Ahwee, S. (2001). Professional development programs in reading: A national survey of district directors. In J. V. Hoffman, D. L. Schallert, C. M. Fairbanks, J. Worthy, & B. Maloch (Eds.), *Fiftieth yearbook of the National Reading Conference* (pp. 275–286). Chicago: National Reading Conference.

Ivey, G., & Broaddus, K. (2001). "Just plain reading": A survey of what makes students want to read in middle school classrooms. *Reading Research Quarterly, 36,* 350–377.

Jaeger, R. M. (1997). Survey research methods in education. In R. M. Jaeger (Ed.), *Complementary methods for research in education* (2nd ed., pp. 449–476). Washington, DC: American Educational Research Association.

Kalton, G. (1983). *Introduction to survey sampling*. Beverly Hills, CA: Sage.

Kraemer, H. C., & Thiemann, S. (1987). *How many subjects? Statistical power analysis in research*. Thousand Oaks, CA: Sage.

Krosnick, J. A. (1999). Survey research. *Annual Review of Psychology, 50,* 537–567.

Krueger, R. A., & Casey, M. A. (2000). *Focus groups: A practical guide for applied research* (3rd ed.). Thousand Oaks, CA: Sage.

Link, M. W., & Oldendick, R. W. (1999). Call screening: Is it really a problem for survey research? *Public Opinion Quarterly, 63,* 577–589.

Matthewson, G. C. (1994). Model of attitude influence upon reading and learning to read. In R. B. Ruddell, M. R. Ruddell, & H. Singer (Eds.), *Theoretical models and processes of reading* (4th ed., pp. 1131–1161). Newark, DE: International Reading Association.

McKenna, M. C. (1994). Toward a model of reading attitude acquisition. In E. H. Cramer & M. Castle (Eds.), *Fostering the life-long love of reading: The affective domain in reading education* (pp. 18–40). Newark, DE: International Reading Association.

McKenna, M. C., & Kear, J. D. (1990). Measuring attitude toward reading: A new tool for teachers. *The Reading Teacher, 43,* 626–639.

McKenna, M. C., Kear, D. J., & Ellsworth, R. A. (1995). Children's attitudes toward reading: A national survey. *Reading Research Quarterly, 30,* 934–956.

More about mail surveys. (1997). American Statistical Association brochures about survey research. Retrieved online February 6, 2003, from *http://www.amstat.org/sections/srms/brochures/Mail.pdf*

Morrison, C. (1963). *A critical analysis of reported and recommended reading practices in the elementary schools.* Unpublished doctoral dissertation, Harvard Graduate School of Education, Cambridge, MA.

Morrison, C., & Austin, M. C. (1977). *The torch lighters revisited.* Newark, DE: International Reading Association.

Nachmias, D., & Nachmias, C. (1981). *Research methods in the social sciences.* New York: St. Martin's Press.

Publication manual of the American Psychological Association (5th ed.). (2001). Washington, DC: American Psychological Association.

Rose, L. C., & Gallup, A. M. (2002). The 34th annual Phi Delta Kappa/Gallup poll of the public's attitudes toward the public schools. *Phi Delta Kappan, 84*(1), 41–56.

Schaefer, D. R., & Dillman, D. A. (1998). Development of a standard e-mail methodology: Results of an experiment. *Public Opinion Quarterly, 62,* 378–397.

Seidman, I. (1998). *Interviewing as qualitative research: A guide for researchers in education and the social sciences* (2nd ed.). New York: Teachers College Press.

Shulman, L. S. (1997). Disciplines of inquiry in education: A new overview. In R. M. Jaeger (Ed.), *Complementary methods for research in education* (2nd ed., pp. 3–29). Washington, DC: American Educational Research Association.

Strunk, W., & White, E. B. (2000). *The elements of style* (4th ed.). Boston: Allyn & Bacon.

Tucker, C., Lepkowski, J. M., & Piekarski, L. (2002). List-assisted telephone sampling design efficiency. *Public Opinion Quarterly, 66,* 321–338.

Venezky, R. L. (1984). The history of reading research. In R. Barr, M. L. Kamil, P. Mosenthal, & P. D. Pearson (Eds.), *Handbook of reading research* (pp. 3–38). New York: Longman.

Weisberg, H. F., Krosnick, J. A., & Bowen, B. D. (1996). *An introduction to survey research, polling, and data analysis.* Thousand Oaks, CA: Sage.

What are focus groups? (1997). American Statistical Association brochures about survey research. Retrieved online February 6, 2003, from *http://www.amstat.org/sections/srms/brochures/focusgroups.pdf*

What is a margin of error? (1998). American Statistical Association brochures about survey research. Retrieved online February 6, 2003, from *http://www.amstat.org/sections/srms/brochures/margin.pdf*

What is a survey? (n.d.). American Statistical Association brochures about survey research. Retrieved online February 6, 2003, from *http://www.amstat.org/sections/srms/brochures/survwhat.html*

Wiseman, F. (1972). Methodological bias in public opinion surveys. *Public Opinion Quarterly, 36,* 105–108.

CHAPTER 14

Verbal Protocols of Reading

Michael Pressley
Katherine Hilden

For more than a century, researchers have been listening to people think aloud in formal studies (e.g., Marbe, 1901). Before that Aristotle and Plato urged others to talk about what was on their mind and William James (1890) reported what people had to say about their thinking in the first comprehensive textbook detailing psychological theory. Although the most attention has been given to think-aloud studies of problem solving (see, e.g., Ericsson & Simon, 1984/ 1993), a growing body of research has implemented verbal protocol methodology to study adult reading processes. Fewer studies have used verbal protocols to examine the developing nature of reading in emerging readers. As it turns out, people are actually quite good at reporting the contents of their working memory (i.e., what they are currently consciously thinking about). That was much of the point of Ericsson and Simon's (1984/1993) book-length conceptual treatment of verbal protocols of thinking. One reason that is true is that working memory cannot contain much at any one moment. (Recall the 7 +/- 2 formula that George Miller put forth in his 1956 article?) Thus, it is possible in a comment or two to get out what is in one's mind.

WHAT HAS VERBAL PROTOCOL METHODOLOGY TAUGHT US ABOUT READING?

With more than 40 reasonably independent verbal protocol analyses in the literature, Pressley and Afflerbach (1995) reasoned that there was a good chance that all important conscious processes of reading would have been captured in at least one of them. Thus, Pressley and Afflerbach catalogued all the processes reported in the various verbal protocols of adult reading available in the early 1990s, using grounded theory analysis (Strauss & Corbin, 1998) resulting in a theory of expert reading. The major claim of this theory is that the nature of constructively responsive reading is that good readers are constantly shifting their processing in response to text. To borrow Keene and Zimmermann's (1997) description, readers' minds resemble mosaics of thinking. The following consists of an extremely brief introduction to Pressley and Afflerbach's (1995) findings. Table 14.1 summarizes the processes detectable when readers think aloud as they read.

From Pressley and Afflerbach's (1995) summative work and the studies they reviewed, we now know that expert comprehenders actively make sense of a text before, during, and after reading. We have learned from verbal protocols that expert readers often preview a text before reading. Previewing can include skimming headers and illustrations to decide whether a text informs their reading goals. An initial preview can also activate prior knowledge related to topics covered in the text, which later aids in comprehension. Expert readers also use a repertoire of comprehension strategies while reading. Although readers normally read text from beginning to end, they often change their reading speed or skip around a text, depending on their interest in specific points covered in the text and the difficulty of the text. Also, expert readers often attempt to identify main ideas. They consciously make inferences by filling in gaps or make guesses about the author's intentions. As reading proceeds, active readers integrate ideas across the text (e.g., reflecting on the actions of a story in relation to the setting). Skilled readers also interpret texts and ideas in them: They summarize, generate visual images, and empathize (or not) with the ideas expressed by the author.

Finally, and most critically, expert readers monitor whether their strategies and text processings are producing the understanding they want. If expert readers feel they are not understanding a text, they may reread confusing parts, skip problematic sections, or look ahead for clarification. Because expert readers do not know the definition of every word in the texts they read, they look for content clues pertaining to the meaning of unfamiliar words or look up unknown words in a dictionary.

In short, when Pressley and Afflerbach (1995) reviewed existing verbal protocols of reading, they found that expert readers are massively active as they read. They are also massively aware, with their awareness affecting their processing of text. Such awareness is not

TABLE 14.1. Conscious Processes of Reading Reflected in Verbal Protocols of Reading

Before reading

Constructing a goal for reading
Overviewing (skimming text)
Deciding to read/focus on only particular sections of text
Deciding to not read the text
Activating prior knowledge and related knowledge
Summarizing what was gained from previewing
Generating an initial hypothesis about content of the text

During initial reading of text

Generally beginning to end reading of text
Reading only sections believed to contain critical information
Skimming
If text is easy, read with automatic processes and few conscious strategies
Reading aloud
Repeating/restating text to hold in working memory
Repeating/restating a thought that occurred during reading
Making notes
Pausing to reflect on text
Paraphrasing part of text
Explicitly looking for related words, concepts, or ideas in text and using them
     to construct main idea, gist, or summary
Looking for patterns in the text
Predicting/substantiating predictions about content of text
Resetting reading/learning goals at a different level of understanding because
     text suggests more appropriate goal
Identifying important information in text (e.g., looking for what is "news" in
     text and looking for keywords, topic sentences, topic paragraphs)
Conscious inference making (e.g., inferring referents of pronouns, filling in
     gaps, inferring the meanings of unfamiliar vocabulary words, making
     inferences about the author, and deducing implied conclusions)
Integrating different parts of text (e.g., by holding representations of different
     parts of text in working memory, looking back and forth in text to pull
     meanings together, rereading text to increase connections, and making
     notes to assist integrative understanding)
Interpreting the text
Monitoring characteristics of text and the processing of the text (especially
     problems in processing text)
Reacting when problems during reading are detected (e.g., rereading for
     clarification, deciding to slow down and read more carefully, and
     deciding to just keep reading in hope that the meaning will become
     clearer later in the reading)
Evaluating (e.g., accepting and being skeptical—about both style and content
     of text)

(continued)

TABLE 14.1 *(continued)*

After reading

Monitoring that the text is understood and deciding not to process text
    additionally or monitoring that more processing is required to get the
    meaning of the text
Rereading after the first reading
Recitation of text to increase memory of it
Listing pieces of information in text
Constructing cohesive summaries of text
Self-questioning, self-testing over content of text
Imagining how hypothetical situations might be viewed in light of information
    in text
Reflecting on information in text, with possibility of shift in interpretations as
    reflection proceeds
Rereading parts of text following reflection in order to rethink text based on
    insights gained during reflection
Continually evaluating and possibly reconstructing an understanding of the text
Changing one's response to a text as the understanding is reconstructed
Reflecting on/mentally recoding text in anticipation of using it later

cold cognition, with expert readers often evaluating the style of the
text (e.g., deciding whether it was poorly or well written) and its content (e.g., whether or not points made are valid). Sometimes readers'
reactions are so charged that they literally stand up and cheer during
reading or, alternatively, throw a text down in disgust.

An Exemplar Study: Wyatt et al. (1993)

Wyatt et al. (1993) conducted a verbal protocol study that made
clear the complex nature of conscious reading processes. Those researchers wanted to discover how skilled social scientists read in their
areas of expertise. They had 15 professors in the social sciences read
aloud an article of their choosing. Why 15 participants? The investigators' goal was to describe all the strategies used by social scientists
as they read. Thus, the researchers listened to professors read until
no new reading processes were identified. By the 10th reader, little
new was being heard or observed. By the 15th reader, nothing new
seemed to be entering the conclusions.

Why did Wyatt and colleagues decide to allow professors to read
an article of their choosing instead of holding the article constant?
This allowed each professor to select a piece that matched his or her
very particular expertise and interest and therefore more closely mir-
rored how social scientists actually read. The professors had no diffi-

culty talking aloud as they read the article. Based on direct observations of the reading (i.e., the researchers watched, listened, took notes, and reviewed audiotapes), the researchers coded the data, inventing the coding categories as needed. In other words, the authors used a grounded theory approach (Strauss & Corbin, 1990) to drive the data analysis. The coding scheme was constructed based on the reports of the readers, with the researchers revisiting the data until they were confident that every single process reported by readers was captured by coding categories. Three overarching categories were identified: text processing and comprehension strategies, monitoring of reading, and evaluation of the reading.

Compared to most other verbal protocols of reading, Wyatt et al. (1993) captured a greater diversity of reading processes. In particular, previously reported verbal protocols of reading conducted by information processing-oriented psychologists tended to report that readers used strategies and monitored. In contrast, verbal protocol studies carried out by rhetoricians reported reader evaluations more. Wyatt et al. succeeded in capturing in one study a fuller range of responses because of their general methodological tactics, particularly their use of grounded theory to construct categories rather than coming to the study with preformed categories (which was the universal approach to coding of data in previous research).

The careful reader might notice that the individual strategies that composed the general categories in the Wyatt et al. study closely resemble those summarized in Table 14.1, based on the analyses of 40+ verbal protocol studies by Pressley and Afflerbach (1995). We think this congruence reflects that in both studies, data were imputed to a point when no new categories of verbal self-report were emerging. In addition, our reading of verbal protocol studies produced since 1995 (e.g., Crain-Thorenson, Lippma, & McClendon-Magnuson, 1997; Shearer, Lundeberg, & Coballes-Vega, 1997) is that they contain no processes not included in Pressley and Afflerbach (1995). Our confidence is high that Table 14.1 captures just about all the conscious processes during reading, at least those that can be verbalized.

QUESTIONS ABOUT CONDUCTING VERBAL PROTOCOLS IN READING

As with any methodology used to study reading, collecting verbal protocols has its advantages and disadvantages. This methodology can enlighten our understanding of such factors as reader characteristics—processes and strategies used by readers, readers' motivation and affect, the interaction of readers' motivation and affect with their cognitive responses—and the examination of contextual variables: text task, setting, and readability. By examining these factors as they relate to reading comprehension processes, verbal protocols research can be used to refine existing theory and break ground for new theory (Afflerbach, 2000). However, many questions remain related to collection, analysis, and interpretation of verbal protocols of reading.

Should Verbal Protocols Occur Retrospectively or Concurrently with Reading?

Frankly, the procedures and directions in verbal protocol studies have varied greatly from study to study. Sometimes readers are urged to report what they are thinking as they read, and sometimes reports are collected retrospectively. Ericsson and Simon (1984/1993) claimed that verbal protocols should be concurrent, for verbal protocols are intended to reflect the contents of short-term memory—that is, what is currently in consciousness. From that perspective, only concurrent reports make sense, asking participants to report the thoughts in their head while they are having them. So, what can be made of retrospective reports, for example, when readers are cued to stop after so much reading and report what they have been doing since last they were stopped by the researcher? In that case, whatever is being reported is stored in long-term memory, rather than a report of current consciousness. Does that mean that retrospective reports are necessarily less accurate or complete? The answer is that we do not know with respect to protocols of reading, although Ericsson and Simon (1984/1993), based largely on data from verbal protocol studies of problem solving, believed that retrospective reports were likely less complete and accurate than concurrent reports. There is a need for research to determine whether the conclusions about reading are different if protocols are collected concurrently versus retrospectively.

That said, we are going to take a stance on concurrent versus retrospective reports. Often, retrospective reporting involves a reader reporting recent processing on cue (e.g., when a blue dot occurs in the text; Olshavsky, 1976–1977). Crain-Thoreson et al. (1997) reported the only true experimental evaluation of the effects of prompted versus unprompted reports. They found that requiring readers to stop and report, rather than letting them report as they read and when they wished, affected the reports obtained from lower-ability college readers but not higher-ability college readers. Specifically, the low-ability readers were more likely to report that they were confused when they were reading passages that required them to stop at intervals and report processing. With high-ability readers, the requirement to stop did not have this effect. Thus, based on available evidence, at this point, a recommendation to collect concurrent or retrospective reports must be conditionalized: If the readers are capable and reading text that should cause few problems, concurrent reports probably are better. If the readers are less capable, reading texts that might be challenging to them, more valid reports might be obtained by signaling the readers to provide reports of their processing (i.e., with blue dots or some other place markers).

Should Verbal Protocols Be Interpretations of Processes or Direct Reports of Thinking?

Ericsson and Simon (1984/1993) recommended think-alouds as exact reports of what the thinker is thinking, rather than reader interpretations of their processing. From their perspective, a report such as, "I can see a really frightened Scrooge!" would be more acceptable than a report such as, "I'm making mental images of what is in the story." Both types of reports, however, have been collected in studies. We know of no analyses that are revealing about how conclusions about reading processes are affected by whether readers report what they are thinking or report their thinking processes by name. After reading and reflecting on the verbal protocols of reading covered by Pressley and Afflerbach (1995) and some that have appeared since then, we do not have a firm stand on this issue, except that we think that readers should be allowed to speak their own minds. Thus, we advise researchers to instruct readers to report what they are thinking as they read without attempting to shape their reports further. Researchers should record the readers' verbal reports and then make sense of them.

Verbal Protocol Limitation: Cueing Reader to Researchers' Expectations

Perhaps the most objectionable situation occurs when a researcher telegraphs to the reader in advance of collecting the verbal protocol just which processes he or she is interested in. Pressley and Afflerbach (1995) reported examples of researchers letting readers know that they should be focusing on main ideas or summarizing or report what they are looking for as they go through text. In contrast are studies such as that of Wyatt et al. (1993) in which researchers were very careful not to cue readers to use particular processes. Our position is that this is the most defensible tactic if the goal is to understand readers' natural reading processes.

Thus, with respect to directions to participants, after thinking about many, many verbal protocols of reading, we recommend keeping instructions to participants general (e.g., "Please think aloud as you read. . . . Tell me what you are thinking as you read the text"). Definitely do not prompt particular processes.

Can Verbal Protocols Be Collected with Young Children as Developing Readers?

While quite a few studies exist in which children and adolescents have provided verbal protocols, there seems to be an enduring question of whether less able readers and young children are capable of providing useful verbal protocols (Afflerbach & Johnston, 1984). Afflerbach and Johnston reasoned that because verbal ability is confounded with reading ability, younger and less verbal participants may produce poor think-alouds. They reasoned that young readers may not provide accurate think-alouds because they may not have sufficient metacognitive awareness of what they are thinking while reading. However, there are published verbal protocols with younger, developing readers. For example, Brown, Pressley, Van Meter, and Schuder (1996) studied the verbal protocols of second graders over the course of a year as a measure of improved reading comprehension. We are also currently collecting verbal protocols with first graders. In particular, we believe that such protocols can be revealing about when instruction intended to stimulate comprehension processing in first-grade students actually succeeds in doing so. Using verbal protocols, we have been able to identify when first graders make predictions based on prior knowledge, evaluative interpretations of text, and summaries (Hilden & Pressley, 2004). We suggest that when conducting verbal protocols of reading with younger students, researchers should have students read text within their reading level. If the students are asked to read overly difficult texts, their cognitive resources may be so taxed by reading that they cannot accurately verbalize their thoughts.

At the very least, we need more research about how early elementary school children are able to verbalize their thoughts while reading. This work is important for it has potential to inform developmental theories of reading. We look forward to learning much about how students' reading comprehension processes shift during development, expecting think-aloud data to prove very useful in illuminating developmental reading processes.

DETAILED REPORTING OF VERBAL PROTOCOL STUDIES

Although educational researchers have collected verbal protocols for a century, this is a not a standardized methodology yet, making it daunting to compare findings across studies. Moreover, we do not think it makes sense for verbal protocol analyses to become standardized based on what is now known.

Indeed, the hallmark of this methodology is its open-ended nature, with a great strength being that verbal protocol studies can be flexibly fitted to the questions posed by the researcher rather than the questions needing to be adjusted to research methodology.

We do agree with Afflerbach (2000), however, that researchers should provide substantial detail about how they did their study and why they made the decisions they did with respect to text, participants, directions provided to participants, and analyses—including transcription, raters, how raters categorized participant responses, and reliability of ratings. We consider briefly each of these aspects of research design in this section.

Text Factors

When designing a verbal protocol study in reading, the researcher must decide what type of texts will be read. In the Wyatt et al. (1993) study, the goal was to investigate, as naturalistically as possible, how social scientists read for professional purposes. Therefore, each professor read an article of his or her choosing, within his or her area of professional interest. In the Brown et al. (1996) study the goal was to compare reading comprehension of students who had experienced strategy instruction to those who had not. Therefore, all participants read the same passage, a fairly easy but definitely grade-2-level story. The researchers wanted the readers to be able to read the story fluently, so that some of their cognitive capacity would be available for sense making rather than consumed by word-recognition demands (LaBerge & Samuels, 1974). In addition, if a researcher decided to have students read texts that were at a higher reading level than the students' reading level, verbal protocols might include more word-level strategies. Because there would probably be more miscomprehension than with texts that can be read fluently, there might also be more reports of fix-up strategies. In short, because the strategies reported might vary as a function of text features, at a minimum, the report of a study must include information about the text being read in relation to the reader. Wyatt et al. (1993) did that, as did Brown et al. (1996).

Participants

It is always good to be clear about who is being studied before studying them. With respect to reading, the need is especially urgent. Thus, if it is a study of adult reading, much needs to be known about the participants besides the fact that they are adults: What is their educational level and previous reading achievement?

Are cultural, vocational, or avocational backgrounds relevant to the texts read in the study? With the exception of the vocational question, all the same issues pertain to child readers. Given the variety of educational approaches to reading, and the possibility that comprehension processing varies as a function of the reading program a child has experienced, often it will make sense to be clear about the type of reading instruction that participants experienced.

Given the intense, current interest in readers with learning disabilities, we are anticipating think-aloud studies involving readers who have difficulty reading. Researchers should be exceptionally clear about the nature of the reading difficulties of such participants, being as specific as possible.

Directions

Because of the potential for directions to bias the processing of participants in think-aloud studies, the researcher should be very clear about what is said to participants. Our advisement earlier in this chapter boils down to directing the participant's processing as little as possible. Simply ask participants to think aloud while they read, reporting what they are doing and thinking as they go through a text. Mention of specific reading or thinking processes has the potential to prompt participants to use those processes. Similarly, explaining thinking aloud by modeling with a short text can send the message to do as I do.

That said, often more is going to have to be said for participants to know what is meant by "thinking aloud." In particular, it has been known since Piaget's early research, the younger the children, the greater the difficulty in getting them to think about thinking. Based on experience in the Brown et al. (1996) study, we know that it takes awhile for some second graders to warm up to talking about what they are thinking as they read, at least in ways that obviously map to reading processes. Whatever is required to inform participants about their task in a study should be reported in detail so that consumers of the study can appraise whether the directions may have biased the results in one direction or another. Of course, the only way to know whether directions bias is to do experiments varying the degree of explicitness of directions given to participants, a direction we think should be pursued in the near future.

Tasks

An issue that has arisen repeatedly in the verbal protocols of reading literature is whether readers should be cued when to report their processing. Should participants be asked to stop reading at particular points to report on their processing or allowed to make reports of processing when they choose to do so? Certainly, the latter results in more natural reading, while the former provides greater research control, with it possible to more easily compare the processing of two readers, because, at least, they will have provided reports of processing at the same points in text.

If a decision is made to cue, it is necessary to decide when to cue. For example, some studies cue at the sentence or individual line-level (e.g., McGuire & Yewchuck, 1996; Myers, Lytle, Paladino, Devenpeck, & Green, 1990; Wade, 1990) whereas others cue at the paragraph or section level (e.g., Loxterman, Beck, & McKeown, 1994). Also, the researcher must decide whether to show readers the whole passage at once, or have them read the passage a line at a time (using note cards or by clicking through succeeding computer screens). Again, presenting the whole passage is more naturalistic than providing the passage a line at a time. Reading a line at a time interrupts the natural flow of reading, prevents readers from previewing texts by skimming, and prevents them from going back and re-reading important parts of texts. On the other hand, the latter situation allows the researcher to know better just what the participant is reacting to at the moment.

Analysis Plan

What do researchers do with the verbal reports? At one level, the answer is obvious—they categorize them in order to characterize the reader's processing. But, are these categories that were decided in advance (e.g., if the researcher is interested in self-questioning during reading, he or she may have come to the study with various categories of self-questions that might occur) or are they decided in light of the data (e.g., if the readers never self-question while reading the focal text, there would be no self-questioning category in the results)?

If the researcher is really interested in capturing the "mosaic" quality of the processing (Keene & Zimmermann, 1997), he or she might want to focus on strings of processes, for example, seeing how often a reader's thinking or strategies shifted during reading of a sentence or in a minute of reading or while reading the caption of an illustration. The researcher often will have to make decisions about whether the data can be quantified. Often this will be challenging, with Wyatt et al. (1993) a case in point: They decided that processes could be classified as never occurring, observed once, observed a few times (i.e., 2 to 4 times), or observed a lot (i.e., 5 or more times). Any more fine grained classification resulted in unreliable quantification. Whatever analysis decisions are made, the researcher must specify them clearly and explain the rationale for the decisions. Often, it is going to take some effort to come up with a reliable, credible analysis plan, one that can convince other scientists.

FINAL THOUGHTS

Verbal protocols of reading have provided valuable insights about the nature of constructively responsive reading. We know of no other method that reveals quite as much about active, strategic processes during reading. Although not a completely clear window on how the mind processes text, it is a window that admits a great deal of light.

Nonetheless, we look forward to the day when there are many more verbal protocol of reading studies. For example, conducting additional verbal protocol studies of reading with different age groups could affect developmental theories of reading. In addition to focusing on younger readers, we also need more information on how various reader, text, and methodological factors influence readers' comprehension processes as measured by verbal protocols. Reader factors that require further study employing this method include readers' motivation, purpose for reading, and ability levels. How do differently abled readers actively make sense of the text that they read? The following text factors also deserve further research attention: text genres and text organization. Studies of reading comprehension of hypertext are also needed. Finally, the field of verbal protocol research in reading needs methodological studies to fill in existing gaps concerning the issues of probing and training.

We realize that we have focused exclusively on verbal protocols of reading. This is because we know of little research that uses verbal protocols to study writing processes. However, we believe that many of the factors involved in reading would also be important in writing. We look forward to research in this area as well.

REFERENCES

Afflerbach, P. (2000). Verbal reports and protocol analysis. In M. L. Kamil, P. B. Mosenthal, P. D. Pearson, & R. Barr (Eds.), *Handbook of reading research* (pp. 163–179). Mahwah, NJ: Erlbaum.

Afflerbach, P., & Johnston, P. (1984). Research methodology: On the use of verbal reports in reading research. *Journal of Reading Behavior, 22,* 307–322.

Brown, R., Pressley, M., VanMeter., & Schuder, T. (1996). A quasi-experimental validation of Transactional Strategy Instruction with low achieving second-grade readers. *Journal of Educational Psychology, 88,* 18–37.

Crain-Thorenson, C., Lippman, M. Z., & McClendon-Magnuson, D. (1997). Windows on comprehension: Reading comprehension processes as revealed by two think-aloud procedures. *Journal of Educational Psychology, 89,* 579–591.

Ericsson, K. A., & Simon, H. A. (1993). *Protocol analysis: Verbal reports as data.* Cambridge MA: MIT Press. (Original work published 1984)

Hilden, K., & Pressley, M. (2004). *Can reading comprehension strategies be taught in first grade?* East Lansing: College of Education, Michigan State University.

James, W. (1890). *The principles of psychology.* New York: Holt.

Keene, E., & Zimmermann, S. (1997). *Mosaic of thought: Teaching comprehension in a reader's workshop.* Portsmouth, NH: Heinemann.

LaBerge, D., & Samuels, S. J. (1974). Toward a theory of automatic information processing in reading. *Cognitive Psychology, 6,* 293–323.

Loxterman, J. A., Beck, I. L., & McKeown, M. G. (1994). The effects of thinking aloud during reading on students' comprehension of more or less coherent texts. *Reading Research Quarterly, 29,* 352–365.

Marbe, K. (1901). *Experimentell-psychologische: Untersuchungen uber das Urteil.* Leipzig: Engelmann. (Reprinted and translated in J. Mandler & G. Mandler [Eds.], *Thinking: From association to gestalt* [pp. 143–148]. New York: Wiley.)

McGuire, K. L., & Yewchuk, C. R. (1996). Use of metacognitive reading strategies by gifted learning disabled students: An exploratory study. *Journal of Education of the Gifted, 19,* 293–314.

Meyers, J., Lytle, S., Palladino, D., Devenpeck, G., & Green, M. (1990). Think-aloud protocol analysis: An investigation of reading comprehension strategies in fourth- and fifth-grade students. *Journal of Psychoeducational Assessment, 8,* 112–127.

Miller, G. A. (1956). The magical number seven, plus-or-minus two: Some limits on our capacity for processing information. *Psychological Review, 63,* 81–97.

Olshavsky, J. L. (1976–1977). Reading as problem solving: An investigation of strategies. *Reading Research Quarterly, 4,* 655–675.

Pressley, M., & Afflerbach, P. (1995). *Verbal protocols of reading: The nature of constructively responsive reading.* Hillsdale, NJ: Erlbaum.

Shearer, B. A., Lundeberg, M. A., & Coballes-Vega, C. (1997). Making the connection between research and reality: Strategies teachers use to read and evaluate journal articles. *Journal of Educational Psychology, 89,* 592–598.

Strauss, A., & Corbin, J. (1990). *Basics of qualitative research: Grounded theory procedures and techniques.* Newbury Park, CA: Sage.

Strauss, A., & Corbin, J. (1998). *Basics of qualitative research: Grounded theory procedures and techniques* (2nd ed.). Newbury Park, CA: Sage.

Wade, S. E. (1990). Using think-alouds to assess comprehension. *The Reading Teacher, 43,* 442–451.

Wyatt, D., Pressley, M., El-Dinary, P. B., Stein, S., Evans, P., & Brown, R. (1993). Comprehension strategies, worth and credibility monitoring, and evaluations: Cold and hot cognition when experts read professional articles that are important to them. *Learning and Individual Differences, 5,* 49–72.

CHAPTER 15

Toward a Pragmatics
of Epistemology, Methodology,
and Other People's Theories
in Literacy Research

Mark Dressman
Sarah J. McCarthey

This chapter represents our best attempt, as literacy researchers first and predominantly qualitative researchers and theorists second, to outline a pragmatic approach toward the development of literacy research practices that makes conscious use of both epistemological concerns and theory across a broad range of methodologies, or ways of doing, literacy research. Our view of pragmatism derives from the school of philosophy commonly known as American Pragmatism, a school founded in the latter half of the 19th and early 20th centuries by Charles Sanders Peirce, Henry James, and John Dewey. Its principles include the following:

> a metaphysics that emphasizes processes and relations; a naturalistic and evolutionary understanding of human existence; an analysis of intellectual activity as problem-oriented and as benefiting from historically developed methods; and an emphasis upon the democratic reconstruction of society through educational and other institutions. (Campbell, 1995, p. 14)

In addition, American Pragmatism eschews "ultimate" questions about the nature of reality such as whether objective truth exists and instead focuses on what the consequences of acting from a position of positive objectivity or taking a more tentative stance toward an observed phenomenon might be for individuals within a given situation.

By arguing for a *pragmatics* of literacy research, then, we mean that we intend to examine the relations among epistemology, theory, and methodology from a stance that is grounded in as full a view as possible of the actual conditions in which research is likely to be conducted, rather than in hypothetical conditions removed from the logistical, cultural, historical, and sociopolitical realities of actual schools, homes, and even laboratory settings. Moreover, a pragmatics of literacy research would focus on a broad consideration of the ways in which a research project's epistemological assumptions, methods, and grounding in prior research and/or theory transactionally influence each other as well as others' likely interpretations and uses of the knowledge generated from the activity of the research.

In this chapter we also take into consideration the uses of theory, or "theoretical frames," in literacy research. We acknowledge at the outset that the terms *theory* and *theoretical* have many possible meanings among literacy researchers and have traditionally referred to explanations of specific phenomena, such as phonemic awareness and its relationship to learning to decode text fluently or schema theory and its implications for comprehension, that are grounded in the empirical evidence of research into the specific phenomena. When we use these terms in our discussion, however, they specifically refer to the more recent practice on the part of qualitative researchers to apply "other people's theories"—that is, theories originating external to the phenomenon on which the researcher is focusing, such as Vygotsky's (1978) theory of the zone of proximal development, Foucauldian theories of language and power (Foucault, 1984), or feminist theories of discourse (e.g., Walkerdine, 1990). Although the use of theoretical frames in literacy research is becoming an increasingly frequent feature of literacy research and has considerable implications for many epistemological and methodological approaches to research, it has received little direct attention or systematic scrutiny as an investigative practice. In this chapter we consider how the use of such external grand narratives may have pragmatic consequences for the ways that knowledge about literacy is both conceptualized and produced.

Our plan for discussing the issues we have outlined proceeds in three sections. In the first, we consider the epistemological implications of four methods of investigating an enduring and important research question, the effect of class size on teaching and learning. In the second section, we consider the current and possible roles of theoretical frames as methodological tools. In our third and concluding section, we summarize our arguments and suggest some broad pragmatic principles for the improvement of literacy research as an epistemological, methodological, and theory-building enterprise.

EPISTEMOLOGY AND METHODOLOGY: CONSIDERING FOUR APPROACHES

To illustrate the relationship between epistemology and methodology, we explore one topic—class size and literacy teaching and learning—using methods described in four chapters of this book. We became interested in using this issue to frame our discussion after reading the report of the National Research Council (2002), *Scientific Research in Education*, in which the debate about class size within the research literature is used to illustrate one of its six principles for conducting educational research: "using methods that permit direct investigation of the question" (p. 62). The authors of the report phrased the research question regarding class size and educational outcome in these terms: "Does reducing class size improve students' achievement?" (pp. 64–65).

From our perspective as former teachers, we found it puzzling that none of these studies or the report itself ever asked how a reduction or expansion in class size might positively, negatively, or neutrally affect the nature of instruction offered by teachers of smaller classes. Our conversations about the strengths and limitations of their review of the research on class size and its effects suggested to us that here was an issue that could provide a consistent context across which four research approaches and their implied epistemological perspectives might be considered. In this section, then, we consider four *hypothetical* studies based on the underlying assumptions of each research method. We do not consider issues such as cost or site selection but focus only on the methods and the underlying epistemologies implicit in their designs. Through our discussion we hope to illustrate the epistemological strengths and weaknesses of each method and to demonstrate the importance of using all kinds of methods to understand literacy teaching and learning.

Experimental and Quasi-Experimental Designs

The primary concern in any experimental study is to control the procedures of investigation and a number of relevant variables in such a way that in the end, any effects of the experimental condition can be logically attributed to the variable or variables under investigation. Experimental studies of human behavior rely on a number of key elements or principles in their design in order to ensure procedural control of possible external influences on outcomes. Among these are (1) the randomized selection and assignment of subjects; (2) the comparative use of at least two, and frequently more, groups, one of which is used as the "control" and one of which is identical to the control in all ways except in its addition of the "independent" variable under investigation; (3) contextual uniformity and procedural regularity across experimental groups, including clear operational definitions of all variables; and (4) measurement procedures that exclude or compensate for any human error or bias, and that are nearly always quantitative in nature.

An experimental study of the relations among class size, instructional practice, and student achievement would, at minimum, require the comparison of two groups in which the factor of instructional practice was varied and two groups in which the factor of class size was varied. Let us suppose that the instructional context of the study was 11th-grade American literature, that a large class was defined as having 30 students and a small class 15 students, that the two instructional practices to be compared were lecture/discussion and small-group literature study circles, and that the effects of the experiment were to be measured by a final 50-item multiple-choice test covering factual, interpretive, and critical comprehension of the novel. In an experimental study, the population would be defined as 11th-grade students of approximately the same age within that particular high school. Sixty students would be randomly selected and randomly assigned to four treatment groups (large class-lecture/discussion; small class-lecture/discussion; large class-study circles; small class-study circles) so that distribution of characteristics such as gender, ethnicity, social class, IQ, grade point average, and any other variable that might be confounded with the effects of class size and instructional practice on achievement would be distributed equally across the four groups. All four groups would need to read the same novel over the same period in identical physical conditions, using highly standardized instructional procedures for both the lecture/discussion and literature study format. Descriptive statistics of test scores for each group would be computed, and statistical procedures would be used to determine whether the differences between mean scores were significant. However, because the cell size for the small-group condition is relatively small, the experiment would probably need to be performed multiple times and the numbers and scores from identical groups would need to be combined before any parametric analyses could be validly performed.

The logistical problems inherent in conducting such an experiment within the context of a comprehensive high school, however, should be fairly obvious, necessitating the likelihood that the experiment would have to be conducted across multiple settings. For instance, in typical high school settings students are not randomly assigned to classes and may be uncooperative, teachers are likely to be less than enthusiastic about following an experimenter's scripted procedures, and administrative regulations and scheduling seldom allow for the regularity required by an experiment that is several weeks long. As a result, experimental literacy research of the type described previously may take two approaches. One approach is likely to be quasi-experimental, which as many intervening variables as possible are controlled for but the selection and/or assignment of subjects is not randomized, instructional procedures may not be completely identical, and less powerful, sometimes nonparametric, statistical procedures are needed. In the other approach, the unit of analysis is considered not to be individual students but individual classrooms, which are, in turn, randomly selected and assigned to either the experimental or control condition. Despite these challenges, some studies such as the Tennessee studies (Ritter & Boruch, 1999) have been conducted and shed light on the relationship between class size and student achievement.

The epistemological perspective embedded in this example enacts a view of human behavior which assumes that students and readers, like all other physical objects in a universe of discreet but classifiable physical objects, are above all else physical entities subject to dynamic laws of behavior. At the level of complex human behavior, these laws may not be the same as those that govern the physical universe; but because variables of human behavior are typically assumed to be normally distributed in the population there is also assumed to be a regularity, or at least a normative pattern of distribution to them, that would allow the detection of predictable patterns among them. Patterned predictability in human behavior is the knowledge that experimentalists in literacy research seek, for when a prediction that is planned for comes true more times than chance will allow, then a true pattern—one that may not consider history or culture or individual experience—has been found and certainty has been obtained, at least for the population as it has been defined. Such knowledge, like knowledge about the laws of planetary movements or genetic heritability, remains true in all circumstances and is free of the emotional or cultural distortions that characterized belief about the heavens in Ptolemy's time or bloodlines in the middle ages. Thus, a fully randomized and procedurally controlled experiment testing the effects of two different class sizes and two different instructional practices on an objective measure of student achievement should yield reliable information—information that can be used to produce higher student performance in future 11th-grade American literature classrooms, and that may be extended, with further experimentation, to other grade levels, student populations, and literary content.

The principal strengths of this epistemological perspective are its emphasis on the rationality of knowledge, the clarity of its argument that predictable patterns of human behavior can be known, and the trustworthiness and utilitarian value of knowledge that is not invented but essentially *discovered* through its methods. If the previously described experiment yielded findings, for example, of higher performance in smaller classes but no effect for instructional practice, then school systems interested in improving student performance in literature classes would rationally be expected to reduce class size without concern for other changes that would be necessary to take instructional advantage of having fewer students in classes. Decision making based on what is generalizable beyond its immediate context is clearly the most powerful kind of knowledge from this perspective.

However, the enactment of such an epistemological perspective also has significant pragmatic limitations. As already mentioned, the need for full control of the experimental context may be practically impossible, or where possible, may produce a condition so significantly different from the actual school contexts that the experimental context itself becomes a threat to validity. Under quasi-experimental conditions, every compromise in control becomes a possible source of bias, which must be investigated and compensated for through statistical techniques and multiple experiments. Another limitation of the method revolves around the generalizability of findings. Suppose in the previous example that the student body of the high school or high schools in which the study was conducted was largely suburban, middle- to upper-middle class, and white with a small minority of Latino but few African-American students. Would findings from the study be generalizable to suburban African-American populations? To rural white populations? To bilingual urban populations? In the past 20 years, a significant body of research has demonstrated that variables such as ethnicity and linguistic background may interact significantly with variables such as class size and instructional practice. Today an awareness of the effect of these and other variables on educational outcomes would have to be controlled for necessitating experiments with multiple student populations across multiple settings before the evidence could be supported and generalized. But when the First Grade Studies of the 1960s were conducted, their effects were unknown and so were not considered in the studies' design, yet their findings were generalized to all students in the United States (Willis & Harris, 1997). This raises the question of what other as yet unforeseen variables may inadvertently bias findings whose epistemological foundations and practices provide a rational "guarantee" of their general effectiveness across any and all populations.

Finally, the need to operationally define a variable may produce an artificial rigidity in the practical application of a variable under experimental conditions and in the generalizability of findings. In other words, beyond the boundaries of its experimental definition, what constitutes a "large" class versus a "small" class? Is it 30 versus 15 students, as in the present example, or would a difference of 25 versus 20 or 40 versus 10 or 29 versus 17 students produce the same results? What constitutes instructional practice? Is it the size of small groups? The nature of the questions the teacher asks during whole-class discussion? The amount of interaction allowed during lectures? Or, is it the teacher's enthusiasm for one practice over the other—and if so, how does one go about objectively measuring, much less controlling for, "enthusiasm"? Experimentalists might agree that generalizing the effects of a variable as defined beyond its boundaries should not be done, but in practice and policy these types of generalizations occur regularly.

In short, one pragmatic consequence of the epistemological perspective embedded within experimentalism is that it can encourage a false confidence about the ecological validity and the generalizability of findings beyond the experimental context in which they occurred. Moreover, the need for control within approaches that enact such an epistemology ultimately requires much manipulation of contexts and comparative replication across contexts to assure the generalizability of findings within actual contexts. The defense of truth claims from such studies can become such an overriding preoccupation that experimentalists may attempt to account for more and more variability in their results and design ever more controlled conditions that are increasingly remote from the actual conditions of classrooms and instructional practice. Despite these limitations, controlled experiments continue to be used and provide useful information about aspects of literacy learning and teaching. Like other research methods, experimental designs address certain questions well, while being less effective at illuminating other important issues.

Formative Experiments

In Chapter 8 of this volume, Reinking and Bradley provide six characteristics of formative experiments: (1) theoretical—"theory . . . is used to justify the importance of the inquiry, to provide a rationale for the intervention, interpret findings, contextualize conclusions . . ." (p. 159); (2) interventionist and goal-oriented—there is a planned intervention with the promise of improving education and a justification of the goal; (3) iterative—"the initial intervention is implemented within a continuous cycle of data collection and analysis aimed at determining what contextual factors enhance or inhibit the intervention's effectiveness" (p. 159); (4) transformational—"intervention may transform the educational environment in some way" (p. 160) including unintended consequences; (5) methodologically inclusive and flexible—it is likely that both quantitative and qualitative data will be collected and data collection may be adapted to the setting; and (6) pragmatic—"valuing of intuitive knowledge, and an investment in democratic ideals . . ." (p. 160) with the likelihood of involving practitioners as well as researchers.

If we were to design a formative experiment to evaluate the effects of class size and instructional practice on students' achievement, we might begin by inviting four teachers within, say, an upper elementary setting, to collaborate with us. Through an agreement with the school administration, the size of two teachers' classes during the period that reading was taught would be reduced to approximately half—15 students—its usual size. With the teachers, we would select a number of texts to be used in all four classrooms over the experimental period. The instructional intervention that we would be testing, literature study circles (e.g., Day, Spiegel, McLellan, & Brown, 2002; McMahon & Raphael, 1997), is grounded in both reader response theory (Rosenblatt, 1968) and theories of small-group interaction derived from the work of Vygotsky (1978) and other social constructivists. To collect baseline data, prior to the intervention we would observe the teaching of reading in each teacher's classroom, interview each teacher about his or her practices and philosophy, and collect test scores and survey data from the students about their attitudes toward reading in general and in class. We would share this theoretical rationale and the principles of literature study circles with the teachers and together design a plan for teaching one novel. During the instructional period, we would keep field notes of how each teacher actually arranged his or her class and students' interaction and collect any written responses to the reading or other artifacts that were produced. We would also collect quantitative information, such as tests of comprehension and vocabulary development given as summative assessments of the novel, and, if feasible, collect standardized reading test information. This information would be provided to teachers as feedback; a new plan for reading that addressed concerns and issues raised by the teachers, students, and researchers would be formulated for the reading of a second novel, and the process of reading and data collection would be repeated, and so on, through several trials.

As Reinking and Bradley note in Chapter 8, the epistemological origins of formative experiments are multiple, ranging from design experiments in engineering to neo-Vygotskian research. But perhaps the best articulated perspective of those they name is that of American Pragmatist John Dewey (Dewey & Bentley, 1949). For Dewey, the world is not made up of discrete objects "bumping into" each other with causal effect; rather, what appear to be discrete objects are actually only temporary assemblages in transactional relation—entities whose encounters with other entities result in changes to both. One may describe and be able to predict the interaction of one entity with another when examined in isolation; but the full effects of any interaction are unforeseeable. Thus, the earth beneath us appears solid but is actually a shifting mass of continental plates whose collision in turn affects climate patterns, ocean currents, and biological evolution; a surge in one species' population reduces others and sows the seeds of its own extinction; one nation colonizes another but then must adapt itself to the mores and practices of its colony; and a single shift in a school's curriculum might produce not only an intended consequence but many others, both positive and negative, as well. Moreover, objective knowledge of phenomena such as plate techtonics, evolution, political science, or instructional theory may or may not allow one to predict the future shape of continents, how or which organisms will evolve, how two cultures will affect each other, or what the full outcome of an educational innovation might be. From a Pragmatist view, broad, general theoretical knowledge may have its function, but it is to inform, not direct, the development of understanding about a particular situation. What matters most is what Reinking and Bradley term *conditional knowledge*, that is, knowledge/information gained from a situation that can be used in future instances of that situation to produce a beneficial outcome locally, and with further modification and development, in other similar situations.

It is from an evaluation of the strengths and the limitations of an epistemology strongly influenced by the tenets of American Pragmatism that its consequences for formative experiments as knowledge-producing activities may best be observed. We begin by noting that philosophers have not named the school founded by Dewey, Charles Sanders Pierce, and Henry James *American* Pragmatism out of historical or nationalist impulse but, rather, as a way of describing it as something quintessentially and culturally *American*. That is why, as Americans ourselves, and we suspect to other American readers, formative experiments, with their focus on problem solving and practicality, their mention of theory but focus on local situations, and the inclusion of a broad range of shareholders as well as a broad range of measurements, seem to make so much common sense. What makes common sense seem common, however, is often not a sharing of meanings or ideas but, rather, meanings and ideas that are so adaptable and open to interpretation that they can appeal to many different points of view without upsetting the sensibilities of a broad range of constituents. For example, in its heyday, whole language represented such a commonsense approach to literacy (see Dressman, McCarty, & Benson, 1998, for a discussion of its multiple meanings and implied practices), but its commonsense rationale may also explain why as a practice it was so hard to pin down and so hard to determine exactly what about its practices were effective and ineffective. So, too, in the foregoing example, practices such as "literature study circles" and "reader response" may be hard, with so many stakeholders involved, to accurately describe. Not only may such "fuzziness" have an epistemological benefit, it may also have a rhetorical and political benefit in that it keeps different groups with different interests and different ways of exercising power—that is, teachers, administrators, and researchers—seemingly collaborative and communicative, even though each may not be aware of the other's actual practices or reasoning.

A second, related attribute of the epistemology enacted by formative and design experiments that seems very American and also double-edged is the tension—some would say balance—between attention to theoretical (constitutional, federal) issues and local (historical, regional, state) circumstances. This tension, or balance, can be read from the wording of Reinking and Bradley's description of their first principle of formative and design experiments, when they note that theory "plays a predominant role [which is] to provide a rationale for the intervention, interpret findings, contextualize conclusions, and so forth" (Chapter 8, p. 159), but also quote Cobb, Comfrey, diSessa, Lehrer, and Schauble (2003) to note that "theory 'must do real work' by being *'accountable to the activity of design'* " (p. 159; italics in original). Thus, an epistemologically pragmatic compromise is arrived at whereby the status and existence of theory as an external form of knowledge is acknowledged but the organic integrity of local conditions is practically allowed to prevail. We would also point out that in this case, keeping theory and practice separate in ways that limit the interaction of one with the other is distinctly out of character with American Pragmatism, but its consequence—the development of a rationalized insularity that acts to resist the insights of external criticism that theory can provide—may still be a distinctly *American* flaw.

Case Studies

In Chapter 2 of this volume, Diane Barone describes case studies as investigations of bounded systems such as an individual child or teacher (and all of his or her topic-related relations) or a particular setting, such as a classroom. Barone also cites Merriam (1998), who characterized case studies as having four additional characteristics. They are (1) particularistic (i.e., "the study is centered on a particular situation, program, event, phenomenon, or person," p. 8); (2) descriptive (i.e., "the researcher gathers rich description of the object of study," p. 8); (3) heuristic (i.e., they enrich a reader's understanding); and (4) inductive (i.e., "the data drive the understandings that emerge from the study," p. 8). The primary characteristic of a case-study report is a strong narrative whose credibility is established through collecting multiple sources of data over time, creating a chain of evidence and analysis, and considering ethical issues that often include the likely biases/frame of reference of the researcher.

Case-study research has its origins in multiple disciplines, including anthropology (which, in turn, derived its methods from natural history), sociology (largely from a school of research developed at the University of Chicago in the 1930s), and clinical psychology and medicine, in which the case histories of individuals with striking psychological or medical problems are recorded, either as illustrative (teaching) examples of a phenomena or, for example, in Freudian psychoanalysis, as the grounds for theory building. Barone (Chapter 2) also cites Dyson's (1995) argument that case studies "do not offer information about causality regarding teaching practices" (p. 7), because the focus is on understanding a particular setting or individual within that setting. If the terms *causality* and *generalizability* imply a set of rules or laws that can be applied in circumstances that will produce a predictable outcome, as in genetics or physics, we would agree that case studies are not about causality or generalizability. However, we also would argue that there are other traditions and ways of understanding causality and generalizability such as the study of evolutionary biology or the geophysics of plate techtonics, that, while not highly predictive, may be more powerful in their capacity for reconceptualizing the dynamics of a system and for generating hypotheses about a generalized phenomenon than the positivistic traditions of experimentalism or the commonsense pragmatism of formative experiments. Our task in this section, then, is to suggest how case studies allow us to understand certain phenomenon, to reconceptualize some dynamics such as student–teacher interactions, and contribute to supporting or challenging theories. Additionally, through an outline of the epistemological assumptions that operate within the conceptualization, the data collection and analysis, and the "writing up" of case-study research, we highlight some of the limitations of this method.

As a hypothetical case study, let us consider a situation in which a middle school teacher and two classes are observed and interviewed as they read the novel *Roll of Thunder, Hear My Cry* (Taylor, 1976). One class has 27 students, but the other is considerably smaller, with 17 students. The teacher organizes instruction in the smaller class using a literature-study-groups approach and uses more of a lecture/discussion method with the larger class. The focus is to understand how students in each of the classes experience instruction. Unlike formative experiments, the role of the researcher in this case study is not to participate in instructional decision making. Rather, she collects data naturalistically, through field notes and videotapes of both classes and interviews that are as nondirective as possible. In addition, four students from the smaller class and seven students from the larger class are interviewed about their reading preferences and histories, artifacts such as their writing in response to the novel are collected, and test data and information from parent interviews and other classmates are gathered. Demographic characteristics, such as the race, gender, linguistic background, ethnicity, and social class of the class in general and of the focal students in particular are also noted. During the analytical phase of the research, connections among the teacher's comments about his instructional practice and observations about the students, student behavior, and student comments; artifacts such as the student writing; transcripts of small-group and whole-class discussions; and demographic data are noted. In writing up the study, the researcher weaves these connections and their supporting data together to produce a clear and consistent account of events in both classrooms and draws conclusions about the experience of the teacher and students within literature-study-groups versus lecture/discussion formats with both small- and large-size classes. The narrative may be partly diachronic—focused on sequentiality over the course of the novel—but it is more likely to be more synchronic, or focused on broader dynamic principles observed in both classes and their likely influences on the reading of the focal students in both classes. Rather than compare outcomes in both classes in terms of student achievement, the researcher focuses on a comparative discussion of qualitative differences in participation level and the nature of students' responses to the novel, with specific reference to the focal students in each class.

The epistemology enacted through a case study such as the foregoing depends on three assumptions about how the human social world is organized, knowledge of that world is validated, and the nature of knowledge about social experience in general. First, in the social world of human experience, people are not conceived of as free-standing individuals but as members of many different normative groups or categories that share a specific history of social, cultural, economic, political, religious, gendered, cognitive, or physical (to name the most prevalent types) experience. This shared experience is also assumed to have created structural conditions that produce behaviors, attitudes, and beliefs that the members themselves and/or outsiders identify as characteristic of that group. To identify an individual in a case study as a member of that group—to identify the teacher in the foregoing example as an active participant in the state affiliate of the National Council of Teachers of English (NCTE), for example, or to describe the setting of the school as suburban, or one focal student as Latino and another as a "struggling" reader—is to invoke, either implicitly or explicitly, powerful norms about the active members of NCTE, social class, race, language, and students with reading disabilities that can have a powerful influence on the sense a researcher gives, and the sense a reader takes, from a case study. Consequently, a second epistemological assumption is that individuals of a particular group stand in metonymic relation to the group(s) of which they are a part: Thus, to name a student as Latino is implicitly to generalize one's observations about that individual to Latino students in general, or to name a student as female or male is to suggest that all females or males may share some if not all of that student's gendered behavior. Thus, while the author of a case study may overtly claim that his or her findings cannot be generalized, the implicit message to readers might be that if an instructional practice worked in one setting or with one group of middle school students, it will work in a broad range of settings and with most groups of middle schoolers. This is even more powerfully so in cases in which little or no attention is paid by the researcher to the group characteristics of individuals or settings, and thus readers are left to assume that the findings of the study are applicable across a broader range of circumstances or conditions than is warranted. For example, although as Barone (Chapter 2) notes, Bissex's (1980) study of her son's literacy development has been used to argue for emergent literacy practices across a broad range of sociocultural settings, the social and cultural capital that Bissex and her husband, two PhD students at Harvard University at the time of the study, brought to their son's education would not be a set of conditions that many other parents or schools might be able to reproduce.

When these two powerful epistemological assumptions are combined with the readability of case study narratives, not only may they encourage the overgeneralization of instructional approaches such as literature study groups in all settings and with all populations, they may also have the negative practical consequence of reifying stereotypes about the assumed strengths or weaknesses of particular student groups or school settings. This may be the most problematic epistemological aspect of case-study research. Yet this is not necessarily the case, particularly in studies in which the researcher is careful to make the multiplicity of groups that make up the identity of an individual or setting as a bounded system and their interaction (or transaction) a focus of the analysis and reporting.

A third epistemological assumption of more recent case studies, and in particular of those that take a poststructural perspective (see, e.g., Dressman, 1997; McCarthey, 1998; Foley, 1990) is that the behavior of individuals or groups within particular settings cannot usually be explained as either the additive or integrative result of all the groups to which they belong (e.g., gender, race, religion, linguistic background, and social class together) but, rather, as the practices and beliefs of these groups interact with *and contradict* one another in ways that challenge rather than uphold stereotypical views. Thus, in the aforementioned study, although the Latino focal student in the case study is bilingual and has only been in the United States for 2 years, he has been very successful in this context. Analyses of the data demonstrate that prior to coming to the United States, he was a highly proficient reader and writer of Spanish and has been encouraged to maintain his Spanish-language proficiency in his home; moreover, transcripts of interviews with the researcher and of his interaction with peers in class show that he has found unexpected connections between his family's experiences in rural Mexico and the experiences of the Logans in the rural Great Depression setting of *Roll of Thunder, Hear My Cry* (Taylor, 1976). One of the greatest epistemological strengths of case-study research, then, is its capacity to interrupt stereotypical assumptions about groups of students and settings, thus refining the normative findings of experimental and formative research (and accounting for the many exceptional cases that are often not reported in such studies), as well as suggesting new relationships among important social factors.

These epistemological features of case studies have another pragmatic element in common—the ways that case studies are often used to develop theories (in the sense of "grand narratives") about learning and, subsequently, to challenge or support them. Piaget's (1969) work, of course, is a compelling example of the development of theory from case studies; his theory of the development of cognitive structures is derived from his observations of his own three children. Case studies of individual children have also led to the development of theories (in the sense that they are grounded in the empirical evidence) about the ways in which children learn to read and write (e.g., Baghban, 1984; Bissex, 1980; Calkins, 1983). These case studies offer the opportunities to generalize to theory. In addition, some researchers (e.g., Lensmire, 2000; McCarthey, 1994, in press) have begun with "grand narratives" such as Bakhtin's (1981) theory of dialogism and used case studies to support or challenge aspects of those theories. Case-study research lends itself to both the development and challenge of theories because of the potential to examine the particular within the general and vice versa. However, like other methods, the case-study approach is effective for examining some questions and not as appropriate for addressing others.

Discourse Analysis: Conversation

Conversational discourse analysis focuses on conversation as it is acquired, as it works in everyday life, as it evidences particular cultural norms, as it is constituent of activities, and as it reflects and reflexively sustains particular social order and relations (Florio-Ruane & Morrell, Chapter 4, this volume). Its methodology is rooted in the fields of anthropology, linguistics, sociology, and cultural studies, among others, and involves processes not so much of design or data collection as of analysis and interpretation. As Florio-Ruane and Morell also note, discourse analysis also has a long developmental history in the field of literacy studies—a history that complicates attempts to identify its epistemological assumptions. What began in the 1960s and early 1970s as a study of patterns of conversational exchange between teachers and students became, by the late 1970s and 1980s, a study of the role of culture as a mediator of communication and has since come to developed to include a study of discourse(s) as exercises in power relations. With each shift in focus has come a new, increasingly broad definition of what discourse is, and with it a concurrent broadening of the scope of its epistemological assumptions.

A study of class size and its relation to instructional approach that relied largely on discourse analysis would focus largely on qualitative differences in conversations between a teacher and students and among students in two classes of different sizes. Suppose, as in the example presented of case studies, a teacher were reading *Roll of Thunder, Hear My Cry* (Taylor, 1976) with two middle school classes of different sizes, and as a way of evaluating not the outcomes of student learning as measured by test scores but the quality of the discussions generated by lecture/discussion versus literature study groups, a researcher arranged to videotape all novel-related conversations in both settings, as well as keep field notes from direct observation of most, if not all, relevant classes. In the preanalytical stage, each videotape would be transcribed and in addition the researcher might watch each videotape and annotate the written transcript to record visual information (i.e., how students were sitting, the position of the teacher relative to the students, and gestures) alongside the written transcript. In the second phase of analysis, the transcripts would be "coded" in some way to record salient features of the conversations between/among the teacher and students; preliminary hypotheses about the underlying issues, such as the dominance of one gender of speaker or the direction of the conversation and its relation to individuals in each tape, might be formed. In the third phase of analysis, repetitions of specific patterns might be identified, along with their relation to the broader context of the classroom. The researcher might "test" his or her hypotheses by allowing colleagues to view the tapes and comparing their observations/interpretations of exchanges with the researcher's. These hypotheses might be compared to findings from other similar studies or to critical theoretical descriptions of discourse patterns, as a way of establishing the generality of this "type" of conversation within classroom contexts. After the researcher was satisfied that he or she had identified a *pattern* of conversational exchange, he or she would begin to "write up" the study, most likely framing its findings in a combined review of previous research and a review of theories of discourse that supported the broader point that he or she believed the analysis aligned with or challenged.

The epistemological axis on which assumptions about knowledge and knowing hinge in discourse analysis is, obviously, language. In early studies of conversation, language was frequently conceived of as the medium, or bearer, of meanings and therefore of knowing, a useful but inert tool of human invention that was separate from the world and from thinking about the world. In later conceptualizations, language and thought remained separate, but language was seen to operate as a constructive agent in its own right, through its syntactic logic and morphological, semantic roots of history, culture, and perception for its users. Following the precepts of Ferdinand de Saussure (1916/1966), linguists distinguished between two aspects of language, *la langue*, or the formal study of languages as systems, and *la parole*, or the study of language in everyday use—a distinction that also parallels the epistemological distinction between having formal, articulated knowledge *about* a phenomenon and having a more informal, practical competence that comes from *being of* a phenomenon. Although some analysts of discourse focus on the competencies of *la parole*, those who focus on the ways in which language use constitutes power relations among its users also emphasize the systemic, structural (and structuring) aspects of language as a practice. For these latter analysts (e.g., Fairclough, 1989; Foucault, 1984; Gee, 1999), people's use of language structures not only how they make sense of the world but whether their understandings will be valorized within their societies; thus, language not only structures ways of knowing but also affects the power that individuals are able to exercise in their political and economic lives.

How a discourse analyst conceives of the role of language in coming to know about the world is likely to influence the focus of his or her research. In the foregoing example, for instance, a researcher with a view of language as a tool of thought would likely focus on identifying typical patterns of interaction such as IRE (teacher Initiates; student Responds; teacher Evaluates; Mehan, 1979), students' participation, and the types of exchanges among individuals in classes of two different sizes. A researcher with a more "constructivist" view of thought and language might examine patterns of interaction but might focus as well on the semantic and syntactic quality of the exchanges (i.e., on how thoughts or ideas embodied in the utterances of a teacher or student or in the text of the novel were repeated or altered in the utterances of other students, either in conversation or in writing. Finally, a discourse analyst who saw language as structuring power relations would also examine patterns of interaction and the ways in which words and phrases as well as larger structures such as plot and character circulated among classroom participants, but the focus in this case might be how the knowledge (i.e., written or verbal comments) displayed by some students was valorized while others' knowledge was not acknowledged by the teacher and by peers, or perhaps how power relations as described within the novel itself (e.g., the Logans' status as African American landowners; Cassie's run-in with a white child) were responded to by the teacher, individual students, and the class as a whole.

A pragmatic strength of an epistemological view of research anchored in language is the power it gives a researcher to pinpoint precisely and concretely where learning occurs or breaks down within an instructional event. Experimentalist and formative experimentalists may produce causal explanations for the outcomes of instructional events, but their capacity to pinpoint exactly where and how related factors operate within an instructional event remains limited. Similarly, case-study approaches may allow a researcher to identify the causal factors within a bounded system after the fact, but they do not necessarily provide the insight into the dynamics of an instructional event needed to influence future outcomes. Discourse analysis offers insight into how patterns of interaction within a classroom might be redesigned or reengineered to produce more equitable and/or more productive learning for students. However—and as discourse theorists from Derrida (1976) to Foucault (1984) to Bourdieu (1977) to Gee (1999) to Fairclough (1989) would likely agree—because knowledge *about* a phenomenon is distinct from and not usually easily translated into the practical knowledge, or competence, that accrues from *being of* a phenomenon, knowing *about* patterns of discourse or the structures of discourse that also structure inequitable educational outcomes may not lead to changes in the actual practices of teachers or students within classroom settings.

Through the use of four illustrative studies, we have demonstrated the epistemological strengths and weaknesses of particular research methods. Each method can be powerful in illuminating some aspects of literacy teaching and learning but limited in its ability to inform us in other ways. For example, experimental designs, despite their limitations to generalize to all populations and their lack of consideration of culture and the individual can still be used to produce predictable patterns about class size, instructional practices, and student achievement. Formative experiments, because of their pragmatic features, adaptability and political benefits can help address questions of what literacy practices work in what settings. Although case studies might be used to overgeneralize to theory or to reify stereotypes, they have the potential to provide rich data for understanding how individuals and groups experience different types of instructional practices. Likewise, discourse analysis can help us not only to understand differences in conversational exchanges in large and small classes but to show how those patterns are mediated by power relationships. Yet, the patterns in the classrooms studied may differ substantially from patterns in other classrooms and prevent us from using the information in ways that lead to changing inequitable practices. Underlying each of these methods is a view of knowledge that influences the development of research questions, the data sources, the data-collection procedures, and types of analyses. By examining the underlying epistemologies of their methods, researchers can improve the formulation of their questions, procedures, and analyses.

OTHER PEOPLE'S THEORIES
AS EPISTEMOLOGICAL RESOURCES

Beyond the epistemological assumptions enacted through the methodologies that literacy researchers use in their investigations, another source of assumptions about how the world is known and what constitutes knowledge has become quite commonplace in the last 20 years, particularly within qualitative methodologies. Unlike traditional reviews of literature which focus on previous empirical studies related to a research topic, theoretical frames typically make reference to theories and theorists whose perspectives are related to but removed from the immediate context of the research setting. For example, while a study of class size and instructional practice might traditionally rely on previous studies of class size and findings from studies of instructional practices related to lecture/discussion and/or literature study groups, its theoretical frame might consist of a review of related concepts from the work of Russian literary theorist Mikhail Bakhtin (1981) as a way of framing an analysis of students' observed appropriation of language and ideas in their discourse about the novel they read, the work of social constructivists such as Vygotsky (1978) and Leon'tev (1981) to characterize the analysis of small-group interactions, or the work of feminists and of Gee (1989) and Fairclough (1999) to support their analysis of power relations among participants.

We take the position that where they are employed with rigor and thoroughness, theoretical frames represent an important trans-methodological innovation in the field of literacy research, for they provide additional epistemological resources that can strengthen the truth claims of research findings derived through a broad range of methodological approaches in at least three interrelated ways. First, theoretical frames can help to expand the significance and implications of a research project beyond its immediate practical boundaries so that the project is comprehensive within, and more relevant to, the context of broader theoretical, social scientific issues. A study of class size considered within the structuralist perspective of Pierre Bourdieu's *Outline of a Theory of Practice* (1977), for example, becomes a study of the ways that space, time, and cultural logic interact within specific material, historical conditions. Similarly, the analysis of instructional practices in the teaching of *Roll of Thunder, Hear My Cry* (Taylor, 1976), when framed by a consideration of critical race theory and/or the discourse theories of Gee (1999) and Fairclough (1989), becomes a study in the ways that issues of power and racism are mediated by discourse conventions. A second related benefit is the external source of comparison and contrast for the analysis of data that theoretical frames can provide. Feminist theories of discourse, for example, might be used to account for gender differences in the ways that students participate in discussions conducted in whole-class versus small-group settings, but they may also provide an occasion for exploring contradictions, when findings do not align with what theory would predict. Moreover, where findings align with a particular theoretical frame or do not align, or where a theoretical frame is used for the first time to account for a particular phenomenon, not only the findings of the study but the theory used is itself expanded or refined or revised. Thus, a third benefit of the use of theoretical frames in literacy research is the opportunity for literacy researchers to contribute to the building of "grand" theories of human social behavior.

However, we would also argue that the realization of the epistemological benefits of using other people's theories in literacy research depends not merely on the use, or mention, of theory in the report of a study but instead on the quality, or nature, of that use. In an ongoing study of the uses of theoretical frames in literacy research conducted by one of us (Dressman, 2003), 49 studies published in major literacy research journals that made use of theoretical frames were studied to identify the types, extent, and functions of theory use. Four patterns of use and function were found for the studies. Ten of the 49 articles used theoretical frames as a "foundational platform," in which the discussion of the frame appeared in the introduction or early sections of the article and was not referred to again. In these instances, the larger significance of a study to the broad theoretical principles of its frame was alluded to but never fully developed. Nine of the remaining 39 articles used theoretical frames as a "focal apparatus," in which the theoretical frame was developed in the introduction of the article and referred back to in its concluding discussion but did not figure into the report of the study's design or methods, its analysis, or its report of findings. In these instances, readers were reminded of the significance of the study to larger theoretical issues, but again, the theoretical frame was not well integrated into the analysis of data.

Twenty-two of the remaining 30 studies used or made mention of a theoretical frame as a "discursive scaffold." In these articles, the theoretical frame was identifiable, either implicitly or explicitly, throughout most if not all sections of a research article, including the introduction, methods, analysis, discussion, and concluding parts of the published study. In these cases, the larger social scientific implications of the study were usually clearly apparent and the use of theory as a comparative structure—that is, as a way of "making sense" of the data and providing interpretive insight that might otherwise not be perceived—was evident. Yet it would be difficult in many of these cases to argue that this use of theory contributed much to the building or refinement of social theory itself. In fact, in a few (but not all) instances a case could be made that the conclusions of the paper were grounded more in the theoretical frame than in an analysis of the data—in other words, that the data and its analysis supported the theory rather than that the theory illuminated or supported the data.

Of the 49 studies, then, only 8 made use of a theoretical frame as a "dialectical scaffold," in which theory was both compared, or aligned with findings, and contrasted—that is, in which theory was used analytically to both interrogate, and be interrogated by, the study's data. In these studies, the epistemological use of assumptions about how the world is known and the nature of knowledge itself not only foregrounded the broader social scientific implications of the study through the full use of the frame in most if not all sections of the published study but also provided an important "other" point of view against which to compare and contrast findings from the data, and in the process contribute to the expansion, refinement, or revision of the theoretical frame itself.

CONCLUSION: PROCEED WITH CAUTION

In our pragmatic consideration of epistemology and theory in research methods, we have emphasized the ways in which research is actually conducted within schools and attempted to uncover the assumptions behind conducting various types of research. By analyzing the epistemological strengths and weaknesses of each of four research methods, we have noted that different methods are based on different epistemological assumptions, and that is one reason why they have different strengths and weaknesses from one another. We have also implied that within the epistemological strengths of a particular method lie some of its weaknesses. For example, on closer examination of the generalizability of experimental and quasi-experimental methods, we see that, in fact, it is nearly impossible to generalize the findings of a study to all groups; further, the predictive nature and rationality of knowledge that is assumed using these methods may call for artificial conditions that are almost impossible to create in actual schools resulting in knowledge that is limited in its utility to classrooms. The problem-solving focus within local settings available through the formative experiments addresses many of the issues created by experimental designs. Yet, the collaborative, adaptable nature of the design makes the findings difficult to replicate but can also hide the underlying tensions between theory and practice or mask unintended consequences. While case studies are intended to be particularistic and descriptive using narrative as the vehicle for communication, they may have the unintended consequence of encouraging unwarranted generalization. Potential gains in insight by focusing on language and equity issues through discourse analysis could be lost if those same insights do not lead to changes or the establishment of more equitable relationships within classrooms.

We argue that despite the limitations of each, every method has something valuable to contribute to literacy research, yet, no one method can address the range of issues researchers need to address literacy teaching and learning. Differences in epistemological assumptions among the methods are a strength rather than a liability because they produce different types of knowledge. Experimental studies can provide some generalizable information with the possibilities of predicting outcomes in a wide range of settings. Formative methods have the capability of solving curricular problems within local settings as information is produced in collaborative relationships. Case studies provide detailed narratives about particular individuals within a social setting with the power to generate hypotheses. Discourse analysis provides insight about where and how learning occurs within particular settings while embracing diversity and the power of language.

Our investigation of epistemological assumptions among research method and the use of theory by literacy researchers has led us to three implications. First, we argue for a rigorous skepticism and humility in any approach to conducting research in literacy. Researchers need to be aware of the assumptions underlying the methods they choose and consider the benefits and unintended consequences of their methods, not only from a practical point of view but also from an epistemological perspective. Researchers need to ask:

What are the bases for the claims made? When we focus on these aspects of human interaction, what are we leaving out? What can we learn from this design? What are the limitations of what we can learn? Realizing that each method has a range of strengths and weaknesses, we hope that researchers will question their own assumptions as well as those of the designs they choose to employ.

Second, although it may be tempting to recommend that researchers mix a variety of research methods to ensure that a given topic is well covered, we argue against simply mixing methods. The ways in which researchers consider the nature of knowledge may conflict with one another; therefore, simply combining methods together may not produce the types of useful data we need to make classrooms better places for our students but may result in a hodge-podge of information without theoretical grounding. The purposes of the research and the research questions frame the types of data to be collected and analyzed; the results of those analyses need to be represented in different forms such as tables, models, narratives, or themes that are consistent with the epistemological assumptions and research designs. Research questions, sources of data, and types of analyses and interpretations should be aligned with one another and rest on clear, but carefully examined, epistemological assumptions. While we caution against mixing methods, we do recommend "triangulation" (a metaphor from qualitative methods; Stake, 1995) of research methods to improve educational policy and practices. For example, triangulation of research methods would include using multiple methods to study the same general topic, but the actual research questions and designs would differ from one another in scope, type of data collected, and forms of analyses and representations. Triangulation also involves using alternative means of confirming interpretations; therefore, researchers using different tools would check their findings on the same topic with one another. For example, experimentalists could look at what discourse analysts have found in specific classroom settings and vice versa. An additional aspect of triangulation is the idea of involving researchers in an examination of other researchers' raw data and interpretations. Why not have researchers who are designing formative experiments read the narratives of classrooms case study researchers have written?

Our third implication relates to the use of theory in research methods. While theoretical alignment can contribute to the readability of a research report, it does not substitute for validity. The benefits of theoretical frames in research reports include expanding the significance and implications of reports, providing opportunities for comparisons and contrasts of data, and building grand theories of social interaction, yet they need to be employed with greater caution than we have done previously. Just as we are suggesting that researchers need to consider and question the epistemologies of their methods, they also need to interrogate the theories they use to make their arguments. Literacy researchers need to not only build on the work of others from a variety of perspectives and methods but also continually engage in dialogue about the assumptions, interpretations, and consequences of their methods.

REFERENCES

Baghdan, M. (1984). *Our daughter learns to read and write: A case study from birth to three*. Newark, DE: International Reading Association.

Bakhtin, M. M. (1981). *The dialogic imagination*. Austin: University of Texas Press.

Bissex, G. (1980). *Gnyx at wrk*. Cambridge, MA: Harvard University Press.

Bourdieu, P. (1977). *Outline of a theory of practice*. Cambridge, UK: Cambridge University Press.

Calkins, L. (1983). *Lessons from a child: On the teaching and learning of writing*. Exeter, NH: Heinemann.

Campbell, J. (1995). *Understanding John Dewey: Nature and cooperative intelligence*. Chicago: Open Court.

Cobb, P., Confrey, J., diSessa, A., Lehrer, R., & Schauble, L. (2003). Design experiments in education research. *Educational Researcher, 32*(1), 9–13.

Day, J. P., Spiegel, D. L., McLellan, J., & Brown, V. B. (2002). *Moving forward with literature circles*. New York: Scholastic.

Derrida, J. (1976). *Of grammatology*. Baltimore: Johns Hopkins University Press.

de Saussure, F. (1966). *Course in general linguistics* (W. Baskin, Trans.). New York: McGraw-Hill. (Original work published 1916)

Dewey, J., & Bentley, A. E. (1949). *Knowing and the known*. Boston: Beacon Press

Dressman, M. (1997). Preference as performance: Doing social class and gender in three school libraries. *Journal of Literacy Research, 29*, 319–361.

Dressman, M. (2003). *Theoretically framed: Investigating the tropics of literacy research and reporting*. Chicago: American Educational Research Association.

Dressman, M., McCarty, L., & Benson, J. (1998). "Whole language" as signifier: Considering the semantic field of school literacy. *Journal of Literacy Research, 30*, 9–52.

Dyson, A. H. (1995). Children out of bounds: the power of case studies in expanding visions of literacy development. In K. Hinchman, D. Leu, & C. Kinzer (Eds.), *Perspectives on literacy research and practice* (pp. 39–53). Chicago: National Reading Conference.

Fairclough, N. (1989). *Language and power.* London: Longman.

Foley, D. (1990). *Learning capitalist culture: Deep in the heart of Tejas.* Philadelphia: University of Pennsylvania Press.

Foucault, M. (1984). *The Foucault reader* (P. Rabinow, Ed.). New York: Pantheon.

Gee, J. P. (1999). *An introduction to discourse analysis: Theory and method.* New York: Routledge.

Lensmire, T. (2000). *Powerful writing, responsible teaching.* New York: Teachers College Press.

Leont'ev, A. N. (1981). The problem of activity in psychology. In J. Wertsch (Ed.), *The concept of activity in Soviet psychology.* Armonk, NY: Sharpe.

McCarthey, S. J. (1994). Authors, text, and talk: The internalization of dialogue from social interaction during writing. *Reading Research Quarterly, 29*(3), 201–231.

McCarthey, S. J. (1998). Constructing multiple subjectivities in classroom learning contexts, *Research in the Teaching of English, 32,* 126–160.

McCarthey, S. J. (in press). Bakhtin's dialogism in a preschooler's talk. *Literacy Teaching and Learning.*

McMahon, S. I., & Raphael, T. E. (Eds.). (1997). *The Book Club connection.* New York: Teachers College Press.

Mehan, H. (1979). *Learning lessons.* Cambridge, MA: Harvard University Press.

Merriam, S. (1998). *Case study research in education: A qualitative approach.* San Francisco: Jossey-Bass.

National Research Council. (2002). *Scientific research in education.* Washington, DC: National Academy Press.

Piaget, J. (1969). *Psychology of intelligence.* Paterson, NJ: Littlefield, Adams.

Ritter, G. W., & Boruch, R. F. (1999). The political and institutional origins of a randomized controlled trial on elementary school class size: Tennessee's Project STAR. *Educational Evaluation and Policy Analysis, 21*(2), 111–125.

Rosenblatt, L. (1968). *The reader, the text, and the poem.* Carbondale: Southern Illinois University Press.

Stake, R, E. (1995). *The art of case study research.* Thousand Oaks, CA: Sage.

Taylor, M. D. (1976). *Roll of thunder, hear my cry.* New York: Dial Books.

Vygotsky, L. (1978). *Mind in society: the development of higher psychological processes* (M. Cole, V. John-Steiner, S. Scribner, & E. Souberman, Eds. and Trans.). Cambridge, MA: Harvard University Press. (Original work published 1934)

Walkerdine, V. (1990). *Schoolgirl fictions.* New York: Verso.

Willis, A. I., & Harris, V. J. (1997). Expanding the boundaries: A reaction to the First-Grade Studies. *Reading Research Quarterly, 32,* 439–445.

CHAPTER 16

Conclusion

Nell K. Duke
Marla H. Mallette

What do we hope you take away from this book? Many things, of course, but there are five overarching messages that we believe are especially important:

• *Message 1: Many different research methodologies, in fact each research methodology discussed in this book and others, have valuable contributions to make to the study of literacy.* We believe that each chapter of this book helps to make this point. Each methodology featured includes references to studies that it is hard to deny are important—that have provided new insights, confirmed or disconfirmed previous thinking, moved research forward, and/or influenced classroom practice. Our field would be a lesser place were that type of research unavailable. What we would understand about literacy and literacy learning would be diminished.

Chapters in this book are not, of course, the only source of evidence for the value of many different research methodologies in our understanding of literacy. Perusal of seminal volumes in literacy, such as the *Handbook of Reading Research: Volume III* (Kamil, Mosenthal, Pearson, & Barr, 2000), demonstrate that many different types of research have influenced our understanding across the field. Studies widely cited within literacy include a vast array of different methodologies. Awards bestowed in the field, such as the International Reading Association Outstanding Dissertation Award, Dina Feitelson Award, and Albert J. Harris Award have been given to studies of a wide range of research methods. And many well-respected literacy

347

scholars are on record espousing the value of many different types of research (e.g., Pearson, 2002; Pressley, Duke, & Boling, 2004; Purcell-Gates, 2001; Readence & Barone, 1996).

The contribution of a variety of research methodologies to understanding literacy is not simply an "in house" phenomenon. Studies that have reached beyond the literacy research community to influence classroom practices in real schools with real children also include a range of methodologies. Take, for example, Shanahan and Neuman's (1997) list of the 13 studies that they believe have had the greatest influence on classroom practice:

Atwell, N. (1987). *In the middle*. Portsmouth, NH: Boynton/Cook, Heinemann.

Bond, G. L., & Dykstra, R. (1967). The cooperative research program in first-grade reading instruction. *Reading Research Quarterly, 2*, 5–142.

Children's Television Workshop. (1969). *Sesame Street*. New York: Public Broadcasting System.

Clay, M. M. (1979/1985). *The early detection of reading difficulties*. Auckland, New Zealand: Heinemann.

Durkin, D. (1966). *Children who read early*. New York: Teachers College Press.

Durkin, D. (1978–1979). What classroom observations reveal about reading comprehension instruction. *Reading Research Quarterly, 14*, 481–533.

Freire, P. (1970). *Pedagogy of the oppressed* (M. B. Ramos, Trans.). New York: Herder & Herder.

Goodman, K. S. (1965). A linguistic study of cues and miscues in reading. *Elementary English, 42*, 639–643.

Graves, D. H. (1981). *A case study observing the development of primary children's composing, spelling, and motor behaviors during the writing process. Final report* (NIE Grant No. G-78-0174). Durham, NH: University of New Hampshire. (ERIC Document Reproduction Service No. 218 653)

Pichert, J. W., & Anderson, R. C. (1977). Taking different perspectives on a story. *Journal of Educational Psychology, 69*, 309–315.

Read, C. (1971). Preschool children's knowledge of English phonology. *Harvard Educational Review, 41*, 1–34.

Stein, N. L., & Glenn, C. G. (1977). An analysis of story comprehension in elementary school children. In R. Freedle (Ed.), *New directions in discourse processing: Vol. 2. Advances in discourse processing* (pp. 53–120). Norwood, NJ: Ablex.

Sticht, T. G., Gaylor, J. S., Kern, R. P., & Fox, L. C. (1972). Project REALISTIC: Determination of adult functional literacy skill levels. *Reading Research Quarterly, 7*, 424–465.

Methodologies used in these studies include oral miscue analysis, correlation, case study, experiment and quasi-experiment, design or formative experiment, ethnography, descriptive observational research (with and without numbers), instrument development, and discourse analysis. Even if one does not agree with all the articles on Shanahan and Neuman's list, or with the list of methodologies we have identified as represented in their list, this exercise certainly suggests that no one research methodology has a monopoly on high impact research in literacy.

• *Message 2: Different types of research are for different types of questions and claims. The match of research methodology to research questions and resulting claims is essential.* This message too should be evident in chapter after chapter of this book. Chapter authors discuss the types of questions to which their methodology is well suited, and the types of claims that can be made on the basis of that methodology. If you want to understand what goes on in literature circle discussions, you surely will not turn to neuroimaging techniques. If you want to know whether and how neural activity differs for good and poor readers, discourse analysis is not the best choice. If you want to know when and how a reader brings prior knowledge to bear in his or her reading, verbal protocol analysis leaps out as a methodology to use. If your interest is in whether one method of spelling instruction results in better spelling performance than another, experimental research is likely the appropriate methodology. This may seem obvious, yet we routinely read studies in which the question asked and/or the claims made do not in fact match well the research methodology used. And we encounter rhetoric suggesting that some research methodologies are inherently best, rather than best *for what*. As a field we must demand that qualifier in discussions of research methodology.

• *Message 3: There are standards of quality for every type of research. There is better- and poorer-quality research of every methodology*. A danger of arguing for the value of many different kinds of research and research perspectives is to imply that anything goes. We hope this book has resoundingly countered that implication. For each methodology chapter, authors were asked to identify standards of quality for research using that methodology. Each has done so, and without balking at the task. In the minds of these authors, well-known and well respected for their use of their assigned methodology, there are indeed hallmarks of quality research. Anything does not go.

We may in fact be more discerning of the quality and contribution of a given study when we seriously value many different research methodologies. Suppose, for example, that one is writing a review of literature on emergent literacy development. Assuming that there are limitations of space and reader attention, if one restricts the review primarily or exclusively to case study and ethnographic research, more attention to studies of those methodologies can be given than if the review includes as well findings from experimental and correlational studies. One might have to be more selective, then, about the studies of each methodology included. Of course, as we suggested in Message 2, one's question should be a driving force in determining what studies are afforded attention. But the quality of the work and its contribution can also be discriminating factors. Even in our everyday reading as scholars, the sheer number and range of different types of research that cross our desks means that we cannot attend to all studies; considerations of quality should help us decide which to attend to more closely.

• *Message 4: Synergy across research methodologies is possible, powerful, and advisable.* What if, starting tomorrow, we conducted nothing but high-quality, exemplary work within each of the research methodologies in this book? What if the standards of quality identified by authors in this volume were instantiated in each and every study? That would be fantastic, but it would not be enough. We need to work not only within but *across* these methods—what we call synergy of research methods.

Among the audience likely to read this book, at least, it seems a platitude to say this, but no number of experiments, in the absence of other types of research, will help us learn what we need to learn about literacy. Similarly, no number of case studies can, in themselves, help us understand everything we want to understand. Our richest and most productive knowledge base will come when different studies involving different research methodologies inform one another—when the whole of what we know in an area is built of many different kinds of parts, each doing what they do best, and together being much more than their sum.

Of course, synergy of research methodologies has occurred. In literacy we have many examples in which different studies conducted with different methodologies have informed one another and led to greater insight than could have come with one or the other. In the following paragraphs, we present two such examples. The examples are presented only briefly, and undoubtedly incompletely. Our intent is not so much to focus on the historical particulars or particulars in content but, rather simply to illustrate that this happens, and should happen more often.

One insight made possible, we believe, by research of a variety of methodologies is the insight that teaching children that the speech stream is composed of phonemes can improve their word reading. *Research using technologies* designed to examine the speech stream revealed that phonemes in speech are not separate and distinct, as implied to our written orthography, but rather influence one another. Thus it may be challenging for children to learn to tease out individual phonemes in words associated with particular letters (e.g., Liberman, Cooper, Shankweiler, & Studder-Kennedy, 1967). *Research examining children's written text*, in particular their spellings, indicated that indeed part of what children are developing when developing literacy is an understanding of relationship between the speech stream and orthography (e.g., Read, 1971; Chomsky, 1970). *Correlational studies* revealed relationships between the degree to which children were aware of the speech stream and their achievement and growth in literacy (e.g., Ehri, 1979; Share, Jorm, Maclean, & Matthews, 1984). *Experimental studies* indicated that if one engages children in activities to become more aware phonemes in the speech stream, their reading and writing is improved (e.g., Ball & Blachman, 1991; Williams, 1980).

Another insight made possible by studies of a variety of methodologies is that teaching children about text structure improves their comprehension. *Verbal protocols* demonstrated that good readers attend to text structure when they read (see Pressley & Afflerbach, 1995, for a review). *Research comparing good and poor comprehenders* (in a sense a form of correlational research) found that good comprehenders attend more readily to text structure than do poor comprehenders (e.g., Meyer, Brandt, & Bluth, 1980). *Experimental studies* revealed that teaching children to attend to text structure leads to better comprehension (Armbruster, Anderson, & Ostertatg, 1987; Taylor & Beach, 1984). As with the phonemic awareness insight, it is not that each of these studies led independently to the insight but that they informed and built on one another. The researchers cited research of other methodologies and were clearly influenced by that work. Neither the richness nor the rapidity of identifying the insight could likely have occurred without the synergy of these different research methodologies.

We want to be clear that we are not talking here about mixing methodologies within a study, but about different studies, of different methodologies, informing one another and larger insights. Of course, in some cases, mixed methodologies within a study is quite appropriate to a research question or set of questions and have important contributions to make (e.g., Tashakkori & Teddlie, 2003). However, we concur with the caution in mixing methods given by Dressman and McCarthey (Chapter 15, this volume). It will not serve the field well to mix methodologies if standards of quality and theoretical consistency are not met throughout the study.

• **Message 5: We must urgently and actively pursue synergy across research methodologies.** In our commentary in *Journal of Literacy Research* discussed at the outset of this book, we argued that the field of literacy is in danger of increasing fragmentation (Duke & Mallette, 2001). For example, we cited Trika Smith-Burke's concern about the "splintering off" of the National Reading Conference into subgroups such as the American Reading Forum and the Society for the Scientific Study of Reading. We pointed out how Stanovich referred to the field of literacy as being, "fractious." This trend toward fragmentation is of particular concern to us when research methodology is confounded with particular areas of study. For example, one finds few experimental studies around critical literacy and few case studies in the area of phonemic awareness, yet we believe it is possible to conduct high-quality research in both and see potential contributions to the field in both. For example, we might ask how comprehension achievement differs for children taught with and without critical literacy approaches (our hypothesis being that one would see higher comprehension achievement among students whose teachers taught with an emphasis on critical literacy). Or we might ask how a child with very strong or very weak phonemic awareness experiences phonemic awareness instruction in school (our interest in understanding whether a child whose phonemic awareness is extremely different from most of his or her peers experiences phonemic awareness instruction differently than intended). Of course, we are not advocating doing research of every particular kind in every particular area just for the sake of doing it, but we are arguing that particular research methodologies should not be dismissed out of hand as possible contributors to research in a particular area, and rather that we should actively seek a variety of questions, and thus methodologies, that could contribute to work in a particular area. We believe this is an important step in reversing the trend of fragmentation in the field.

To close, we want to thank again the contributors of this book, whose work individually and collectively has powerfully supported the five messages we have offered here:

- Message 1: Many different research methodologies, in fact each research methodology discussed in this book and others, have valuable contributions to make to the study of literacy.
- Message 2: Different types of research are for different types of questions and claims. The match of research methodology to research questions and resulting claims is essential.
- Message 3: There are standards of quality for every type of re-

search. There is better and poorer-quality research of every methodology.

- Message 4: Synergy across research methodologies is possible, powerful, and advisable.
- Message 5: We must urgently and actively pursue synergy across research methodologies.

We hope that our work, and yours, will do justice to the high bar that they have set.

REFERENCES

Armbruster, B. B., Anderson, T. H., & Ostertag, J. (1987). Does text structure/sumamrizatoOn instruction facilitate learning from expository text? *Reading Research Quarterly, 22,* 331–346.

Atwell, N. (1987). *In the middle.* Portsmouth, NH: Boynton/Cook, Heinemann.

Ball, E. W., & Blachman, B. A. (1991). Does phoneme awareness training in kindergarten make a difference in early word recognition and developmental spelling? *Reading Research Quarterly, 26,* 49–66.

Bond, G. L., & Dykstra, R. (1967). The cooperative research program in the first-grade reading instruction. *Reading Research Quarterly, 2,* 5–142.

Children's Television Workshop. (1969). *Sesame Street.* New York: Public Broadcasting System.

Chomsky, C. (1970). Reading, writing and phonology. *Harvard Educational Review, 40,* 287–309.

Clay, M. M. (1985). *The early detection of reading difficulties.* Auckland, New Zealand: Heinemann. (Original work published 1979)

Duke, N. K., & Mallette, M. H. (2001). Critical Issues: Preparation for new literacy researchers in multi-epistemological, multi-methodological times. *Journal of Literacy Research, 33,* 345–360.

Durkin, D. (1966). *Children who read early.* New York: Teachers College Press.

Durkin, D. (1978–1979). What classroom observations reveal about reading comprehension instruction. *Reading Research Quarterly, 14,* 481–533.

Ehri, L. (1979). *Orthography and the amalgamation of word identities in beginning readers: Final report.* Davis: University of California. (ERIC Document Reproduction Service No. ED 188145)

Freire, P. (1970). *Pedagogy of the oppressed* (M. B. Ramos, Trans.). New York: Herder & Herder.

Goodman, K. S. (1965). A linguistic study of cues and miscues in reading. *Elementary English, 42,* 639–643.

Graves, D. H. (1981). *A case study observing the development of primary children's composing, spelling, and motor behaviors during the writing process. Final report* (NIE Grant No. G-78–0174). Durham, NH: University of New Hampshire. (ERIC Document Reproduction Service No. 218 653)

Kamil, M. L., Mosenthal, P. M., Pearson, P. D., & Barr, R. (2000). *Handbook of reading research: Volume III.* Mahwah, NJ: Erlbaum.

Liberman, A. M., Cooper, F., Shankweiler, D., & Studdert-Kennedy, M. (1967). Perception of the speech code. *Psychological Review, 74,* 431–461.

Meyer, B. J. F., Brandt, D. M., & Bluth, G. J. (1980). Use of top-level structure in text: Key for reading comprehension of ninth-grade students. *Reading Research Quarterly, 16,* 72–103.

Pearson, P. D. (2002, May). *Up the down staircase: The role of research in policy and practice.* Paper presented at the annual convention of the International Reading Association, San Francisco.

Pichert, J. W., & Anderson, R. C. (1977). Taking different perspectives on a story. *Journal of Educational Psychology, 69,* 309–315.

Pressley, M., & Afflerbach, P. (1995). *Verbal protocols of reading: The nature of constructively responsive reading.* Hillsdale, NJ: Erlbaum.

Pressley, M., Duke, N. K., & Boling, E. C. (2004). The educational science and scientifically-based instruction we need: Lessons from reading research and policy making. *Harvard Educational Review, 74*(1), 30–61.

Purcell-Gates, V. (2001). The role of qualitative and ethnographic research. *Reading Online.* http://www.readingonline.org/articles/art_index.asp?HREF= purcellgates/index.html

Read, C. (1971). Preschool children's knowledge of English phonology. *Harvard Educational Review, 41,* 1–34.

Readence, J., & Barone, D. (1996). Expectations and directions for *Reading Research Quarterly*: Broadening the lens. *Reading Research Quarterly, 31*(1), 8–10.

Shanahan, T., & Neuman, S. (1997). Literacy research that makes a difference. *Reading Research Quarterly, 32*(2), 202–210.

Share, D. L., Jorm, A. F., Maclean, R., & Matthews, R. (1984). Sources of individual differences in reading acquisition. *Journal of Educational Psychology, 76,* 1309–1324.

Stein, N. L., & Glenn, C. G. (1977). An analysis of story comprehension in elementary school children. In R. Freedle (Ed.), *New directions in discourse processing: Vol. 2. Advances in discourse processing* (pp. 53–120). Norwood, NJ: Ablex.

Sticht, T. G., Gaylor, J. S., Kern, R. P., & Fox, L. C. (1972). Project REALISTIC: Determination of adult functional literacy skill levels. *Reading Research Quarterly, 7,* 424–465.

Tashakkori, A., & Teddlie, C (2003). *Handbook of mixed methods in social and behavioral research.* Thousand Oaks, CA: Sage.

Taylor, B. M., & Beach, R. W. (1984). The effects of text structure instruction on middle-grade students' comprehension and production of expository text. *Reading Research Quarterly, 19,* 134–146.

Williams, J. P. (1980). Teaching decoding with a special emphasis on phoneme analysis and phoneme blending. *Journal of Educational Psychology, 72,* 1–15.

APPENDIX

Alphabetical Listing of the Exemplars

Baumann, J. F., Hoffman, J. V., Duffy-Hester, A. M., & Ro, J. M. (2000). *The First R* yesterday and today: U.S. elementary reading instruction practices reported by teachers and administrators. *Reading Research Quarterly, 35,* 338–377. (**Survey**)

Brown, R., Pressley, M., Van Meter, P., & Schuder, T. (1996). A quasi-experimental validation of transactional strategies instruction with low-achieving second grade readers. *Journal of Educational Psychology, 88,* 18–37. (**Verbal Protocols**)

Bus, A. G., & van IJzendoorn, M. H. (1999). Phonological awareness and early reading: A meta-analysis of experimental training studies. *Journal of Educational Psychology, 91,* 403–414. (**Meta-Analysis**)

Compton-Lilly, C. (2002). *Reading families: The literate lives of urban children.* New York: Teachers College Press. (**Case Study**)

Coté, N., & Goldman, S. R. (1999). Building representations of informational text: Evidence from children's think-aloud protocols. In H. Van Oostendorp & S. R. Goldman (Eds.), *The construction of mental representations during reading* (pp. 169–193). Mahwah, NJ: Erlbaum. (**Discourse Analysis: Written Text**)

Coté, N., Goldman, S. R., & Saul, E. U. (1998). Students making sense of informational text: Relations between processing and representation. *Discourse Processes, 25,* 1–53. (**Discourse Analysis: Written Text**)

Cunningham, A. E., & Stanovich, K. E. (1997). Early reading acquisition and its relation to reading experience and ability ten years later. *Developmental Psychology, 33,* 934–945. (**Correlational**)

Dyson, A. H., (2003). *The brothers and sisters learn to write: Popular literacies in childhood and school cultures.* New York: Teachers College Press. (**Ethnography**)

Foorman, B. R., Francis, D. J., Fletcher, J. M., Schatschneider, C., & Mehta, P. (1998). The role of instruction in learning to read: Preventing reading failure in at-risk children. *Journal of Educational Psychology, 90,* 37–55. (**Experimental and Quasi-Experimental**)

Henk, W. A., & Melnick, S. A. (1995). The Reader Self-Perception Scale (RSPS): A new tool for measuring how children feel about themselves as readers. *The Reading Teacher, 48,* 470–482. **(Instrumentation [Affective])**

Lewis, C. (2001). *Literacy practices as social acts: Power, status, and cultural norms in the classroom.* Mahwah, NJ: Erlbaum. **(Ethnography)**

McKenna, M. C., Kear, D. J., & Ellsworth, R. A. (1995). Children's attitudes toward reading: A national survey. *Reading Research Quarterly, 30,* 934–956. **(Survey)**

Michaels, S. (1981). "Sharing time": Children's narrative styles and differential access to literacy. *Language in Society, 10,* 423–443. **(Discourse Analysis: Conversation)**

Morrell, E. (2002). Toward a critical pedagogy of popular culture: Literacy development among urban youth. *Journal of Adolescent and Adult Literacy, 46*(1), 72–77. **(Discourse Analysis: Conversation)**

Purcell-Gates, V. (1995). *Other people's words: The cycle of low literacy.* Cambridge, MA: Harvard University Press. **(Ethnography)**

Reinking, D., & Watkins, J. (2000). A formative experiment investigating the use of multimedia book reviews to increase elementary students' independent reading. *Reading Research Quarterly 35,* 384–419. **(Formative and Design Experiments)**

Simos, P. G., Fletcher, J. M., Sarkari, S., Billingsley, R. L., Francis, D. J., Castillo, E. M., Denton, C., & Papanicolaou, A. C. (2004). *Early development of neuropsychological processes involved in normal reading and reading disability.* **(Neuroimaging)**

Vellutino, F. R., & Scanlon, D. M. (1987). Phonological coding, phonological awareness, and reading ability: Evidence from a longitudinal and experimental study. *Merrill–Palmer Quarterly, 33,* 321–363. **(Experimental and Quasi-Experimental)**

Wyatt, D., Pressley, M., El-Dinary, P. B., Stein, S., Evans, P., & Brown, R. (1993). Comprehension strategies, worth and credibility monitoring, and evaluations: Cold and hot cognition when experts read professional articles that are important to them. *Learning and Individual Differences, 5,* 49–72. **(Verbal Protocols)**

Index

Achievement, sense of
  causation and, 200
  meta-analyses of, 243–246
Activity theory, 157–158
Affective instrumentation
  attributes of, 205–208
  description, 197–199
  exemplars of, 201–203
  importance of, 199–201
  lessons learned from, 220–222
  purposes and uses of, 203–205
  steps for validating, 208t–211, 212f, 213–
    220, 216t
American Pragmatism. *See also* Pragmatism
  description, 322–323
  formative experiments and, 330–332
Analysis of data
  in ethnographic research, 106–108
  in survey research, 297–298
  in verbal protocol research, 312, 318–319
Analysis of discourse. *See also* Discourse, oral;
    Discourse, written
  critical discourse analysis, 54–57
  description, 49–51, 51–52, 59–60, 85–86,
    343
  epistemological features of, 336–340
  exemplars of, 57–59, 83–85
  specific to written texts, 62–66, 67–71, 69f,
    70f, 72f, 73–78, 76t, 79t–80t, 80–82
Analytic research, formative experiments and,
  160
Angular gyrus. *See also* Neuroimaging
  fMRI studies of, 268–269
  interventions and, 277–278, 279f
  reading disabilities and, 266
Archival data, in ethnographic research, 106.
  See also Data collection
Arguments, 68–69. *See also* Propositions
Artifacts, in ethnographic research, 106. *See
  also* Data collection
Atomic level of analysis, 70. *See also*
  Discourse, written; Propositions
Atomic propositions. *See* Propositions
Attitudes regarding literacy
  description, 200
  survey research regarding, 299, 301t–303
Attrition, 120. *See also* Validity

Basal regions, 263–264. *See also*
  Neuroimaging
Beginning observation, 103–104. *See also*
  Observational method of data collection
Beliefs and literacy, 200
Bibliographic notes, 182–183. *See also*
  Historical research
Bilingual education, 232t
Binominal effect size display (BESD), 236–
  238
Bounded system, 8
Brain structure and functioning, 258–260. *See
  also* Neuroimaging

Case-study research
  description, 7–10, 25, 343
  epistemological features of, 332–336, 339
  exemplars of, 23–25
  history of, 10–21
  questions answered by, 21–22
  regarding phonemic awareness, 352
  standards for quality in, 23
Causation
  between achievement and affect, 199–200
  case-study research and, 332–333
  correlational data and, 28–30, 40–41
  ethnography and, 94
  experimental design and, 114–115, 117–
    119
  validity and, 127
Ceiling effects, 121. *See also* Validity
Cerebral tomography (CT), 254. *See also*
  Neuroimaging
Children's Social Desirability Questionnaire
  (CSDQ), 219
Class size
  case-study research and, 332–336
  discourse analysis and, 336–340
  experimental and quasi-experimental design
    and, 324–328
  formative experiments and, 329–332
  structuralist perspective of, 341
Classroom environment. *See also* Education
  effect of intervention on, 164–165
  ethnography and, 102–103
  meta-analyses of, 232t
  oral discourse and, 52–54

Code-oriented instruction
    experimental design regarding, 135–141, 138*t*
    quasi-experimental design regarding, 141–
        145
Coding of data. *See also* Data analysis
    in ethnographic research, 109
    in meta-analysis, 235, 238, 244–245
    in verbal protocol research, 312
Cognitive development, 33–38, 35*t*, 36*t*, 37*t*
Cognitive efficiency hypothesis, 32–33
Cognitive measurement. *See* Affective
        instrumentation
Coherence, discourse analysis and, 71, 73
Coherence relations, 65. *See also* Discourse,
        written
Coherent pattern matching, 132–133
Cohesiveness, 71, 73
Collection of data
    in ethnographic research, 101–106
    in survey research, 296–297, 297–298
    in verbal protocol research, 312
Collective case-study research, 9–10. *See also*
        Case-study research
Comparative research, 9
Comparison, 28–29
Comprehension
    brain structure and, 263
    functional neuroimaging studies of, 266
    lifelong reading habits and, 38–39*t*
    meta-analyses of, 231*t*, 240–242, 241*f*
    print exposure and, 40–41
    text structure and, 351
    verbal protocol research and, 308–309, 312
Computer-assisted interviews, 293. *See also*
        Survey research
Conditional knowledge, 330. *See also*
        Knowledge
Conferencing in writing, 12–13
Confounds, control of, 131–132
Connectives, 65–66. *See also* Discourse,
        written
Construct validity. *See also* Validity
    affective instrumentation and, 204–205,
        215
    in experimental design, 121–123, 139–140
    interrelationships with other types of
        validity, 127
    in survey research, 296
Content notes, 182–183. *See also* Historical
        research
Contrastive sampling, 100–101. *See also*
        Sampling
Control
    correlational data and, 28–29
    minimizing threats to validity with, 131–
        132
    type 1 errors and, 144
Conversation. *See also* Discourse, oral
    in the classroom, 52–54
    culture and, 47–49
    pragmatism and, 336–340
Corpus callosum, 258. *See also* Neuroimaging
Correlational data
    description, 39–42
    difficulties in interpreting, 31–33

    dilemma of, 28–30
    hierarchical multiple regression analysis,
        33–38, 35*t*, 36*t*, 37*t*
    of lifelong reading habits, 38–39*t*
    need for, 30–31
    speech and, 351
Counterfactual inference. *See also*
        Experimental design
    adequacy of, 133–134
    description, 116–117
Critical approach, 97. *See also* Ethnography
Critical discourse analysis. *See also* Analysis of
        discourse; Discourse, oral
    description, 54–57
    exemplars of, 57–59
Criticism, internal, 181–182. *See also*
        Historical research
CT (cerebral tomography) scanning, 254. *See
        also* Neuroimaging
Culture
    conversation and, 47–49
    ethnography and, 92–93

Data analysis
    in ethnographic research, 106–108
    in survey research, 297–298
    in verbal protocol research, 312, 318–319
Data, coding of. *See also* Data analysis
    in ethnographic research, 109
    in meta-analysis, 235, 238, 244–245
    in verbal protocol research, 312
Data collection
    in ethnographic research, 101–106
    in survey research, 296–297, 297–298
    in verbal protocol research, 312
Data, correlational
    description, 39–42
    difficulties in interpreting, 31–33
    dilemma of, 28–30
    hierarchical multiple regression analysis,
        33–38, 35*t*, 36*t*, 37*t*
    of lifelong reading habits, 38–39*t*
    need for, 30–31
    speech and, 351
Decoding skills, 34–35*t*
Definition of methodology, 1–3
Descriptive research
    affective instrumentation and, 204–205
    case-study research as, 8
    description of, 332
Design experiments. *See also* Formative
        experiments
    difference between formative experiments
        and, 151–152
Directionality problem, 29–30. *See also*
        Correlational data
Disabilities, learning. *See also* Reading
        disabilities
    meta-analyses of, 232*t*, 239
    structural neuroimaging and, 257–260
Disabilities, reading. *See also* Disabilities,
        learning
    meta-analyses of, 232*t*
    MSI studies regarding, 269–271*f*
    structural neuroimaging and, 257–260

Discourse analysis. *See also* Discourse, oral;
  Discourse, written
  critical discourse analysis, 54–57
  description, 49–51, 51–52, 59–60, 85–86,
    343
  epistemological features of, 336–340
  exemplars of, 57–59, 83–85
  specific to written texts, 62–66, 67–71, 69*f*,
    70*f*, 72*f*, 73–78, 76*t*, 79*t*–80*t*, 80–82
Discourse, oral
  critical discourse analysis and, 54–57
  culture and, 47–49
  description, 46–47, 51–52, 59–60
  education and, 49–51
  exemplars of, 52–54, 57–59
  pragmatism and, 336–340
Discourse, written
  analysis of, 67–71, 69*f*, 70*f*, 72*f*, 73–78,
    76*t*, 79*t*–80*t*, 80–82
  description, 62–66, 85–86
  exemplars of, 83–85
Discriminant validity, 133. *See also* Validity
Drawing, compared to writing, 14

Ecological approach, 96. *See also* Ethnography
Economic development, correlational data
  regarding, 31–32
Editing in writing, case-study research
  regarding, 12–13
Education. *See also* Classroom environment;
  Instructional practice
  critical discourse analysis and, 57–59
  oral discourse and, 49–51, 52–54
Effect size, in meta-analysis, 236–238, 242–
  243, 245
Elementary Reading Attitude Survey (ERAS).
  See also Affective instrumentation
  description, 201, 301–302
  directions of, 207
  factor analysis of, 215–217
  social desirability of, 218
  validity and, 217
Engagement, 200
Environment, classroom. *See also* Education
  effect of intervention on, 164–165
  ethnography and, 102–103
  meta-analyses of, 232*t*
  oral discourse and, 52–54
Environment, home
  case-study research regarding, 19–21
  print exposure and, 40–41
Environmental opportunity hypothesis, 32
Epistemology. *See also* Pragmatism
  case-study research and, 332–336
  discourse analysis and, 336–340
  experimental and quasi-experimental design
    and, 324–328
  formative experiments and, 329–332
  importance of, 2–3
  pragmatism of, 342–345
  theoretical frames and, 340–342
Equal-appearing interval scaling, 211
Error analysis
  case-study research regarding, 12–13
  in survey research, 296

Ethnic minorities, case-study research and, 25
Ethnography
  approaches to, 95–97
  data analysis, 106–110
  data collection and, 101–106
  description, 92–93
  essential elements of, 97–100
  questions answered by, 93–95
  sampling and, 100–101
  standards for quality in, 111–112
  writing up the results of, 110–111
Evidence, in historical research, 177–184
Expectations regarding literacy, 200
Experimental design
  affective instrumentation and, 203–204
  description, 116–119, 128–133, 145–146
  epistemological features of, 324–328, 339
  exemplars of, 135–141, 138*t*, 141–145
  generalizability of, 343
  history of, 114–116
  regarding critical literacy, 352
  standards for quality in, 133–134
  validity in, 119–127
Experimental effect, 118–119. *See also*
  Experimental design
Exploratory experimentation, 153–154. *See
  also* Formative experiments
Expository structure, 64–66. *See also*
  Discourse, written
External validity. *See also* Validity
  in experimental design, 123–127, 139–140
  interrelationships with other types of
    validity, 127

Face-to-face surveys, 290. *See also* Survey
  research
Factor analysis, in affective instrumentation,
  215
Feminism
  discourse analysis and, 57
  theories of discourse and, 341
Fidelity of treatment problems, 121. *See also*
  Validity
Field notes. *See also* Data collection;
  Ethnography
  data analysis of, 108–109
  description, 99–100
  in ethnographic research, 104–105
Flexibility, in formative experiments, 158–
  159, 160
Floor effects, 121. *See also* Validity
Fluency, functional neuroimaging studies of,
  266
fMRI (functional MRI). *See also* Functional
  neuroimaging; Neuroimaging
  description, 255, 261–265*f*
  structural neuroimaging and, 257–260
  studies using, 267–269, 268*f*
Focus groups, 290. *See also* Survey research
Formative experiments
  description, 151–155, 343
  epistemological features of, 329–332, 339
  exemplar of, 161–165
  history of, 155–158
  instructional practice and, 149–151

Formative experiments (*continued*)
  methodological characteristics of, 158–161
  need for, 165–166
Frame, sampling. *See also* Sampling
  description, 294
  in survey research, 296–297
Frontal cortex, 259. *See also* Neuroimaging
Functional MRI (fMRI). *See also* Functional
    neuroimaging; Neuroimaging
  description, 255, 261–265*f*
  structural neuroimaging and, 257–260
  studies using, 267–269, 268*f*
Functional neuroimaging. *See also*
    Neuroimaging
  description, 253
  exemplars of, 274–280, 279*f*
  methods of, 260–265*f*, 264*f*
  reading acquisition and, 265–274, 268*f*,
    271*f*, 273*f*

Generalization
  in case-study research, 332–333, 334–335
  from ethnographic research, 101
  of experimental and quasi-experimental
    design, 343
  in experimental design, 327–328
  external validity and, 124–127
  from a sample to a population, 294
Goal orientation, 159
Grounded theory, 312
Grouping, meta-analyses of, 232*t*

Heuristic characteristic
  of case-study research, 8
  description of, 332
Hidden bias, 131–132
Hierarchical linear modeling, 143
Hierarchical multiple regression analysis. *See
  also* Correlational data
  description, 33–38, 35*t*, 36*t*, 37*t*, 39–42
  of lifelong reading habits, 38–39*t*
Higher criticism, 181–182. *See also* Historical
    research
Historical research
  description, 170–174
  exemplar of, 186–190
  opportunities for, 190–193
  oral history, 186–190
  process of, 177–186
  reasons for, 176–177
  regarding literacy, 174–176

History effect, 120, 130. *See also* Validity
History of methodologies. *See also* *individual
    methodologies*
  affective instrumentation, 201
  case-study research, 10–21
  discourse analysis, 51–52, 336–337
  experimental design, 114–116
  formative and design experiments, 155–
    158
  historical research, 173–174
  meta-analysis, 228–230, 231*t*–232*t*, 233
  neuroimaging, 252–255
  survey research, 288–289

Home environment
  case-study research regarding, 19–21
  print exposure and, 40–41
Homework, case-study research regarding, 18
Hypothesis formation
  meta-analysis and, 238
  in survey research, 295–296
Hypothesis testing. *See also* Formative
    experiments
  description, 153–154
  discourse analysis and, 337
  experimental design and, 132–133
  meta-analysis and, 228, 245–246

Hypothetical counterfactual. *See also*
    Experimental design
  adequacy of, 133–134
  description, 116–117

Independence assumption, 143
Independent reading, 161–165
Inductive characteristic
  case-study research and, 8
  description, 332
Inferior frontal areas. *See also* Neuroimaging
  fMRI studies of, 269
  interventions and, 277–278, 279*f*
  reading disabilities and, 266
Inferior parietal areas, 263–264. *See also*
    Neuroimaging
Instruction, code-oriented
  experimental design regarding, 135–141,
    138*t*
  quasi-experimental design regarding, 141–
    145
Instructional practice. *See also* Interventions
  affective instrumentation and, 205
  case-study research and, 332–336
  discourse analysis and, 336–340
  experimental and quasi-experimental design
    and, 141–145, 324–328
  formative and design experiments and,
    149–151
  formative experiments and, 329–332
  meta-analyses of, 231*t*
  neuroimaging studies regarding, 281
  regarding phonics, 18, 135–141, 138*t*, 239–
    240
  survey research regarding, 301*t*–303, 303–
    304
Instrumental case-study research, 9. *See also*
    Case-study research
Instrumentation, 120. *See also* Validity
Insula, 259. *See also* Neuroimaging
Intelligence, correlational data regarding, 32–
    33
Internal criticism, 181–182. *See also* Historical
    research
Internal validity. *See also* Validity
  in experimental design, 119–120, 139–140
  interrelationships with other types of
    validity, 127
  threats to, 130
Internet surveys, 292–293. *See also* Survey
    research

Interpretation of data, 109–110. *See also* Data analysis
Intersubjectivity, 107–108
Interventions. *See also* Instructional practice
design experiments and, 152–153
formative experiments and, 159
independent reading and, 161–165
neuroimaging studies regarding, 271–274, 273*f*, 274–280, 279*f*
Interviews, 105–106. *See also* Data collection
Intrinsic case-study research, 8–9. *See also* Case-study research
Invented spelling, 12–13, 15–16
Item analysis, 214–215
Iterative process, 159–160

Knowledge
construction of in discourse, 55
formative experiments and, 154, 330–332
language and, 338–339
oral discourse and, 50
spontaneous writing and, 82
written discourse and, 73–74

Language
acquisition of, 50
brain structure and, 263
critical discourse analysis and, 59–60
culture and, 47–49
discourse analysis and, 337–338
exposure to, 41
processing of, 258
Lateral occipitotemporal region, 277–278, 279*f*. *See also* Neuroimaging
Learning
assessment of, 74
formative experiments and, 159
Learning disabilities. *See also* Reading disabilities
meta-analyses of, 232*t*, 239
structural neuroimaging and, 257–260
Lifelong reading habits, 38–39*t*
Likert scale. *See also* Scaling techniques
in affective instrumentation, 210
response format and, 213
Linguistic cues, 65–66. *See also* Discourse, written
Literacy events, 47. *See also* Discourse, oral
Low power, 121. *See also* Validity

Magnetic resonance imaging (MRI). *See also* Neuroimaging
description, 254–255
structural neuroimaging and, 257–260
Magnetic resonance spectroscopy (MRS). *See also* Functional neuroimaging
description, 261–265*f*
interventions and, 271–274, 273*f*
Magnetic source imaging (MSI). *See also* Functional neuroimaging; Neuroimaging
description, 255, 261–265*f*, 264*f*
interventions and, 271–274, 273*f*, 276–280, 279*f*
studies using, 269–271*f*

Magnetoencephalography. *See also* Functional neuroimaging; Neuroimaging
description, 255, 261–265*f*
interventions and, 271–274, 273*f*, 276–280, 279*f*
studies using, 269–271*f*
Mail surveys, 291–292. *See also* Survey research
Manipulation, correlational data and, 28–29
Memory
demonstrated in written responses, 77–78, 79*t*–80*t*, 80–81
learning and, 74
Mental model, 73–74. *See also* Knowledge
Meta-analysis
description, 227–228, 229*f*, 246
exemplars of, 243–246
history of, 228–230, 231*t*–232*t*, 233
questions appropriate for, 238–243
standards for quality in, 233–238
Methodologies, history of. *See also* individual methodologies
affective instrumentation, 201
case-study research, 10–21
discourse analysis, 51–52, 336–337
experimental design, 114–116
formative and design experiments, 155–158
historical research, 173–174
meta-analysis, 228–230, 231*t*–232*t*, 233
neuroimaging, 252–255
survey research, 288–289
Methodology. *See also* individual methodologies; Pragmatism
definition of, 1–3
pragmatism of, 342–345
risks of combining, 344
synergy across, 3, 350–351, 352
values of different types of, 347–349
Middle temporal gyri, 263–264. *See also* Neuroimaging
Motivation for Reading Questionnaire, 202. *See also* Affective instrumentation
Motivation to Read Profile (MRP), 202. *See also* Affective instrumentation
Move-testing experimentation, 153–154. *See also* Formative experiments
MRI (magnetic resonance imaging) scanning. *See also* Neuroimaging
description, 254–255
structural neuroimaging and, 257–260
MRS (magnetic resonance spectroscopy). *See also* Functional neuroimaging
description, 261–265*f*
interventions and, 271–274
MSI (magnetic source imaging). *See also* Functional neuroimaging; Neuroimaging
description, 255, 261–265*f*, 264*f*
interventions and, 271–274, 273*f*, 276–280, 279*f*
studies using, 269–271*f*
Multiple-case research, 22. *See also* Case-study research
Multiple regression analysis. *See also* Correlational data
description, 33–38, 35*t*, 36*t*, 37*t*, 39–42
of lifelong reading habits, 38–39*t*

Narrative structure, 64–66. *See also* Discourse, written
National Reading Conference oral history project, 186–190. *See also* Historical research
National Reading Panel, meta-analyses conducted by, 230, 233
Network approach, 97. *See also* Ethnography
Neuroimaging. *See also* Functional neuroimaging
exemplar of, 274–280
history of, 252–255
reading acquisition and, 256–257
relevance of to reading research, 280–282
structural, 257–260
Nonsampling errors, 295. *See also* Survey research

Observational method of data collection, 101–104. *See also* Data collection
Oral discourse
critical discourse analysis and, 54–57
culture and, 47–49
description, 46–47, 51–52, 59–60
education and, 49–51
exemplars of, 52–54, 57–59
pragmatism and, 336–340
Oral history, 186–190. *See also* Historical research
Orthographic analysis, 267–268

Participant observation, 101–103. *See also* Observational method of data collection
Particularistic characteristic
of case-study research, 8
description of, 332
PET (positron emission tomography). *See also* Functional neuroimaging; Neuroimaging
description, 255, 261–265f
reading disabilities and, 266
Phenomenological approach, 96. *See also* Ethnography
Phonemic awareness, 231t, 240, 241–242, 243–246, 352
experimental design regarding, 135–141, 138t
speech and, 350–351

Phonics instruction
case-study research regarding, 18
experimental design regarding, 135–141, 138t
meta-analysis and, 239–240
Phonological coding skills
hierarchical multiple regression analysis of, 34–35t
quasi-experimental design regarding, 141–145
Planum temporale, 258–259. *See also* Neuroimaging
Population, 293–295, 297. *See also* Sampling
Positron emission tomography (PET). *See also* Functional neuroimaging; Neuroimaging
description, 255, 261–265f
reading disabilities and, 266

Postcolonial theory, 57
Posterior brain regions. *See also* Neuroimaging
reading acquisition and, 263–264
reading disabilities and, 259
Pragmatism
case-study research and, 332–336
description, 322–324, 342–345
discourse analysis and, 336–340
experimental and quasi-experimental design and, 324–328
formative experiments and, 160–161, 329–332
Predicates, 68–69. *See also* Propositions
Preschool intervention, 231t
Presentation of research, 185–186
Presentism, 185
Print exposure
correlational data regarding, 32, 40
hierarchical multiple regression analysis of, 34–38, 35t, 36t, 37t
Probability sample, 294. *See also* Sampling
Propositional scheme. *See* Propositions
Propositions, 68–71, 69f, 70f, 72f, 73–78, 76t, 79t–80t, 80–82. *See also* Discourse, written
Providential sampling, 101. *See also* Sampling
Purposive sampling. *See also* Sampling
description, 101
external validity and, 126–127

Qualitative interviews, 288. *See also* Survey research
Quality of research methodologies
case-study research, 23
ethnographic research, 111–112
experimental and quasi-experimental design, 133–134
meta-analysis, 233–238, 242–243
survey research, 298–299
types of methodologies and, 349–350
Quantitative research, 9
Quasi-experimental design. *See also* Experimental design
counterfactual inference and, 116–117
description, 128–133, 145–146
epistemological features of, 324–328
exemplars of, 141–145
generalizability of, 343
standards for quality in, 133–134
Questionnaires, 205–208. *See also* affective instrumentation

Random sampling. *See also* Sampling
description, 294
in experimental design, 128–130, 139, 145–146, 325
external validity and, 126–127
in survey research, 297
Readability, 67–68
Reader Self-Perception Scale (RSPS). *See also* Affective instrumentation
content validity of, 211, 212f
description, 201
factor analysis of, 215–217, 216t
lessons learned from, 220
scaling technique of, 210–211

theoretical framework of, 209
validity and, 217
Reading disabilities. *See also* Disabilities,
    learning
    meta-analyses of, 232t
    MSI studies regarding, 269–271f
    structural neuroimaging and, 257–260
Reading habits, lifelong, 38–39t
Reading process, 308–309, 310t–311t
Recall, 77–78, 79t–80t, 80–81
Recording technology
    in ethnographic research, 104–105
    historical research and, 179
    oral discourse recording and, 48–49
    recording of oral histories, 189
Regional cerebral blood flow, 255. *See also*
    Neuroimaging
Regression analysis. *See also* Correlational data
    description, 33–38, 35t, 36t, 37t, 39–42
    of lifelong reading habits, 38–39t
Regression to the mean. *See also* Validity
    affective instrumentation and, 204–205
    description, 120
    internal validity and, 130
Regularity effect, 239
Reliability
    in affective instrumentation, 214
    in ethnographic research, 98–99
Representative sampling, 100–101. *See also*
    Sampling
Restriction of range, 121. *See also* Validity
Revision in writing, 12–13
Rhetorical structure of text, 64–65. *See also*
    Discourse, written

Sample statistic, 294. *See also* Sampling
Sampling
    in ethnographic research, 100–101
    in experimental design, 128–130, 139,
        145–146, 325
    external validity and, 124–126
    in meta-analysis, 236
    purposive, 101, 126–127
    survey research and, 293–295, 296, 297
    in verbal protocol research, 317
Sampling error. *See also* Sampling
    description, 294–295
    in survey research, 296
Sampling frame. *See also* Sampling
    description, 294
    in survey research, 296–297
Sampling, random. *See also* Sampling
    description, 294
    in experimental design, 128–130, 139,
        145–146, 325
    external validity and, 126–127
    in survey research, 297
Satisficing, 296. *See also* Survey research
Scaling techniques
    in affective instrumentation, 210–211
    response format and, 213
    social desirability and, 218
Selection bias. *See also* Validity
    description, 120
    internal validity and, 130

Semantic differential scaling, 210–211. *See
    also* Scaling techniques
Semistructured interviews, 288. *See also*
    Survey research
Sight reading instruction, 135–141, 138t
Signaling devices, 66. *See also* Discourse,
    written
Simple random sample, 294. *See also* Random
    sampling; Sampling
Single positron emission computed
    tomography (SPECT), 255. *See also*
    Neuroimaging
Single-subject design
    case-study research and, 22
    compared to case-study research, 8
Situated evaluations, 157. *See also* Formative
    experiments
Situational model, 73–74. *See also* Knowledge
Social desirability
    in affective instrumentation, 218–219
    in mail surveys, 291
Social network approach, 97. *See also*
    Ethnography
Socioeconomic status, 13–15, 19–21
Specificity, 158–159
SPECT (single positron emission computed
    tomography), 255. *See also* Neuroimaging
Speech stream, 350–351
Spontaneous writing, 81–82. *See also* Writing
    process
Statistical conclusion validity. *See also* Validity
    description, 121
    in experimental design, 120–121
    interrelationships with other types of
        validity, 127
    in quasi-experimental design, 143
Stratified random sample, 294. *See also*
    Random sampling; Sampling
Structural neuroimaging, 253, 257–260. *See
    also* Neuroimaging
Structuralist perspective, 341
Structured personal interviews, 290. *See also*
    Survey research
Structured surveys, 288. *See also* Survey
    research
Superior temporal gyri. *See also* Neuroimaging
    fMRI studies of, 268–269
    interventions and, 277–278, 279f
    reading acquisition and, 263–264
    reading disabilities and, 270
Supramarginal gyrus, 277–278, 279f. *See also*
    Neuroimaging
Survey research. *See also* Structured surveys
    description, 287–288, 304–305
    design process of, 295–298
    evaluation of, 300t
    exemplars of, 299, 301t–304
    history of, 288–289
    sampling and, 293–295
    standards for quality in, 298–299
    types of surveys used, 290–293
Synergy across methodologies
    importance of, 3
    value of, 350–351, 352
Systemic research, 160

Teaching. *See* Instructional practice
Technology
  in ethnographic research, 104–105
  historical research and, 179
  oral discourse recording and, 48–49
  recording of oral histories, 189
Technology-enhanced survey methods, 292–
    293. *See also* Survey research
Telephone surveys. *See also* Survey research
  computer assisted, 293
  description, 290–291
Temporoparietal areas, 258, 266, 270. *See also*
    Neuroimaging
Testing, 120. *See also* Validity
Text structure, 351
Textbase, 73–74. *See also* Knowledge
Theory. *See also* Pragmatism
  as epistemological resources, 340–342
  formative and design experiments and, 159
  meaning of, 323
  pragmatism of, 342–345
Third-variable problem, 29. *See also*
    Correlational data
Transformation, 160
Treatment diffusion, 123. *See also* Validity
Triangulation, 98, 344. *See also* Validity
Tutoring, 232*t*
Type error, controlling for, 144

Unreliability of measurement, 121. *See also*
    Validity

Vagueness, in historical research, 185
Validity. *See also* Construct validity
  of affective instrumentation, 208*t*–211,
    212*f*, 213–220, 216*t*
  in ethnographic research, 98
  in experimental design, 119–127, 139–140,
    146
  intersubjectivity and, 107–108
  minimizing threats to, 131–132
  in quasi-experimental design, 143
  in survey research, 296
  threats to, 130, 134
Validity, construct. *See also* Validity
  affective instrumentation and, 204–205,
    215
  in experimental design, 121–123, 139–140
  interrelationships with other types of
    validity, 127
  in survey research, 296
Validity, external. *See also* Validity
  in experimental design, 123–127, 139–140
  interrelationships with other types of
    validity, 127

Validity, internal. *See also* Validity
  in experimental design, 119–120, 139–140
  interrelationships with other types of
    validity, 127
  threats to, 130
Ventral occipitotemporal regions. *See also*
    Neuroimaging
  interventions and, 277–278, 279*f*
  reading acquisition and, 263–264
  reading disabilities and, 270
Verbal protocol research
  description, 308–309, 310*t*–311*t*, 319
  exemplars of, 311–312
  process of, 312–315
  reporting of, 316–319
  text structure and, 351
Violation of assumptions of statistical tests,
    121. *See also* Validity
Visuospatial analysis, 267–268
Vocabulary development
  correlational data regarding, 32–33, 40
  hierarchical multiple regression analysis of,
    34–35*t*
  language exposure and, 41
  meta-analyses of, 231*t*

Web surveys, 292–293. *See also* Survey
    research
Wernicke's area, 277–278, 279*f*. *See also*
    Neuroimaging
Whole-language, 235
Word-meaning-based instruction, 135–141,
    138*t*
Word recognition
  fMRI studies of, 267–268
  functional neuroimaging studies of, 265–
    266
  meta-analyses of, 240–242, 241*f*
  MSI studies regarding, 270
Writer Self-Perception Scale (WSPS). *See also*
    Affective instrumentation
  description, 201
  development of, 221
Writing Attitude Survey (WAS), 202. *See also*
    Affective instrumentation
Writing process
  case-study research regarding, 12–13
  compared to drawing, 14
  discourse analysis and, 74–78, 76*t*, 79*t*–80*t*,
    80–82
Written discourse
  analysis of, 67–71, 69*f*, 70*f*, 72*f*, 73–78,
    76*t*, 79*t*–80*t*, 80–82
  description, 62–66, 85–86
  exemplars of, 83–85